Everyman, I will go with thee,
and be thy guide

Hereward College

LEARNING RESOURCES
CENTRE

John Keats

SELECTED POEMS

Edited by
NICHOLAS ROE
University of St Andrews

EVERYMAN
J. M. DENT · LONDON
CHARLES E. TUTTLE
VERMONT

This edition first published in Everyman in 1995
Reprinted 2000

J. M. Dent
Orion Publishing Group
Orion House
5 Upper St Martin's Lane
London WC2H 9EA
and
Tuttle Publishing
Airport Industrial Park, 364 Innovation Drive,
North Clarendon, VT, 05759-9436 USA

Typeset in Sabon by Deltatype Ltd, Ellesmere Port, Cheshire
Printed in Great Britain by
The Guernsey Press Co. Ltd, Guernsey, C.I.

British Library Cataloguing-in-Publication Data
is available upon request.

ISBN 0 460 87549 3

CONTENTS

NOTE ON THE AUTHOR AND EDITOR

JOHN KEATS was born in London on 31 October 1795, the son of Frances Jennings and Thomas Keats, who managed the Swan and Hoop Inn, Moorgate. Keats was sent to Enfield School, which had a strongly dissenting and republican culture, where he enjoyed a liberal and enlightened education subsequently reflected in his poetry. Orphaned at the age of fourteen, he became a surgeon's apprentice before enrolling, in 1815, as a student at Guy's Hospital. Keats's earliest poems date from 1814 and his first volume, *Poems*, was published in 1817. During this year Keats gave up his medical training and devoted himself full-time to a literary career. His experimental poem *Endymion*, which he thought of as a 'test' of his creative powers, was published in April 1818. In summer of that year, Keats and his friend Charles Brown began a walking tour of the Lake District and Western Highlands of Scotland. While crossing the Island of Mull, Keats contracted a bad sore throat, displaying the first symptoms of the tuberculosis that would eventually kill him. He returned to London by sea, and took up residence in Hampstead where he met and fell in love with Fanny Brawne. During autumn 1818 he started work on *Hyperion*, and in 1819 he wrote *The Eve of St Agnes*, *Lamia*, and his great sequence of odes. These were published during 1820 in his third volume, although by this time Keats's illness had become more severe. He left England for Italy, in search of a warmer climate that would help him recover his health. He died in Rome on 23 February 1821, aged twenty-five, and was buried there in the Protestant Cemetery.

NICHOLAS ROE is Professor of English at the University of St Andrews, Scotland. His books include *Wordsworth and Coleridge, The Radical Years* (1988), *The Politics of Nature* (1992), *Keats and History* (1995) and *John Keats and the Culture of Dissent* (1997).

CHRONOLOGY OF KEATS'S LIFE

Year	Age	Life
1795		John Keats born 31 October and baptised at St Botolph's, Bishopsgate
1797	1/2	George Keats born 28 February
1799	3/4	Thomas Keats born 18 November
1801	5/6	Edward Keats born 28 April, but dies before he is one year old
1802	6/7	Thomas Keats (John's father), becomes manager of the Swan and Hoop and stables
1803	7/8	Frances Keats born 3 June. John and his brother George are taken to board at John Clarke's School at Enfield (August)
1804	8/9	Thomas Keats (K's father) is killed in a horse-riding accident (April)

CHRONOLOGY OF HIS TIMES

Year	Artistic Events	Historical Events
1795	Helen Maria Williams *Letters Containing a Sketch of the Politics of France* published	Treasonable Practices and Seditious Meetings Bills passed into law (December)
1796	Coleridge *Poems on Various Subjects* published (April)	
1797	Coleridge writes *Kubla Khan*, and first version of *Ancient Mariner* (November)	British Navy mutinies at Spithead and The Nore (April–June)
		Burke dies (July)
1798	*Lyrical Ballads* published anonymously (September)	French invasion of republican Switzerland (January)
1799		Washington dies (December)
1800	Edgeworth *Castle Rackrent* Bloomfield *Farmer's Boy*	Herschel discovers infra-red rays Volta invents first electric battery
1801		Toussaint L'Ouverture takes command of Spanish Santo Domingo, liberates black slaves (January)
		Jefferson elected third President of US
1802		Bonaparte becomes Life Consul (August)
1804		Bonaparte proclaimed Emperor (May)
		Coronation of Bonaparte (November)

Year	Age	Life

1810   14/15   Frances Keats (K's mother) dies from tuberculosis
                 (March). In this year (or possibly 1811) K is
                 apprenticed to Thomas Hammond and occupies a
                 room above Hammond's surgery at Edmonton. His
                 education continues informally at Enfield

1812   16/17   K quarrels with Hammond and moves into lodgings

1814   18/19   Early spring K reads Spenser's *Epithalamion* with
                 CCC and moves swiftly on to *The Faerie Queene*.
                 Writes *On Peace* (April)

1815   19/20   K writes a sonnet *Written on the day that Mr Leigh
                 Hunt left Prison* (February) and shows it to CCC.
                 K registers as a student at Guy's Hospital and
                 becomes an assistant surgeon (October)

1816   20/21   K's first published poem 'O Solitude' appears in the
                 Examiner (May). He passes examination at
                 Apothecaries' Hall and becomes eligible to practise as
                 apothecary (July). Writes *On first looking into
                 Chapman's Homer*, published December in Leigh
                 Hunt's article 'Young Poets' in the *Examiner*.
                 Decides to abandon his medical career

Year	Artistic Events	Historical Events
1805		Battle of Trafalgar, death of Nelson (21 October) Discovery of morphine
1806	Elizabeth Barrett (Browning) born (March)	
1807	Wordsworth *Poems in Two Volumes*	Abolition of slave trading in British ships (March)
1808	Leigh Hunt founds the *Examiner*	Peninsular War between France and Britain in Spain begins
1809	*Quarterly Review* founded Byron *English Bards and Scotch Reviewers*	British victory at Talavera in Spain
1811		Prince of Wales made Regent
1812	Byron *Childe Harold* I & II Final shipment of Elgin marbles arrives in London	Luddite Riots Bonaparte invades Russia
1813	Leigh Hunt imprisoned for libel on Prince Regent (till 1815) Shelley *Queen Mab*	Mass Luddite trial in York; many hangings and transportations
1814	Wordsworth's *Excursion* published	Bonaparte exiled to Elba
1815	Wordsworth *Poems*	Bonaparte marches on Paris; defeated at Waterloo (June) and exiled to St Helena
1816	Byron leaves England, travels to Geneva, and meets Shelley, Mary Godwin and Claire Clairmont in Geneva. That summer a ghost-story competition between them initiates Mary's writing of *Frankenstein* Leigh Hunt *Rimini* Shelley *Alastor and Other Poems*	End of Napoleonic Wars followed in Britain by economic depression, unemployment, rise in price of bread Spa Fields riot (December)

Year	Age	Life
1817	21/22	Hunt shows some of K's poetry to Shelley, William Godwin, and Hazlitt at a dinner party (February). Haydon takes Keats to see the Elgin Marbles in the British Museum (March). K's *Poems* published; abandons medical career. Taylor and Hessey decide to publish his future poetry (April). K travels to the Isle of Wight and begins *Endymion* (finished November). Returns to London and meets Wordsworth, sees Kean in *Richard III* at Drury Lane (December)
1818	22/23	K's brother Tom spitting blood (January). K writes *Isabella* (February–April). *Endymion* published (late April). June–August: K embarks on a walking tour of the Lakes and Scotland. He calls at Rydal Mount to see Wordsworth and is disappointed to find Wordsworth away campaigning for the Tory candidate in the Westmorland election. K is unwell, cuts short the Scottish tour and returns to London by boat. Tom's condition has worsened in his absence. Meets Fanny Brawne (September). This autumn at work on *Hyperion* and nursing Tom. Tom Keats dies 1 December
1819	23/24	The 'Annus Mirabilis'. Writes *The Eve of St Agnes* (January–February). April–May: writes *La belle dame sans merci*, all the major odes except *To Autumn*. Gives up *Hyperion*, worried about financial position, and considers becoming a ship's surgeon. June: begins work on *Lamia*. August: at work on *The Fall of Hyperion*. September: finishes *Lamia*. Joins the crowd welcoming Henry Hunt in the Strand, London (13 September). 19 September: writes *To Autumn* in Winchester after visit to London. Abandons *The Fall of Hyperion* and returns to London. November: moves to live near Fanny Brawne, Wentworth Place, Hampstead. December: unwell again. 25 December: becomes engaged to Fanny Brawne after failing to 'wean' himself from her in the autumn

Year	Artistic Events	Historical Events
1817	Byron *Manfred* Coleridge *Biographia Literaria* and *Sibylline Leaves* *Blackwood's Edinburgh Magazine* founded; one of its early articles is an attack on the 'Cockney School' (October)	Civil unrest continues; Prince Regent attacked
1818	Byron *Beppo, Childe Harold IV* Mary Shelley *Frankenstein* Jane Austen *Northanger Abbey, Persuasion* Emily Brontë born (April) Lockhart's fourth 'Cockney School' essay attacks K (August) Croker's attack on *Endymion* in the *Quarterly Review* appears in September The *Examiner* reprints Reynolds' defence of *Endymion* (October)	Karl Marx born (May)
1819	Byron *Don Juan* I–II (July) Shelley writes *Ode to the West Wind*	16 August: Peterloo Massacre, Manchester; militia ride on peaceful crowd which had gathered to hear Henry Hunt speak on the subject of Parliamentary Reform. 400 civilians injured, 11 killed. There is a public outcry. Hunt travels from Manchester to London where crowds gather to greet him (September) Parliament passes the Six Acts to prevent sedition Laënnec invents the stethoscope

Year	Age	Life
1820	24/25	February: K suffers a severe haemorrhage, offers to break off his engagement with Fanny, who refuses. K is confined to his house. July: *Lamia, Isabella, The Eve of St Agnes, and other Poems* published. K moves to Leigh Hunt's house so that he can be looked after, but he is ordered to go to Italy by his doctor. Shelley invites K to stay with him in Italy. K's departure from England is delayed by bad weather. 21–31 October: K's ship is held in quarantine at Naples. 15 November: K and his friend Joseph Severn reach Rome and take lodgings by the 'Spanish Steps'
1821	25	Nursed by Severn, K dies on 23 February. 26 February: buried in the Protestant Cemetery, Rome. 17 March: news of his death reaches London. Severn designed K's tombstone with the symbol of a lyre 'with only half the strings – to show his classical genius cut off by death before its maturity'. As K had wished, his epitaph read: 'Here lies one whose name was writ in water'

Year	Artistic Events	Historical Events
1820	Whilst writing a prose defence against attacks on himself and *Don Juan* in *Blackwood's*, Byron includes a critique of K's poetry – especially K's disregard for Pope. This article is not published in either of their lifetimes	Death of George III (January); accession of Prince Regent as George IV The Cato Street Conspiracy to murder the cabinet is 'uncovered' George IV's attempts to discredit and divorce his wife, Caroline, prove vastly unpopular. Her trial becomes a focus for popular discontent with the Establishment
1821	De Quincey *The Confessions of an English Opium Eater* Shelley composes *Adonais* (published July) Byron orders Murray to remove all mentions of K from his manuscripts and publications on the grounds that he 'cannot war with the dead – particularly those already killed by criticism'	Bonaparte dies on St Helena (May)

EDITOR'S PREFACE AND ACKNOWLEDGEMENTS

Keats's writing career was brief but, from 1814 until his death in February 1821, he produced some of the best-loved and most widely anthologised poems of the Romantic period. This volume offers a comprehensive selection of Keats's poems, placing the well-known *Hyperion* poems and the odes alongside the earlier, experimental poetry of his 1817 collection and *Endymion*. The annotations have been designed to assist the reader in approaching some of the complexities of Keats's early style and his many classical allusions. In the Introduction and Notes, I emphasise the way in which Keats's poetry is concerned to 'think of the earth', counterbalancing the idea of the 'unworldly' Keats which has been an enduring legacy from the nineteenth century to the present day.

Like all who work on the poetry of Keats, I am indebted to the textual scholarship of Jack Stillinger. His standard edition of *The Poems of John Keats* and his monograph *The Texts of Keats's Poems* have been valuable guides and references in the preparation of this volume. I thank the staff of the following libraries for assistance in locating material: Bibliothèque Nationale de Paris, The British Library, The National Library of Scotland, St Andrews University Library. I am grateful to the following for their support in the preparation of this volume: Michael Alexander, Dorothy Black and Jane Sommerville in the School of English, St Andrews University; Christine Gascoigne in the Special Collections Department of St Andrews University Library; Christina Gee and Roberta Davis at Keats House, Hampstead; Jane and Simon Taylor, Chelsea, London. My wife Jane Stabler contributed to all sections of this book in the course of its preparation, and she has been an encouraging presence throughout.

NICHOLAS ROE

ABBREVIATIONS

1817	John Keats, *Poems* (1817)
1820	John Keats, *Lamia, Isabella, the Eve of St Agnes, and other Poems* (1820)
Barnard	John Barnard, *John Keats* (1987)
Bate	Walter Jackson Bate, *John Keats* (1963)
CCC	Charles Cowden Clarke
Dickstein	Morris Dickstein, *Keats and His Poetry. A Study in Development* (1971)
Gittings	Robert Gittings, *John Keats* (1968)
Gittings (1954)	Robert Gittings, *John Keats. The Living Year* (1954)
Howe	*The Complete Works of William Hazlitt*, ed. P. P. Howe (21 vols, 1930–34)
Jack	Ian Jack, *Keats and the Mirror of Art* (1967)
JK	*John Keats. Poetry Manuscripts at Harvard. A Facsimile Edition*, ed. Jack Stillinger (1990)
Jones	John Jones, *John Keats's Dream of Truth* (1969)
K	John Keats
K & H	*Keats and History*, ed. Nicholas Roe (1995)
KC	*The Keats Circle*, ed. Hyder Edward Rollins (2 edn, 2 vols, 1965)
KCH	*Keats. The Critical Heritage*, ed. Geoffrey M. Matthews (1971)
KHM	Jerome McGann, 'Keats and the Historical Method in Literary Criticism' in Jerome McGann, *The Beauty of Inflections* (1985)
KP	'Keats and Politics: A Forum', *Studies in Romanticism* (Summer, 1986)
L	J. Lemprière, *Bibliotheca Classica; or, A Classical Dictionary* (3rd edn, London, 1797)

L&L	*Life, Letters, and Literary Remains, of John Keats*, ed. Richard Monckton Milnes (2 vols, 1848)
Letters	*The Letters of John Keats. A Selection*, ed. Robert Gittings (1970)
Newey (1989)	Vincent Newey, ' "Alternate uproar and sad peace": Keats, Politics, and the Idea of Revolution', MHRA *Yearbook of English Studies* (1989)
Newey (1995)	Vincent Newey, 'Keats, History, and the Poets', *Keats and History*, ed. Nicholas Roe (1995)
OED	*The Oxford English Dictionary* (2nd edn)
Recollections	Charles Cowden Clarke, 'Recollections of John Keats', in Charles and Mary Cowden Clarke, *Recollections of Writers* (1878)
Sperry	Stuart M. Sperry, *Keats the Poet* (1973)
TKP	Jack Stillinger, *The Texts of Keats's Poems* (1974)
Vendler	Helen Vendler, *The Odes of John Keats* (1983)
Ward	Aileen Ward, *John Keats. The Making of a Poet* (1963)
Watkins	Daniel P. Watkins, *Keats's Poetry and the Politics of the Imagination* (1989)

INTRODUCTION

When Keats died in Rome of tuberculosis, 23 February 1821, at the age of twenty-five, he was already becoming a mythical figure. Shelley's magnificent elegy *Adonais*, published the following July, lamented Keats as a 'delicate and fragile genius' who had been assassinated by malicious reviewers – namely John Lockhart in *Blackwood's Magazine* and John Wilson Croker in the *Quarterly Review*.[1] Byron's pungent quip in *Don Juan*,

> 'Tis strange the mind, that very fiery particle,
> Should let itself be snuff'd out by an Article
> (XI. 60)

only served to fix the sickly image of Keats by giving it very wide circulation. Less than ten years after Keats's death, the preface to the first collected edition of his poems, published by Galignani in Paris in 1829, affirmed that Keats's 'fragile vitality' had been unable to bear the 'party malice' of his critics: 'the excitement of spirit was too much for his frame to sustain'.[2]

The idea of Keats's vulnerable genius conformed to a potent myth that Wordsworth, in *Resolution and Independence*, had associated with Chatterton and Burns, poets whose 'glad' youth was consumed by 'despondency and madness'. Keats was readily admitted to this tragic pantheon and, in the process, he was removed from the turbulent historical period in which he had lived and written his poems to become the poet merely of ideal beauty, a 'joy forever' because uncontaminated by worldly concerns. As Keats's friend and poetic mentor Leigh Hunt wrote in 1844:

> Keats was a born poet of the most poetical kind. All his feelings came to him through a poetical medium, or were specially coloured by it. He enjoyed a jest as heartily as any one, and sympathized with the lowliest common-place; but the next minute his thoughts were in a garden of enchantment, with nymphs, and fauns, and shapes of exalted humanity.[3]

An 'enchanted' other-worldly Keats served the requirements of nineteenth-century publishers and readers alike. By insulating Keats from relevance to human affairs, he became a poet who might safely be anthologised and marketed in particular for the ever-growing numbers of women readers who, it was believed, would (should) not concern themselves with politics, economics, or public life.[4] An extreme, but nevertheless wholly representative portrait of the 'unworldly' Keats appears in Stopford Brooke's dismissive account of Keats as a poet who had no regard whatsoever for humanity or 'the excitement [and] the turmoil' of contemporary events:

> He has, in spite of a few passages and till quite the end of his career, no vital interest in the present, none in man as a whole, none in the political movement of human thought, none in the future of mankind, none in liberty, equality, or fraternity, no interest in anything but beauty.[5]

Those final comments suggest that Keats, as poet of beauty, was debarred from any relation to the revolutionary upheavals that had taken place during his lifetime.

Since Edmund Burke's influential *A Philosophical Enquiry into the Origin of our Ideas of the Sublime and Beautiful* (1757), 'beauty' had been classified as a property of femininity. Moreover, according to Burke, beauty

> almost always carries with it an idea of weakness and imperfection. Women are very sensible of this; for which reason, they learn to lisp, to totter in their walk, to counterfeit weakness, and even sickness. In all this, they are guided by nature. Beauty in distress is much the most affecting beauty.[6]

Throughout the nineteenth century, many readers identified 'Keats' with the changeless beauty of his own Grecian urn, but also, following Burke, with the 'affecting' passive status frequently imposed on middle-class Victorian women. For Matthew Arnold, the publication in 1878 of the letters Keats wrote to Fanny Brawne demonstrated 'the complete enervation of the writer' –'the abandonment of . . . the merely sensuous man' who was also suffering 'under the throttling and unmanning grasp of mortal disease'.[7] Recent feminist readings have engaged rewardingly with issues of gender in Keats's poetry and critical reception.[8] Yet elsewhere Brooke's and Arnold's image of Keats still persists in popular understanding and also among professional scholars and critics. One of the purposes of this new Everyman selection of Keats is to offer, for the first time in an edition of its kind, an opportunity for the reader to reconsider Keats's achievement, encouraging a more accurate assessment of a poet who described himself as resolutely intent upon effecting some 'public good'.

Poems from all stages of Keats's career are included in this volume with (unusually in a selected Keats) parallel texts of *La belle dame sans merci* from Keats's letter of February to May 1819 and the revised version of the poem published in Hunt's *Indicator*, 10 May 1820. The contents are arranged chronologically by date of composition, revealing Keats's development from the luxurious, Spenserian idiom of the early work to the more directed and sustained cadences of the odes and the Miltonic blank verse of the Hyperion poems. Such an arrangement also serves to highlight Keats's growing mastery of poetic forms and his challenge to critical opinions about poetry.

Typical of his early, longer poems 'I stood tip-toe', *Sleep and Poetry*, and *Endymion* is a welcome for the chancey 'happiness' of composition which lends these poems a provisional, open-ended quality. Nearly halfway through 'I stood tip-toe', for instance, Keats appears at a loss as to the direction in which his poem is moving:

> What next? A tuft of evening primroses,
> O'er which the mind may hover till it dozes;
> O'er which it well might take a pleasant sleep . . .
> (107–9)

Croker, writing in the *Quarterly* (September 1818), objected that Keats 'seems to us to write a line at random, and then he follows not the thought excited by this line, but that suggested by the *rhyme* with which it concludes'.[9] Reviewers found that (like Wordsworth's and Coleridge's *Lyrical Ballads* twenty years before) Keats's poetry did not conform to received ideas of what literature should be: 'he seems to have written directly in despite of our preconceived notions of the *manner* in which a poet ought to write; and he is continually shocking our ideas of poetical decorum, at the very time when we are acknowledging the hand of genius'.[10] In *Endymion*, however, the poem's licentious form is intrinsic to its meaning as a 'poetic romance' in pursuit of elusive beauty – a knowingly wayward, meandering response to Shelley's recent quest poem, *Alastor* (1816). Yet here too, Keats's verse can suddenly sharpen to a vision of intense pain,

> the trembling knee
> And frantic gape of lonely Niobe,
> Poor, lonely Niobe! when her lovely young
> Were dead and gone, and her caressing tongue
> Lay a lost thing upon her paly lip,
> And very, very deadliness did nip
> Her motherly cheeks.
>
> (*Endymion*, i. 337–43)

The passage shows us Keats's facility with weak verbal counters such as 'trembling knee', 'lovely young', 'dead and gone'. Similarly, the repetition of 'lonely Niobe' has its own music, but scant emotive pressure. Her 'frantic gape' has a truly arresting presence, however, and this carries over two further lines, before coming into focus as an unsettling image of tenderness deprived of its own purpose to comfort. It is 'caressing tongue' which achieves this effect: shockingly intimate, oral, sensual, the words unexpectedly open a scene of maternal grief to the loss of erotic possibility – a 'very deadliness' akin to that of the knight-at-arms, 'palely loitering' in *La belle dame sans merci*.

Keats never abandoned his trust that his 'unmisgiving' approach to poetic composition would yield the 'happy lot' of an achieved poem. As he told the painter Benjamin Robert Haydon, 10 May 1817, he seemed to have a 'good Genius' – Shakespeare – presiding over his writing, in as much that 'things which [I] do half at Random are afterwards confirmed by my judgment in a dozen features of Propriety' (*Letters*, 12). He wrote his early poems quickly, at times in contest with friends like Leigh Hunt, or, in *Endymion*, with himself as 'a test, a trial of my Powers of Imagination and chiefly of my invention which is a rare thing indeed – by which I must make 4000 Lines of one bare circumstance and fill them with Poetry' (*Letters*, 27). His need to write *Endymion* as a 'trial' of his imagination was characteristic of his poetic ambitions after that poem was published in April 1818. It was sustained (for example) in his experiments with the sonnet form during spring 1819, in *To Sleep* and 'If by dull rhymes'. These shorter lyrics cleared the way for and merged with the more complex dynamics of the odes of spring 1819, most of which were published in Keats's third collection, *Lamia, Isabella, and The Eve of St Agnes* (1820). The odes, with *Hyperion* and *The Fall of Hyperion* have for many years formed the essential 'canonical' Keats. In a different direction, however, Keats's developing skill as a narrative poet in *Isabella* and in *The Eve of St Agnes* is also demonstrated by the contrast between the exuberance of the couplets in *Endymion* and the more calculated finesse of the heroic couplets in *Lamia*. Throughout, this selection seeks to call attention to Keats's steadily compassionate feel for humanity, and the tough, unillusioned stance before life that braces and invigorates his poetry.

The selection begins with the early (and neglected) sonnet *On Peace*, written in April 1814 to celebrate the Peace of Paris – which appeared to conclude the age of revolution and war in Europe that had been the inescapable milieu of Keats's early life. The sonnet may be a little awkward in places, conventionally phrased in others. Yet, in contrast to the triumphalist 'Waterloo poems' written by Wordsworth and Southey the following year, Keats's poem announces clearly a humane voice, responding to and addressing contemporary events, and reaffirming democratic rights over the despotism of 'sceptred tyrants'. *On Peace* serves as a reminder that, as much as Helen Maria Williams and William Blake, Mary Wollstonecraft or Percy Shelley, Keats was a poet of the 'Revolutionary Idea':

> With England's happiness proclaim Europa's liberty.
> Oh Europe! let not sceptred tyrants see
> That thou must shelter in thy former state;
> Keep thy chains burst, and boldly say thou art free . . .
>
> (9–12)

Sentiments such as these encouraged the Romantic scholar and editor H. W. Garrod to suggest that with Keats

> these sympathies went deeper, and lasted longer, than is usually recognized. Keats . . . is more the child of the Revolutionary Idea than we commonly suppose. That is true, even in politics. But the Revolutionary Idea is neither wholly, nor primarily, political.[11]

So often read as 'escapist' lyrics, Keats's poems were inflected by the pressures of his times no less than the young Coleridge's *Religious Musings* (1796), the democratic sentiments of *Lyrical Ballads* (1798), or Mary Shelley's daemonic commentary on political revolution, *Frankenstein* (1818). All of Keats's poems were written at a period that in many respects closely resembles our own times: the aftermath of the global conflict with Napoleonic France which – like the 'Cold War' against the Soviet Empire – had focused the country's attention, and drained its resources for decades. As for us at this end of the twentieth century, the 'new world order' in Keats's lifetime was unsettled and anxious. In Britain, economic and social dislocations were exacerbated, releasing an acute introspective preoccupation with the wellbeing of domestic society. One obvious manifestation of this was the revival of demands for parliamentary reform, hitherto firmly suppressed by the government from the mid 1790s. In fact, the repression had begun within weeks of Keats's birth when, in December 1795, the notorious 'Two Acts' were passed, making criticism of the King or his heirs or successors treason, and limiting the size of public meetings called for political discussion.

Keats's mother, Frances Jennings, was the eldest child of Alice Whalley and John Jennings, who leased the prosperous Swan and Hoop Inn and stables at Moorgate, London. As Robert Gittings says, Frances's background was 'one of comfortable affluence and good education', such that when on 9 October 1794 she married Thomas Keats (who may have been employed at the Swan and Hoop) their future prospects must have looked extremely good.[12] Their eldest son John was born on 31 October 1795, followed by George in 1797, Tom in 1799, and Frances in June 1803. From 1802, Thomas Keats was brought in by John Jennings to manage the stables at the Swan and Hoop, and this financial security encouraged hopes of sending John and his brothers to prestigious Harrow School (where they would have met the young Lord Byron, a pupil there from 1801–5). Fortunately, Keats was not sent to Harrow; from August 1803 he attended a school that represented some aspects of advanced intellectual and political life in England at that period.

Enfield School, founded in 1786 by the eminent Baptist minister John Ryland, was an enlightened, independent establishment which developed from the vigorous dissenting culture of the later eighteenth century – the engine of advanced intellectual and political life in England at that period. Leading dissenters and reformists of the time had been associated with Keats's school, among them Joseph Priestley, George Dyer, Major John Cartwright and Gilbert Wakefield. These names are sufficient to indicate that John Clarke, Keats's headmaster, had links with the radical intelligentsia of the day and that he moved in circles where, in the 1790s, Coleridge, Wordsworth, Thelwall, Blake, Southey, Mary Wollstonecraft and William Godwin could also be found. It was at Enfield School that Keats's imaginative and political identity was formed, in an environment where the progressive, liberal ideals of the American and French Revolutions remained intact during the less optimistic years beyond the turn of the century.

The school's influence on Keats's subsequent career was profound, especially following his father's fatal accident in 1804 and, later, his mother's death from tuberculosis in 1810. Most notably, perhaps, Enfield School brought Keats the friendship of Charles Cowden Clarke, the headmaster's son, who encouraged his earliest poetry and his reading of Spenser, the strongest early influence on his verse. In his *Recollections of Writers*, Charles Cowden Clarke recalled Keats 'ramping' through the first volume of *The Faerie Queene* and 'singling out epithets' like 'a true poet': 'He *hoisted* himself up, and looked burly and dominant, as he said, "what an image that is – '*sea-shouldering whales*!'" '[13] Clarke also remembered that in his last years at Enfield Keats had 'exhausted the school library', devouring an extraordinary range of literary, historical, scientific and travel writings, as well as liberal and republican texts which reflected the political and religious opinions of the school's founder. Furthermore, the school at Enfield fostered Keats's receptivity to the liberal *Examiner* newspaper many years before he met the editor, Leigh Hunt, who in the columns of the *Examiner* would bring Keats's poems to public critical notice for the first time.

Although biographers have noted that Enfield School provided a 'liberal' curriculum for its pupils, they have omitted to stress its crucial role in transmitting to Keats the dynamic intellectual life of English dissent, and the progressive, reformist politics which had gained so much encouragement from revolutionary changes in France in 1789–92. The idea of Keats as a poet with no grasp of recent historical events is all the more untenable in view of the numerous instances where the poems give voice explicitly to Keats's political and social opinions. The sonnets to the Polish patriot Kosciusko and to Leigh Hunt celebrate two prominent figures in contemporary radical life, clearly demonstrating where Keats's sympathies were aligned. Brief but forceful, *Lines Written on 29 May* expresses Keats's admiration of the English republican tradition stemming from the English Revolution and commonwealth in the seventeenth century. The opening of *Endymion* III – an accomplished display of 'cockney' versification and rhyming – conveys Keats's contempt for those

> who lord it o'er their fellow-men
> With most prevailing tinsel: who unpen
> Their baaing vanities, to browse away
> The comfortable green and juicy hay
> From human pastures . . .
>> With unladen breasts,
> Save of blown self-applause, they proudly mount
> To their spirit's perch, their being's high account,
> Their tiptop nothings, their dull skies, their thrones –
> Amid the fierce intoxicating tones
> Of trumpets, shoutings, and belabour'd drums
> And sudden cannon.
>
> (III.1–5, 12–18)

Here, the juxtaposition of 'loose' run-on couplets and liberal political sentiment helps us to understand how contemporary readers – such as Lockhart – identified a distinct and subversive politics of style in poetry that later readers have dismissed out of hand as 'vulgar', or just downright 'bad writing'. Elsewhere, stanzas 15–18 of *Isabella; or, the Pot of Basil* expose the lethal employment which underwrites the mercantile empire of those 'ledger-men', Isabella's brothers:

> For them the Ceylon diver held his breath,
>> And went all naked to the hungry shark;
> For them his ears gush'd blood
>
> (113–15)

Even in this medieval 'Story from Boccaccio', political and economic concerns surface with unexpected power. Keats allows his readers to realise the human cost of commercial prosperity, the exploitation which made possible the rich interiors depicted in Pre-Raphaelite paintings inspired by his poems; Holman Hunt's *Isabella* on the cover of this book is a good example. Keats's disturbingly physical realisation of the damage wrought by the scramble for profit led George Bernard Shaw to claim that, in a later time, the poet of *Isabella; or, the Pot of Basil* might have become a Bolshevik revolutionary.[14]

At the beginning of *Hyperion,* Book I, Saturn appears as a king dethroned and ruined – no longer aware, even, of his former regal identity:

> Upon the sodden ground
> His old right hand lay nerveless, listless, dead,
> Unsceptred; and his realmless eyes were closed;
> While his bow'd head seem'd list'ning to the Earth,
> His ancient mother, for some comfort yet.

> It seem'd no force could wake him from his place;
> But there came one, who with a kindred hand
> Touch'd his wide shoulders, after bending low
> With reverence, though to one who knew it not.
> (I.17–25)

As these lines suggest, one of Saturn's literary forebears is Shakespeare's poor, mad, despised old king, Lear, and the relationship is worth attending to in some detail. After the execution of Louis XVI in January 1793, any portrait of a dethroned monarch was regarded in Britain as potentially subversive – an incitement to treason. In fact, during the last years of George III's reign (he died in 1820), *King Lear* was kept off the stage because it was feared that audiences would relate Lear's insanity and weakening hold on power to the mental instability of the King. But Keats's description of Saturn engages with the world in more ways than the obvious concern with the riddance of monarchy. Just as Lear gradually recovers his sanity under the kindly ministration of Cordelia and her doctors, so Saturn – for all his massive, sepulchral presence – has fallen from divinity to become only too human: a patient on a hospital bed, in need of 'some comfort yet'. His hand is 'nerveless, listless', his eyes 'closed', his tongue 'palsied'. So he rests, 'postured motionless . . . still couchant on the earth' (1.85–7).

Like Hunt, numerous critics have found Keats's verse luxuriant, sensual, fancifully self-indulgent – and not without cause: scenes of feasting appear in *Sleep and Poetry* ('Feed upon apples red, and strawberries', 103) and in *The Eve of St Agnes* ('lucent syrops, tinct with cinnamon', 267); in *Lamia* ('loaded with a feast the tables stood' II. 189), and in *The Fall of Hyperion* 'a feast of summer fruits' (I. 29). Yet Keats's poetry is also, and almost from the first, vividly alert to the physical manifestations of bodily health or disease – 'paly lip', 'quiet breathing', 'tender-taken breath', 'anguish moist and fever dew', 'eyes in torture fixed and anguish drear'. The 'Beadsman' in *The Eve of St Agnes* is an invalid, 'meagre, barefoot, wan' (12); old Angela dies 'palsy-twitch'd (376); Moneta in *The Fall of Hyperion* reveals 'a wan face, . . . bright-blanch'd / By an immortal sickness which kills not' (I. 256–8). Keats's distinctive vision – as unique as the Wordsworthian universe of childhood and nature – presents the world as a gigantic hospital, a global sickroom populated with 'effigies of pain' (*Hyperion*, I. 228). A representative instance appears in one of Keats's most critically analysed and widely anthologised poems, where Keats longs to 'quite forget'

> The weariness, the fever, and the fret
> Here, where men sit and hear each other groan;
> Where palsy shakes a few, sad, last gray hairs,
> Where youth grows pale, and spectre-thin, and dies;
> Where but to think is to be full of sorrow
> And leaden-eyed despairs,
> Where Beauty cannot keep her lustrous eyes,
> Or new Love pine at them beyond to-morrow.
>
> (23–30)

These famous lines from *Ode to a Nightingale* have often been cited as Keats's response to the death of his youngest brother Tom, destroyed by tuberculosis, 1 December 1818. This may well have been so: the ode was composed only five months after Tom died. More far-reaching, however, is the way in which these lines extend beyond the particular, the personal, to accommodate the ills of humanity at large – which Keats was never able entirely to forget or escape.

On leaving school in 1810, Keats had been apprenticed to the physician Thomas Hammond at Edmonton – sufficiently near to Enfield for Keats to remain in close touch with his friends the Clarkes. He subsequently continued his medical training at Guy's Hospital up to March 1817, the month when his first collection – entitled simply, *Poems* – was published in London. For a time, therefore, Keats's two careers of medicine and poetry overlapped in a way that the more specialised disciplines of our own time may no longer permit. This point is worth making, for Keats himself evidently saw a real continuity between his medical background and his developing sense of what he had to do as a poet.

It is difficult to exaggerate the horrific scenes Keats would have witnessed at Guy's. Smallpox could be vaccinated against, but most illnesses were incurable and, in any case, the favoured treatment of 'bleeding' the patient (even in cases where wounds had already caused severe loss of blood), usually hastened death. There was no anaesthetic and the few operations that were possible – setting bones, amputating limbs, cutting for gallstones – meant excruciating pain for the patient (unless drowsy with opium, numb with drink or knocked out before the first incision). The outcome was frequently – though not always – fatal. When Keats wrote in *Hyperion* of the Titans' 'big hearts / Heaving in pain, and horribly convuls'd' (II. 26–7), of 'horrors, portion'd to a giant nerve' (I. 175), he sought to amplify the intensity of pain which he knew, from walking the wards at Guy's, as the limit of human endurance. When he abandoned his medical training this powerful apprehension of human suffering, witnessed over and over again at first hand, was transferred to become a principal focus of his poetry. The cure of suffering that had not proved feasible through political revolution or medical practice might be possible through the pharmacy of imagination; in this way medicine and politics were united in Keats's aspiration to become a poet who might prove ' "a sage/ A humanist, physician to all men" ' (*The Fall of Hyperion*, I. 189–90).

In his *Autobiography* (1850), Leigh Hunt drew attention to the 'transcendental cosmopolitics' of *Hyperion*, suggesting how the battle between Olympians and Titans might be read as a sublime recapitulation of recent political revolutions.[15] And, certainly, one can read Oceanus's speech in *Hyperion*, Book II as an account of the liberal progressive ideology characteristic of Enfield School and, more broadly, of the revolutionary period as a whole:

> '‘tis the eternal law
> That first in beauty should be first in might:
> Yea, by that law, another race may drive
> Our conquerors to mourn as we do now.
> Have ye beheld the young God of the Seas,
> My dispossessor? Have ye seen his face?
> Have ye beheld his chariot, foam'd along
> By noble winged creatures he hath made?
> I saw him on the calmed waters scud,
> With such a glow of beauty in his eyes,
> That it enforc'd me to bid sad farewell
> To all my empire: farewell sad I took,
> And hither came, to see how dolorous fate

> Had wrought upon ye; and how I might best
> Give consolation in this woe extreme.
> Receive the truth, and let it be your balm.'
> (II.228–43)

In Oceanus's account, ' "Nature's law, not force" ' (II. 181) brought about Neptune's succession as god of the seas, Jupiter's dispossession of Saturn, and the expectation that Hyperion, god of the sun, will soon give place to his beautiful young successor, Apollo. Instead of Tom Paine's 'eternal law', *The Rights of Man* (1791–2), which had convinced a generation that the present 'is an age of Revolutions, in which everything may be looked for',[16] Keats presents a militant aesthetic in which 'might' – and consequent historical change – becomes the prerogative of youth and 'beauty'. Oceanus's speech is complicated, however, in that it is made from the perspective of the defeated party, the victims, those who have lost out in a period of tumultuous upheaval.

In one respect keyed to the ascendancy of ideal beauty, Oceanus's speech is also a token of 'comfort', 'consolation', 'balm', and 'woe extreme'. If this is not quite Keats's ideal of 'negative capability' (see *Letters*, 43), a Shakespearean hospitality to all aspects of the question, it is nevertheless more than a partisan commitment to the idea of revolutionary progress. The deification of Apollo, with which *Hyperion*, III abruptly breaks off, does not appear as an immaculate ascent, but a 'dying into life' through experience of all that is common to humanity:

> 'Names, deeds, gray legends, dire events, rebellions,
> Majesties, sovran voices, agonies,
> Creations and destroyings, all at once
> Pour into the wide hollows of my brain,
> And deify me, as if some blithe wine
> Or bright elixir peerless I had drunk,
> And so become immortal.'
> (III. 114–20)

As the god of poetry, medicine, and music (as well as the sun), Apollo's initiation is in some respects a parallel to Keats's own attainment of poetic selfhood, a link that is made more evident when Keats recast his poem in *The Fall of Hyperion* to include a personal rite of passage (see especially 1.118–149). The point seems to be that, for all Keats's belief in historical progress outlined in his letter of September 1819 – 'civil[iz]ed countries become gradually more enlighten'd and there should be a continual change for the better' (*Letters*, 312) – an awareness of human frailties and susceptibilities might have a tempering, salutary effect on unrestrained idealism: 'I hope sincerely I shall be able to put a Mite of help to the Liberal side of the Question before I die' (*Letters*, 302). Put another way, one can say that the 'revolutionary idea' and the experience of the wards at Guy's Hospital contributed much to the unique voice of Keats's poems.

Less well known than Hunt's remark about 'transcendental cosmopolitics', but just as pertinent, is the observation by William Maginn ('R. T. S.' in his contributions to *Blackwood's Magazine*) describing the 'pharmacopolitical poet of *Endymion*'. Maginn was writing to William Blackwood on hearing of Keats's death, and regretting Lockhart's attacks on Keats in the 'Cockney School' essays, where Keats's medical training and poetical ambitions had been ridiculed.[17] Maginn could not have known it, but his awkward term 'pharmacopolitical poet' strikes very close indeed to Keats's own conception of the poet as 'physician to all men' – one who, in Moneta's words in *The Fall of Hyperion* ' "pours out a balm upon the world" ' (I. 201). Critical estimates of Keats's poetry have emphasised how its soothing qualities may succeed in 'numbing pain', rather than its accompanying purpose in leading humankind to recognise 'how necessary a World of Pains and troubles is to school an Intelligence and make it a soul. A Place where the heart must feel and suffer in a thousand diverse ways!' (*Letters*, 250). Keats's belief that poetry offered a mode of intervention amid 'the agonies, the strife / Of human hearts' (*Sleep and Poetry*, 124–5) has been displaced in favour of a view of his poetry as wholly aesthetic in orientation, evading 'life' for the 'Cold Pastoral' of the Grecian urn, the 'immortal bird' of *Ode to a Nightingale*, or the tranquil impersonality of *To Autumn*. As a result, we have lost sight of the tough, mischievous Keats – a 'malcontent' who was angry and impatient with 'things as they are' and intent upon a poetic career as a means to transform that state of affairs. We forget that Keats's poetry – much more so than that of any of his contemporaries – was viewed from the outset as transparently political in meaning and purpose, one token of the democratisation of political and cultural life that is still continuing today. If we can once again read and respond to the unsettling, disconcerting poetry of 'I stood tip-toe' and *Endymion*, as well as the canonical favourites such as *To Autumn* and 'Bright Star', we attune ourselves to a restless creative energy which is one of the unacknowledged legislators of our pluralistic, multicultural society today.

NICHOLAS ROE

References

1   See *Shelley's Poetry and Prose*, ed. D. Reiman and S. Powers (1977), p. 390.
2   *The Poetical Works of Coleridge, Shelley, and Keats. Complete in One Volume* (1829), pp. v–vi.
3   Leigh Hunt, *Imagination and Fancy* (1844), p. 312.
4   Susan Wolfson, 'Feminizing Keats', *Critical Essays on John Keats*, ed. H. de Almeida (1990), pp. 317–56.
5   Stopford A. Brooke, *Studies in Poetry* (1907), p. 204.
6   Edmund Burke, *A Philosophical Enquiry into the Origin of our Ideas of the Sublime and Beautiful*, ed. A. Philips (1990), p. 100.
7   Matthew Arnold, Preface to *Keats*, Ward's *English Poets* Series (1880).
8   See for example *Romanticism and Feminism*, ed. A. Mellor (1988); Margaret Homans, 'Keats Reading Women, Women Reading Keats', SIR, 29 (Fall, 1990), pp. 341–70; Anne Mellor, *Romanticism and Gender* (1993).
9   *Quarterly Review* (Sept. 1818), rpt KCH, p. 112.
10 The *Weekly Repository, or Literary Gazette* (3–10 Sept. 1820), p. 23. This was a reprint of an unsigned review in the *Monthly Review* (July, 1820), KCH, 159–63. Its appearance in the *Weekly Repository*, published by Galignani in Paris, indicates one view of Keats circulated widely on the continent.
11 H. W. Garrod, *Keats* (1926), p. 68.
12 Robert Gittings, *John Keats* (1968), p. 31.
13 *Recollections*, p. 126.
14 *The John Keats Memorial Volume* (1921), pp. 175–6.
15 *The Autobiography of Leigh Hunt, with Reminiscences of Friends and Contemporaries* (3vols, 1850), II p. 202.
16 *The Rights of Man Part I*, ed. H. Collins (1969), p. 168.
17 William Maginn to William Blackwood, 10 April 1821, National Library of Scotland, MS 4007. For Lockhart on Keats, see in particular 'Cockney School of Poetry. No. IV', *Blackwood's Magazine* (Aug. 1818), rpt KCH, pp. 97–110.

SELECTED POEMS

On Peace

O Peace! and dost thou with thy presence bless
    The dwellings of this war-surrounded isle;
Soothing with placid brow our late distress,
    Making the triple kingdom brightly smile?
Joyful I hail thy presence; and I hail   5
    The sweet companions that await on thee;
Complete my joy – let not my first wish fail,
    Let the sweet mountain nymph thy favorite be,
With England's happiness proclaim Europa's liberty.
O Europe! let not sceptred tyrants see   10
    That thou must shelter in thy former state;
Keep thy chains burst, and boldly say thou art free;
    Give thy kings law – leave not uncurbed the great;
    So with the horrors past thou'lt win thy happier fate.

Lines Written on 29 May, the Anniversary of Charles's Restoration, on Hearing the Bells Ringing

Infatuate Britons, will you still proclaim
His memory, your direst, foulest shame?
    Nor patriots revere?
Ah! when I hear each traitorous lying bell,
'Tis gallant Sydney's, Russell's, Vane's sad knell,   5
    That pains my wounded ear.

Written on the day that Mr Leigh Hunt left Prison

What though, for showing truth to flatter'd state
    Kind Hunt was shut in prison, yet has he,
    In his immortal spirit, been as free
As the sky-searching lark, and as elate.
Minion of grandeur! think you he did wait?   5

Think you he nought but prison walls did see,
    Till, so unwilling, thou unturn'dst the key?
Ah, no! far happier, nobler was his fate!
In Spenser's halls he strayed, and bowers fair,
    Culling enchanted flowers; and he flew   10
With daring Milton through the fields of air:
    To regions of his own his genius true
Took happy flights. Who shall his fame impair
    When thou art dead, and all thy wretched crew?

To Charles Cowden Clarke

Oft have you seen a swan superbly frowning,
And with proud breast his own white shadow crowning;
He slants his neck beneath the waters bright
So silently, it seems a beam of light
Come from the galaxy: anon he sports, –
With outspread wings the Naiad Zephyr courts,
Or ruffles all the surface of the lake
In striving from its crystal face to take
Some diamond water drops, and them to treasure
In milky nest, and sip them off at leisure.   10
But not a moment can he there insure them,
Nor to such downy rest can he allure them;
For down they rush as though they would be free,
And drop like hours into eternity.
Just like that bird am I in loss of time,
Whene'er I venture on the stream of rhyme;
With shatter'd boat, oar snapt, and canvass rent,
I slowly sail, scarce knowing my intent;
Still scooping up the water with my fingers,
In which a trembling diamond never lingers.   20

By this, friend Charles, you may full plainly see
Why I have never penn'd a line to thee:
Because my thoughts were never free, and clear,
And little fit to please a classic ear;
Because my wine was of too poor a savour

For one whose palate gladdens in the favour
Of sparkling Helicon: – small good it were
To take him to a desert rude, and bare,
Who had on Baiæ's shore reclin'd at ease,
While Tasso's page was floating in a breeze   30
That gave soft music from Armida's bowers,
Mingled with fragrance from her rarest flowers:
Small good to one who had by Mulla's stream
Fondled the maidens with the breasts of cream;
Who had beheld Belphœbe in a brook,
And lovely Una in a leafy nook,
And Archimago leaning o'er his book:
Who had of all that's sweet tasted, and seen,
From silv'ry ripple, up to beauty's queen;
From the sequester'd haunts of gay Titania,   40
To the blue dwelling of divine Urania:
One, who, of late, had ta'en sweet forest walks
With him who elegantly chats, and talks –
The wrong'd Libertas, – who has told you stories
Of laurel chaplets, and Apollo's glories;
Of troops chivalrous prancing through a city,
And tearful ladies made for love, and pity:
With many else which I have never known.
Thus have I thought; and days on days have flown
Slowly, or rapidly – unwilling still   50
For you to try my dull, unlearned quill.
Nor should I now, but that I've known you long;
That you first taught me all the sweets of song:
The grand, the sweet, the terse, the free, the fine;
What swell'd with pathos, and what right divine:
Spenserian vowels that elope with ease,
And float along like birds o'er summer seas;
Miltonian storms, and more, Miltonian tenderness;
Michael in arms, and more, meek Eve's fair slenderness.
Who read for me the sonnet swelling loudly   60
Up to its climax and then dying proudly?
Who found for me the grandeur of the ode,
Growing, like Atlas, stronger from its load?
Who let me taste that more than cordial dram,
The sharp, the rapier-pointed epigram?
Shew'd me that epic was of all the king,

Round, vast, and spanning all like Saturn's ring?
You too upheld the veil from Clio's beauty,
And pointed out the patriot's stern duty;
The might of Alfred, and the shaft of Tell;   70
The hand of Brutus, that so grandly fell
Upon a tyrant's head. Ah! had I never seen,
Or known your kindness, what might I have been?
What my enjoyments in my youthful years,
Bereft of all that now my life endears?
And can I e'er these benefits forget?
And can I e'er repay the friendly debt?
No, doubly no; – yet should these rhymings please,
I shall roll on the grass with two-fold ease:
For I have long time been my fancy feeding   80
With hopes that you would one day think the reading
Of my rough verses not an hour mispent;
Should it e'er be so, what a rich content!
Some weeks have pass'd since last I saw the spires
In lucent Thames reflected: – warm desires
To see the sun o'er peep the eastern dimness,
And morning shadows streaking into slimness
Across the lawny fields, and pebbly water;
To mark the time as they grow broad, and shorter;
To feel the air that plays about the hills,   90
And sips its freshness from the little rills;
To see high, golden corn wave in the light
When Cynthia smiles upon a summer's night,
And peers among the cloudlet's jet and white,
As though she were reclining in a bed
Of bean blossoms, in heaven freshly shed.
No sooner had I stepp'd into these pleasures
Than I began to think of rhymes and measures:
The air that floated by me seem'd to say
'Write! thou wilt never have a better day.'   100
And so I did. When many lines I'd written,
Though with their grace I was not oversmitten,
Yet, as my hand was warm, I thought I'd better
Trust to my feelings, and write you a letter.
Such an attempt required an inspiration
Of a peculiar sort, – a consummation; –
Which, had I felt, these scribblings might have been

Verses from which the soul would never wean:
But many days have past since last my heart
Was warm'd luxuriously by divine Mozart;   110
By Arne delighted, or by Handel madden'd;
Or by the song of Erin pierc'd and sadden'd:
What time you were before the music sitting,
And the rich notes to each sensation fitting.
Since I have walk'd with you through shady lanes
That freshly terminate in open plains,
And revel'd in a chat that ceased not
When at night-fall among your books we got:
No, nor when supper came, nor after that, –
Nor when reluctantly I took my hat;   120
No, nor till cordially you shook my hand
Mid-way between our homes: – your accents bland
Still sounded in my ears, when I no more
Could hear your footsteps touch the grav'ly floor.
Sometimes I lost them, and then found again;
You chang'd the footpath for the grassy plain.
In those still moments I have wish'd you joys
That well you know to honour: – 'Life's very toys
With him,' said I, 'will take a pleasant charm;
It cannot be that ought will work him harm.'   130
These thoughts now come o'er me with all their might: –
Again I shake your hand, – friend Charles, good night.

September, 1816

On first looking into Chapman's Homer

Much have I travell'd in the realms of gold,
   And many goodly states and kingdoms seen;
   Round many western islands have I been
Which bards in fealty to Apollo hold.
Oft of one wide expanse had I been told   5
   That deep-brow'd Homer ruled as his demesne;
   Yet did I never breathe its pure serene
Till I heard Chapman speak out loud and bold:
Then felt I like some watcher of the skies

When a new planet swims into his ken;   10
Or like stout Cortez when with eagle eyes
   He star'd at the Pacific – and all his men
Look'd at each other with a wild surmise –
   Silent, upon a peak in Darien.

'Keen, fitful gusts are whisp'ring'

Keen, fitful gusts are whisp'ring here and there
   Among the bushes half leafless, and dry;
   The stars look very cold about the sky,
And I have many miles on foot to fare.
Yet feel I little of the cool bleak air,   5
   Or of the dead leaves rustling drearily,
   Or of those silver lamps that burn on high,
Or of the distance from home's pleasant lair:
For I am brimfull of the friendliness
   That in a little cottage I have found;   10
Of fair-hair'd Milton's eloquent distress,
   And all his love for gentle Lycid drown'd;
Of lovely Laura in her light green dress,
   And faithful Petrarch gloriously crown'd.

Addressed to the same ['Great spirits']

Great spirits now on earth are sojourning;
   He of the cloud, the cataract, the lake,
   Who on Helvellyn's summit, wide awake,
Catches his freshness from Archangel's wing:
He of the rose, the violet, the spring,   5
   The social smile, the chain for Freedom's sake:
   And lo! – whose stedfastness would never take
A meaner sound than Raphael's whispering.
And other spirits there are standing apart
   Upon the forehead of the age to come;   10
These, these will give the world another heart,

And other pulses. Hear ye not the hum
Of mighty workings? –
Listen awhile ye nations, and be dumb.

To Kosciusko

Good Kosciusko, thy great name alone
  Is a full harvest whence to reap high feeling;
  It comes upon us like the glorious pealing
Of the wide spheres – an everlasting tone.
And now it tells me, that in worlds unknown,   5
  The names of heroes, burst from clouds concealing,
  Are changed to harmonies, for ever stealing
Through cloudless blue, and round each silver throne.
It tells me too, that on a happy day,
  When some good spirit walks upon the earth,
  Thy name with Alfred's, and the great of yore
Gently commingling, gives tremendous birth
To a loud hymn, that sounds far, far away
  To where the great God lives for evermore.

Sleep and Poetry

'As I lay in my bed slepe full unmete
Was unto me, but why that I ne might
Rest I ne wist, for there n'as erthly wight
[As I suppose] had more of hertis ese
Than I, for I n'ad sicknesse nor disese.'

CHAUCER

What is more gentle than a wind in summer?
What is more soothing than the pretty hummer
That stays one moment in an open flower,
And buzzes cheerily from bower to bower?
What is more tranquil than a musk-rose blowing
In a green island, far from all men's knowing?
More healthful than the leafiness of dales?
More secret than a nest of nightingales?
More serene than Cordelia's countenance?
More full of visions than a high romance? 10
What, but thee Sleep? Soft closer of our eyes!
Low murmurer of tender lullabies!
Light hoverer around our happy pillows!
Wreather of poppy buds, and weeping willows!
Silent entangler of a beauty's tresses!
Most happy listener! when the morning blesses
Thee for enlivening all the cheerful eyes
That glance so brightly at the new sun-rise.

But what is higher beyond thought than thee?
Fresher than berries of a mountain tree? 20
More strange, more beautiful, more smooth, more regal,
Than wings of swans, than doves, than dim-seen eagle?
What is it? And to what shall I compare it?
It has a glory, and nought else can share it:
The thought thereof is awful, sweet, and holy,
Chacing away all worldliness and folly;
Coming sometimes like fearful claps of thunder,
Or the low rumblings earth's regions under;
And sometimes like a gentle whispering
Of all the secrets of some wond'rous thing 30
That breathes about us in the vacant air;

So that we look around with prying stare,
Perhaps to see shapes of light, aerial lymning,
And catch soft floatings from a faint-heard hymning;
To see the laurel wreath, on high suspended,
That is to crown our name when life is ended.
Sometimes it gives a glory to the voice,
And from the heart up-springs, rejoice! rejoice!
Sounds which will reach the Framer of all things,
And die away in ardent mutterings.   40

No one who once the glorious sun has seen,
And all the clouds, and felt his bosom clean
For his great Maker's presence, but must know
What 'tis I mean, and feel his being glow:
Therefore no insult will I give his spirit,
By telling what he sees from native merit.

O Poesy! for thee I hold my pen
That am not yet a glorious denizen
Of thy wide heaven – Should I rather kneel
Upon some mountain-top until I feel   50
A glowing splendour round about me hung,
And echo back the voice of thine own tongue?
O Poesy! for thee I grasp my pen
That am not yet a glorious denizen
Of thy wide heaven; yet, to my ardent prayer,
Yield from thy sanctuary some clear air,
Smoothed for intoxication by the breath
Of flowering bays, that I may die a death
Of luxury, and my young spirit follow
The morning sun-beams to the great Apollo   60
Like a fresh sacrifice; or, if I can bear
The o'erwhelming sweets, 'twill bring to me the fair
Visions of all places: a bowery nook
Will be elysium – an eternal book
Whence I may copy many a lovely saying
About the leaves, and flowers – about the playing
Of nymphs in woods, and fountains; and the shade
Keeping a silence round a sleeping maid;
And many a verse from so strange influence
That we must ever wonder how, and whence   70

It came. Also imaginings will hover
Round my fire-side, and haply there discover
Vistas of solemn beauty, where I'd wander
In happy silence, like the clear meander
Through its lone vales; and where I found a spot
Of awfuller shade, or an enchanted grot,
Or a green hill o'erspread with chequered dress
Of flowers, and fearful from its loveliness,
Write on my tablets all that was permitted,
All that was for our human senses fitted.   80
Then the events of this wide world I'd seize
Like a strong giant, and my spirit teaze
Till at its shoulders it should proudly see
Wings to find out an immortality.

Stop and consider! life is but a day;
A fragile dew-drop on its perilous way
From a tree's summit; a poor Indian's sleep
While his boat hastens to the monstrous steep
Of Montmorenci. Why so sad a moan?
Life is the rose's hope while yet unblown;   90
The reading of an ever-changing tale;
The light uplifting of a maiden's veil;
A pigeon tumbling in clear summer air;
A laughing school-boy, without grief or care,
Riding the springy branches of an elm.

O for ten years, that I may overwhelm
Myself in poesy; so I may do the deed
That my own soul has to itself decreed.
Then will I pass the countries that I see
In long perspective, and continually   100
Taste their pure fountains. First the realm I'll pass
Of Flora, and old Pan: sleep in the grass,
Feed upon apples red, and strawberries,
And choose each pleasure that my fancy sees;
Catch the white-handed nymphs in shady places,
To woo sweet kisses from averted faces, —
Play with their fingers, touch their shoulders white
Into a pretty shrinking with a bite
As hard as lips can make it: till agreed,

A lovely tale of human life we'll read.   110
And one will teach a tame dove how it best
May fan the cool air gently o'er my rest;
Another, bending o'er her nimble tread,
Will set a green robe floating round her head,
And still will dance with ever varied ease,
Smiling upon the flowers and the trees:
Another will entice me on, and on
Through almond blossoms and rich cinnamon;
Till in the bosom of a leafy world
We rest in silence, like two gems upcurl'd   120
In the recesses of a pearly shell.

And can I ever bid these joys farewell?
Yes, I must pass them for a nobler life,
Where I may find the agonies, the strife
Of human hearts: for lo! I see afar,
O'er sailing the blue cragginess, a car
And steeds with streamy manes – the charioteer
Looks out upon the winds with glorious fear:
And now the numerous tramplings quiver lightly
Along a huge cloud's ridge; and now with sprightly   130
Wheel downward come they into fresher skies,
Tipt round with silver from the sun's bright eyes.
Still downward with capacious whirl they glide,
And now I see them on a green-hill's side
In breezy rest among the nodding stalks.
The charioteer with wond'rous gesture talks
To the trees and mountains; and there soon appear
Shapes of delight, of mystery, and fear,
Passing along before a dusky space
Made by some mighty oaks: as they would chase   140
Some ever-fleeting music on they sweep.
Lo! how they murmur, laugh, and smile, and weep:
Some with upholden hand and mouth severe;
Some with their faces muffled to the ear
Between their arms; some, clear in youthful bloom,
Go glad and smilingly athwart the gloom;
Some looking back, and some with upward gaze;
Yes, thousands in a thousand different ways
Flit onward – now a lovely wreath of girls

Dancing their sleek hair into tangled curls;   150
And now broad wings. Most awfully intent
The driver of those steeds is forward bent,
And seems to listen: O that I might know
All that he writes with such a hurrying glow.
The visions all are fled – the car is fled
Into the light of heaven, and in their stead
A sense of real things comes doubly strong,
And, like a muddy stream, would bear along
My soul to nothingness: but I will strive
Against all doubtings, and will keep alive   160
The thought of that same chariot, and the strange
Journey it went.

                  Is there so small a range
In the present strength of manhood, that the high
Imagination cannot freely fly
As she was wont of old? prepare her steeds,
Paw up against the light, and do strange deeds
Upon the clouds? Has she not shewn us all?
From the clear space of ether, to the small
Breath of new buds unfolding? From the meaning
Of Jove's large eye-brow, to the tender greening   170
Of April meadows? Here her altar shone,
E'en in this isle; and who could paragon
The fervid choir that lifted up a noise
Of harmony, to where it aye will poise
Its mighty self of convoluting sound,
Huge as a planet, and like that roll round,
Eternally around a dizzy void?
Ay, in those days the Muses were nigh cloy'd
With honors; nor had any other care
Than to sing out and sooth their wavy hair.   180

Could all this be forgotten? Yes, a scism
Nurtured by foppery and barbarism,
Made great Apollo blush for this his land.
Men were thought wise who could not understand
His glories: with a puling infant's force
They sway'd about upon a rocking horse,
And thought it Pegasus. Ah dismal soul'd!

The winds of heaven blew, the ocean roll'd
Its gathering waves – ye felt it not. The blue
Bared its eternal bosom, and the dew   190
Of summer nights collected still to make
The morning precious: beauty was awake!
Why were ye not awake? But ye were dead
To things ye knew not of, – were closely wed
To musty laws lined out with wretched rule
And compass vile: so that ye taught a school
Of dolts to smooth, inlay, and clip, and fit,
Till, like the certain wands of Jacob's wit,
Their verses tallied. Easy was the task:
A thousand handicraftsmen wore the mask   200
Of Poesy. Ill-fated, impious race!
That blasphemed the bright Lyrist to his face,
And did not know it, – no, they went about,
Holding a poor, decrepid standard out
Mark'd with most flimsy mottos, and in large
The name of one Boileau!

                                        O ye whose charge
It is to hover round our pleasant hills!
Whose congregated majesty so fills
My boundly reverence, that I cannot trace
Your hallowed names, in this unholy place,   210
So near those common folk; did not their shames
Affright you? Did our old lamenting Thames
Delight you? Did ye never cluster round
Delicious Avon, with a mournful sound,
And weep? Or did ye wholly bid adieu
To regions where no more the laurel grew?
Or did ye stay to give a welcoming
To some lone spirits who could proudly sing
Their youth away, and die? 'Twas even so:
But let me think away those times of woe: 220
Now 'tis a fairer season; ye have breathed
Rich benedictions o'er us; ye have wreathed
Fresh garlands: for sweet music has been heard
In many places; – some has been upstirr'd
From out its crystal dwelling in a lake,
By a swan's ebon bill; from a thick brake,

Nested and quiet in a valley mild,
Bubbles a pipe; fine sounds are floating wild
About the earth: happy are ye and glad.

These things are doubtless: yet in truth we've had   230
Strange thunders from the potency of song;
Mingled indeed with what is sweet and strong,
From majesty: but in clear truth the themes
Are ugly clubs, the Poets Polyphemes
Disturbing the grand sea. A drainless shower
Of light is poesy; 'tis the supreme of power;
'Tis might half slumb'ring on its own right arm.
The very archings of her eye-lids charm
A thousand willing agents to obey,
And still she governs with the mildest sway: 240
But strength alone though of the Muses born
Is like a fallen angel: trees uptorn,
Darkness, and worms, and shrouds, and sepulchres
Delight it; for it feeds upon the burrs,
And thorns of life; forgetting the great end
Of poesy, that it should be a friend
To sooth the cares, and lift the thoughts of man.

    Yet I rejoice: a myrtle fairer than
E'er grew in Paphos, from the bitter weeds
Lifts its sweet head into the air, and feeds   250
A silent space with ever sprouting green.
All tenderest birds there find a pleasant screen,
Creep through the shade with jaunty fluttering,
Nibble the little cupped flowers and sing.
Then let us clear away the choaking thorns
From round its gentle stem; let the young fawns,
Yeaned in after times, when we are flown,
Find a fresh sward beneath it, overgrown
With simple flowers: let there nothing be
More boisterous than a lover's bended knee;   260
Nought more ungentle than the placid look
Of one who leans upon a closed book;
Nought more untranquil than the grassy slopes
Between two hills. All hail delightful hopes!
As she was wont, th' imagination

Into most lovely labyrinths will be gone,
And they shall be accounted poet kings
Who simply tell the most heart-easing things.
O may these joys be ripe before I die.

Will not some say that I presumptuously   270
Have spoken? that from hastening disgrace
'Twere better far to hide my foolish face?
That whining boyhood should with reverence bow
Ere the dread thunderbolt could reach? How!
If I do hide myself, it sure shall be
In the very fane, the light of Poesy:
If I do fall, at least I will be laid
Beneath the silence of a poplar shade;
And over me the grass shall be smooth shaven;
And there shall be a kind memorial graven.   280
But off Despondence! miserable bane!
They should not know thee, who athirst to gain
A noble end, are thirsty every hour.
What though I am not wealthy in the dower
Of spanning wisdom; though I do not know
The shiftings of the mighty winds that blow
Hither and thither all the changing thoughts
Of man: though no great minist'ring reason sorts
Out the dark mysteries of human souls
To clear conceiving: yet there ever rolls   290
A vast idea before me, and I glean
Therefrom my liberty; thence too I've seen
The end and aim of Poesy. 'Tis clear
As any thing most true; as that the year
Is made of the four seasons – manifest
As a large cross, some old cathedral's crest,
Lifted to the white clouds. Therefore should I
Be but the essence of deformity,
A coward, did my very eye-lids wink
At speaking out what I have dared to think.   300
Ah! rather let me like a madman run
Over some precipice; let the hot sun
Melt my Dedalian wings, and drive me down
Convuls'd and headlong! Stay! an inward frown
Of conscience bids me be more calm awhile,

An ocean dim, sprinkled with many an isle,
Spreads awfully before me. How much toil!
How many days! what desperate turmoil!
Ere I can have explored its widenesses.
Ah, what a task! upon my bended knees,   310
I could unsay those — no, impossible!
Impossible!

              For sweet relief I'll dwell
On humbler thoughts, and let this strange assay
Begun in gentleness die so away.
E'en now all tumult from my bosom fades:
I turn full hearted to the friendly aids
That smooth the path of honour; brotherhood,
And friendliness the nurse of mutual good.
The hearty grasp that sends a pleasant sonnet
Into the brain ere one can think upon it;   320
The silence when some rhymes are coming out;
And when they're come, the very plesant rout:
The message certain to be done to-morrow.
'Tis perhaps as well that it should be to borrow
Some precious book from out its snug retreat,
To cluster round it when we next shall meet.
Scarce can I scribble on; for lovely airs
Are fluttering round the room like doves in pairs;
Many delights of that glad day recalling,
When first my senses caught their tender falling.   330
And with these airs come forms of elegance
Stooping their shoulders o'er a horse's prance,
Careless, and grand — fingers soft and round
Parting luxuriant curls; — and the swift bound
Of Bacchus from his chariot, when his eye
Made Ariadne's cheek look blushingly.
Thus I remember all the pleasant flow
Of words at opening a portfolio.

Things such as these are ever harbingers
To trains of peaceful images: the stirs   340
Of a swan's neck unseen among the rushes:
A linnet starting all about the bushes:
A butterfly, with golden wings broad parted,

Nestling a rose, convuls'd as though it smarted
With over pleasure – many, many more,
Might I indulge at large in all my store
Of luxuries: yet I must not forget
Sleep, quiet with his poppy coronet:
For what there may be worthy in these rhymes
I partly owe to him: and thus, the chimes   350
Of friendly voices had just given place
To as sweet a silence, when I 'gan retrace
The pleasant day, upon a couch at ease.
It was a poet's house who keeps the keys
Of pleasure's temple. Round about were hung
The glorious features of the bards who sung
In other ages – cold and sacred busts
Smiled at each other. Happy he who trusts
To clear Futurity his darling fame!
Then there were fauns and satyrs taking aim   360
At swelling apples with a frisky leap
And reaching fingers, 'mid a luscious heap
Of vine leaves. Then there rose to view a fane
Of liny marble, and thereto a train
Of nymphs approaching fairly o'er the sward:
One, loveliest, holding her white hand toward
The dazzling sun-rise: two sisters sweet
Bending their graceful figures till they meet
Over the trippings of a little child:
And some are hearing, eagerly, the wild   370
Thrilling liquidity of dewy piping.
See, in another picture, nymphs are wiping
Cherishingly Diana's timorous limbs; –
A fold of lawny mantle dabbling swims
At the bath's edge, and keeps a gentle motion
With the subsiding crystal: as when ocean
Heaves calmly its broad swelling smoothiness o'er
Its rocky marge, and balances once more
The patient weeds; that now unshent by foam
Feel all about their undulating home.   380
Sappho's meek head was there half smiling down
At nothing; just as though the earnest frown
Of over thinking had that moment gone
From off her brow, and left her all alone.

Great Alfred's too, with anxious, pitying eyes,
As if he always listened to the sighs
Of the goaded world; and Kosciusko's worn
By horrid suffrance – mightily forlorn.

Petrarch, outstepping from the shady green,
Starts at the sight of Laura; nor can wean   390
His eyes from her sweet face. Most happy they!
For over them was seen a free display
Of out-spread wings, and from between them shone
The face of Poesy: from off her throne
She overlook'd things that I scarce could tell.
The very sense of where I was might well
Keep Sleep aloof: but more than that there came
Thought after thought to nourish up the flame
Within my breast; so that the morning light
Surprised me even from a sleepless night;   400
And up I rose refresh'd, and glad, and gay,
Resolving to begin that very day
These lines; and howsoever they be done,
I leave them as a father does his son.

'I stood tip-toe upon a little hill'

'Places of nestling green for Poets made.'
Story of Rimini

I stood tip-toe upon a little hill,
The air was cooling, and so very still,
That the sweet buds which with a modest pride
Pull droopingly, in slanting curve aside,
Their scanty leaved, and finely tapering stems,
Had not yet lost those starry diadems
Caught from the early sobbing of the morn.
The clouds were pure and white as flocks new shorn,
And fresh from the clear brook; sweetly they slept
On the blue fields of heaven, and then there crept   10
A little noiseless noise among the leaves,
Born of the very sigh that silence heaves:
For not the faintest motion could be seen
Of all the shades that slanted o'er the green.
There was wide wand'ring for the greediest eye,
To peer about upon variety;
Far round the horizon's crystal air to skim,
And trace the dwindled edgings of its brim;
To picture out the quaint, and curious bending
Of a fresh woodland alley, never ending;   20
Or by the bowery clefts, and leafy shelves,
Guess where the jaunty streams refresh themselves.
I gazed awhile, and felt as light, and free
As though the fanning wings of Mercury
Had played upon my heels: I was light-hearted,
And many pleasures to my vision started;
So I straightaway began to pluck a posey
Of luxuries bright, milky, soft and rosy.

A bush of May flowers with the bees about them;
Ah, sure no tasteful nook would be without them;   30
And let a lush laburnum oversweep them,
And let long grass grow round the roots to keep them
Moist, cool and green; and shade the violets,
That they may bind the moss in leafy nets.

A filbert hedge with wild briar overtwined,
And clumps of woodbine taking the soft wind
Upon their summer thrones; there too should be
The frequent chequer of a youngling tree,
That with a score of light green brethren shoots
From the quaint mossiness of aged roots: 40
Round which is heard a spring-head of clear waters
Babbling so wildly of its lovely daughters
The spreading blue bells: it may haply mourn
That such fair clusters should be rudely torn
From their fresh beds, and scattered thoughtlessly
By infant hands, left on the path to die.

Open afresh your round of starry folds,
Ye ardent marigolds!
Dry up the moisture from your golden lids,
For great Apollo bids   50
That in these days your praises should be sung
On many harps, which he has lately strung;
And when again your dewiness he kisses,
Tell him, I have you in my world of blisses:
So haply when I rove in some far vale,
His mighty voice may come upon the gale.

Here are sweet peas, on tip-toe for a flight:
With wings of gentle flush o'er delicate white,
And taper fingers catching at all things,
To bind them all about with tiny rings.   60

Linger awhile upon some bending planks
That lean against a streamlet's rushy banks,
And watch intently Nature's gentle doings:
They will be found softer than ring-dove's cooings.
How silent comes the water round that bend;
Not the minutest whisper does it send
To the o'erhanging sallows: blades of grass
Slowly across the chequer'd shadows pass.
Why, you might read two sonnets, ere they reach
To where the hurrying freshnesses aye preach   70
A natural sermon o'er their pebbly beds;
Where swarms of minnows show their little heads,

Staying their wavy bodies 'gainst the streams,
To taste the luxury of sunny beams
Temper'd with coolness. How they ever wrestle
With their own sweet delight, and ever nestle
Their silver bellies on the pebbly sand.
If you but scantily hold out the hand,
That very instant not one will remain;
But turn your eye, and they are there again.   80
The ripples seem right glad to reach those cresses,
And cool themselves among the em'rald tresses;
The while they cool themselves, they freshness give,
And moisture, that the bowery green may live :
So keeping up an interchange of favours,
Like good men in the truth of their behaviours.
Sometimes goldfinches one by one will drop
From low hung branches; little space they stop;
But sip, and twitter, and their feathers sleek;
Then off at once, as in a wanton freak: 90
Or perhaps, to show their black, and golden wings,
Pausing upon their yellow flutterings.
Were I in such a place, I sure should pray
That nought less sweet might call my thoughts away,
Then the soft rustle of a maiden's gown
Fanning away the dandelion's down;
Than the light music of her nimble toes
Patting against the sorrel as she goes.
How she would start, and blush, thus to be caught
Playing in all her innocence of thought.   100
O let me lead her gently o'er the brook,
Watch her half-smiling lips, and downward look;
O let me for one moment touch her wrist;
Let me one moment to her breathing list;
And as she leaves me may she often turn
Her fair eyes looking through her locks aubùrne.

What next? A tuft of evening primroses,
O'er which the mind may hover till it dozes;
O'er which it well might take a pleasant sleep,
But that 'tis ever startled by the leap   110
Of buds into ripe flowers; or by the flitting
Of diverse moths, that aye their rest are quitting;

Or by the moon lifting her silver rim
Above a cloud, and with a gradual swim
Coming into the blue with all her light.
O Maker of sweet poets, dear delight
Of this fair world, and all its gentle livers;
Spangler of clouds, halo of crystal rivers,
Mingler with leaves, and dew and tumbling streams,
Closer of lovely eyes to lovely dreams,   120
Lover of loneliness, and wandering,
Of upcast eye, and tender pondering!
Thee must I praise above all other glories
That smile us on to tell delightful stories.
For what has made the sage or poet write
But the fair paradise of Nature's light?
In the calm grandeur of a sober line,
We see the waving of the mountain pine;
And when a tale is beautifully staid,
We feel the safety of a hawthorn glade: 130
When it is moving on luxurious wings,
The soul is lost in pleasant smotherings:
Fair dewy roses brush against our faces,
And flowering laurels spring from diamond vases;
O'er head we see the jasmine and sweet briar,
And bloomy grapes laughing from green attire;
While at our feet, the voice of crystal bubbles
Charms us at once away from all our troubles:
So that we feel uplifted from the world,
Walking upon the white clouds wreath'd and curl'd.   140
So felt he, who first told, how Psyche went
On the smooth wind to realms of wonderment;
What Psyche felt, and Love, when their full lips
First touch'd; what amorous, and fondling nips
They gave each other's cheeks; with all their sighs,
And how they kist each other's tremulous eyes:
The silver lamp, – the ravishment, – the wonder –
The darkness, – loneliness, – the fearful thunder;
Their woes gone by, and both to heaven upflown,
To bow for gratitude before Jove's throne.   150
So did he feel, who pull'd the boughs aside,
That we might look into a forest wide,
To catch a glimpse of Fawns, and Dryades

Coming with softest rustle through the trees;
And garlands woven of flowers wild, and sweet,
Upheld on ivory wrists, or sporting feet:
Telling us how fair, trembling Syrinx fled
Arcadian Pan, with such a fearful dread.
Poor nymph, – poor Pan, – how he did weep to find,
Nought but a lovely sighing of the wind   160
Along the reedy stream; a half heard strain,
Full of sweet desolation – balmy pain.

What first inspired a bard of old to sing
Narcissus pining o'er the untainted spring?
In some delicious ramble, he had found
A little space, with boughs all woven round;
And in the midst of all, a clearer pool
Than e'er reflected in its pleasant cool
The blue sky here, and there, serenely peeping
Through tendril wreaths fantastically creeping.   170
And on the bank a lonely flower he spied,
A meek and forlorn flower, with naught of pride,
Drooping its beauty o'er the watery clearness,
To woo its own sad image into nearness:
Deaf to light Zephyrus it would not move;
But still would seem to droop, to pine, to love.
So while the Poet stood in this sweet spot,
Some fainter gleamings o'er his fancy shot;
Nor was it long ere he had told the tale
Of young Narcissus, and sad Echo's bale.   180

Where had he been, from whose warm head out-flew
That sweetest of all songs, that ever new,
That aye refreshing, pure deliciousness,
Coming ever to bless
The wanderer by moonlight? to him bringing
Shapes from the invisible world, unearthly singing
From out the middle air, from flowery nests,
And from the pillowy silkiness that rests
Full in the speculation of the stars.
Ah! surely he had burst our mortal bars;   190
Into some wond'rous region he had gone,
To search for thee, divine Endymion!

He was a Poet, sure a lover too,
Who stood on Latmus' top, what time there blew
Soft breezes from the myrtle vale below;
And brought in faintness solemn, sweet, and slow
A hymn from Dian's temple; while upswelling,
The incense went to her own starry dwelling.
But though her face was clear as infant's eyes,
Though she stood smiling o'er the sacrifice,   200
The Poet wept at her so piteous fate,
Wept that such beauty should be desolate:
So in fine wrath some golden sounds he won,
And gave meek Cynthia her Endymion.

Queen of the wide air; thou most lovely queen
Of all the brightness that mine eyes have seen!
As thou exceedest all things in thy shine,
So every tale, does this sweet tale of thine.
O for three words of honey, that I might
Tell but one wonder of thy bridal night!   210

Where distant ships do seem to show their keels,
Phœbus awhile delayed his mighty wheels,
And turned to smile upon thy bashful eyes,
Ere he his unseen pomp would solemnize.
The evening weather was so bright, and clear,
That men of health were of unusual cheer;
Stepping like Homer at the trumpet's call,
Or young Apollo on the pedestal:
And lovely women were as fair and warm,
As Venus looking sideways in alarm.   220
The breezes were ethereal, and pure,
And crept through half closed lattices to cure
The languid sick; it cool'd their fever'd sleep,
And soothed them into slumbers full and deep.
Soon they awoke clear eyed: nor burnt with thirsting,
Nor with hot fingers, nor with temples bursting:
And springing up, they met the wond'ring sight
Of their dear friends, nigh foolish with delight;
Who feel their arms, and breasts, and kiss and stare,
And on their placid foreheads part the hair.   230
Young men, and maidens at each other gaz'd

With hands held back, and motionless, amaz'd
To see the brightness in each other's eyes;
And so they stood, fill'd with a sweet surprise,
Until their tongues were loos'd in poesy.
Therefore no lover did of anguish die:
But the soft numbers, in that moment spoken,
Made silken ties, that never may be broken.
Cynthia! I cannot tell the greater blisses,
That follow'd thine, and thy dear shepherd's kisses: 240
Was there a Poet born? — but now no more,
My wand'ring spirit must no further soar. —

On receiving a laurel crown from Leigh Hunt

Minutes are flying swiftly, and as yet
   Nothing unearthly has enticed my brain
   Into a delphic labyrinth — I would fain
Catch an immortal thought to pay the debt
I owe to the kind poet who has set   5
   Upon my ambitious head a glorious gain.
   Two bending laurel sprigs — 'tis nearly pain
To be conscious of such a coronet.
Still time is fleeting, and no dream arises
   Gorgeous as I would have it — only I see   10
A trampling down of what the world most prizes,
   Turbans and crowns, and blank regality;
And then I run into most wild surmises
   Of all the many glories that may be.

To Leigh Hunt, Esq.

Glory and loveliness have passed away;
   For if we wander out in early morn,
   No wreathed incense do we see upborne
Into the east, to meet the smiling day:
No crowd of nymphs soft voic'd and young, and gay,   5
   In woven baskets bringing ears of corn,
   Roses, and pinks, and violets, to adorn
The shrine of Flora in her early May.
But there are left delights as high as these,
   And I shall ever bless my destiny,   10
That in a time, when under pleasant trees
   Pan is no longer sought, I feel a free
A leafy luxury, seeing I could please
   With these poor offerings, a man like thee.

On seeing the Elgin Marbles

My spirit is too weak – mortality
  Weighs heavily on me like unwilling sleep,
  And each imagined pinnacle and steep
Of godlike hardship tells me I must die
Like a sick eagle looking at the sky.   5
  Yet 'tis a gentle luxury to weep
  That I have not the cloudy winds to keep
Fresh for the opening of the morning's eye.
Such dim-conceived glories of the brain
  Bring round the heart an undescribable feud;   10
So do these wonders a most dizzy pain
  That mingles Grecian grandeur with the rude
Wasting of old time – with a billowy main –
  A sun – a shadow of a magnitude.

On the Sea

It keeps eternal whisperings around
  Desolate shores, and with its mighty swell
  Gluts twice ten thousand caverns; till the spell
Of Hecate leaves them their old shadowy sound.
Often 'tis in such gentle temper found   5
  That scarcely will the very smallest shell
  Be moved for days from whence it sometime fell,
When last the winds of heaven were unbound.
O ye who have your eyeballs vext and tir'd,
  Feast them upon the wideness of the sea;   10
O ye whose ears are dinned with uproar rude
  Or fed too much with cloying melody –
Sit ye near some old cavern's mouth and brood
  Until ye start as if the sea nymphs quired.

Endymion: A Poetic Romance
'The stretched metre of an antique song'
Inscribed to the Memory of Thomas Chatterton

BOOK I

A thing of beauty is a joy for ever:
Its loveliness increases; it will never
Pass into nothingness; but still will keep
A bower quiet for us, and a sleep
Full of sweet dreams, and health, and quiet breathing.
Therefore, on every morrow, are we wreathing
A flowery band to bind us to the earth,
Spite of despondence, of the inhuman dearth
Of noble natures, of the gloomy days,
Of all the unhealthy and o'er-darkened ways   10
Made for our searching: yes, in spite of all,
Some shape of beauty moves away the pall
From our dark spirits. Such the sun, the moon,
Trees old and young, sprouting a shady boon
For simple sheep; and such are daffodils
With the green world they live in; and clear rills
That for themselves a cooling covert make
'Gainst the hot season; the mid forest brake,
Rich with a sprinkling of fair musk-rose blooms:
And such too is the grandeur of the dooms   20
We have imagined for the mighty dead;
All lovely tales that we have heard or read:
An endless fountain of immortal drink,
Pouring unto us from the heaven's brink.

Nor do we merely feel these essences
For one short hour; no, even as the trees
That whisper round a temple become soon
Dear as the temple's self, so does the moon,
The passion poesy, glories infinite,
Haunt us till they become a cheering light   30
Unto our souls, and bound to us so fast,

That, whether there be shine, or gloom o'ercast,
They alway must be with us, or we die.

   Therefore, 'tis with full happiness that I
Will trace the story of Endymion.
The very music of the name has gone
Into my being, and each pleasant scene
Is growing fresh before me as the green
Of our own vallies: so I will begin
Now while I cannot hear the city's din;   40
Now while the early budders are just new,
And run in mazes of the youngest hue
About old forests; while the willow trails
Its delicate amber; and the dairy pails
Bring home increase of milk. And, as the year
Grows lush in juicy stalks, I'll smoothly steer
My little boat, for many quiet hours,
With streams that deepen freshly into bowers.
Many and many a verse I hope to write,
Before the daisies, vermeil rimm'd and white,   50
Hide in deep herbage; and ere yet the bees
Hum about globes of clover and sweet peas,
I must be near the middle of my story.
O may no wintry season, bare and hoary,
See it half finished: but let Autumn bold,
With universal tinge of sober gold,
Be all about me when I make an end.
And now at once, adventuresome, I send
My herald thought into a wilderness:
There let its trumpet blow, and quickly dress   60
My uncertain path with green, that I may speed
Easily onward, thorough flowers and weed.

   Upon the sides of Latmos was outspread
A mighty forest; for the moist earth fed
So plenteously all weed-hidden roots
Into o'er-hanging boughs, and precious fruits.
And it had gloomy shades, sequestered deep,
Where no man went; and if from shepherd's keep
A lamb strayed far a-down those inmost glens,
Never again saw he the happy pens   70

Whither his brethren, bleating with content,
Over the hills at every nightfall went.
Among the shepherds, 'twas believed ever,
That not one fleecy lamb which thus did sever
From the white flock, but pass'd unworried
By angry wolf, or pard with prying head,
Until it came to some unfooted plains
Where fed the herds of Pan: ay great his gains
Who thus one lamb did lose. Paths there were many,
Winding through palmy fern, and rushes fenny,   80
And ivy banks; all leading pleasantly
To a wide lawn, whence one could only see
Stems thronging all around between the swell
Of turf and slanting branches: who could tell
The freshness of the space of heaven above,
Edg'd round with dark tree tops? through which a dove
Would often beat its wings, and often too
A little cloud would move across the blue.

Full in the middle of this pleasantness
There stood a marble altar, with a tress   90
Of flowers budded newly; and the dew
Had taken fairy phantasies to strew
Daisies upon the sacred sward last eve,
And so the dawned light in pomp receive.
For 'twas the morn: Apollo's upward fire
Made every eastern cloud a silvery pyre
Of brightness so unsullied, that therein
A melancholy spirit well might win
Oblivion, and melt out his essence fine
Into the winds: rain-scented eglantine   100
Gave temperate sweets to that well-wooing sun;
The lark was lost in him; cold springs had run
To warm their chilliest bubbles in the grass;
Man's voice was on the mountains; and the mass
Of nature's lives and wonders puls'd tenfold,
To feel this sun-rise and its glories old.

Now while the silent workings of the dawn
Were busiest, into that self-same lawn
All suddenly, with joyful cries, there sped

A troop of little children garlanded;   110
Who gathering round the altar, seemed to pry
Earnestly round as wishing to espy
Some folk of holiday: nor had they waited
For many months, ere their ears were sated
With a faint breath of music, which ev'n then
Fill'd out its voice, and died away again.
Within a little space again it gave
Its airy swellings, with a gentle wave,
To light-hung leaves, in smoothest echoes breaking
Through copse-clad vallies, – ere their death, o'ertaking   120
The surgy murmurs of the lonely sea.

  And now, as deep into the wood as we
Might mark a lynx's eye, there glimmered light
Fair faces and a rush of garments white,
Plainer and plainer shewing, till at last
Into the widest alley they all past,
Making directly for the woodland altar.
O kindly muse! let not my weak tongue faulter
In telling of this goodly company,
Of their old piety, and of their glee: 130
But let a portion of ethereal dew
Fall on my head, and presently unmew
My soul; that I may dare, in wayfaring,
To stammer where old Chaucer used to sing.

  Leading the way, young damsels danced along,
Bearing the burden of a shepherd song;
Each having a white wicker over brimm'd
With April's tender younglings: next, well trimm'd,
A crowd of shepherds with as sunburnt looks
As may be read of in Arcadian books;   140
Such as sat listening round Apollo's pipe,
When the great deity, for earth too ripe,
Let his divinity o'er-flowing die
In music, through the vales of Thessaly:
Some idly trailed their sheep-hooks on the ground,
And some kept up a shrilly mellow sound
With ebon-tipped flutes: close after these,
Now coming from beneath the forest trees,

A venerable priest full soberly,
Begirt with ministring looks: alway his eye   150
Stedfast upon the matted turf he kept,
And after him his sacred vestments swept.
From his right hand there swung a vase, milk-white,
Of mingled wine, out-sparkling generous light;
And in his left he held a basket full
Of all sweet herbs that searching eye could cull:
Wild thyme, and valley-lilies whiter still
Than Leda's love, and cresses from the rill.
His aged head, crowned with beechen wreath,
Seem'd like a poll of ivy in the teeth   160
Of winter hoar. Then came another crowd
Of shepherds, lifting in due time aloud
Their share of the ditty. After them appear'd,
Up-followed by a multitude that rear'd
Their voices to the clouds, a fair wrought car,
Easily rolling so as scarce to mar
The freedom of three steeds of dapple brown:
Who stood therein did seem of great renown
Among the throng. His youth was fully blown,
Shewing like Ganymede to manhood grown;   170
And, for those simple times, his garments were
A chieftain king's: beneath his breast, half bare,
Was hung a silver bugle, and between
His nervy knees there lay a boar-spear keen.
A smile was on his countenance; he seem'd,
To common lookers on, like one who dream'd
Of idleness in groves Elysian:
But there were some who feelingly could scan
A lurking trouble in his nether lip,
And see that oftentimes the reins would slip   180
Through his forgotten hands: then would they sigh,
And think of yellow leaves, of owlet's cry,
Of logs piled solemnly. – Ah, well-a-day,
Why should our young Endymion pine away!

   Soon the assembly, in a circle rang'd,
Stood silent round the shrine: each look was chang'd
To sudden veneration: women meek
Beckon'd their sons to silence; while each cheek

Of virgin bloom paled gently for slight fear.
Endymion too, without a forest peer,   190
Stood, wan, and pale, and with an awed face,
Among his brothers of the mountain chase.
In midst of all, the venerable priest
Eyed them with joy from greatest to the least,
And, after lifting up his aged hands,
Thus spake he: 'Men of Latmos! shepherd bands!
Whose care it is to guard a thousand flocks:
Whether descended from beneath the rocks
That overtop your mountains; whether come
From vallies where the pipe is never dumb;   200
Or from your swelling downs, where sweet air stirs
Blue hare-bells lightly, and where prickly furze
Buds lavish gold; or ye, whose precious charge
Nibble their fill at ocean's very marge,
Whose mellow reeds are touch'd with sounds forlorn
By the dim echoes of old Triton's horn:
Mothers and wives! who day by day prepare
The scrip, with needments, for the mountain air;
And all ye gentle girls who foster up
Udderless lambs, and in a little cup   210
Will put choice honey for a favoured youth:
Yea, every one attend! for in good truth
Our vows are wanting to our great god Pan.
Are not our lowing heifers sleeker than
Night-swollen mushrooms? Are not our wide plains
Speckled with countless fleeces? Have not rains
Green'd over April's lap? No howling sad
Sickens our fearful ewes; and we have had
Great bounty from Endymion our lord.
The earth is glad: the merry lark has pour'd   220
His early song against yon breezy sky,
That spreads so clear o'er our solemnity.'

    Thus ending, on the shrine he heap'd a spire
Of teeming sweets, enkindling sacred fire;
Anon he stain'd the thick and spongy sod
With wine, in honour of the shepherd-god.
Now while the earth was drinking it, and while
Bay leaves were crackling in the fragrant pile,

And gummy frankincense was sparkling bright
'Neath smothering parsley, and a hazy light   230
Spread greyly eastward, thus a chorus sang:

'O thou, whose mighty palace roof doth hang
From jagged trunks, and overshadoweth
Eternal whispers, glooms, the birth, life, death
Of unseen flowers in heavy peacefulness;
Who lov'st to see the hamadryads dress
Their ruffled locks where meeting hazels darken;
And through whole solemn hours dost sit, and hearken
The dreary melody of bedded reeds —
In desolate places, where dank moisture breeds   240
The pipy hemlock to strange overgrowth;
Bethinking thee, how melancholy loth
Thou wast to lose fair Syrinx — do thou now,
By thy love's milky brow!
By all the trembling mazes that she ran,
Hear us, great Pan!

'O thou, for whose soul-soothing quiet, turtles
Passion their voices cooingly 'mong myrtles,
What time thou wanderest at eventide
Through sunny meadows, that outskirt the side   250
Of thine enmossed realms: O thou, to whom
Broad leaved fig trees even now foredoom
Their ripen'd fruitage; yellow girted bees
Their golden honeycombs; our village leas
Their fairest blossom'd beans and poppied corn;
The chuckling linnet its five young unborn,
To sing for thee; low creeping strawberries
Their summer coolness; pent up butterflies
Their freckled wings; yea, the fresh budding year
All its completions — be quickly near,   260
By every wind that nods the mountain pine,
O forester divine!

'Thou, to whom every faun and satyr flies
For willing service; whether to surprise
The squatted hare while in half sleeping fit;
Or upward ragged precipices flit

To save poor lambkins from the eagle's maw;
Or by mysterious enticement draw
Bewildered shepherds to their path again;
Or to tread breathless round the frothy main,   270
And gather up all fancifullest shells
For thee to tumble into Naiads' cells,
And, being hidden, laugh at their out-peeping;
Or to delight thee with fantastic leaping,
The while they pelt each other on the crown
With silvery oak apples, and fir cones brown –
By all the echoes that about thee ring,
Hear us, O satyr king!

   'O Hearkener to the loud clapping shears,
While ever and anon to his shorn peers   280
A ram goes bleating: Winder of the horn,
When snouted wild-boars routing tender corn
Anger our huntsmen: Breather round our farms,
To keep off mildews, and all weather harms:
Strange ministrant of undescribed sounds,
That come a swooning over hollow grounds,
And wither drearily on barren moors:
Dread opener of the mysterious doors
Leading to universal knowledge – see,
Great son of Dryope,   290
The many that are come to pay their vows
With leaves about their brows!

   'Be still the unimaginable lodge
For solitary thinkings; such as dodge
Conception to the very bourne of heaven,
Then leave the naked brain: be still the leaven,
That spreading in this dull and clodded earth
Gives it a touch ethereal – a new birth:
Be still a symbol of immensity;
A firmament reflected in a sea;   300
An element filling the space between;
An unknown – but no more: we humbly screen
With uplift hands our foreheads, lowly bending,
And giving out a shout most heaven rending,

Conjure thee to receive our humble Pæan,
Upon thy Mount Lycean!'

    Even while they brought the burden to a close,
A shout from the whole multitude arose,
That lingered in the air like dying rolls
Of abrupt thunder, when Ionian shoals   310
Of dolphins bob their noses through the brine.
Meantime, on shady levels, mossy fine,
Young companies nimbly began dancing
To the swift treble pipe, and humming string.
Aye, those fair living forms swam heavenly
To tunes forgotten — out of memory:
Fair creatures! whose young children's children bred
Thermopylæ its heroes — not yet dead,
But in old marbles ever beautiful.
High genitors, unconscious did they cull   320
Time's sweet first-fruits — they danc'd to weariness,
And then in quiet circles did they press
The hillock turf, and caught the latter end
Of some strange history, potent to send
A young mind from its bodily tenement.
Or they might watch the quoit-pitchers, intent
On either side; pitying the sad death
Of Hyacinthus, when the cruel breath
Of Zephyr slew him, — Zephyr penitent,
Who now, ere Phœbus mounts the firmament,   330
Fondles the flower amid the sobbing rain.
The archers too, upon a wider plain,
Beside the feathery whizzing of the shaft,
And the dull twanging bowstring, and the raft
Branch down sweeping from a tall ash top,
Call'd up a thousand thoughts to envelope
Those who would watch. Perhaps, the trembling knee
And frantic gape of lonely Niobe,
Poor, lonely Niobe! when her lovely young
Were dead and gone, and her caressing tongue   340
Lay a lost thing upon her paly lip,
And very, very deadliness did nip
Her motherly cheeks. Arous'd from this sad mood
By one, who at a distance loud halloo'd,

Uplifting his strong bow into the air,
Many might after brighter visions stare:
After the Argonauts, in blind amaze
Tossing about on Neptune's restless ways,
Until, from the horizon's vaulted side,
There shot a golden splendour far and wide,   350
Spangling those million poutings of the brine
With quivering ore: 'twas even an awful shine
From the exaltation of Apollo's bow;
A heavenly beacon in their dreary woe.
Who thus were ripe for high contemplating,
Might turn their steps towards the sober ring
Where sat Endymion and the aged priest
'Mong shepherds gone in eld, whose looks increas'd
The silvery setting of their mortal star.
There they discours'd upon the fragile bar   360
That keeps us from our homes ethereal;
And what our duties there: to nightly call
Vesper, the beauty-crest of summer weather;
To summon all the downiest clouds together
For the sun's purple couch; to emulate
In ministring the potent rule of fate
With speed of fire-tailed exhalations;
To tint her pallid cheek with bloom, who cons
Sweet poesy by moonlight: besides these,
A world of other unguess'd offices.   370
Anon they wander'd, by divine converse,
Into Elysium; vieing to rehearse
Each one his own anticipated bliss.
One felt heart-certain that he could not miss
His quick gone love, among fair blossom'd boughs,
Where every zephyr-sigh pouts, and endows
Her lips with music for the welcoming.
Another wish'd, mid that eternal spring,
To meet his rosy child, with feathery sails,
Sweeping, eye-earnestly, through almond vales: 380
Who, suddenly, should stoop through the smooth wind,
And with the balmiest leaves his temples bind;
And, ever after, through those regions be
His messenger, his little Mercury.
Some were athirst in soul to see again

Their fellow huntsmen o'er the wide champaign
In times long past; to sit with them, and talk
Of all the chances in their earthly walk;
Comparing, joyfully, their plenteous stores
Of happiness, to when upon the moors,   390
Benighted, close they huddled from the cold,
And shar'd their famish'd scrips. Thus all out-told
Their fond imaginations, – saving him
Whose eyelids curtain'd up their jewels dim,
Endymion: yet hourly had he striven
To hide the cankering venom, that had riven
His fainting recollections. Now indeed
His senses had swoon'd off: he did not heed
The sudden silence, or the whispers low,
Or the old eyes dissolving at his woe,   400
Or anxious calls, or close of trembling palms,
Or maiden's sigh, that grief itself embalms:
But in the self-same fixed trance he kept,
Like one who on the earth had never stept.
Aye, even as dead-still as a marble man,
Frozen in that old tale Arabian.

Who whispers him so pantingly and close?
Peona, his sweet sister: of all those,
His friends, the dearest. Hushing signs she made,
And breath'd a sister's sorrow to persuade   410
A yielding up, a cradling on her care.
Her eloquence did breathe away the curse:
She led him, like some midnight spirit nurse
Of happy changes in emphatic dreams,
Along a path between two little streams, –
Guarding his forehead, with her round elbow,
From low-grown branches, and his footsteps slow
From stumbling over stumps and hillocks small;
Until they came to where these streamlets fall,
With mingled bubblings and a gentle rush,   420
Into a river, clear, brimful, and flush
With crystal mocking of the trees and sky.
A little shallop, floating there hard by,
Pointed its beak over the fringed bank;
And soon it lightly dipt, and rose, and sank,

And dipt again, with the young couple's weight, —
Peona guiding, through the water straight,
Towards a bowery island opposite;
Which gaining presently, she steered light
Into a shady, fresh, and ripply cove, 430
Where nested was an arbour, overwove
By many a summer's silent fingering;
To whose cool bosom she was used to bring
Her playmates, with their needle broidery,
And minstrel memories of times gone by.

So she was gently glad to see him laid
Under her favourite bower's quiet shade,
On her own couch, new made of flower leaves,
Dried carefully on the cooler side of sheaves
When last the sun his autumn tresses shook, 440
And the tann'd harvesters rich armfuls took.
Soon was he quieted to slumbrous rest:
But, ere it crept upon him, he had prest
Peona's busy hand against his lips,
And still, a sleeping, held her finger-tips
In tender pressure. And as a willow keeps
A patient watch over the stream that creeps
Windingly by it, so the quiet maid
Held her in peace: so that a whispering blade
Of grass, a wailful gnat, a bee bustling 450
Down in the blue-bells, or a wren light rustling
Among sere leaves and twigs, might all be heard.

O magic sleep! O comfortable bird,
That broodest o'er the troubled sea of the mind
Till it is hush'd and smooth! O unconfin'd
Restraint! imprisoned liberty! great key
To golden palaces, strange minstrelsy,
Fountains grotesque, new trees, bespangled caves,
Echoing grottos, full of tumbling waves
And moonlight; aye, to all the mazy world 460
Of silvery enchantment! — who, upfurl'd
Beneath thy drowsy wing a triple hour,
But renovates and lives? — Thus, in the bower,
Endymion was calm'd to life again.

Opening his eyelids with a healthier brain,
He said: 'I feel this thine endearing love
All through my bosom: thou art as a dove
Trembling its closed eyes and sleeked wings
About me; and the pearliest dew not brings
Such morning incense from the fields of May,   470
As do those brighter drops that twinkling stray
From those kind eyes, – the very home and haunt
Of sisterly affection. Can I want
Aught else, aught nearer heaven, than such tears?
Yet dry them up, in bidding hence all fears
That, any longer, I will pass my days
Alone and sad. No, I will once more raise
My voice upon the mountain-heights; once more
Make my horn parley from their foreheads hoar:
Again my trooping hounds their tongues shall loll   480
Around the breathed boar: again I'll poll
The fair-grown yew tree, for a chosen bow:
And, when the pleasant sun is getting low,
Again I'll linger in a sloping mead
To hear the speckled thrushes, and see feed
Our idle sheep. So be thou cheered sweet,
And, if thy lute is here, softly intreat
My soul to keep in its resolved course.'

   Hereat Peona, in their silver source,
Shut her pure sorrow drops with glad exclaim,   490
And took a lute, from which there pulsing came
A lively prelude, fashioning the way
In which her voice should wander. 'Twas a lay
More subtle cadenced, more forest wild
Than Dryope's lone lulling of her child;
And nothing since has floated in the air
So mournful strange. Surely some influence rare
Went, spiritual, through the damsel's hand;
For still, with Delphic emphasis, she spann'd
The quick invisible strings, even though she saw   500
Endymion's spirit melt away and thaw
Before the deep intoxication.
But soon she came, with sudden burst, upon
Her self-possession – swung the lute aside,

And earnestly said: 'Brother, 'tis vain to hide
That thou dost know of things mysterious,
Immortal, starry; such alone could thus
Weigh down thy nature. Hast thou sinn'd in aught
Offensive to the heavenly powers? Caught
A Paphian dove upon a message sent?   510
Thy deathful bow against some deer-herd bent,
Sacred to Dian? Haply, thou hast seen
Her naked limbs among the alders green;
And that, alas! is death. No, I can trace
Something more high perplexing in thy face!'

    Endymion look'd at her, and press'd her hand,
And said, 'Art thou so pale, who wast so bland
And merry in our meadows? How is this?
Tell me thine ailment: tell me all amiss! –
Ah! thou hast been unhappy at the change   520
Wrought suddenly in me. What indeed more strange?
Or more complete to overwhelm surmise?
Ambition is no sluggard: 'tis no prize,
That toiling years would put within my grasp,
That I have sigh'd for: with so deadly gasp
No man e'er panted for a mortal love.
So all have set my heavier grief above
These things which happen. Rightly have they done:
I, who still saw the horizontal sun
Heave his broad shoulder o'er the edge of the world,   530
Out-facing Lucifer, and then had hurl'd
My spear aloft, as signal for the chace –
I, who, for very sport of heart, would race
With my own steed from Araby; pluck down
A vulture from his towery perching; frown
A lion into growling, loth retire –
To lose, at once, all my toil breeding fire,
And sink thus low! but I will ease my breast
Of secret grief, here in this bowery nest.

    'This river does not see the naked sky,   540
Till it begins to progress silverly
Around the western border of the wood,
Whence, from a certain spot, its winding flood

Seems at the distance like a crescent moon:
And in that nook, the very pride of June,
Had I been used to pass my weary eves;
The rather for the sun unwilling leaves
So dear a picture of his sovereign power,
And I could witness his most kingly hour,
When he doth tighten up the golden reins,   550
And paces leisurely down amber plains
His snorting four. Now when his chariot last
Its beams against the zodiac-lion cast,
There blossom'd suddenly a magic bed
Of sacred ditamy, and poppies red:
At which I wondered greatly, knowing well
That but one night had wrought this flowery spell;
And, sitting down close by, began to muse
What it might mean. Perhaps, thought I, Morpheus,
In passing here, his owlet pinions shook;   560
Or, it may be, ere matron Night uptook
Her ebon urn, young Mercury, by stealth,
Had dipt his rod in it: such garland wealth
Came not by common growth. Thus on I thought,
Until my head was dizzy and distraught.
Moreover, through the dancing poppies stole
A breeze, most softly lulling to my soul;
And shaping visions all about my sight
Of colours, wings, and bursts of spangly light;
The which became more strange, and strange, and dim,   570
And then were gulph'd in a tumultuous swim:
And then I fell asleep. Ah, can I tell
The enchantment that afterwards befel?
Yet it was but a dream: yet such a dream
That never tongue, although it overteem
With mellow utterance, like a cavern spring,
Could figure out and to conception bring
All I beheld and felt. Methought I lay
Watching the zenith, where the milky way
Among the stars in virgin splendour pours;   580
And travelling my eye, until the doors
Of heaven appear'd to open for my flight,
I became loth and fearful to alight
From such high soaring by a downward glance:

So kept me stedfast in that airy trance,
Spreading imaginary pinions wide.
When, presently, the stars began to glide,
And faint away, before my eager view:
At which I sigh'd that I could not pursue,
And dropt my vision to the horizon's verge;   590
And lo! from opening clouds, I saw emerge
The loveliest moon, that ever silver'd o'er
A shell for Neptune's goblet: she did soar
So passionately bright, my dazzled soul
Commingling with her argent spheres did roll
Through clear and cloudy, even when she went
At last into a dark and vapoury tent –
Whereat, methought, the lidless-eyed train
Of planets all were in the blue again.
To commune with those orbs, once more I rais'd   600
My sight right upward: but it was quite dazed
By a bright something, sailing down apace,
Making me quickly veil my eyes and face:
Again I look'd, and, O ye deities,
Who from Olympus watch our destinies!
Whence that completed form of all completeness?
Whence came that high perfection of all sweetness?
Speak, stubborn earth, and tell me where, O where
Hast thou a symbol of her golden hair?
Not oat-sheaves drooping in the western sun;   610
Not – thy soft hand, fair sister! let me shun
Such follying before thee – yet she had,
Indeed, locks bright enough to make me mad;
And they were simply gordian'd up and braided,
Leaving, in naked comeliness, unshaded,
Her pearl round ears, white neck, and orbed brow;
The which were blended in, I know not how,
With such a paradise of lips and eyes,
Blush tinted cheeks, half smiles, and faintest sighs,
That, when I think thereon, my spirit clings   620
And plays about its fancy, till the stings
Of human neighbourhood envenom all.
Unto what awful power shall I call?
To what high fane? – Ah! see her hovering feet,
More bluely vein'd, more soft, more whitely sweet

Than those of sea-born Venus, when she rose
From out her cradle shell. The wind out-blows
Her scarf into a fluttering pavilion;
'Tis blue, and over-spangled with a million
Of little eyes, as though thou wert to shed,   630
Over the darkest, lushest blue-bell bed,
Handfuls of daisies.' – 'Endymion, how strange!
Dream within dream!" – 'She took an airy range,
And then, towards me, like a very maid,
Came blushing, waning, willing, and afraid,
And press'd me by the hand: Ah! 'twas too much;
Methought I fainted at the charmed touch,
Yet held my recollection, even as one
Who dives three fathoms where the waters run
Gurgling in beds of coral: for anon,   640
I felt upmounted in that region
Where falling stars dart their artillery forth,
And eagles struggle with the buffeting north
That balances the heavy meteor-stone; –
Felt too, I was not fearful, nor alone,
But lapp'd and lull'd along the dangerous sky.
Soon, as it seem'd, we left our journeying high,
And straightway into frightful eddies swoop'd;
Such as ay muster where grey time has scoop'd
Huge dens and caverns in a mountain's side: 650
There hollow sounds arous'd me, and I sigh'd
To faint once more by looking on my bliss –
I was distracted; madly did I kiss
The wooing arms which held me, and did give
My eyes at once to death: but 'twas to live,
To take in draughts of life from the gold fount
Of kind and passionate looks; to count, and count
The moments, by some greedy help that seem'd
A second self, that each might be redeem'd
And plunder'd of its load of blessedness.   660
Ah, desperate mortal! I ev'n dar'd to press
Her very cheek against my crowned lip,
And, at that moment, felt my body dip
Into a warmer air: a moment more,
Our feet were soft in flowers. There was store
Of newest joys upon that alp. Sometimes

A scent of violets, and blossoming limes,
Loiter'd around us; then of honey cells,
Made delicate from all white-flower bells;
And once, above the edges of our nest,   670
An arch face peep'd, – an Oread as I guess'd.

    'Why did I dream that sleep o'er-power'd me
In midst of all this heaven? Why not see,
Far off, the shadows of his pinions dark,
And stare them from me? But no, like a spark
That needs must die, although its little beam
Reflects upon a diamond, my sweet dream
Fell into nothing – into stupid sleep.
And so it was, until a gentle creep,
A careful moving caught my waking ears,   680
And up I started: Ah! my sighs, my tears,
My clenched hands; – for lo! the poppies hung
Dew-dabbled on their stalks, the ouzel sung
A heavy ditty, and the sullen day
Had chidden herald Hesperus away,
With leaden looks: the solitary breeze
Bluster'd, and slept, and its wild self did teaze
With wayward melancholy; and I thought,
Mark me, Peona! that sometimes it brought
Faint fare-thee-wells, and sigh-shrilled adieus! –   690
Away I wander'd – all the pleasant hues
Of heaven and earth had faded: deepest shades
Were deepest dungeons; heaths and sunny glades
Were full of pestilent light; our taintless rills
Seem'd sooty, and o'er-spread with upturn'd gills
Of dying fish; the vermeil rose had blown
In frightful scarlet, and its thorns out-grown
Like spiked aloe. If an innocent bird
Before my heedless footsteps stirr'd, and stirr'd
In little journeys, I beheld in it   700
A disguis'd demon, missioned to knit
My soul with under darkness; to entice
My stumblings down some monstrous precipice:
Therefore I eager followed, and did curse
The disappointment. Time, that aged nurse,
Rock'd me to patience. Now, thank gentle heaven!

These things, with all their comfortings, are given
To my down-sunken hours, and with thee,
Sweet sister, help to stem the ebbing sea
Of weary life.'

           Thus ended he, and both   710
Sat silent: for the maid was very loth
To answer; feeling well that breathed words
Would all be lost, unheard, and vain as swords
Against the enchased crocodile, or leaps
Of grasshoppers against the sun. She weeps,
And wonders; struggles to devise some blame;
To put on such a look as would say, *Shame
On this poor weakness!* but, for all her strife,
She could as soon have crush'd away the life
From a sick dove. At length, to break the pause,   720
She said with trembling chance: 'Is this the cause?
This all? Yet it is strange, and sad, alas!
That one who through this middle earth should pass
Most like a sojourning demi-god, and leave
His name upon the harp-string, should achieve
No higher bard than simple maidenhood,
Singing alone, and fearfully, – how the blood
Left his young cheek; and how he used to stray
He knew not where; and how he would say, *nay*,
If any said 'twas love: and yet 'twas love;   730
What could it be but love? How a ring-dove
Let fall a sprig of yew tree in his path;
And how he died: and then, that love doth scathe
The gentle heart, as northern blasts do roses;
And then the ballad of his sad life closes
With sighs, and an alas! – Endymion!
Be rather in the trumpet's mouth, – anon
Among the winds at large – that all may hearken!
Although, before the crystal heavens darken,
I watch and dote upon the silver lakes   740
Pictur'd in western cloudiness, that takes
The semblance of gold rocks and bright gold sands,
Islands, and creeks, and amber-fretted strands
With horses prancing o'er them, palaces
And towers of amethyst, – would I so tease

My pleasant days, because I could not mount
Into those regions? The Morphean fount
Of that fine element that visions, dreams,
And fitful whims of sleep are made of, streams
Into its airy channels with so subtle,   750
So thin a breathing, not the spider's shuttle,
Circled a million times within the space
Of a swallow's nest-door, could delay a trace,
A tinting of its quality: how light
Must dreams themselves be; seeing they're more slight
Than the mere nothing that engenders them!
Then wherefore sully the entrusted gem
Of high and noble life with thoughts so sick?
Why pierce high-fronted honour to the quick
For nothing but a dream?' Hereat the youth   760
Look'd up: a conflicting of shame and ruth
Was in his plaited brow: yet, his eyelids
Widened a little, as when Zephyr bids
A little breeze to creep between the fans
Of careless butterflies: amid his pains
He seem'd to taste a drop of manna-dew,
Full palatable; and a colour grew
Upon his cheek, while thus he lifeful spake.

    'Peona! ever have I long'd to slake
My thirst for the world's praises: nothing base,   770
No merely slumberous phantasm, could unlace
The stubborn canvas for my voyage prepar'd –
Though now 'tis tatter'd; leaving my bark bar'd
And sullenly drifting: yet my higher hope
Is of too wide, too rainbow-large a scope,
To fret at myriads of earthly wrecks.
Wherein lies happiness? In that which becks
Our ready minds to fellowship divine,
A fellowship with essence; till we shine,
Full alchemiz'd, and free of space. Behold   780
The clear religion of heaven! Fold
A rose leaf round thy finger's taperness,
And soothe thy lips: hist, when the airy stress
Of music's kiss impregnates the free winds,
And with a sympathetic touch unbinds

Eolian magic from their lucid wombs:
Then old songs waken from enclouded tombs;
Old ditties sigh above their father's grave;
Ghosts of melodious prophecyings rave
Round every spot where trod Apollo's foot;   790
Bronze clarions awake, and faintly bruit,
Where long ago a giant battle was;
And, from the turf, a lullaby doth pass
In every place where infant Orpheus slept.
Feel we these things? — that moment have we stept
Into a sort of oneness, and our state
Is like a floating spirit's. But there are
Richer entanglements, enthralments far
More self-destroying, leading, by degrees,
To the chief intensity: the crown of these   800
Is made of love and friendship, and sits high
Upon the forehead of humanity.
All its more ponderous and bulky worth
Is friendship, whence there ever issues forth
A steady splendour; but at the tip-top,
There hangs by unseen film, an orbed drop
Of light, and that is love: its influence,
Thrown in our eyes, genders a novel sense,
At which we start and fret; till in the end,
Melting into its radiance, we blend,   810
Mingle, and so become a part of it, —
Nor with aught else can our souls interknit
So wingedly: when we combine therewith,
Life's self is nourish'd by its proper pith,
And we are nurtured like a pelican brood.
Aye, so delicious is the unsating food,
That men, who might have tower'd in the van
Of all the congregated world, to fan
And winnow from the coming step of time
All chaff of custom, wipe away all slime   820
Left by men-slugs and human serpentry,
Have been content to let occasion die,
Whilst they did sleep in love's elysium.
And, truly, I would rather be struck dumb,
Than speak against this ardent listlessness:
For I have ever thought that it might bless

The world with benefits unknowingly;
As does the nightingale, upperched high,
And cloister'd among cool and bunched leaves —
She sings but to her love, nor e'er conceives
How tiptoe Night holds back her dark-grey hood.   830
Just so may love, although 'tis understood
The mere commingling of passionate breath,
Produce more than our searching witnesseth:
What I know not: but who, of men, can tell
That flowers would bloom, or that green fruit would swell
To melting pulp, that fish would have bright mail,
The earth its dower of river, wood, and vale,
The meadows runnels, runnels pebble-stones,
The seed its harvest, or the lute its tones,   840
Tones ravishment, or ravishment its sweet,
If human souls did never kiss and greet?

  'Now, if this earthly love has power to make
Men's being mortal, immortal; to shake
Ambition from their memories, and brim
Their measure of content; what merest whim,
Seems all this poor endeavour after fame,
To one, who keeps within his stedfast aim
A love immortal, an immortal too.
Look not so wilder'd; for these things are true,   850
And never can be born of atomies
That buzz about our slumbers, like brain-flies,
Leaving us fancy-sick. No, no, I'm sure,
My restless spirit never could endure
To brood so long upon one luxury,
Unless it did, though fearfully, espy
A hope beyond the shadow of a dream.
My sayings will the less obscured seem,
When I have told thee how my waking sight
Has made me scruple whether that same night   860
Was pass'd in dreaming. Hearken, sweet Peona!
Beyond the matron-temple of Latona,
Which we should see but for these darkening boughs,
Lies a deep hollow, from whose ragged brows
Bushes and trees do lean all round athwart,

And meet so nearly, that with wings outraught,
And spreaded tail, a vulture could not glide
Past them, but he must brush on every side.
Some moulder'd steps lead into this cool cell,
Far as the slabbed margin of a well,   870
Whose patient level peeps its crystal eye
Right upward, through the bushes, to the sky.
Oft have I brought thee flowers, on their stalks set
Like vestal primroses, but dark velvet
Edges them round, and they have golden pits:
'Twas there I got them, from the gaps and slits
In a mossy stone, that sometimes was my seat,
When all above was faint with mid-day heat.
And there in strife no burning thoughts to heed,
I'd bubble up the water through a reed;   880
So reaching back to bôy-hood: make me ships
Of moulted feathers, touchwood, alder chips,
With leaves stuck in them; and the Neptune be
Of their petty ocean. Oftener, heavily,
When love-lorn hours had left me less a child,
I sat contemplating the figures wild
Of o'er-head clouds melting the mirror through.
Upon a day, while thus I watch'd, by flew
A cloudy Cupid, with his bow and quiver;
So plainly character'd, no breeze would shiver   890
The happy chance: so happy, I was fain
To follow it upon the open plain,
And, therefore, was just going; when, behold!
A wonder, fair as any I have told –
The same bright face I tasted in my sleep,
Smiling in the clear well. My heart did leap
Through the cool depth. – It moved as if to flee –
I started up, when lo! refreshfully,
There came upon my face, in plenteous showers,
Dew-drops, and dewy buds, and leaves, and flowers,   900
Wrapping all objects from my smothered sight,
Bathing my spirit in a new delight.
Aye, such a breathless honey-feel of bliss
Alone preserved me from the drear abyss
Of death, for the fair form had gone again.
Pleasure is oft a visitant; but pain

Clings cruelly to us, like the gnawing sloth
On the deer's tender haunches: late, and loth,
'Tis scar'd away by slow returning pleasure.
How sickening, how dark the dreadful leisure   910
Of weary days, made deeper exquisite,
By a fore-knowledge of unslumbrous night!
Like sorrow came upon me, heavier still,
Then when I wander'd from the poppy hill:
And a whole age of lingering moments crept
Sluggishly by, ere more contentment swept
Away at once the deadly yellow spleen.
Yes, thrice have I this fair enchantment seen;
Once more been tortured with renewed life.
When last the wintry gusts gave over strife   920
With the conquering sun of spring, and left the skies
Warm and serene, but yet with moistened eyes
In pity of the shatter'd infant buds, –
That time thou didst adorn, with amber studs,
My hunting cap, because I laugh'd and smil'd,
Chatted with thee, and many days exil'd
All torment from my breast; – 'twas even then,
Straying about, yet, coop'd up in the den
Of helpless discontent, – hurling my lance
From place to place, and following at chance,   930
At last, by hap, through some young trees it struck,
And, plashing among bedded pebbles, stuck
In the middle of a brook, – whose silver ramble
Down twenty little falls, through reeds and bramble,
Tracing along, it brought me to a cave,
Whence it ran brightly forth, and white did lave
The nether sides of mossy stones and rock, –
'Mong which it gurgled blythe adieus, to mock
Its own sweet grief at parting. Overhead,
Hung a lush screen of drooping weeds, and spread   940
Thick, as to curtain up some wood-nymph's home.
"Ah! impious mortal, whither do I roam?"
Said I, low voic'd: "Ah, whither! 'Tis the grot
Of Proserpine, when Hell, obscure and hot,
Doth her resign; and where her tender hands
She dabbles, on the cool and sluicy sands:
Or 'tis the cell of Echo, where she sits,

And babbles thorough silence, till her wits
Are gone in tender madness, and anon,
Faints into sleep, with many a dying tone   950
Of sadness. O that she would take my vows,
And breathe them sighingly among the boughs,
To sue her gentle ears for whose fair head,
Daily, I pluck sweet flowerets from their bed,
And weave them dyingly — send honey-whispers
Round every leaf, that all those gentle lispers
May sigh my love unto her pitying!
O charitable echo! hear, and sing
This ditty to her! — tell her" — so I stay'd
My foolish tongue, and listening, half afraid,   960
Stood stupefied with my own empty folly,
And blushing for the freaks of melancholy.
Salt tears were coming, when I heard my name
Most fondly lipp'd, and then these accents came:
"Endymion! the cave is secreter
Than the isle of Delos. Echo hence shall stir
No sighs but sigh-warm kisses, or light noise
Of thy combing hand, the while it travelling cloys
And trembles through my labyrinthine hair."
At that oppress'd I hurried in. — Ah! where   970
Are those swift moments? Whither are they fled?
I'll smile no more, Peona; nor will wed
Sorrow the way to death; but patiently
Bear up against it: so farewel, sad sigh;
And come instead demurest meditation,
To occupy me wholly, and to fashion
My pilgrimage for the world's dusky brink.
No more will I count over, link by link,
My chain of grief: no longer strive to find
A half-forgetfulness in mountain wind   980
Blustering about my ears: aye, thou shalt see,
Dearest of sisters, what my life shall be;
What a calm round of hours shall make my days.
There is a paly flame of hope that plays
Where'er I look: but yet, I'll say 'tis naught —
And here I bid it die. Have not I caught,
Already, a more healthy countenance?

By this the sun is setting; we may chance
Meet some of our near-dwellers with my car.'

   This said, he rose, faint-smiling like a star   990
Through autumn mists, and took Peona's hand:
They stept into the boat, and launch'd from land.

BOOK II

O sovereign power of love! O grief! O balm!
All records, saving thine, come cool, and calm,
And shadowy, through the mist of passed years:
For others, good or bad, hatred and tears
Have become indolent; but touching thine,
One sigh doth echo, one poor sob doth pine,
One kiss brings honey-dew from buried days.
The woes of Troy, towers smothering o'er their blaze,
Stiff-holden shields, far-piercing spears, keen blades,
Struggling, and blood, and shrieks – all dimly fades   10
Into some backward corner of the brain;
Yet, in our very souls, we feel amain
The close of Troilus and Cressid sweet.
Hence, pageant history! hence, gilded cheat!
Swart planet in the universe of deeds!
Wide sea, that one continuous murmur breeds
Along the pebbled shore of memory!
Many old rotten-timber'd boats there be
Upon thy vaporous bosom, magnified
To goodly vessels; many a sail of pride,   20
And golden keel'd, is left unlaunch'd and dry.
But wherefore this? What care, though owl did fly
About the great Athenian admiral's mast?
What care, though striding Alexander past
The Indus with his Macedonian numbers?
Though old Ulysses tortured from his slumbers
The glutted Cyclops, what care? – Juliet leaning
Amid her window-flowers, – sighing, – weaning
Tenderly her fancy from its maiden snow,
Doth more avail than these: the silver flow   30
Of Hero's tears, the swoon of Imogen,
Fair Pastorella in the bandit's den,

Are things to brood on with more ardency
Than the death-day of empires. Fearfully
Must such conviction come upon his head,
Who, thus far, discontent, has dared to tread,
Without one muse's smile, or kind behest,
The path of love and poesy. But rest,
In chafing restlessness, is yet more drear
Than to be crush'd, in striving to uprear   40
Love's standard on the battlements of song.
So once more days and nights aid me along,
Like legion'd soldiers.

                   Brain-sick shepherd prince,
What promise hast thou faithful guarded since
The day of sacrifice? Or, have new sorrows
Come with the constant dawn upon thy morrows?
Alas! 'tis his old grief. For many days,
Has he been wandering in uncertain ways:
Through wilderness, and woods of mossed oaks;
Counting his woe-worn minutes, by the strokes   50
Of the lone woodcutter; and listening still,
Hour after hour, to each lush-leav'd rill.
Now he is sitting by a shady spring,
And elbow-deep with feverous fingering
Stems the upbursting cold: a wild rose tree
Pavilions him in bloom, and he doth see
A bud which snares his fancy: lo! but now
He plucks it, dips its stalk in the water: how!
It swells, it buds, it flowers beneath his sight;
And, in the middle, there is softly pight   60
A golden butterfly; upon whose wings
There must be surely character'd strange things,
For with wide eye he wonders, and smiles oft.

Lightly this little herald flew aloft,
Follow'd by glad Endymion's clasped hands:
Onward it flies. From languor's sullen bands
His limbs are loos'd, and eager, on he hies
Dazzled to trace it in the sunny skies.
It seem'd he flew, the way so easy was;
And like a new-born spirit did he pass   70

Through the green evening quiet in the sun,
O'er many a heath, through many a woodland dun,
Through buried paths, where sleepy twilight dreams
The summer time away. One track unseams
A wooded cleft, and, far away, the blue
Of ocean fades upon him; then, anew,
He sinks adown a solitary glen,
Where there was never sound of mortal men,
Saving, perhaps, some snow-light cadences
Melting to silence, when upon the breeze   80
Some holy bark let forth an anthem sweet,
To cheer itself to Delphi. Still his feet
Went swift beneath the merry-winged guide,
Until it reached a splashing fountain's side
That, near a cavern's mouth, for ever pour'd
Unto the temperate air: then high it soar'd,
And, downward, suddenly began to dip,
As if, athirst with so much toil, 'twould sip
The crystal spout-head: so it did, with touch
Most delicate, as though afraid to smutch   90
Even with mealy gold the waters clear.
But, at that very touch, to disappear
So fairy-quick, was strange! Bewildered,
Endymion sought around, and shook each bed
Of covert flowers in vain; and then he flung
Himself along the grass. What gentle tongue,
What whisperer disturb'd his gloomy rest?
It was a nymph uprisen to the breast
In the fountain's pebbly margin, and she stood
'Mong lilies, like the youngest of the brood.   100
To him her dripping hand she softly kist,
And anxiously began to plait and twist
Her ringlets round her fingers, saying: 'Youth!
Too long, alas, hast thou starv'd on the ruth,
The bitterness of love: too long indeed,
Seeing thou art so gentle. Could I weed
Thy soul of care, by heavens, I would offer
All the bright riches of my crystal coffer
To Amphitrite; all my clear-eyed fish,
Golden, or rainbow-sided, or purplish,   110
Vermilion-tail'd, or finn'd with silvery gauze;

Yea, or my veined pebble-floor, that draws
A virgin light to the deep; my grotto-sands
Tawny and gold, ooz'd slowly from far lands
By my diligent springs; my level lilies, shells,
My charming rod, my potent river spells;
Yes, every thing, even to the pearly cup
Meander gave me, – for I bubbled up
To fainting creatures in a desert wild.
But woe is me, I am but as a child   120
To gladden thee; and all I dare to say,
Is, that I pity thee; that on this day
I've been thy guide; that thou must wander far
In other regions, past the scanty bar
To mortal steps, before thou cans't be ta'en
From every wasting sigh, from every pain,
Into the gentle bosom of thy love.
Why it is thus, one knows in heaven above:
But, a poor Naiad, I guess not. Farewel!
I have a ditty for my hollow cell.'   130

   Hereat, she vanished from Endymion's gaze,
Who brooded o'er the water in amaze:
The dashing fount pour'd on, and where its pool
Lay, half asleep, in grass and rushes cool,
Quick waterflies and gnats were sporting still,
And fish were dimpling, as if good nor ill
Had fallen out that hour. The wanderer,
Holding his forehead, to keep off the burr
Of smothering fancies, patiently sat down;
And, while beneath the evening's sleepy frown   140
Glow-worms began to trim their starry lamps,
Thus breath'd he to himself: 'Whoso encamps
To take a fancied city of delight,
O what a wretch is he! and when 'tis his,
After long toil and travelling, to miss
The kernel of his hopes, how more than vile:
Yet for him there's refreshment even in toil;
Another city doth he set about,
Free from the smallest pebble-bead of doubt
That he will seize on trickling honey-combs: 150
Alas, he finds them dry; and then he foams,

And onward to another city speeds.
But this is human life: the war, the deeds,
The disappointment, the anxiety,
Imagination's struggles, far and nigh,
All human; bearing in themselves this good,
That they are still the air, the subtle food,
To make us feel existence, and to shew
How quiet death is. Where soil is men grow,
Whether to weeds or flowers; but for me,   160
There is no depth to strike in: I can see
Nought earthly worth my compassing; so stand
Upon a misty, jutting head of land –
Alone? No, no; and by the Orphean lute,
When mad Eurydice is listening to't;
I'd rather stand upon this misty peak,
With not a thing to sigh for, or to seek,
But the soft shadow of my thrice-seen love,
Than be – I care not what. O meekest dove
Of heaven! O Cynthia, ten-times bright and fair!   170
From thy blue throne, now filling all the air,
Glance but one little beam of temper'd light
Into my bosom, that the dreadful might
And tyranny of love be somewhat scar'd!
Yet do not so, sweet queen; one torment spar'd,
Would give a pang to jealous misery,
Worse than the torment's self: but rather tie
Large wings upon my shoulders, and point out
My love's far dwelling. Though the playful rout
Of Cupids shun thee, too divine art thou,   180
Too keen in beauty, for thy silver prow
Not to have dipp'd in love's most gentle stream.
O be propitious, nor severely deem
My madness impious; for, by all the stars
That tend thy bidding, I do think the bars
That kept my spirit in are burst – that I
Am sailing with thee through the dizzy sky!
How beautiful thou art! The world how deep!
How tremulous-dazzlingly the wheels sweep
Around their axle! Then these gleaming reins,   190
How lithe! When this thy chariot attains
Its airy goal, haply some bower veils

Those twilight eyes? Those eyes! – my spirit fails –
Dear goddess, help! or the wide-gaping air
Will gulph me – help!' – At this with madden'd stare,
And lifted hands, and trembling lips he stood;
Like old Deucalion mountain'd o'er the flood,
Or blind Orion hungry for the morn.
And, but from the deep cavern there was borne
A voice, he had been froze to senseless stone;   200
Nor sigh of his, nor plaint, nor passion'd moan
Had more been heard. Thus swell'd it forth: 'Descend,
Young mountaineer! descend where alleys bend
Into the sparry hollows of the world!
Oft hast thou seen bolts of the thunder hurl'd
As from thy threshold; day by day hast been
A little lower than the chilly sheen
Of icy pinnacles, and dipp'dst thine arms
Into the deadening ether that still charms
Their marble being: now, as deep profound   210
As those are high, descend! He ne'er is crown'd
With immortality, who fears to follow
Where airy voices lead: so through the hollow,
The silent mysteries of earth, descend!'

      He heard but the last words, nor could contend
One moment in reflection: for he fled
Into the fearful deep, to hide his head
From the clear moon, the trees, and coming madness.

      'Twas far too strange, and wonderful for sadness;
Sharpening, by degrees, his appetite   220
To dive into the deepest. Dark, nor light,
The region; nor bright, nor sombre wholly,
But mingled up; a gleaming melancholy;
A dusky empire and its diadems;
One faint eternal eventide of gems.
Aye, millions sparkled on a vein of gold,
Along whose track the prince quick footsteps told,
With all its lines abrupt and angular:
Out-shooting sometimes, like a meteor-star,
Through a vast antre; then the metal woof,   230
Like Vulcan's rainbow, with some monstrous roof

Curves hugely: now, far in the deep abyss,
It seems an angry lightning, and doth hiss
Fancy into belief: anon it leads
Through winding passages, where sameness breeds
Vexing conceptions of some sudden change;
Whether to silver grots, or giant range
Of sapphire columns, or fantastic bridge
Athwart a flood of crystal. On a ridge
Now fareth he, that o'er the vast beneath   240
Towers like an ocean-cliff, and whence he seeth
A hundred waterfalls, whose voices come
But as the murmuring surge. Chilly and numb
His bosom grew, when first he, far away,
Descried an orbed diamond, set to fray
Old darkness from his throne: 'twas like the sun
Uprisen o'er chaos: and with such a stun
Came the amazement, that, absorb'd in it,
He saw not fiercer wonders – past the wit
Of any spirit to tell, but one of those   250
Who, when this planet's sphering time doth close,
Will be its high remembrancers: who they?
The mighty ones who have made eternal day
For Greece and England. While astonishment
With deep-drawn sighs was quieting, he went
Into a marble gallery, passing through
A mimic temple, so complete and true
In sacred custom, that he well nigh fear'd
To search it inwards; whence far off appear'd,
Through a long pillar'd vista, a fair shrine,   260
And, just beyond, on light tiptoe divine,
A quiver'd Dian. Stepping awfully,
The youth approach'd; oft turning his veil'd eye
Down sidelong aisles, and into niches old.
And when, more near against the marble cold
He had touch'd his forehead, he began to thread
All courts and passages, where silence dead
Rous'd by his whispering footsteps murmured faint:
And long he travers'd to and fro, to acquaint
Himself with every mystery, and awe;   270
Till, weary, he sat down before the maw
Of a wide outlet, fathomless and dim

To wild uncertainty and shadows grim.
There, when new wonders ceas'd to float before,
And thoughts of self came on, how crude and sore
The journey homeward to habitual self!
A mad-pursuing of the fog-born elf,
Whose flitting lantern, through rude nettle-briar,
Cheats us into a swamp, into a fire,
Into the bosom of a hated thing.   280

    What misery most drowningly doth sing
In lone Endymion's ear, now he has raught
The goal of consciousness? Ah, 'tis the thought,
The deadly feel of solitude: for lo!
He cannot see the heavens, nor the flow
Of rivers, nor hill-flowers running wild
In pink and purple chequer, nor, up-pil'd,
The cloudy rack slow journeying in the west,
Like herded elephants; nor felt, nor prest
Cool grass, nor tasted the fresh slumberous air;   290
But far from such companionship to wear
An unknown time, surcharg'd with grief, away,
Was now his lot. And must he patient stay,
Tracing fantastic figures with his spear?
'No!' exclaimed he, 'why should I tarry here?'
No! loudly echoed times innumerable.
At which he straightway started, and 'gan tell
His paces back into the temple's chief;
Warming and glowing strong in the belief
Of help from Dian: so that when again   300
He caught her airy form, thus did he plain,
Moving more near the while. 'O Haunter chaste
Of river sides, and woods, and healthy waste,
Where with thy silver bow and arrows keen
Art thou now forested? O woodland Queen,
What smoothest air thy smoother forehead woos?
Where dost thou listen to the wide halloos
Of thy disparted nymphs? Through what dark tree
Glimmers thy crescent? Wheresoe'er it be,
'Tis in the breath of heaven: thou dost taste   310
Freedom as none can taste it, nor dost waste
Thy loveliness in dismal elements;

But, finding in our green earth sweet contents,
There livest blissfully. Ah, if to thee
It feels Elysian, how rich to me,
An exil'd mortal, sounds its pleasant name!
Within my breast there lives a choking flame —
O let me cool it the zephyr-boughs among!
A homeward fever parches up my tongue —
O let me slake it at the running springs!   320
Upon my ear a noisy nothing rings —
O let me once more hear the linnet's note!
Before mine eyes thick films and shadows float —
O let me 'noint them with the heaven's light!
Dost thou now lave thy feet and ankles white?
O think how sweet to me the freshening sluice!
Dost thou now please thy thirst with berry-juice?
O think how this dry palate would rejoice!
If in soft slumber thou dost hear my voice,
O think how I should love a bed of flowers! —   330
Young goddess! let me see my native bowers!
Deliver me from this rapacious deep!'

    Thus ending loudly, as he would o'erleap
His destiny, alert he stood: but when
Obstinate silence came heavily again,
Feeling about for its old couch of space
And airy cradle, lowly bow'd his face
Desponding, o'er the marble floor's cold thrill.
But 'twas not long; for, sweeter than the rill
To its old channel, or a swollen tide   340
To margin sallows, were the leaves he spied,
And flowers, and wreaths, and ready myrtle crowns
Up heaping through the slab: refreshment drowns
Itself, and strives its own delights to hide —
Nor in one spot alone; the floral pride
In a long whispering birth enchanted grew
Before his footsteps; as when heav'd anew
Old ocean rolls a lengthened wave to the shore,
Down whose green back the short-liv'd foam, all hoar,
Bursts gradual, with a wayward indolence.   350

Increasing still in heart, and pleasant sense,
Upon his fairy journey on he hastes;
So anxious for the end, he scarcely wastes
One moment with his hand among the sweets:
Onward he goes — he stops — his bosom beats
As plainly in his ear, as the faint charm
Of which the throbs were born. This still alarm,
This sleepy music, forc'd him walk tiptoe:
For it came more softly than the east could blow
Arion's magic to the Atlantic isles;   360
Or than the west, made jealous by the smiles
Of thron'd Apollo, could breathe back the lyre
To seas Ionian and Tyrian.

O did he ever live, that lonely man,
Who lov'd — and music slew not? 'Tis the pest
Of love, that fairest joys give most unrest;
That things of delicate and tenderest worth
Are swallow'd all, and made a seared dearth,
By one consuming flame: it doth immerse
And suffocate true blessings in a curse.   370
Half-happy, by comparison of bliss,
Is miserable. 'Twas even so with this
Dew-dropping melody, in the Carian's ear;
First heaven, then hell, and then forgotten clear,
Vanish'd in elemental passion.

And down some swart abysm he had gone,
Had not a heavenly guide benignant led
To where thick myrtle branches, 'gainst his head
Brushing, awakened: then the sounds again
Went noiseless as a passing noontide rain   380
Over a bower, where little space he stood;
For as the sunset peeps into a wood
So saw he panting light, and towards it went
Through winding alleys; and lo, wonderment!
Upon soft verdure saw, one here, one there,
Cupids a slumbering on their pinions fair.

After a thousand mazes overgone,
At last, with sudden step, he came upon
A chamber, myrtle wall'd, embowered high,

Full of light, incense, tender minstrelsy,   390
And more of beautiful and strange beside:
For on a silken couch of rosy pride,
In midst of all, there lay a sleeping youth
Of fondest beauty; fonder, in fair sooth,
Than sighs could fathom, or contentment reach:
And coverlids gold-tinted like the peach,
Or ripe October's faded marigolds,
Fell sleek about him in a thousand folds —
Not hiding up an Apollonian curve
Of neck and shoulder, nor the tenting swerve   400
Of knee from knee, nor ankles pointing light;
But rather, giving them to the filled sight
Officiously. Sideway his face repos'd
On one white arm, and tenderly unclos'd,
By tenderest pressure, a faint damask mouth
To slumbery pout; just as the morning south
Disparts a dew-lipp'd rose. Above his head,
Four lily stalks did their white honours wed
To make a coronal; and round him grew
All tendrils green, of every bloom and hue,   410
Together intertwin'd and trammel'd fresh:
The vine of glossy sprout; the ivy mesh,
Shading its Ethiop berries; and woodbine,
Of velvet leaves and bugle-blooms divine;
Convolvulus in streaked vases flush;
The creeper, mellowing for an autumn blush;
And virgin's bower, trailing airily;
With others of the sisterhood. Hard by,
Stood serene Cupids watching silently.
One, kneeling to a lyre, touch'd the strings,   420
Muffling to death the pathos with his wings;
And, ever and anon, uprose to look
At the youth's slumber; while another took
A willow-bough, distilling odorous dew,
And shook it on his hair; another flew
In through the woven roof, and fluttering-wise
Rain'd violets upon his sleeping eyes.

    At these enchantments, and yet many more,
The breathless Latmian wonder'd o'er and o'er;

Until, impatient in embarrassment,   430
He forthright pass'd, and lightly treading went
To that same feather'd lyrist, who straightway,
Smiling, thus whisper'd: 'Though from upper day
Thou art a wanderer, and thy presence here
Might seem unholy, be of happy cheer!
For 'tis the nicest touch of human honour,
When some ethereal and high-favouring donor
Presents immortal bowers to mortal sense;
As now 'tis done to thee, Endymion. Hence
Was I in no wise startled. So recline   440
Upon these living flowers. Here is wine,
Alive with sparkles — never, I aver,
Since Ariadne was a vintager,
So cool a purple: taste these juicy pears,
Sent me by sad Vertumnus, when his fears
Were high about Pomona: here is cream,
Deepening to richness from a snowy gleam;
Sweeter than that nurse Amalthea skimm'd
For the boy Jupiter: and here, undimm'd
By any touch, a bunch of blooming plums   450
Ready to melt between an infant's gums:
And here is manna pick'd from Syrian trees,
In starlight, by the three Hesperides.
Feast on, and meanwhile I will let thee know
Of all these things around us.' He did so,
Still brooding o'er the cadence of his lyre;
And thus: 'I need not any hearing tire
By telling how the sea-born goddess pin'd
For a mortal youth, and how she strove to bind
Him all in all unto her doting self.   460
Who would not be so prison'd? but, fond elf,
He was content to let her amorous plea
Faint through his careless arms; content to see
An unseiz'd heaven dying at his feet;
Content, O fool! to make a cold retreat,
When on the pleasant grass such love, lovelorn,
Lay sorrowing; when every tear was born
Of diverse passion; when her lips and eyes
Were clos'd in sullen moisture, and quick sighs
Came vex'd and pettish through her nostrils small.   470

Hush! no exclaim – yet, justly mightst thou call
Curses upon his head. – I was half glad,
But my poor mistress went distract and mad,
When the boar tusk'd him: so away she flew
To Jove's high throne, and by her plainings drew
Immortal tear-drops down the thunderer's beard;
Whereon, it was decreed he should be rear'd
Each summer time to life. Lo! this is he,
That same Adonis, safe in the privacy
Of this still region all his winter-sleep.   480
Aye, sleep; for when our love-sick queen did weep
Over his waned corse, the tremulous shower
Heal'd up the wound, and, with a balmy power,
Medicined death to a lengthened drowsiness:
The which she fills with visions, and doth dress
In all this quiet luxury; and hath set
Us young immortals, without any let,
To watch his slumber through. 'Tis well nigh pass'd,
Even to a moment's filling up, and fast
She scuds with summer breezes, to pant through   490
The first long kiss, warm firstling, to renew
Embower'd sports in Cytherea's isle.
Look! how those winged listeners all this while
Stand anxious: see! behold!' – This clamant word
Broke through the careful silence; for they heard
A rustling noise of leaves, and out there flutter'd
Pigeons and doves: Adonis something mutter'd,
The while one hand, that erst upon his thigh
Lay dormant, mov'd convuls'd and gradually
Up to his forehead. Then there was a hum   500
Of sudden voices, echoing, 'Come! come!
Arise! awake! Clear summer has forth walk'd
Unto the clover-sward, and she has talk'd
Full soothingly to every nested finch:
Rise, Cupids! or we'll give the blue-bell pinch
To your dimpled arms. Once more sweet life begin!'
At this, from every side they hurried in,
Rubbing their sleepy eyes with lazy wrists,
And doubling over head their little fists
In backward yawns. But all were soon alive: 510
For as delicious wine doth, sparkling, dive

In nectar'd clouds and curls through water fair,
So from the arbour roof down swell'd an air
Odorous and enlivening; making all
To laugh, and play, and sing, and loudly call
For their sweet queen: when lo! the wreathed green
Disparted, and far upward could be seen
Blue heaven, and a silver car, air-borne,
Whose silent wheels, fresh wet from clouds of morn,
Spun off a drizzling dew, — which falling chill   520
On soft Adonis' shoulders, made him still
Nestle and turn uneasily about.
Soon were the white doves plain, with necks stretch'd out,
And silken traces tighten'd in descent;
And soon, returning from love's banishment,
Queen Venus leaning downward open arm'd:
Her shadow fell upon his breast, and charm'd
A tumult to his heart, and a new life
Into his eyes. Ah, miserable strife,
But for her comforting! unhappy sight,   530
But meeting her blue orbs! Who, who can write
Of these first minutes? The unchariest muse
To embracements warm as theirs makes coy excuse.

   O it has ruffled every spirit there,
Saving Love's self, who stands superb to share
The general gladness: awfully he stands;
A sovereign quell is in his waving hands;
No sight can bear the lightning of his bow;
His quiver is mysterious, none can know
What themselves think of it; from forth his eyes   540
There darts strange light of varied hues and dyes:
A scowl is sometimes on his brow, but who
Look full upon it feel anon the blue
Of his fair eyes run liquid through their souls.
Endymion feels it, and no more controls
The burning prayer within him; so, bent low,
He had begun a plaining of his woe.
But Venus, bending forward, said: 'My child,
Favour this gentle youth; his days are wild
With love — he — but alas! too well I see   550
Thou know'st the deepness of his misery.

Ah, smile not so, my son: I tell thee true,
That when through heavy hours I used to rue
The endless sleep of this new-born Adon',
This stranger ay I pitied. For upon
A dreary morning once I fled away
Into the breezy clouds, to weep and pray
For this my love: for vexing Mars had teaz'd
Me even to tears: thence, when a little eas'd,
Down-looking, vacant, through a hazy wood,   560
I saw this youth as he despairing stood:
Those same dark curls blown vagrant in the wind;
Those same full fringed lids a constant blind
Over his sullen eyes: I saw him throw
Himself on wither'd leaves, even as though
Death had come sudden; for no jot he mov'd,
Yet mutter'd wildly. I could hear he lov'd
Some fair immortal, and that his embrace
Had zoned her through the night. There is no trace
Of this in heaven: I have mark'd each cheek,   570
And find it is the vainest thing to seek;
And that of all things 'tis kept secretest.
Endymion! one day thou wilt be blest:
So still obey the guiding hand that fends
Thee safely through these wonders for sweet ends.
'Tis a concealment needful in extreme;
And if I guess'd not so, the sunny beam
Thou shouldst mount up to with me. Now adieu!
Here must we leave thee.' — At these words up flew
The impatient doves, up rose the floating car,   580
Up went the hum celestial. High afar
The Latmian saw them minish into nought;
And, when all were clear vanish'd, still he caught
A vivid lightning from that dreadful bow.
When all was darkened, with Etnean throe
The earth clos'd — gave a solitary moan —
And left him once again in twilight lone.

    He did not rave, he did not stare aghast,
For all those visions were o'ergone, and past,
And he in loneliness: he felt assur'd   590
Of happy times, when all he had endur'd

Would seem a feather to the mighty prize.
So, with unusual gladness, on he hies
Through caves, and palaces of mottled ore,
Gold dome, and crystal wall, and turquois floor,
Black polish'd porticos of awful shade,
And, at the last, a diamond balustrade,
Leading afar past wild magnificence,
Spiral through ruggedest loopholes, and thence
Stretching across a void, then guiding o'er   600
Enormous chasms, where, all foam and roar,
Streams subterranean tease their granite beds;
Then heighten'd just above the silvery heads
Of a thousand fountains, so that he could dash
The waters with his spear; but at the splash,
Done heedlessly, those spouting columns rose
Sudden a poplar's height, and 'gan to enclose
His diamond path with fretwork, streaming round
Alive, and dazzling cool, and with a sound,
Haply, like dolphin tumults, when sweet shells   610
Welcome the float of Thetis. Long he dwells
On this delight; for, every minute's space,
The streams with changed magic interlace;
Sometimes like delicatest lattices,
Cover'd with crystal vines; then weeping trees,
Moving about as in a gentle wind,
Which, in a wink, to watery gauze refin'd,
Pour'd into shapes of curtain'd canopies,
Spangled, and rich with liquid broideries
Of flowers, peacocks, swans, and naiads fair.   620
Swifter than lightning went these wonders rare;
And then the water, into stubborn streams
Collecting, mimick'd the wrought oaken beams,
Pillars, and frieze, and high fantastic roof,
Of those dusk places in times far aloof
Cathedrals call'd. He bade a loth farewel
To these founts Protean, passing gulph, and dell,
And torrent, and ten thousand jutting shapes,
Half seen through deepest gloom, and griesly gapes,
Blackening on every side, and overhead   630
A vaulted dome like Heaven's, far bespread
With starlight gems: aye, all so huge and strange,

The solitary felt a hurried change
Working within him into something dreary, –
Vex'd like a morning eagle, lost, and weary,
And purblind amid foggy, midnight wolds.
But he revives at once: for who beholds
New sudden things, nor casts his mental slough?
Forth from a rugged arch, in the dusk below,
Came mother Cybele! alone – alone –   640
In sombre chariot; dark foldings thrown
About her majesty, and front death-pale,
With turrets crown'd. Four maned lions hale
The sluggish wheels; solemn their toothed maws,
Their surly eyes brow-hidden, heavy paws
Uplifted drowsily, and nervy tails
Cowering their tawny brushes. Silent sails
This shadowy queen athwart, and faints away
In another gloomy arch.

                  Wherefore delay,
Young traveller, in such a mournful place?   650
Art thou wayworn, or canst not further trace
The diamond path? And does it indeed end
Abrupt in middle air? Yet earthward bend
Thy forehead, and to Jupiter cloud-borne
Call ardently! He was indeed wayworn;
Abrupt, in middle air, his way was lost;
To cloud-borne Jove he bowed, and there crost
Towards him a large eagle, 'twixt whose wings,
Without one impious word, himself he flings,
Committed to the darkness and the gloom: 660
Down, down, uncertain to what pleasant doom,
Swift as a fathoming plummet down he fell
Through unknown things; till exhaled asphodel,
And rose, with spicy fannings interbreath'd,
Came swelling forth where little caves were wreath'd
So thick with leaves and mosses, that they seem'd
Large honey-combs of green, and freshly teem'd
With airs delicious. In the greenest nook
The eagle landed him, and farewel took.

It was a jasmine bower, all bestrown   670
With golden moss. His every sense had grown
Ethereal for pleasure; 'bove his head
Flew a delight half-graspable; his tread
Was Hesperean; to his capable ears
Silence was music from the holy spheres;
A dewy luxury was in his eyes;
The little flowers felt his pleasant sighs
And stirr'd them faintly. Verdant cave and cell
He wander'd through, oft wondering at such swell
Of sudden exaltation: but, 'Alas!'   680
Said he, 'will all this gush of feeling pass
Away in solitude? And must they wane,
Like melodies upon a sandy plain,
Without an echo? Then shall I be left
So sad, so melancholy, so bereft!
Yet still I feel immortal! O my love,
My breath of life, where art thou? High above,
Dancing before the morning gates of heaven?
Or keeping watch among those starry seven,
Old Atlas' children? Art a maid of the waters,   690
One of shell-winding Triton's bright-hair'd daughters?
Or art, impossible! a nymph of Dian's,
Weaving a coronal of tender scions
For very idleness? Where'er thou art,
Methinks it now is at my will to start
Into thine arms; to scare Aurora's train,
And snatch thee from the morning; o'er the main
To scud like a wild bird, and take thee off
From thy sea-foamy cradle; or to doff
Thy shepherd vest, and woo thee mid fresh leaves.   700
No, no, too eagerly my soul deceives
Its powerless self: I know this cannot be.
O let me then by some sweet dreaming flee
To her entrancements: hither sleep awhile!
Hither most gentle sleep! and soothing foil
For some few hours the coming solitude.'

  Thus spake he, and that moment felt endued
With power to dream deliciously; so wound
Through a dim passage, searching till he found

The smoothest mossy bed and deepest, where 710
He threw himself, and just into the air
Stretching his indolent arms, he took, O bliss!
A naked waist: 'Fair Cupid, whence is this?'
A well-known voice sigh'd, 'Sweetest, here am I!'
At which soft ravishment, with doating cry
They trembled to each other. – Helicon!
O fountain'd hill! Old Homer's Helicon!
That thou wouldst spout a little streamlet o'er
These sorry pages; then the verse would soar
And sing above this gentle pair, like lark 720
Over his nested young: but all is dark
Around thine aged top, and thy clear fount
Exhales in mists to heaven. Aye, the count
Of mighty Poets is made up; the scroll
Is folded by the Muses; the bright roll
Is in Apollo's hand: our dazed eyes
Have seen a new tinge in the western skies:
The world has done its duty. Yet, oh yet,
Although the sun of poesy is set,
These lovers did embrace, and we must weep 730
That there is no old power left to steep
A quill immortal in their joyous tears.
Long time in silence did their anxious fears
Question that thus it was; long time they lay
Fondling and kissing every doubt away;
Long time ere soft caressing sobs began
To mellow into words, and then there ran
Two bubbling springs of talk from their sweet lips.
'O known Unknown! from whom my being sips
Such darling essence, wherefore may I not 740
Be ever in these arms? in this sweet spot
Pillow my chin for ever? ever press
These toying hands and kiss their smooth excess?
Why not for ever and for ever feel
That breath about my eyes? Ah, thou wilt steal
Away from me again, indeed, indeed –
Thou wilt be gone away, and wilt not heed
My lonely madness. Speak, delicious fair!
Is – is it to be so? No! Who will dare
To pluck thee from me? And, of thine own will, 750

Full well I feel thou wouldst not leave me. Still
Let me entwine thee surer, surer — now
How can we part? Elysium! who art thou?
Who, that thou canst not be for ever here,
Or lift me with thee to some starry sphere?
Enchantress! tell me by this soft embrace,
By the most soft completion of thy face,
Those lips, O slippery blisses, twinkling eyes,
And by these tenderest, milky sovereignties —
These tenderest, and by the nectar-wine,　　　　　760
The passion' — 'O dov'd Ida the divine!
Endymion! dearest! Ah, unhappy me!
His soul will 'scape us — O felicity!
How he does love me! His poor temples beat
To the very tune of love — how sweet, sweet, sweet.
Revive, dear youth, or I shall faint and die;
Revive, or these soft hours will hurry by
In tranced dulness; speak, and let that spell
Affright this lethargy! I cannot quell
Its heavy pressure, and will press at least　　　　　770
My lips to thine, that they may richly feast
Until we taste the life of love again.
What! dost thou move? dost kiss? O bliss! O pain!
I love thee, youth, more than I can conceive;
And so long absence from thee doth bereave
My soul of any rest: yet must I hence:
Yet, can I not to starry eminence
Uplift thee; nor for very shame can own
Myself to thee. Ah, dearest, do not groan
Or thou wilt force me from this secrecy,　　　　　780
And I must blush in heaven. O that I
Had done it already; that the dreadful smiles
At my lost brightness, my impassion'd wiles,
Had waned from Olympus' solemn height,
And from all serious Gods; that our delight
Was quite forgotten, save of us alone!
And wherefore so ashamed? 'Tis but to atone
For endless pleasure, by some coward blushes:
Yet must I be a coward! — Horror rushes
Too palpable before me — the sad look　　　　　790
Of Jove — Minerva's start — no bosom shook

With awe of purity – no Cupid pinion
In reverence veiled – my crystalline dominion
Half lost, and all old hymns made nullity!
But what is this to love? O I could fly
With thee into the ken of heavenly powers,
So thou wouldst thus, for many sequent hours,
Press me so sweetly. Now I swear at once
That I am wise, that Pallas is a dunce –
Perhaps her love like mine is but unknown –   800
O I do think that I have been alone
In chastity: yes, Pallas has been sighing,
While every eve saw me my hair uptying
With fingers cool as aspen leaves. Sweet love,
I was as vague as solitary dove,
Nor knew that nests were built. Now a soft kiss –
Aye, by that kiss, I vow an endless bliss,
An immortality of passion's thine:
Ere long I will exalt thee to the shine
Of heaven ambrosial; and we will shade   810
Ourselves whole summers by a river glade;
And I will tell thee stories of the sky,
And breathe thee whispers of its minstrelsy.
My happy love will overwing all bounds!
O let me melt into thee; let the sounds
Of our close voices marry at their birth;
Let us entwine hoveringly – O dearth
Of human words! roughness of mortal speech!
Lispings empyrean will I sometime teach
Thine honied tongue – lute-breathings, which I gasp   820
To have thee understand, now while I clasp
Thee thus, and weep for fondness – I am pain'd,
Endymion: woe! woe! is grief contain'd
In the very deeps of pleasure, my sole life?' –
Hereat, with many sobs, her gentle strife
Melted into a languor. He return'd
Entranced vows and tears.

                        Ye who have yearn'd
With too much passion, will here stay and pity,
For the mere sake of truth; as 'tis a ditty
Not of these days, but long ago 'twas told   830

By a cavern wind unto a forest old;
And then the forest told it in a dream
To a sleeping lake, whose cool and level gleam
A poet caught as he was journeying
To Phœbus' shrine; and in it he did fling
His weary limbs, bathing an hour's space,
And after, straight in that inspired place
He sang the story up into the air,
Giving it universal freedom. There
Has it been ever sounding for those ears   840
Whose tips are glowing hot. The legend cheers
Yon centinel stars; and he who listens to it
Must surely be self-doomed or he will rue it:
For quenchless burnings come upon the heart,
Made fiercer by a fear lest any part
Should be engulphed in the eddying wind.
As much as here is penn'd doth always find
A resting place, thus much comes clear and plain;
Anon the strange voice is upon the wane –
And 'tis but echo'd from departing sound,   850
That the fair visitant at last unwound
Her gentle limbs, and left the youth asleep. –
Thus the tradition of the gusty deep.

    Now turn we to our former chroniclers. –
Endymion awoke, that grief of hers
Sweet paining on his ear: he sickly guess'd
How lone he was once more, and sadly press'd
His empty arms together, hung his head,
And most forlorn upon that widow'd bed
Sat silently. Love's madness he had known: 860
Often with more than tortured lion's groan
Moanings had burst from him; but now that rage
Had pass'd away: no longer did he wage
A rough-voic'd war against the dooming stars.
No, he had felt too much for such harsh jars:
The lyre of his soul Eolian tun'd
Forgot all violence, and but commun'd
With melancholy thought: O he had swoon'd
Drunken from pleasure's nipple; and his love
Henceforth was dove-like. – Loth was he to move   870

From the imprinted couch, and when he did,
'Twas with slow, languid paces, and face hid
In muffling hands. So temper'd, out he stray'd
Half seeing visions that might have dismay'd
Alecto's serpents; ravishments more keen
Than Hermes' pipe, when anxious he did lean
Over eclipsing eyes: and at the last
It was a sounding grotto, vaulted, vast,
O'er studded with a thousand, thousand pearls,
And crimson mouthed shells with stubborn curls,   880
Of every shape and size, even to the bulk
In which whales arbour close, to brood and sulk
Against an endless storm. Moreover too,
Fish-semblances, of green and azure hue,
Ready to snort their streams. In this cool wonder
Endymion sat down, and 'gan to ponder
On all his life: his youth, up to the day
When 'mid acclaim, and feasts, and garlands gay,
He stept upon his shepherd throne: the look
Of his white palace in wild forest nook,   890
And all the revels he had lorded there:
Each tender maiden whom he once thought fair,
With every friend and fellow-woodlander –
Pass'd like a dream before him. Then the spur
Of the old bards to mighty deeds: his plans
To nurse the golden age 'mong shepherd clans:
That wondrous night: the great Pan-festival:
His sister's sorrow; and his wanderings all,
Until into the earth's deep maw he rush'd:
Then all its buried magic, till it flush'd   900
High with excessive love. 'And now,' thought he,
'How long must I remain in jeopardy
Of blank amazements that amaze no more?
Now I have tasted her sweet soul to the core
All other depths are shallow: essences,
Once spiritual, are like muddy lees,
Meant but to fertilize my earthly root,
And make my branches lift a golden fruit
Into the bloom of heaven: other light,
Though it be quick and sharp enough to blight   910

The Olympian eagle's vision, is dark,
Dark as the parentage of chaos. Hark!
My silent thoughts are echoing from these shells;
Or they are but the ghosts, the dying swells
Of noises far away? – list!' – Hereupon
He kept an anxious ear. The humming tone
Came louder, and behold, there as he lay,
On either side outgush'd, with misty spray,
A copious spring; and both together dash'd
Swift, mad, fantastic round the rocks, and lash'd   920
Among the conchs and shells of the lofty grot,
Leaving a trickling dew. At last they shot
Down from the ceiling's height, pouring a noise
As of some breathless racers whose hopes poize
Upon the last few steps, and with spent force
Along the ground they took a winding course.
Endymion follow'd – for it seem'd that one
Ever pursued, the other strove to shun –
Follow'd their languid mazes, till well nigh
He had left thinking of the mystery, –   930
And was now rapt in tender hoverings
Over the vanish'd bliss. Ah! what is it sings
His dream away? What melodies are these?
They sound as through the whispering of trees,
Not native in such barren vaults. Give ear!

      'O Arethusa, peerless nymph! why fear
Such tenderness as mine? Great Dian, why,
Why didst thou hear her prayer? O that I
Were rippling round her dainty fairness now,
Circling about her waist, and striving how   940
To entice her to a dive! then stealing in
Between her luscious lips and eyelids thin.
O that her shining hair was in the sun,
And I distilling from it thence to run
In amorous rillets down her shrinking form!
To linger on her lily shoulders, warm
Between her kissing breasts, and every charm
Touch raptur'd! – See how painfully I flow:
Fair maid, be pitiful to my great woe.
Stay, stay thy weary course, and let me lead,   950

A happy wooer, to the flowery mead
Where all that beauty snar'd me.' – 'Cruel god,
Desist! or my offended mistress' nod
Will stagnate all thy fountains: – tease me not
With syren words – Ah, have I really got
Such power to madden thee? And is it true –
Away, away, or I shall dearly rue
My very thoughts: in mercy then away,
Kindest Alpheus, for should I obey
My own dear will, 'twould be a deadly bane. –   960
O, Oread-Queen! would that thou hadst a pain
Like this of mine, then would I fearless turn
And be a criminal. – Alas, I burn,
I shudder – gentle river, get thee hence.
Alpheus! thou enchanter! every sense
Of mine was once made perfect in these woods.
Fresh breezes, bowery lawns, and innocent floods,
Ripe fruits, and lonely couch, contentment gave;
But ever since I heedlessly did lave
In thy deceitful stream, a panting glow   970
Grew strong within me: wherefore serve me so,
And call it love? Alas, 'twas cruelty.
Not once more did I close my happy eye
Amid the thrush's song. Away! Avaunt!
O 'twas a cruel thing.' – 'Now thou dost taunt
So softly, Arethusa, that I think
If thou wast playing on my shady brink,
Thou wouldst bathe once again. Innocent maid!
Stifle thine heart no more; – nor be afraid
Of angry powers: there are deities   980
Will shade us with their wings. Those fitful sighs
'Tis almost death to hear: O let me pour
A dewy balm upon them! – fear no more,
Sweet Arethusa! Dian's self must feel
Sometimes these very pangs. Dear maiden, steal
Blushing into my soul, and let us fly
These dreary caverns for the open sky.
I will delight thee all my winding course,
From the green sea up to my hidden source
About Arcadian forests; and will shew   990
The channels where my coolest waters flow

Through mossy rocks; where, 'mid exuberant green,
I roam in pleasant darkness, more unseen
Than Saturn in his exile; where I brim
Round flowery islands, and take thence a skim
Of mealy sweets, which myriads of bees
Buzz from their honied wings: and thou shouldst please
Thyself to choose the richest, where we might
Be incense-pillow'd every summer night.
Doff all sad fears, thou white deliciousness,   1000
And let us be thus comforted; unless
Thou couldst rejoice to see my hopeless stream
Hurry distracted from Sol's temperate beam,
And pour to death along some hungry sands.' —
'What can I do, Alpheus? Dian stands
Severe before me: persecuting fate!
Unhappy Arethusa! thou wast late
A huntress free in' — At this, sudden fell
Those two sad streams adown a fearful dell.
The Latmian listen'd, but he heard no more,   1010
Save echo, faint repeating o'er and o'er
The name of Arethusa. On the verge
Of that dark gulph he wept, and said: 'I urge
Thee, gentle Goddess of my pilgrimage,
By our eternal hopes, to soothe, to assuage,
If thou art powerful, these lovers' pains;
And make them happy in some happy plains.'

    He turn'd — there was a whelming sound — he stept,
There was a cooler light; and so he kept
Towards it by a sandy path, and lo!   1020
More suddenly than doth a moment go,
The visions of the earth were gone and fled —
He saw the giant sea above his head.

BOOK III

There are who lord it o'er their fellow-men
With most prevailing tinsel: who unpen
Their baaing vanities, to browse away
The comfortable green and juicy hay

From human pastures; or, O torturing fact!
Who, through an idiot blink, will see unpack'd
Fire-branded foxes to sear up and singe
Our gold and ripe-ear'd hopes. With not one tinge
Of sanctuary splendour, not a sight
Able to face an owl's, they still are dight   10
By the blear-eyed nations in empurpled vests,
And crowns, and turbans. With unladen breasts,
Save of blown self-applause, they proudly mount
To their spirit's perch, their being's high account,
Their tiptop nothings, their dull skies, their thrones —
Amid the fierce intoxicating tones
Of trumpets, shoutings, and belabour'd drums,
And sudden cannon. Ah! how all this hums,
In wakeful ears, like uproar past and gone —
Like thunder clouds that spake to Babylon,   20
And set those old Chaldeans to their tasks. —
Are then regalities all gilded masks?
No, there are throned seats unscalable
But by a patient wing, a constant spell,
Or by ethereal things that, unconfin'd,
Can make a ladder of the eternal wind,
And poise about in cloudy thunder-tents
To watch the abysm-birth of elements.
Aye, 'bove the withering of old-lipp'd Fate
A thousand Powers keep religious state,   30
In water, fiery realm, and airy bourne;
And, silent as a consecrated urn,
Hold sphery sessions for a season due.
Yet few of these far majesties, ah, few!
Have bared their operations to this globe —
Few, who with gorgeous pageantry enrobe
Our piece of heaven — whose benevolence
Shakes hand with our own Ceres; every sense
Filling with spiritual sweets to plenitude,
As bees gorge full their cells. And, by the feud   40
'Twixt Nothing and Creation, I here swear,
Eterne Apollo! that thy Sister fair
Is of all these the gentlier-mightiest.
When thy gold breath is misting in the west,
She unobserved steals unto her throne,

And there she sits most meek and most alone;
As if she had not pomp subservient;
As if thine eye, high Poet! was not bent
Towards her with the Muses in thine heart;
As if the ministring stars kept not apart,   50
Waiting for silver-footed messages.
O Moon! the oldest shades 'mong oldest trees
Feel palpitations when thou lookest in:
O Moon! old boughs lisp forth a holier din
The while they feel thine airy fellowship.
Thou dost bless every where, with silver lip
Kissing dead things to life. The sleeping kine,
Couched in thy brightness, dream of fields divine:
Innumerable mountains rise, and rise,
Ambitious for the hallowing of thine eyes;   60
And yet thy benediction passeth not
One obscure hiding-place, one little spot
Where pleasure may be sent: the nested wren
Has thy fair face within its tranquil ken,
And from beneath a sheltering ivy leaf
Takes glimpses of thee; thou art a relief
To the poor patient oyster, where it sleeps
Within its pearly house. – The mighty deeps,
The monstrous sea is thine – the myriad sea!
O Moon! far-spooming Ocean bows to thee,   70
And Tellus feels his forehead's cumbrous load.

    Cynthia! where art thou now? What far abode
Of green or silvery bower doth enshrine
Such utmost beauty? Alas, thou dost pine
For one as sorrowful: thy cheek is pale
For one whose cheek is pale: thou dost bewail
His tears, who weeps for thee. Where dost thou sigh?
Ah! surely that light peeps from Vesper's eye,
Or what a thing is love! 'Tis She, but lo!
How chang'd, how full of ache, how gone in woe!   80
She dies at the thinnest cloud; her loveliness
Is wan on Neptune's blue: yet there's a stress
Of love-spangles, just off yon cape of trees,
Dancing upon the waves, as if to please
The curly foam with amorous influence.

O, not so idle: for down-glancing thence
She fathoms eddies, and runs wild about
O'erwhelming water-courses; scaring out
The thorny sharks from hiding-holes, and fright'ning
Their savage eyes with unaccustomed lightning.   90
Where will the splendor be content to reach?
O love! how potent hast thou been to teach
Strange journeyings! Wherever beauty dwells,
In gulf or aerie, mountains or deep dells,
In light, in gloom, in star or blazing sun,
Thou pointest out the way, and straight 'tis won.
Amid his toil thou gav'st Leander breath;
Thou leddest Orpheus through the gleams of death;
Thou madest Pluto bear thin element;
And now, O winged Chieftain! thou hast sent   100
A moon-beam to the deep, deep water-world,
To find Endymion.

                  On gold sand impearl'd
With lily shells, and pebbles milky white,
Poor Cynthia greeted him, and sooth'd her light
Against his pallid face: he felt the charm
To breathlessness, and suddenly a warm
Of his heart's blood: 'twas very sweet; he stay'd
His wandering steps, and half-entranced laid
His head upon a tuft of straggling weeds,
To taste the gentle moon, and freshening beads,   110
Lashed from the crystal roof by fishes' tails.
And so he kept, until the rosy veils
Mantling the east, by Aurora's peering hand
Were lifted from the water's breast, and fann'd
Into sweet air; and sober'd morning came
Meekly through billows: — when like taper-flame
Left sudden by a dallying breath of air,
He rose in silence, and once more 'gan fare
Along his fated way.

                      Far had he roam'd,
With nothing save the hollow vast, that foam'd   120

Above, around, and at his feet; save things
More dead than Morpheus' imaginings:
Old rusted anchors, helmets, breast-plates large
Of gone sea-warriors; brazen beaks and targe;
Rudders that for a hundred years had lost
The sway of human hand; gold vase emboss'd
With long-forgotten story, and wherein
No reveller had ever dipp'd a chin
But those of Saturn's vintage; mouldering scrolls,
Writ in the tongue of heaven, by those souls　　　　　130
Who first were on the earth; and sculptures rude
In ponderous stone, developing the mood
Of ancient Nox; — then skeletons of man,
Of beast, behemoth, and leviathan,
And elephant, and eagle, and huge jaw
Of nameless monster. A cold leaden awe
These secrets struck into him; and unless
Dian had chaced away that heaviness,
He might have died: but now, with cheered feel,
He onward kept; wooing these thoughts to steal　　　140
About the labyrinth in his soul of love.

'What is there in thee, Moon! that thou shouldst move
My heart so potently? When yet a child
I oft have dried my tears when thou hast smil'd.
Thou seem'dst my sister: hand in hand we went
From eve to morn across the firmament.
No apples would I gather from the tree,
Till thou hadst cool'd their cheeks deliciously:
No tumbling water ever spake romance,
But when my eyes with thine thereon could dance:　　150
No woods were green enough, no bower divine,
Until thou liftedst up thine eyelids fine:
In sowing time ne'er would I dibble take,
Or drop a seed, till thou wast wide awake;
And, in the summer tide of blossoming,
No one but thee hath heard me blithely sing
And mesh my dewy flowers all the night.
No melody was like a passing spright
If it went not to solemnize thy reign.
Yes, in my boyhood, every joy and pain　　　　　160

By thee were fashion'd to the self-same end;
And as I grew in years, still didst thou blend
With all my ardours: thou wast the deep glen;
Thou wast the mountain-top – the sage's pen –
The poet's harp – the voice of friends – the sun;
Thou wast the river – thou wast glory won;
Thou wast my clarion's blast – thou wast my steed –
My goblet full of wine – my topmost deed: –
Thou wast the charm of women, lovely Moon!
O what a wild and harmonized tune   170
My spirit struck from all the beautiful!
On some bright essence could I lean, and lull
Myself to immortality: I prest
Nature's soft pillow in a wakeful rest.
But, gentle Orb! there came a nearer bliss –
My strange love came – Felicity's abyss!
She came, and thou didst fade, and fade away –
Yet not entirely; no, thy starry sway
Has been an under-passion to this hour.
Now I begin to feel thine orby power   180
Is coming fresh upon me: O be kind,
Keep back thine influence, and do not blind
My sovereign vision. – Dearest love, forgive
That I can think away from thee and live! –
Pardon me, airy planet, that I prize
One thought beyond thine argent luxuries!
How far beyond!' At this a surpris'd start
Frosted the springing verdure of his heart;
For as he lifted up his eyes to swear
How his own goddess was past all things fair,   190
He saw far in the concave green of the sea
An old man sitting calm and peacefully.
Upon a weeded rock this old man sat,
And his white hair was awful, and a mat
Of weeds were cold beneath his cold thin feet;
And, ample as the largest winding-sheet,
A cloak of blue wrapp'd up his aged bones,
O'erwrought with symbols by the deepest groans
Of ambitious magic: every ocean-form
Was woven in with black distinctness; storm,   200
And calm, and whispering, and hideous roar,

Quicksand and whirlpool, and deserted shore
Were emblem'd in the woof; with every shape
That skims, or dives, or sleeps, 'twixt cape and cape.
The gulphing whale was like a dot in the spell,
Yet look upon it, and 'twould size and swell
To its huge self; and the minutest fish
Would pass the very hardest gazer's wish,
And shew his little eye's anatomy.
Then there was pictur'd the regality   210
Of Neptune; and the sea nymphs round his state,
In beauteous vassalage, look up and wait.
Beside this old man lay a pearly wand,
And in his lap a book, the which he conn'd
So stedfastly, that the new denizen
Had time to keep him in amazed ken,
To mark these shadowings, and stand in awe.

    The old man rais'd his hoary head and saw
The wilder'd stranger – seeming not to see,
His features were so lifeless. Suddenly   220
He woke as from a trance; his snow-white brows
Went arching up, and like two magic ploughs
Furrow'd deep wrinkles in his forehead large,
Which kept as fixedly as rocky marge,
Till round his wither'd lips had gone a smile.
Then up he rose, like one whose tedious toil
Had watch'd for years in forlorn hermitage,
Who had not from mid-life to utmost age
Eas'd in one accent his o'er-burden'd soul,
Even to the trees. He rose: he grasp'd his stole,   230
With convuls'd clenches waving it abroad,
And in a voice of solemn joy, that aw'd
Echo into oblivion, he said: –

    'Thou art the man! Now shall I lay my head
In peace upon my watery pillow: now
Sleep will come smoothly to my weary brow.
O Jove! I shall be young again, be young!
O shell-borne Neptune, I am pierc'd and stung
With new-born life! What shall I do? Where go,
When I have cast this serpent-skin of woe? –   240

I'll swim to the syrens, and one moment listen
Their melodies, and see their long hair glisten;
Anon upon that giant's arm I'll be,
That writhes about the roots of Sicily:
To northern seas I'll in a twinkling sail,
And mount upon the snortings of a whale
To some black cloud; thence down I'll madly sweep
On forked lightning, to the deepest deep,
Where through some sucking pool I will be hurl'd
With rapture to the other side of the world!   250
O, I am full of gladness! Sisters three,
I bow full hearted to your old decree!
Yes, every god be thank'd, and power benign,
For I no more shall wither, droop, and pine.
Thou art the man!' Endymion started back
Dismay'd; and, like a wretch from whom the rack
Tortures hot breath, and speech of agony,
Mutter'd: 'What lonely death am I to die
In this cold region? Will he let me freeze,
And float my brittle limbs o'er polar seas?   260
Or will he touch me with his searing hand,
And leave a black memorial on the sand?
Or tear me piece-meal with a bony saw,
And keep me as a chosen food to draw
His magian fish through hated fire and flame?
O misery of hell! resistless, tame,
Am I to be burnt up? No, I will shout,
Until the gods through heaven's blue look out! —
O Tartarus! but some few days agone
Her soft arms were entwining me, and on   270
Her voice I hung like fruit among green leaves:
Her lips were all my own, and — ah, ripe sheaves
Of happiness! ye on the stubble droop,
But never may be garner'd. I must stoop
My head, and kiss death's foot. Love! love, farwel!
Is there no hope from thee! This horrid spell
Would melt at thy sweet breath. — By Dian's hind
Feeding from her white fingers, on the wind
I see thy streaming hair! and now, by Pan,
I care not for this old mysterious man!'   280

He spake, and walking to that aged form,
Look'd high defiance. Lo! his heart 'gan warm
With pity, for the grey-hair'd creature wept.
Had he then wrong'd a heart where sorrow kept?
Had he, though blindly contumelious, brought
Rheum to kind eyes, a sting to humane thought,
Convulsion to a mouth of many years?
He had in truth; and he was ripe for tears.
The penitent shower fell, as down he knelt
Before that care-worn sage, who trembling felt   290
About his large dark locks, and faultering spake:

'Arise, good youth, for sacred Phœbus' sake!
I know thine inmost bosom, and I feel
A very brother's yearning for thee steal
Into mine own: for why? thou openest
The prison gates that have so long opprest
My weary watching. Though thou know'st it not,
Thou art commission'd to this fated spot
For great enfranchisement. O weep no more;
I am a friend to love, to loves of yore: 300
Aye, hadst thou never lov'd an unknown power,
I had been grieving at this joyous hour.
But even now most miserable old,
I saw thee, and my blood no longer cold
Gave mighty pulses: in this tottering case
Grew a new heart, which at this moment plays
As dancingly as thine. Be not afraid,
For thou shalt hear this secret all display'd,
Now as we speed towards our joyous task.'

So saying, this young soul in age's mask   310
Went forward with the Carian side by side:
Resuming quickly thus; while ocean's tide
Hung swollen at their backs, and jewel'd sands
Took silently their foot-prints.

                                'My soul stands
Now past the midway from mortality,
And so I can prepare without a sigh

To tell thee briefly all my joy and pain.
I was a fisher once, upon this main,
And my boat danc'd in every creek and bay;
Rough billows were my home by night and day, —   320
The sea-gulls not more constant; for I had
No housing from the storm and tempests mad,
But hollow rocks, — and they were palaces
Of silent happiness, of slumberous ease:
Long years of misery have told me so.
Aye, thus it was one thousand years ago.
One thousand years! — Is it then possible
To look so plainly through them? to dispel
A thousand years with backward glance sublime?
To breathe away as 'twere all scummy slime   330
From off a crystal pool, to see its deep,
And one's own image from the bottom peep?
Yes: now I am no longer wretched thrall,
My long captivity and moanings all
Are but a slime, a thin-pervading scum,
The which I breathe away, and thronging come
Like things of yesterday my youthful pleasures.

'I touch'd no lute, I sang not, trod no measures:
I was a lonely youth on desert shores.
My sports were lonely, 'mid continuous roars,   340
And craggy isles, and sea-mew's plaintive cry
Plaining discrepant between sea and sky.
Dolphins were still my playmates; shapes unseen
Would let me feel their scales of gold and green,
Nor be my desolation; and, full oft,
When a dread waterspout had rear'd aloft
Its hungry hugeness, seeming ready ripe
To burst with hoarsest thunderings, and wipe
My life away like a vast sponge of fate,
Some friendly monster, pitying my sad state,   350
Has dived to its foundations, gulph'd it down,
And left me tossing safely. But the crown
Of all my life was utmost quietude:
More did I love to lie in cavern rude,
Keeping in wait whole days for Neptune's voice,
And if it came at last, hark, and rejoice!

There blush'd no summer eve but I would steer
My skiff along green shelving coasts, to hear
The shepherd's pipe come clear from aery steep,
Mingled with ceaseless bleatings of his sheep: 360
And never was a day of summer shine,
But I beheld its birth upon the brine:
For I would watch all night to see unfold
Heaven's gates, and Æthon snort his morning gold
Wide o'er the swelling streams: and constantly
At brim of day-tide, on some grassy lea,
My nets would be spread out, and I at rest.
The poor folk of the sea-country I blest
With daily boon of fish most delicate:
They knew not whence this bounty, and elate   370
Would strew sweet flowers on a sterile beach.

'Why was I not contented? Wherefore reach
At things which, but for thee, O Latmian!
Had been my dreary death? Fool! I began
To feel distemper'd longings: to desire
The utmost privilege that ocean's sire
Could grant in benediction: to be free
Of all his kingdom. Long in misery
I wasted, ere in one extremest fit
I plung'd for life or death. To interknit   380
One's senses with so dense a breathing stuff
Might seem a work of pain; so not enough
Can I admire how crystal-smooth it felt,
And buoyant round my limbs. At first I dwelt
Whole days and days in sheer astonishment;
Forgetful utterly of self-intent;
Moving but with the mighty ebb and flow.
Then, like a new fledg'd bird that first doth shew
His spreaded feathers to the morrow chill,
I tried in fear the pinions of my will.   390
'Twas freedom! and at once I visited
The ceaseless wonders of this ocean-bed.
No need to tell thee of them, for I see
That thou hast been a witness — it must be —
For these I know thou canst not feel a drouth,
By the melancholy corners of that mouth.

So I will in my story straightway pass
To more immediate matter. Woe, alas!
That love should be my bane! Ah, Scylla fair!
Why did poor Glaucus ever — ever dare   400
To sue thee to his heart! Kind stranger-youth!
I lov'd her to the very white of truth,
And she would not conceive it. Timid thing!
She fled me swift as sea-bird on the wing,
Round every isle, and point, and promontory,
From where large Hercules wound up his story
Far as Egyptian Nile. My passion grew
The more, the more I saw her dainty hue
Gleam delicately through the azure clear:
Until 'twas too fierce agony to bear;   410
And in that agony, across my grief
It flash'd, that Circe might find some relief —
Cruel enchantress! So above the water
I rear'd my head, and look'd for Phœbus' daughter.
Æœa's isle was wondering at the moon: —
It seem'd to whirl around me, and a swoon
Left me dead-drifting to that fatal power.

  'When I awoke, 'twas in a twilight bower;
Just when the light of morn, with hum of bees,
Stole through its verdurous matting of fresh trees.   420
How sweet, and sweeter! for I heard a lyre,
And over it a sighing voice expire.
It ceased — I caught light footsteps; and anon
The fairest face that morn e'er look'd upon
Push'd through a screen of roses. Starry Jove!
With tears, and smiles, and honey-words she wove
A net whose thraldom was more bliss than all
The range of flower'd Elysium. Thus did fall
The dew of her rich speech: "Ah! Art awake?
O let me hear thee speak, for Cupid's sake!   430
I am so oppress'd with joy! Why, I have shed
An urn of tears, as though thou wert cold dead;
And now I find thee living, I will pour
From these devoted eyes their silver store,
Until exhausted of the latest drop,
So it will pleasure thee, and force thee stop

Here, that I too may live: but if beyond
Such cool and sorrowful offerings, thou art fond
Of soothing warmth, of dalliance supreme;
If thou art ripe to taste a long love dream;   440
If smiles, if dimples, tongues for ardour mute,
Hang in thy vision like a tempting fruit,
O let me pluck it for thee." Thus she link'd
Her charming syllables, till indistinct
Their music came to my o'er-sweeten'd soul;
And then she hover'd over me, and stole
So near, if no nearer it had been
This furrow'd visage thou hadst never seen.

'Young man of Latmos! thus particular
Am I, that thou may'st plainly see how far   450
This fierce temptation went: and thou may'st not
Exclaim, How then, was Scylla quite forgot?

'Who could resist? Who in this universe?
She did so breathe ambrosia; so immerse
My fine existence in a golden clime.
She took me like a child of suckling time,
And cradled me in roses. Thus condemn'd,
The current of my former life was stemm'd,
And to this arbitrary queen of sense
I bow'd a tranced vassal: nor would thence   460
Have mov'd, even though Amphion's harp had woo'd
Me back to Scylla o'er the billows rude.
For as Apollo each eve doth devise
A new appareling for western skies;
So every eve, may every spendthrift hour
Shed balmy consciousness within that bower.
And I was free of haunts umbrageous;
Could wander in the mazy forest-house
Of squirrels, foxes shy, and antler'd deer,
And birds from coverts innermost and drear   470
Warbling for very joy mellifluous sorrow –
To me new born delights!

                    'Now let me borrow,
For moments few, a temperament as stern

As Pluto's sceptre, that my words not burn
These uttering lips, while I in calm speech tell
How specious heaven was changed to real hell.

  'One morn she left me sleeping: half awake
I sought for her smooth arms and lips, to slake
My greedy thirst with nectarous camel-draughts;
But she was gone. Whereat the barbed shafts   480
Of disappointment stuck in me so sore,
That out I ran and search'd the forest o'er.
Wandering about in pine and cedar gloom
Damp awe assail'd me; for there 'gan to boom
A sound of moan, an agony of sound,
Sepulchral from the distance all around.
Then came a conquering earth-thunder, and rumbled
That fierce complain to silence: while I stumbled
Down a precipitous path, as if impell'd.
I came to a dark valley. — Groanings swell'd   490
Poisonous about my ears, and louder grew,
The nearer I approach'd a flame's gaunt blue,
That glar'd before me through a thorny brake.
This fire, like the eye of gordian snake,
Bewitch'd me towards; and I soon was near
A sight too fearful for the feel of fear:
In thicket hid I curs'd the haggard scene —
The banquet of my arms, my arbour queen,
Seated upon an uptorn forest root;
And all around her shapes, wizard and brute,   500
Laughing, and wailing, groveling, serpenting,
Shewing tooth, tusk, and venom-bag, and sting!
O such deformities! Old Charon's self,
Should he give up awhile his penny pelf,
And take a dream 'mong rushes Stygian,
It could not be so phantasied. Fierce, wan,
And tyrannizing was the lady's look,
As over them a gnarled staff she shook.
Oft-times upon the sudden she laugh'd out,
And from a basket emptied to the rout   510
Clusters of grapes, the which they raven'd quick
And roar'd for more; with many a hungry lick
About their shaggy jaws. Avenging, slow,

Anon she took a branch of mistletoe,
And emptied on't a black dull-gurgling phial:
Groan'd one and all, as if some piercing trial
Was sharpening for their pitiable bones.
She lifted up the charm: appealing groans
From their poor breasts went sueing to her ear
In vain; remorseless as an infant's bier   520
She whisk'd against their eyes the sooty oil.
Whereat was heard a noise of painful toil,
Increasing gradual to a tempest rage,
Shrieks, yells, and groans of torture-pilgrimage;
Until their grieved bodies 'gan to bloat
And puff from the tail's end to stifled throat:
Then was appalling silence: then a sight
More wildering than all that hoarse affright;
For the whole herd, as by a whirlwind writhen,
Went through the dismal air like one huge Python   530
Antagonizing Boreas, – and so vanish'd.
Yet there was not a breath of wind: she banish'd
These phantoms with a nod. Lo! from the dark
Came waggish fauns, and nymphs, and satyrs stark,
With dancing and loud revelry, – and went
Swifter than centaurs after rapine bent. –
Sighing an elephant appear'd and bow'd
Before the fierce witch, speaking thus aloud
In human accent: "Potent goddess! chief
Of pains resistless! make my being brief,   540
Or let me from this heavy prison fly:
Or give me to the air, or let me die!
I sue not for my happy crown again;
I sue not for my phalanx on the plain;
I sue not for my lone, my widow'd wife;
I sue not for my ruddy drops of life,
My children fair, my lovely girls and boys!
I will forget them; I will pass these joys;
Ask nought so heavenward, so too – too high:
Only I pray, as fairest boon, to die,   550
Or be deliver'd from this cumbrous flesh,
From this gross, detestable, filthy mesh,
And merely given to the cold bleak air.
Have mercy, Goddess! Circe, feel my prayer!"

'That curst magician's name fell icy numb
Upon my wild conjecturing: truth had come
Naked and sabre-like against my heart.
I saw a fury whetting a death-dart;
And my slain spirit, overwrought with fright,
Fainted away in that dark lair of night.   560
Think, my deliverer, how desolate
My waking must have been! disgust, and hate,
And terrors manifold divided me
A spoil amongst them. I prepar'd to flee
Into the dungeon core of that wild wood:
I fled three days – when lo! before me stood
Glaring the angry witch. O Dis, even now,
A clammy dew is beading on my brow,
At mere remembering her pale laugh, and curse.
"Ha! ha! Sir Dainty! there must be a nurse   570
Made of rose leaves and thistledown, express,
To cradle thee my sweet, and lull thee: yes,
I am too flinty-hard for thy nice touch:
My tenderest squeeze is but a giant's clutch.
So, fairy-thing, it shall have lullabies
Unheard of yet; and it shall still its cries
Upon some breast more lily-feminine.
Oh, no – it shall not pine, and pine, and pine
More than one pretty, trifling thousand years;
And then 'twere pity, but fate's gentle shears   580
Cut short its immortality. Sea-flirt!
Young dove of the waters! truly I'll not hurt
One hair of thine: see how I weep and sigh,
That our heart-broken parting is so nigh.
And must we part? Ah, yes, it must be so.
Yet ere thou leavest me in utter woe,
Let me sob over thee my last adieus,
And speak a blessing: Mark me! Thou hast thews
Immortal, for thou art of heavenly race:
But such a love is mine, that here I chase   590
Eternally away from thee all bloom
Of youth, and destine thee towards a tomb.
Hence shalt thou quickly to the watery vast;
And there, ere many days be overpast,
Disabled age shall seize thee; and even then

Thou shalt not go the way of aged men;
But live and wither, cripple and still breathe
Ten hundred years: which gone, I then bequeath
Thy fragile bones to unknown burial.
Adieu, sweet love, adieu!" — As shot stars fall,   600
She fled ere I could groan for mercy. Stung
And poisoned was my spirit: despair sung
A war-song of defiance 'gainst all hell.
A hand was at my shoulder to compel
My sullen steps; another 'fore my eyes
Moved on with pointed finger. In this guise
Enforced, at the last by ocean's foam
I found me; by my fresh, my native home.
Its tempering coolness, to my life akin,
Came salutary as I waded in;   610
And, with a blind voluptuous rage, I gave
Battle to the swollen billow-ridge, and drave
Large froth before me, while there yet remain'd
Hale strength, nor from my bones all marrow drain'd.

'Young lover, I must weep — such hellish spite
With dry cheek who can tell? While thus my might
Proving upon this element, dismay'd,
Upon a dead thing's face my hand I laid;
I look'd — 'twas Scylla! Cursed, cursed Circe!
O vulture-witch, hast never heard of mercy?   620
Could not thy harshest vengeance be content,
But thou must nip this tender innocent
Because I lov'd her? — Cold, O cold indeed
Were her fair limbs, and like a common weed
The sea-swell took her hair. Dead as she was
I clung about her waist, nor ceas'd to pass
Fleet as an arrow through unfathom'd brine,
Until there shone a fabric crystalline,
Ribb'd and inlaid with coral, pebble, and pearl.
Headlong I darted; at one eager swirl   630
Gain'd its bright portal, enter'd, and behold!
'Twas vast, and desolate, and icy-cold;
And all around — But wherefore this to thee
Who in few minutes more thyself shalt see? —
I left poor Scylla in a niche and fled.

My fever'd parchings up, my scathing dread
Met palsy half way: soon these limbs became
Gaunt, wither'd, sapless, feeble, cramp'd, and lame.

'Now let me pass a cruel, cruel space,
Without one hope, without one faintest trace   640
Of mitigation, or redeeming bubble
Of colour'd phantasy; for I fear 'twould trouble
Thy brain to loss of reason: and next tell
How a restoring chance came down to quell
One half of the witch in me.

                'On a day,
Sitting upon a rock above the spray,
I saw grow up from the horizon's brink
A gallant vessel: soon she seem'd to sink
Away from me again, as though her course
Had been resum'd in spite of hindering force –   650
So vanish'd: and not long, before arose
Dark clouds, and muttering of winds morose.
Old Eolus would stifle his mad spleen,
But could not: therefore all the billows green
Toss'd up the silver spume against the clouds.
The tempest came: I saw that vessel's shrouds
In perilous bustle; while upon the deck
Stood trembling creatures. I beheld the wreck;
The final gulphing; the poor struggling souls:
I heard their cries amid loud thunder-rolls.   660
O they had all been sav'd but crazed eld
Annull'd my vigorous cravings: and thus quell'd
And curb'd, think on't, O Latmian! did I sit
Writhing with pity, and a cursing fit
Against that hell-born Circe. The crew had gone,
By one and one, to pale oblivion;
And I was gazing on the surges prone,
With many a scalding tear and many a groan,
When at my feet emerg'd an old man's hand,
Grasping this scroll, and this same slender wand.   670
I knelt with pain – reached out my hand – had grasp'd
These treasures – touch'd the knuckles – they unclasp'd –
I caught a finger: but the downward weight

O'erpowered me – it sank. Then 'gan abate
The storm, and through chill aguish gloom outburst
The comfortable sun. I was athirst
To search the book, and in the warming air
Parted its dripping leaves with eager care.
Strange matters did it treat of, and drew on
My soul page after page, till well-nigh won   680
Into forgetfulness; when, stupefied,
I read these words, and read again, and tried
My eyes against the heavens, and read again.
O what a load of misery and pain
Each Atlas-line bore off! – a shine of hope
Came gold around me, cheering me to cope
Strenuous with hellish tyranny. Attend!
For thou hast brought their promise to an end.

   'In the wide sea there lives a forlorn wretch,
Doom'd with enfeebled carcase to outstretch   690
His loath'd existence through ten centuries,
And then to die alone. Who can devise
A total opposition? No one. So
One million times ocean must ebb and flow,
And he oppressed. Yet he shall not die,
These things accomplish'd: – If he utterly
Scans all the depths of magic, and expounds
The meanings of all motions, shapes, and sounds;
If he explores all forms and substances
Straight homeward to their symbol-essences;   700
He shall not die. Moreover, and in chief,
He must pursue this task of joy and grief
Most piously – all lovers tempest-tost,
And in the savage overwhelming lost,
He shall deposit side by side, until
Time's creeping shall the dreary space fulfil:
Which done, and all these labours ripened,
A youth, by heavenly power lov'd and led,
Shall stand before him; whom he shall direct
How to consummate all. The youth elect   710
Must do the thing, or both will be destroy'd.' –

   'Then,' cried the young Endymion, overjoy'd,
'We are twin brothers in this destiny!

Say, I intreat thee, what achievement high
Is, in this restless world, for me reserv'd.
What! if from thee my wandering feet had swerv'd,
Had we both perish'd?' – 'Look!' the sage replied,
'Dost thou not mark a gleaming through the tide,
Of divers brilliances? 'tis the edifice
I told thee of, where lovely Scylla lies;   720
And where I have enshrined piously
All lovers, whom fell storms have doom'd to die
Throughout my bondage.' Thus discoursing, on
They went till unobscur'd the porches shone;
Which hurryingly they gain'd, and enter'd straight.
Sure never since king Neptune held his state
Was seen such wonder underneath the stars.
Turn to some level plain where haughty Mars
Has legion'd all his battle; and behold
How every soldier, with firm foot, doth hold   730
His even breast: see, many steeled squares,
And rigid ranks of iron – whence who dares
One step? Imagine further, line by line,
These warrior thousands on the field supine: –
So in that crystal place, in silent rows,
Poor lovers lay at rest from joys and woes. –
The stranger from the mountains, breathless, trac'd
Such thousands of shut eyes in order plac'd;
Such ranges of white feet, and patient lips
All ruddy, – for here death no blossom nips.   740
He mark'd their brows and foreheads; saw their hair
Put sleekly on one side with nicest care;
And each one's gentle wrists, with reverence,
Put cross-wise to its heart.

'Let us commence,'
Whisper'd the guide, stuttering with joy, 'even now.'
He spake, and, trembling like an aspen-bough,
Began to tear his scroll in pieces small,
Uttering the while some mumblings funeral.
He tore it into pieces small as snow
That drifts unfeather'd when bleak northerns blow;   750
And having done it, took his dark blue cloak
And bound it round Endymion: then struck
His wand against the empty air times nine. –

'What more there is to do, young man, is thine:
But first a little patience; first undo
This tangled thread, and wind it to a clue.
Ah, gentle! 'tis as weak as spider's skein;
And shouldst thou break it – What, is it done so clean?
A power overshadows thee! Oh, brave!
The spite of hell is tumbling to its grave.   760
Here is a shell; 'tis pearly blank to me,
Nor mark'd with any sign or charactery –
Canst thou read aught? O read for pity's sake!
Olympus! we are safe! Now, Carian, break
This wand against yon lyre on the pedestal.'

'Twas done: and straight with sudden swell and fall
Sweet music breath'd her soul away, and sigh'd
A lullaby to silence. – 'Youth! now strew
These minced leaves on me, and passing through
Those files of dead, scatter the same around,   770
And thou wilt see the issue.' – 'Mid the sound
Of flutes and viols, ravishing his heart,
Endymion from Glaucus stood apart,
And scatter'd in his face some fragments light.
How lightning-swift the change! a youthful wight
Smiling beneath a coral diadem,
Out-sparkling sudden like an upturn'd gem,
Appear'd, and, stepping to a beauteous corse,
Kneel'd down beside it, and with tenderest force
Press'd its cold hand, and wept, – and Scylla sigh'd!   780
Endymion, with quick hand, the charm applied –
The nymph arose: he left them to their joy,
And onward went upon his high employ,
Showering those powerful fragments on the dead.
And, as he pass'd, each lifted up its head,
As doth a flower at Apollo's touch.
Death felt it to his inwards: 'twas too much:
Death fell a weeping in his charnel-house.
The Latmian persever'd along, and thus
All were re-animated. There arose   790
A noise of harmony, pulses and throes
Of gladness in the air – while many, who
Had died in mutual arms devout and true,

Sprang to each other madly; and the rest
Felt a high certainty of being blest.
They gaz'd upon Endymion. Enchantment
Grew drunken, and would have its head and bent.
Delicious symphonies, like airy flowers,
Budded, and swell'd, and, full-blown, shed full showers
Of light, soft, unseen leaves of sounds divine.   800
The two deliverers tasted a pure wine
Of happiness, from fairy-press ooz'd out.
Speechless they eyed each other, and about
The fair assembly wander'd to and fro,
Distracted with the richest overflow
Of joy that ever pour'd from heaven.

                        — 'Away!'
Shouted the new born god; 'Follow, and pay
Our piety to Neptunus supreme!' —
Then Scylla, blushing sweetly from her dream,
They led on first, bent to her meek surprise,   810
Through portal columns of a giant size,
Into the vaulted, boundless emerald.
Joyous all follow'd, as the leader call'd,
Down marble steps; pouring as easily
As hour-glass sand, – and fast, as you might see
Swallows obeying the south summer's call,
Or swans upon a gentle waterfall.

    Thus went that beautiful multitude, nor far,
Ere from among some rocks of glittering spar,
Just within ken, they saw descending thick   820
Another multitude. Whereat more quick
Moved either host. On a wide sand they met,
And of those numbers every eye was wet;
For each their old love found. A murmuring rose,
Like what was never heard in all the throes
Of wind and waters: 'tis past human wit
To tell; 'tis dizziness to think of it.

    This mighty consummation made, the host
Mov'd on for many a league; and gain'd, and lost
Huge sea-marks; vanward swelling in array,   830
And from the rear diminishing away, –

Till a faint dawn surpris'd them. Glaucus cried,
'Behold! behold, the palace of his pride!
God Neptune's palaces!' With noise increas'd,
They shoulder'd on towards that brightening east.
At every onward step proud domes arose
In prospect, – diamond gleams, and golden glows
Of amber 'gainst their faces levelling.
Joyous, and many as the leaves in spring,
Still onward; still the splendour gradual swell'd.   840
Rich opal domes were seen, on high upheld
By jasper pillars, letting through their shafts
A blush of coral. Copious wonder-draughts
Each gazer drank; and deeper drank more near:
For what poor mortals fragment up, as mere
As marble was there lavish, to the vast
Of one fair palace, that far far surpass'd,
Even for common bulk, those olden three,
Memphis, and Babylon, and Nineveh.

As large, as bright, as colour'd as the bow   850
Of Iris, when unfading it doth shew
Beyond a silvery shower, was the arch
Through which this Paphian army took its march,
Into the outer courts of Neptune's state:
Whence could be seen, direct, a golden gate,
To which the leaders sped: but not half raught
Ere it burst open swift as fairy thought,
And made those dazzled thousands veil their eyes
Like callow eagles at the first sunrise.
Soon with an eagle nativeness their gaze   860
Ripe from hue-golden swoons took all the blaze,
And then, behold! large Neptune on his throne
Of emerald deep: yet not exalt alone;
At his right hand stood winged Love, and on
His left sat smiling Beauty's paragon.

Far as the mariner on highest mast
Can see all round upon the calmed vast,
So wide was Neptune's hall: and as the blue
Doth vault the waters, so the waters drew
Their doming curtains, high, magnificent,   870
Aw'd from the throne aloof; – and when storm-rent

Disclos'd the thunder-gloomings in Jove's air;
But sooth'd as now, flash'd sudden everywhere,
Noiseless, sub-marine cloudlets, glittering
Death to a human eye: for there did spring
From natural west, and east, and south, and north,
A light as of four sunsets, blazing forth
A gold-green zenith 'bove the Sea-God's head.
Of lucid depth the floor, and far outspread
As breezeless lake, on which the slim canoe   880
Of feather'd Indian darts about, as through
The delicatest air: air verily,
But for the portraiture of clouds and sky:
This palace floor breath-air, — but for the amaze
Of deep-seen wonders motionless, — and blaze
Of the dome pomp, reflected in extremes,
Globing a golden sphere.

                They stood in dreams
Till Triton blew his horn. The palace rang;
The Nereids danc'd; the Syrens faintly sang;
And the great Sea-King bow'd his dripping head.   890
Then Love took wing, and from his pinions shed
On all the multitude a nectarous dew.
The ooze-born Goddess beckoned and drew
Fair Scylla and her guides to conference;
And when they reach'd the throned eminence
She kist the sea-nymph's cheek, — who sat her down
A toying with the doves. Then, — 'Mighty crown
And sceptre of this kingdom!' Venus said,
'Thy vows were on a time to Nais paid:
Behold!' — Two copious tear-drops instant fell   900
From the God's large eyes; he smil'd delectable,
And over Glaucus held his blessing hands. —
'Endymion! Ah! still wandering in the bands
Of love? Now this is cruel. Since the hour
I met thee in earth's bosom, all my power
Have I put forth to serve thee. What, not yet
Escap'd from dull mortality's harsh net?
A little patience, youth! 'twill not be long,
Or I am skilless quite: an idle tongue,
A humid eye, and steps luxurious,   910

Where these are new and strange, are ominous.
Aye, I have seen these signs in one of heaven,
When others were all blind; and were I given
To utter secrets, haply I might say
Some pleasant words: – but Love will have his day.
So wait awhile expectant. Pr'ythee soon,
Even in the passing of thine honey-moon,
Visit my Cytherea: thou wilt find
Cupid well-natured, my Adonis kind;
And pray persuade with thee – Ah, I have done,   920
All blisses be upon thee, my sweet son!' –
Thus the fair goddess: while Endymion
Knelt to receive those accents halcyon.

Meantime a glorious revelry began
Before the Water-Monarch. Nectar ran
In courteous fountains to all cups outreach'd;
And plunder'd vines, teeming exhaustless, pleach'd
New growth about each shell and pendent lyre;
The which, in disentangling for their fire,
Pull'd down fresh foliage and coverture   930
For dainty toying. Cupid, empire-sure,
Flutter'd and laugh'd, and oft-times through the throng
Made a delighted way. Then dance, and song,
And garlanding grew wild; and pleasure reign'd.
In harmless tendril they each other chain'd,
And strove who should be smother'd deepest in
Fresh crush of leaves.

O 'tis a very sin
For one so weak to venture his poor verse
In such a place as this. O do not curse,
High Muses! let him hurry to the ending.   940

All suddenly were silent. A soft blending
Of dulcet instruments came charmingly;
And then a hymn.

'King of the stormy sea!
Brother of Jove, and co-inheritor
Of elements! Eternally before

Thee the waves awful bow. Fast, stubborn rock,
At thy fear'd trident shrinking, doth unlock
Its deep foundations, hissing into foam.
All mountain-rivers lost; in the wide home
Of thy capacious bosom ever flow. 950
Thou frownest, and old Eolus thy foe
Skulks to his cavern, 'mid the gruff complaint
Of all his rebel tempests. Dark clouds faint
When, from thy diadem, a silver gleam
Slants over blue dominion. Thy bright team
Gulphs in the morning light, and scuds along
To bring thee nearer to that golden song
Apollo singeth, while his chariot
Waits at the doors of heaven. Thou art not
For scenes like this: an empire stern hast thou; 960
And it hath furrow'd that large front: yet now,
As newly come of heaven, dost thou sit
To blend and interknit
Subdued majesty with this glad time.
O shell-borne King sublime!
We lay our hearts before thee evermore –
We sing, and we adore!

   'Breathe softly, flutes;
Be tender of your strings, ye soothing lutes;
Nor be the trumpet heard! O vain, O vain; 970
Not flowers budding in an April rain,
Nor breath of sleeping dove, nor river's flow, –
No, nor the Eolian twang of Love's own bow,
Can mingle music fit for the soft ear
Of goddess Cytherea!
Yet deign, white Queen of Beauty, thy fair eyes
On our souls' sacrifice.

   'Bright-winged Child!
Who has another care when thou hast smil'd?
Unfortunates on earth, we see at last 980
All death-shadows, and glooms that overcast
Our spirits, fann'd away by thy light pinions.
O sweetest essence! sweetest of all minions!
God of warm pulses, and dishevell'd hair,
And panting bosoms bare!

Dear unseen light in darkness! eclipser
Of light in light! delicious poisoner!
Thy venom'd goblet will we quaff until
We fill – we fill!
And by thy Mother's lips –'

                Was heard no more   990
For clamour, when the golden palace door
Opened again, and from without, in shone
A new magificence. On oozy throne
Smooth-moving came Oceanus the old,
To take a latest glimpse at his sheep-fold,
Before he went into his quiet cave
To muse for ever – Then a lucid wave,
Scoop'd from its trembling sisters of mid-sea,
Afloat, and pillowing up the majesty
Of Doris, and the Egean seer, her spouse –   1000
Next, on a dolphin, clad in laurel boughs,
Theban Amphion leaning on his lute:
His fingers went across it – All were mute
To gaze on Amphitrite, queen of pearls,
And Thetis pearly too. –

                The palace whirls
Around giddy Endymion; seeing he
Was there far strayed from mortality.
He could not bear it – shut his eyes in vain;
Imagination gave a dizzier pain.
'O I shall die! sweet Venus, be my stay!   1010
Where is my lovely mistress? Well-away!
I die – I hear her voice – I feel my wing –'
At Neptune's feet he sank. A sudden ring
Of Nereids were about him, in kind strife
To usher back his spirit into life:
But still he slept. At last they interwove
Their cradling arms, and purpose'd to convey
Towards a crystal bower far away.

  Lo! while slow carried through the pitying crowd,
To his inward senses these words spake aloud;   1020
Written in star-light on the dark above:

Dearest Endymion! my entire love!
How have I dwelt in fear of fate: 'tis done –
Immortal bliss for me too hast thou won.
Arise then! for the hen-dove shall not hatch
Her ready eggs, before I'll kissing snatch
Thee into endless heaven. Awake! awake!

   The youth at once arose: a placid lake
Came quiet to his eyes; and forest green,
Cooler than all the wonders he had seen,   1030
Lull'd with its simple song his fluttering breast.
How happy once again in grassy nest!

BOOK IV

Muse of my native land! loftiest Muse!
O first-born on the mountains! by the hues
Of heaven on the spiritual air begot:
Long didst thou sit alone in northern grot,
While yet our England was a wolfish den;
Before our forests heard the talk of men;
Before the first of Druids was a child; –
Long didst thou sit amid our regions wild
Rapt in a deep prophetic solitude.
There came an eastern voice of solemn mood: –   10
Yet wast thou patient. Then sang forth the Nine,
Apollo's garland: – yet didst thou divine
Such home-bred glory, that they cry'd in vain,
'Come hither, Sister of the Island!' Plain
Spake fair Ausonia; and once more she spake
A higher summons: – still didst thou betake
Thee to thy native hopes. O thou hast won
A full accomplishment! The thing is done,
Which undone, these our latter days had risen
On barren souls. Great Muse, thou know'st what prison,   20
Of flesh and bone, curbs, and confines, and frets
Our spirit's wings: despondency besets
Our pillows; and the fresh to-morrow morn
Seems to give forth its light in very scorn
Of our dull, uninspired, snail-paced lives.

Long have I said, how happy he who shrives
To thee! But then I thought on poets gone,
And could not pray: – nor can I now – so on
I move to the end in lowliness of heart. –

'Ah, woe is me! that I should fondly part   30
From my dear native land! Ah, foolish maid!
Glad was the hour, when, with thee, myriads bade
Adieu to Ganges and their pleasant fields!
To one so friendless the clear freshet yields
A bitter coolness; the ripe grape is sour:
Yet I would have, great gods! but one short hour
Of native air – let me but die at home.'

Endymion to heaven's airy dome
Was offering up a hecatomb of vows,
When those words reach'd him. Whereupon he bows   40
His head through thorny-green entanglement
Of underwood, and to the sound is bent,
Anxious as hind towards her hidden fawn.

'Is no one near to help me? No fair dawn
Of life from charitable voice? No sweet saying
To set my dull and sadden'd spirit playing?
No hand to toy with mine? No lips so sweet
That I may worship them? No eyelids meet
To twinkle on my bosom? No one dies
Before me, till from these enslaving eyes   50
Redemption sparkles! – I am sad and lost.'

Thou, Carian lord, hadst better have been tost
Into a whirlpool. Vanish into air,
Warm mountaineer! for canst thou only bear
A woman's sigh alone and in distress?
See not her charms! Is Phœbe passionless?
Phœbe is fairer far – O gaze no more: –
Yet if thou wilt behold all beauty's store,
Behold her panting in the forest grass!
Do not those curls of glossy jet surpass   60
For tenderness the arms so idly lain
Amongst them? Feelest not a kindred pain,

To see such lovely eyes in swimming search
After some warm delight, that seems to perch
Dovelike in the dim cell lying beyond
Their upper lids? – Hist!

        'O for Hermes' wand,
To touch this flower into human shape!
That woodland Hyacinthus could escape
From his green prison, and here kneeling down
Call me his queen, his second life's fair crown!   70
Ah me, how I could love! – My soul doth melt
For the unhappy youth – Love! I have felt
So faint a kindness, such a meek surrender
To what my own full thoughts had made too tender,
That but for tears my life had fled away! –
Ye deaf and senseless minutes of the day,
And thou, old forest, hold ye this for true,
There is no lightning, no authentic dew
But in the eye of love: there's not a sound,
Melodious howsoever, can confound   80
The heavens and earth in one to such a death
As doth the voice of love: there's not a breath
Will mingle kindly with the meadow air,
Till it has panted round, and stolen a share
Of passion from the heart!' –

        Upon a bough
He leant, wretched. He surely cannot now
Thirst for another love: O impious,
That he can even dream upon it thus! –
Thought he, 'Why am I not as are the dead,
Since to a woe like this I have been led   90
Through the dark earth, and through the wondrous
      sea?
Goddess! I love thee not the less: from thee
By Juno's smile I turn not – no, no, no –
While the great waters are at ebb and flow. –
I have a triple soul! O fond pretence –
For both, for both my love is so immense,
I feel my heart is cut for them in twain.'

And so he groan'd, as one by beauty slain.

The lady's heart beat quick, and he could see
Her gentle bosom heave tumultuously.   100
He sprang from his green covert: there she lay,
Sweet as a muskrose upon new-made hay;
With all her limbs on tremble, and her eyes
Shut softly up alive. To speak he tries.
'Fair damsel, pity me! forgive that I
Thus violate thy bower's sanctity!
O pardon me, for I am full of grief –
Grief born of thee, young angel! fairest thief!
Who stolen hast away the wings wherewith
I was to top the heavens. Dear maid, sith   110
Thou art my executioner, and I feel
Loving and hatred, misery and weal,
Will in a few short hours be nothing to me,
And all my story that much passion slew me;
Do smile upon the evening of my days:
And, for my tortur'd brain begins to craze,
Be thou my nurse; and let me understand
How dying I shall kiss that lily hand. –
Dost weep for me? Then should I be content.
Scowl on, ye fates! until the firmament   120
Outblackens Erebus, and the full-cavern'd earth
Crumbles into itself. By the cloud girth
Of Jove, those tears have given me a thirst
To meet oblivion.' – As her heart would burst
The maiden sobb'd awhile, and then replied:
'Why must such desolation betide
As that thou speakest of? Are not these green nooks
Empty of all misfortune? Do the brooks
Utter a gorgon voice? Does yonder thrush,
Schooling its half-fledg'd little ones to brush   130
About the dewy forest, whisper tales? –
Speak not of grief, young stranger, or cold snails
Will slime the rose to night. Though if thou wilt,
Methinks 'twould be a guilt – a very guilt –
Not to companion thee, and sigh away
The light – the dusk – the dark – till break of day!'
'Dear lady,' said Endymion, ' 'tis past:
I love thee! and my days can never last.
That I may pass in patience still speak:

Let me have music dying, and I seek   140
No more delight – I bid adieu to all.
Didst thou not after other climates call,
And murmur about Indian streams?' – Then she,
Sitting beneath the midmost forest tree,
For pity sang this roundelay —

     'O Sorrow,
     Why dost borrow
The natural hue of health, from vermeil lips? –
     To give maiden blushes
     To the white rose bushes?   150
Or is it thy dewy hand the daisy tips?

     'O Sorrow,
     Why dost borrow
The lustrous passion from a falcon-eye? –
     To give the glow-worm light?
     Or, on a moonless night,
To tinge, on syren shores, the salt sea-spry?

     'O Sorrow,
     Why dost borrow
The mellow ditties from a mourning tongue? –   160
     To give at evening pale
     Unto the nightingale,
That thou mayst listen the cold dews among?

     'O Sorrow,
     Why dost borrow
Heart's lightness from the merriment of May? –
     A lover would not tread
     A cowslip on the head,
Though he should dance from eve till peep of day –
     Nor any drooping flower   170
     Held sacred for thy bower,
Wherever he may sport himself and play.

     'To Sorrow,
     I bade good-morrow,
And thought to leave her far away behind;

But cheerly, cheerly,
    She loves me dearly;
She is so constant to me, and so kind:
        I would deceive her
        And so leave her,
But ah! she is so constant and so kind.

'Beneath my palm trees, by the river side,
I sat a weeping: in the whole world wide
There was no one to ask me why I wept, —
        And so I kept
Brimming the water-lily cups with tears
        Cold as my fears.

'Beneath my palm trees, by the river side,
I sat a weeping: what enamour'd bride,
Cheated by shadowy wooer from the clouds,
        But hides and shrouds
Beneath dark palm trees by a river side?

'And as I sat, over the light blue hills
There came a noise of revellers: the rills
Into the wide stream came of purple hue —
        'Twas Bacchus and his crew!
The earnest trumpet spake, and silver thrills
From kissing cymbals made a merry din —
        'Twas Bacchus and his kin!
Like to a moving vintage down they came,
Crown'd with green leaves, and faces all on flame;
All madly dancing through the pleasant valley,
        To scare thee, Melancholy!
O then, O then, thou wast a simple name!
And I forgot thee, as the berried holly
By shepherds is forgotten, when, in June,
Tall chestnuts keep away the sun and moon: —
        I rush'd into the folly!

'Within his car, aloft, young Bacchus stood,
Trifling his ivy-dart, in dancing mood,
        With sidelong laughing;
And little rills of crimson wine imbrued

180

190

200

210

His plump white arms, and shoulders, enough white
    For Venus' pearly bite:
And near him rode Silenus on his ass,
Pelted with flowers as he on did pass
    Tipsily quaffing.

'Whence came ye, merry Damsels! whence came ye!
So many, and so many, and such glee?
Why have ye left your bowers desolate,   220
    Your lutes, and gentler fate? –
"We follow Bacchus! Bacchus on the wing,
    A conquering!
Bacchus, young Bacchus! good or ill betide,
We dance before him thorough kingdoms wide: –
Come hither, lady fair, and joined be
    To our wild minstrelsy!'

'Whence came ye, jolly Satyrs! whence came ye!
So many, and so many, and such glee?
Why have ye left your forest haunts, why left   230
    Your nuts in oak-tree cleft? –
"For wine, for wine we left our kernel tree;
For wine we left our heath, and yellow brooms,
    And cold mushrooms;
For wine we follow Bacchus through the earth;
Great God of breathless cups and chirping mirth! –
Come hither, lady fair, and joined be
    To our mad minstrelsy!'

'Over wide streams and mountains great we went,
And, save when Bacchus kept his ivy tent,   240
Onward the tiger and the leopard pants,
    With Asian elephants:
Onward these myriads – with song and dance,
With zebras striped, and sleek Arabians' prance,
Web-footed alligators, crocodiles,
Bearing upon their scaly backs, in files,
Plump infant laughers mimicking the coil
Of seamen, and stout galley-rowers' toil:
With toying oars and silken sails they glide,
    Nor care for wind and tide.   250

'Mounted on panthers' furs and lions' manes,
From rear to van they scour about the plains;
A three days' journey in a moment done:
And always, at the rising of the sun,
About the wilds they hunt with spear and horn,
          On spleenful unicorn.

'I saw Osirian Egypt kneel adown
          Before the vine-wreath crown!
I saw parch'd Abyssinia rouse and sing
          To the silver cymbal's ring!   260
I saw the whelming vintage hotly pierce
          Old Tartary the fierce!
The kings of Inde their jewel-sceptres vail,
And from their treasures scatter pearled hail;
Great Brahma from his mystic heaven groans,
          And all his priesthood moans;
Before young Bacchus' eye-wink turning pale. –
Into these regions came I following him,
Sick hearted, weary – so I took a whim
To stray away into these forests drear   270
          Alone, without a peer:
And I have told thee all thou mayest hear.

          'Young stranger!
          I've been a ranger
In search of pleasure throughout every clime:
          Alas, 'tis not for me!
          Bewitch'd I sure must be,
To lose in grieving all my maiden prime.

          'Come then, Sorrow!
          Sweetest Sorrow!   280
Like an own babe I nurse thee on my breast:
          I thought to leave thee
          And deceive thee,
But now of all the world I love thee best.

          'There is not one,
          'No, no, not one
But thee to comfort a poor lonely maid;

Thou art her mother,
    And her brother,
Her playmate, and her wooer in the shade.'   290

O what a sigh she gave in finishing,
And look, quite dead to every worldly thing!
Endymion could not speak, but gazed on her;
And listened to the wind that now did stir
About the crisped oaks full drearily,
Yet with as sweet a softness as might be
Remember'd from its velvet summer song.
At last he said: 'Poor lady, how thus long
Have I been able to endure that voice?
Fair Melody! kind Syren! I've no choice;   300
I must be thy sad servant evermore:
I cannot choose but kneel here and adore.
Alas, I must not think – by Phœbe, no!
Let me not think, soft Angel! shall it be so?
Say, beautifullest, shall I never think?
O thou could'st foster me beyond the brink
Of recollection! make my watchful care
Close up its bloodshot eyes, nor see despair!
Do gently murder half my soul, and I
Shall feel the other half so utterly! –   310
I'm giddy at that cheek so fair and smooth;
O let it blush so ever! let it soothe
My madness! let it mantle rosy-warm
With the tinge of love, panting in safe alarm. –
This cannot be thy hand, and yet it is;
And this is sure thine other softling – this
Thine own fair bosom, and I am so near!
Wilt fall asleep? O let me sip that tear!
And whisper one sweet word that I may know
This is this world – sweet dewy blossom!' – *Woe!*   320
Woe! Woe to that Endymion! Where is he? –
Even these words went echoing dismally
Through the wide forest – a most fearful tone,
Like one repenting in his latest moan;
And while it died away a shade pass'd by,
As of a thunder cloud. When arrows fly
Through the thick branches, poor ring-doves sleek forth

Their timid necks and tremble; so these both
Leant to each other trembling, and sat so
Waiting for some destruction – when lo,   330
Foot-feather'd Mercury appear'd sublime
Beyond the tall tree tops; and in less time
Than shoots the slanted hail-storm, down he dropt
Towards the ground; but rested not, nor stopt
One moment from his home: only the sward
He with his wand light touch'd, and heavenward
Swifter than sight was gone – even before
The teeming earth a sudden witness bore
Of his swift magic. Diving swans appear
Above the crystal circlings white and clear;   340
And catch the cheated eye in wide surprise,
How they can dive in sight and unseen rise –
So from the turf outsprang two steeds jet-black,
Each with large dark blue wings upon his back.
The youth of Caria plac'd the lovely dame
On one, and felt himself in spleen to tame
The other's fierceness. Through the air they flew,
High as the eagles. Like two drops of dew
Exhal'd to Phœbus' lips, away they are gone,
Far from the earth away – unseen, alone,   350
Among cool clouds and winds, but that the free,
The buoyant life of song can floating be
Above their heads, and follow them untir'd. –
Muse of my native land, am I inspir'd?
This is the giddy air, and I must spread
Wide pinions to keep here; nor do I dread
Or height, or depth, or width, or any chance
Precipitous: I have beneath my glance
Those towering horses and their mournful freight.
Could I thus sail, and see, and thus await   360
Fearless for power of thought, without thine aid? –

          There is a sleepy dusk, an odorous shade
From some approaching wonder, and behold
Those winged steeds, with snorting nostrils bold
Snuff at its faint extreme, and seem to tire,
Dying to embers from their native fire!

There curl'd a purple mist around them; soon,
It seem'd as when around the pale new moon
Sad Zephyr droops the clouds like weeping willow:
'Twas Sleep slow journeying with head on pillow.   370
For the first time, since he came nigh dead born
From the old womb of night, his cave forlorn
Had he left more forlorn; for the first time,
He felt aloof the day and morning's prime –
Because into his depth Cimmerian
There came a dream, shewing how a young man,
Ere a lean bat could plump its wintery skin,
Would at high Jove's empyreal footstool win
An immortality, and how espouse
Jove's daughter, and be reckon'd of his house.   380
Now was he slumbering towards heaven's gate,
That he might at the threshold one hour wait
To hear the marriage melodies, and then
Sink downward to his dusky cave again.
His litter of smooth semilucent mist,
Diversely ting'd with rose and amethyst,
Puzzled those eyes that for the centre sought;
And scarcely for one moment could be caught
His sluggish form reposing motionless.
Those two on winged steeds, with all the stress   390
Of vision search'd for him, as one would look
Athwart the sallows of a river nook
To catch a glance at silver throated eels, –
Or from old Skiddaw's top, when fog conceals
His rugged forehead in a mantle pale,
With an eye-guess towards some pleasant vale
Descry a favourite hamlet faint and far.

These raven horses, though they foster'd are
Of earth's splenetic fire, dully drop
Their full-veined ears, nostrils blood wide, and stop;   400
Upon the spiritless mist have they outspread
Their ample feathers, are in slumber dead, –
And on those pinions, level in mid air,
Endymion sleepeth and the lady fair.
Slowly they sail, slowly as icy isle
Upon a calm sea drifting: and meanwhile

The mournful wanderer dreams. Behold! he walks
On heaven's pavement; brotherly he talks
To divine powers: from his hand full fain
Juno's proud birds are pecking pearly grain: 410
He tries the nerve of Phœbus' golden bow,
And asketh where the golden apples grow:
Upon his arm he braces Pallas' shield,
And strives in vain to unsettle and wield
A Jovian thunderbolt: arch Hebe brings
A full-brimm'd goblet, dances lightly, sings
And tantalizes long; at last he drinks,
And lost in pleasure at her feet he sinks,
Touching with dazzled lips her starlight hand.
He blows a bugle, – an ethereal band   420
Are visible above: the Seasons four, –
Green-kyrtled Spring, flush Summer, golden store
In Autumn's sickle, Winter frosty hoar,
Join dance with shadowy Hours; while still the blast,
In swells unmitigated, still doth last
To sway their floating morris. 'Whose is this?
Whose bugle?' he inquires: they smile – 'O Dis!
Why is this mortal here? Dost thou not know
Its mistress' lips? Not thou? – 'Tis Dian's: lo!
She rises crescented!' He looks, 'tis she,   430
His very goddess: good-bye earth, and sea,
And air, and pains, and care, and suffering;
Good-bye to all but love! Then doth he spring
Towards her, and awakes – and, strange, o'erhead,
Of those same fragrant exhalations bred,
Beheld awake his very dream: the gods
Stood smiling; merry Hebe laughs and nods;
And Phœbe bends towards him crescented.
O state perplexing! On the pinion bed,
Too well awake, he feels the panting side   440
Of his delicious lady. He who died
For soaring too audacious in the sun,
When that same treacherous wax began to run,
Felt not more tongue-tied than Endymion.
His heart leapt up as to its rightful throne,
To that fair shadow'd passion puls'd its way –
Ah, what perplexity! Ah, well a day!

So fond, so beauteous was his bed-fellow,
He could not help but kiss her: then he grew
Awhile forgetful of all beauty save   450
Young Phœbe's, golden hair'd; and so 'gan crave
Forgiveness: yet he turn'd once more to look
At the sweet sleeper, – all his soul was shook, –
She press'd his hand in slumber; so once more
He could not help but kiss her and adore.
At this the shadow wept, melting away.
The Latmian started up: 'Bright goddess, stay!
Search my most hidden breast! By truth's own tongue,
I have no dædale heart: why is it wrung
To desperation? Is there nought for me,   460
Upon the bourne of bliss, but misery?'

     These words awoke the stranger of dark tresses:
Her dawning love-look rapt Endymion blesses
With 'haviour soft. Sleep yawned from underneath.
'Thou swan of Ganges, let us no more breathe
This murky phantasm! thou contented seem'st
Pillow'd in lovely idleness, nor dream'st
What horrors may discomfort thee and me.
Ah, shouldst thou die from my heart-treachery! –
Yet did she merely weep – her gentle soul   470
Hath no revenge in it: as it is whole
In tenderness, would I were whole in love!
Can I prize thee, fair maid, all price above,
Even when I feel as true as innocence?
I do, I do. – What is this soul then? Whence
Came it? It does not seem my own, and I
Have no self-passion or identity.
Some fearful end must be: where, where is it?
By Nemesis, I see my spirit flit
Alone about the dark – Forgive me, sweet: 480
Shall we away?' He rous'd the steeds: they beat
Their wings chivalrous into the clear air,
Leaving old Sleep within his vapoury lair.

     The good-night blush of eve was waning slow,
And Vesper, risen star, began to throe
In the dusk heavens silverly, when they

Thus sprang direct towards the Galaxy.
Nor did speed hinder converse soft and strange –
Eternal oaths and vows they interchange,
In such wise, in such temper, so aloof   490
Up in the winds, beneath a starry roof,
So witless of their doom, that verily
'Tis well nigh past man's search their hearts to see;
Whether they wept, or laugh'd, or griev'd, or toy'd –
Most like with joy gone mad, with sorrow cloy'd.

   Full facing their swift flight, from ebon streak,
The moon put forth a little diamond peak,
No bigger than an unobserved star,
Or tiny point of fairy scymetar;
Bright signal that she only stoop'd to tie   500
Her silver sandals, ere deliciously
She bow'd into the heavens her timid head.
Slowly she rose, as though she would have fled,
While to his lady meek the Carian turn'd,
To mark if her dark eyes had yet discern'd
This beauty in its birth – Despair! despair!
He saw her body fading gaunt and spare
In the cold moonshine. Straight he seiz'd her wrist;
It melted from his grasp: her hand he kiss'd,
And, horror! kiss'd his own – he was alone.   510
Her steed a little higher soar'd, and then
Dropt hawkwise to the earth.

                There lies a den,
Beyond the seeming confines of the space
Made for the soul to wander in and trace
Its own existence, of remotest glooms.
Dark regions are around it, where the tombs
Of buried griefs the spirit sees, but scarce
One hour doth linger weeping, for the pierce
Of new-born woe it feels more inly smart:
And in these regions many a venom'd dart   520
At random flies; they are the proper home
Of every ill: the man is yet to come
Who hath not journeyed in this native hell.
But few have ever felt how calm and well

Sleep may be had in that deep den of all.
There anguish does not sting; nor pleasure pall:
Woe-hurricanes beat ever at the gate,
Yet all is still within and desolate.
Beset with plainful gusts, within ye hear
No sound so loud as when on curtain'd bier   530
The death-watch tick is stifled. Enter none
Who strive therefore: on the sudden it is won.
Just when the sufferer begins to burn,
Then it is free to him; and from an urn,
Still fed by melting ice, he takes a draught —
Young Semele such richness never quaft
In her maternal longing. Happy gloom!
Dark Paradise! where pale becomes the bloom
Of health by due; where silence dreariest
Is most articulate; where hopes infest;   540
Where those eyes are the brightest far that keep
Their lids shut longest in a dreamless sleep.
O happy spirit-home! O wondrous soul!
Pregnant with such a den to save the whole
In thine own depth. Hail, gentle Carian!
For, never since thy griefs and woes began,
Hast thou felt so content: a grievous feud
Hath led thee to this Cave of Quietude.
Aye, his lull'd soul was there, although upborne
With dangerous speed: and so he did not mourn   550
Because he knew not whither he was going.
So happy was he, not the aerial blowing
Of trumpets at clear parley from the east
Could rouse from that fine relish, that high feast.
They stung the feather'd horse: with fierce alarm
He flapp'd towards the sound. Alas, no charm
Could lift Endymion's head, or he had view'd
A skyey mask, a pinion'd multitude, —
And silvery was its passing: voices sweet
Warbling the while as if to lull and greet   560
The wanderer in his path. Thus warbled they,
While past the vision went in bright array.

'Who, who from Dian's feast would be away?
For all the golden bowers of the day

Are empty left? Who, who away would be
From Cynthia's wedding and festivity?
Not Hesperus: lo! upon his silver wings
He leans away for highest heaven and sings,
Snapping his lucid fingers merrily! —
Ah, Zephyrus! art here, and Flora too!   570
Ye tender bibbers of the rain and dew,
Young playmates of the rose and daffodil,
Be careful, ere ye enter in, to fill
     Your baskets high
With fennel green, and balm, and golden pines,
Savory, latter-mint, and columbines,
Cool parsley, basil sweet, and sunny thyme;
Yea, every flower and leaf of every clime,
All gather'd in the dewy morning: hie
     Away! fly, fly! —   580
Crystalline brother of the belt of heaven,
Aquarius! to whom king Jove has given
Two liquid pulse streams 'stead of feather'd wings,
Two fan-like fountains, — thine illuminings
     For Dian play:
Dissolve the frozen purity of air;
Let thy white shoulders silvery and bare
Shew cold through watery pinions; make more bright
The Star-Queen's crescent on her marriage night:
     Haste, haste away! —   590
Castor has tamed the planet Lion, see!
And of the Bear has Pollux mastery:
A third is in the race! who is the third,
Speeding away swift as the eagle bird?
     The ramping Centaur!
The Lion's mane's on end: the Bear how fierce!
The Centaur's arrow ready seems to pierce
Some enemy: far forth his bow is bent
Into the blue of heaven. He'll be shent,
     Pale unrelentor,   600
When he shall hear the wedding lutes a playing. —
Andromeda! sweet woman! why delaying
So timidly among the stars: come hither!
Join this bright throng, and nimbly follow whither
     They all are going.

Danae's Son, before Jove newly bow'd,
Has wept for thee, calling to Jove aloud.
Thee, gentle lady, did he disenthral:
Ye shall for ever live and love, for all
      Thy tears are flowing. –   610
By Daphne's fright, behold Apollo! –'
                             More
Endymion heard not: down his steed him bore
Prone to the green head of a misty hill.

    His first touch of the earth went nigh to kill.
'Alas!' said he, 'were I but always borne
Through dangerous winds, had but my footsteps worn
A path in hell, for ever would I bless
Horrors which nourish an uneasiness
For my own sullen conquering: to him
Who lives beyond earth's boundary, grief is dim,   620
Sorrow is but a shadow: now I see
The grass; I feel the solid ground – Ah, me!
It is thy voice – divinest! Where? – who? who
Left thee so quiet on this bed of dew?
Behold upon this happy earth we are;
Let us ay love each other; let us fare
On forest-fruits, and never, never go
Among the abodes of mortals here below,
Or be by phantoms duped. O destiny!
Into a labyrinth now my soul would fly,   630
But with thy beauty will I deaden it.
Where didst thou melt to? By thee will I sit
For ever: let our fate stop here – a kid
I on this spot will offer: Pan will bid
Us live in peace, in love and peace among
His forest wildernesses. I have clung
To nothing, lov'd a nothing, nothing seen
Or felt but a great dream! O I have been
Presumptuous against love, against the sky,
Against all elements, against the tie   640
Of mortals each to each, against the blooms
Of flowers, rush of rivers, and the tombs
Of heroes gone! Against his proper glory

Has my own soul conspired: so my story
Will I to children utter, and repent.
There never liv'd a mortal man, who bent
His appetite beyond his natural sphere,
But starv'd and died. My sweetest Indian, here,
Here will I kneel, for thou redeemed hast
My life from too thin breathing: gone and past   650
Are cloudy phantasms. Caverns lone, farewel!
And air of visions, and the monstrous swell
Of visionary seas! No, never more
Shall airy voices cheat me to the shore
Of tangled wonder, breathless and aghast.
Adieu, my daintiest Dream! although so vast
My love is still for thee. The hour may come
When we shall meet in pure elysium.
On earth I may not love thee; and therefore
Doves will I offer up, and sweetest store   660
All through the teeming year: so thou wilt shine
On me, and on this damsel fair of mine,
And bless our simple lives. My Indian bliss!
My river-lily bud! one human kiss!
One sigh of real breath — one gentle squeeze,
Warm as a dove's nest among summer trees,
And warm with dew at ooze from living blood!
Whither didst melt? Ah, what of that! — all good
We'll talk about — no more of dreaming. — Now,
Where shall our dwelling be? Under the brow   670
Of some steep mossy hill, where ivy dun
Would hide us up, although spring leaves were none;
And where dark yew trees, as we rustle through,
Will drop their scarlet berry cups of dew?
O thou wouldst joy to live in such a place;
Dusk for our loves, yet light enough to grace
Those gentle limbs on mossy bed reclin'd:
For by one step the blue sky shouldst thou find,
And by another, in deep dell below,
See, through the trees, a little river go   680
All in its mid-day gold and glimmering.
Honey from out the gnarled hive I'll bring,
And apples, wan with sweetness, gather thee, —
Cresses that grow where no man may them see,

And sorrel untorn by the dew-claw'd stag:
Pipes will I fashion of the syrinx flag,
That thou mayst always know whither I roam,
When it shall please thee in our quiet home
To listen and think of love. Still let me speak;
Still let me dive into the joy I seek, —   690
For yet the past doth prison me. The rill,
Thou haply mayst delight in, will I fill
With fairy fishes from the mountain tarn,
And thou shalt feed them from the squirrel's barn.
Its bottom will I strew with amber shells,
And pebbles blue from deep enchanted wells.
Its sides I'll plant with dew-sweet eglantine,
And honeysuckles full of clear bee-wine.
I will entice this crystal rill to trace
Love's silver name upon the meadow's face.   700
I'll kneel to Vesta, for a flame of fire;
And to god Phœbus, for a golden lyre;
To Empress Dian, for a hunting spear;
To Vesper, for a taper silver-clear,
That I may see thy beauty through the night;
To Flora, and a nightingale shall light
Tame on thy finger; to the River-gods,
And they shall bring thee taper fishing-rods
Of gold, and lines of Naiads' long bright tress.
Heaven shield thee for thine utter loveliness!   710
Thy mossy footstool shall the altar be
'Fore which I'll bend, bending, dear love, to thee:
Those lips shall be my Delphos, and shall speak
Laws to my footsteps, colour to my cheek,
Trembling or stedfastness to this same voice,
And of three sweetest pleasurings the choice:
And that affectionate light, those diamond things,
Those eyes, those passions, those supreme pearl springs,
Shall be my grief, or twinkle me to pleasure.
Say, is not bliss within our perfect seisure?   720
O that I could not doubt!'

                    The mountaineer
Thus strove by fancies vain and crude to clear
His briar'd path to some tranquillity.

It gave bright gladness to his lady's eye,
And yet the tears she wept were tears of sorrow;
Answering thus, just as the golden morrow
Beam'd upward from the vallies of the east:
'O that the flutter of this heart had ceas'd,
Or the sweet name of love had pass'd away.
Young feather'd tyrant! by a swift decay.   730
Wilt thou devote this body to the earth:
And I do think that at my very birth
I lisp'd thy blooming titles inwardly;
For at the first, first dawn and thought of thee,
With uplift hands I blest the stars of heaven.
Art thou not cruel? Ever have I striven
To think thee kind, but ah, it will not do!
When yet a child, I heard that kisses drew
Favour from thee, and so I gave and gave
To the void air, bidding them find out love: 740
But when I came to feel how far above
All fancy, pride, and fickle maidenhood,
All earthly pleasure, all imagin'd good,
Was the warm tremble of a devout kiss, –
Even then, that moment, at the thought of this,
Fainting I fell into a bed of flowers,
And languish'd there three days. Ye milder powers,
Am I not cruelly wrong'd? Believe, believe
Me, dear Endymion, were I to weave
With my own fancies garlands of sweet life,   750
Thou shouldst be one of all. Ah, bitter strife!
I may not be thy love: I am forbidden –
Indeed I am – thwarted, affrighted, chidden,
By things I trembled at, and gorgon wrath.
Twice hast thou ask'd whither I went: henceforth
Ask me no more! I may not utter it,
Nor may I be thy love. We might commit
Ourselves at once to vengeance; we might die;
We might embrace and die: voluptuous thought!
Enlarge not to my hunger, or I'm caught   760
In trammels of perverse deliciousness.
No, no, that shall not be: thee will I bless,
And bid a long adieu.'

The Carian
No word return'd: both lovelorn, silent, wan,
Into the vallies green together went.
Far wandering, they were perforce content
To sit beneath a fair lone beechen tree;
Nor at each other gaz'd, but heavily
Por'd on its hazle cirque of shedded leaves.

    Endymion! unhappy! it nigh grieves   770
Me to behold thee thus in last extreme:
Ensky'd ere this, but truly that I deem
Truth the best music in a first-born song.
Thy lute-voic'd brother will I sing ere long,
And thou shalt aid – hast thou not aided me?
Yes, moonlight Emperor! felicity
Has been thy meed for many thousand years;
Yet often have I, on the brink of tears,
Mourn'd as if yet thou wert a forester; –
Forgetting the old tale.

              He did not stir   780
His eyes from the dead leaves, or one small pulse
Of joy he might have felt. The spirit culls
Unfaded amaranth, when wild it strays
Through the old garden-ground of boyish days.
A little onward ran the very stream
By which he took his first soft poppy dream;
And on the very bark 'gainst which he leant
A crescent he had carv'd, and round it spent
His skill in little stars. The teeming tree
Had swollen and green'd the pious charactery,   790
But not ta'en out. Why, there was not a slope
Up which he had not fear'd the antelope;
And not a tree, beneath whose rooty shade
He had not with his tamed leopards play'd.
Nor could an arrow light, or javelin,
Fly in the air where his had never been –
And yet he knew it not.

              O treachery!
Why does his lady smile, pleasing her eye

With all his sorrowing? He sees her not.
But who so stares on him? His sister sure!   800
Peona of the woods! – Can she endure –
Impossible – how dearly they embrace!
His lady smiles; delight is in her face;
It is no treachery.

              'Dear brother mine!
Endymion, weep not so! Why shouldst thou pine
When all great Latmos so exalt will be?
Thank the great gods, and look not bitterly;
And speak not one pale word, and sigh no more.
Sure I will not believe thou hast such store
Of grief, to last thee to my kiss again.   810
Thou surely canst not bear a mind in pain,
Come hand in hand with one so beautiful.
Be happy both of you! for I will pull
The flowers of autumn for your coronals.
Pan's holy priest for young Endymion calls;
And when he is restor'd, thou, fairest dame,
Shalt be our queen. Now, is it not a shame
To see ye thus, – not very, very sad?
Perhaps ye are too happy to be glad:
O feel as if it were a common day;   820
Free-voic'd as one who never was away.
No tongue shall ask, whence come ye? but ye shall
Be gods of your own rest imperial.
Not even I, for one whole month, will pry
Into the hours that have pass'd us by,
Since in my arbour I did sing to thee.
O Hermes! on this very night will be
A hymning up to Cynthia, queen of light;
For the soothsayers old saw yesternight
Good visions in the air, – whence will befal,   830
As say these sages, health perpetual
To shepherds and their flocks; and furthermore,
In Dian's face they read the gentle lore:
Therefore for her these vesper-carols are.
Our friends will all be there from nigh and far.
Many upon thy death have ditties made;
And many, even now, their foreheads shade

With cypress, on a day of sacrifice.
New singing for our maids shalt thou devise,
And pluck the sorrow from our huntsmen's brows.   840
Tell me, my lady-queen, how to espouse
This wayward brother to his rightful joys!
His eyes are on thee bent, as thou didst poise
His fate most goddess-like. Help me, I pray,
To lure – Endymion, dear brother, say
What ails thee?' He could bear no more, and so
Bent his soul fiercely like a spiritual bow,
And twang'd it inwardly, and calmly said:
'I would have thee my only friend, sweet maid!
My only visitor! not ignorant though,   850
That those deceptions which for pleasure go
'Mong men, are pleasures real as real may be:
But there are higher ones I may not see,
If impiously an earthly realm I take.
Since I saw thee, I have been wide awake
Night after night, and day by day, until
Of the empyrean I have drunk my fill.
Let it content thee, Sister, seeing me
More happy than betides mortality.
A hermit young, I'll live in mossy cave,   860
Where thou alone shalt come to me, and lave
Thy spirit in the wonders I shall tell.
Through me the shepherd realm shall prosper well;
For to thy tongue will I all health confide.
And, for my sake, let this young maid abide
With thee as a dear sister. Thou alone,
Peona, mayst return to me. I own
This may sound strangely: but when, dearest girl,
Thou seest it for my happiness, no pearl
Will trespass down those cheeks. Companion fair!   870
Wilt be content to dwell with her, to share
This sister's love with me?' Like one resign'd
And bent by circumstance, and thereby blind
In self-commitment, thus that meek unknown:
'Aye, but a buzzing by my ears has flown,
Of jubilee to Dian: – truth I heard?
Well then, I see there is no little bird,
Tender soever, but is Jove's own care.

Long have I sought for rest, and, unaware,
Behold I find it! so exalted too!   880
So after my own heart! I knew, I knew
There was a place untenanted in it:
In that same void white Chastity shall sit,
And monitor me nightly to lone slumber.
With sanest lips I vow me to the number
Of Dian's sisterhood; and, kind lady,
With thy good help, this very night shall see
My future days to her fane consecrate.'

    As feels a dreamer what doth most create
His own particular fright, so these three felt: 890
Or like one who, in after ages, knelt
To Lucifer or Baal, when he'd pine
After a little sleep: or when in mine
Far under-ground, a sleeper meets his friends
Who know him not. Each diligently bends
Towards common thoughts and things for very fear;
Striving their ghastly malady to cheer,
By thinking it a thing of yes and no,
That housewives talk of. But the spirit-blow
Was struck, and all were dreamers. At the last   900
Endymion said: 'Are not our fates all cast?
Why stand we here? Adieu, ye tender pair!
Adieu!' Whereat those maidens, with wild stare,
Walk'd dizzily away. Pained and hot
His eyes went after them, until they got
Near to a cypress grove, whose deadly maw,
In one swift moment, would what then he saw
Engulph for ever. 'Stay!' he cried, 'ah, stay!
Turn, damsels! hist! one word I have to say.
Sweet Indian, I would see thee once again.   910
It is a thing I dote on: so I'd fain,
Peona, ye should hand in hand repair
Into those holy groves, that silent are
Behind great Dian's temple. I'll be yon,
At vesper's earliest twinkle – they are gone –
But once, once, once again –' At this he press'd
His hands against his face, and then did rest
His head upon a mossy hillock green,

And so remain'd as he a corpse had been
All the long day; save when he scantly lifted   920
His eyes abroad, to see how shadows shifted
With the slow move of time, – sluggish and weary
Until the poplar tops, in journey dreary,
Had reach'd the river's brim. Then up he rose,
And, slowly as that very river flows,
Walk'd towards the temple grove with this lament:
'Why such a golden eve? The breeze is sent
Careful and soft, that not a leaf may fall
Before the serene father of them all
Bows down his summer head below the west.   930
Now am I of breath, speech, and speed possest,
But at the setting I must bid adieu
To her for the last time. Night will strew
On the damp grass myriads of lingering leaves,
And with them shall I die; nor much it grieves
To die, when summer dies on the cold sward.
Why, I have been a butterfly, a lord
Of flowers, garlands, love-knots, silly posies,
Groves, meadows, melodies, and arbour roses;
My kingdom's at its death, and just it is   940
That I should die with it: so in all this
We miscal grief, bale, sorrow, heartbreak, woe,
What is there to plain of? By Titan's foe
I am but rightly serv'd.' So saying, he
Tripp'd lightly on, in sort of deathful glee;
Laughing at the clear stream and setting sun,
As though they jests had been: nor had he done
His laugh at nature's holy countenance,
Until that grove appear'd, as if perchance,
And then his tongue with sober seemlihed   950
Gave utterance as he entered: 'Ha! I said,
King of the butterflies; but by this gloom,
And by old Rhadamanthus' tongue of doom,
This dusk religion, pomp of solitude,
And the Promethean clay by thief endued,
By old Saturnus' forelock, by his head
Shook with eternal palsy, I did wed
Myself to things of light from infancy;
And thus to be cast out, thus lorn to die,

Is sure enough to make a mortal man   960
Grow impious.' So he inwardly began
On things for which no wording can be found;
Deeper and deeper sinking, until drown'd
Beyond the reach of music: for the choir
Of Cynthia he heard not, though rough briar
Nor muffling thicket interpos'd to dull
The vesper hymn, far swollen, soft and full,
Through the dark pillars of those sylvan aisles.
He saw not the two maidens, nor their smiles,
Wan as primroses gather'd at midnight   970
By chilly finger'd spring. 'Unhappy wight!
Endymion!' said Peona, 'we are here!
What wouldst thou ere we all are laid on bier?'
Then he embrac'd her, and his lady's hand
Press'd, saying: 'Sister, I would have command,
If it were heaven's will, on our sad fate.'
At which that dark-eyed stranger stood elate
And said, in a new voice, but sweet as love,
To Endymion's amaze: 'By Cupid's dove,
And so thou shalt! and by the lily truth   980
Of my own breast thou shalt, beloved youth!'
And as she spake, into her face there came
Light, as reflected from a silver flame:
Her long black hair swell'd ampler, in display
Full golden; in her eyes a brighter day
Dawn'd blue and full of love. Aye, he beheld
Phœbe, his passion! joyous she upheld
Her lucid bow, continuing thus: 'Drear, drear
Has our delaying been; but foolish fear
Withheld me first; and then decrees of fate;   990
And then 'twas fit that from this mortal state
Thou shouldst, my love, by some unlook'd for change
Be spiritualiz'd. Peona, we shall range
These forests, and to thee they safe shall be
As was thy cradle; hither shalt thou flee
To meet us many a time.' Next Cynthia bright
Peona kiss'd, and bless'd with fair good night:
Her brother kiss'd her too, and knelt adown
Before his goddess, in a blissful swoon.
She gave her fair hands to him, and behold,   1000

Before three swiftest kisses he had told,
They vanish'd far away! Peona went
Home through the gloomy wood in wonderment.

THE END

'In drear nighted December'

In drear nighted December,
  Too happy, happy tree,
Thy branches ne'er remember
  Their green felicity –
The north cannot undo them   5
With a sleety whistle through them,
Nor frozen thawings glue them
  From budding at the prime.

In drear nighted December,
  Too happy, happy brook,   10
Thy bubblings ne'er remember
  Apollo's summer look –
But with a sweet forgetting
They stay their crystal fretting,
Never, never petting   15
  About the frozen time.

Ah! would 'twere so with many
  A gentle girl and boy –
But were there ever any
  Writh'd not of passed joy?   20
The feel of not to feel it,
When there is none to heal it,
Nor numbed sense to steel it,
  Was never said in rhyme.

Lines on seeing a Lock of Milton's Hair

Chief of organic numbers!
  Old scholar of the spheres!
Thy spirit never slumbers,
  But rolls about our ears
For ever, and for ever:
O what a mad endeavour
  Worketh he,
Who, to thy sacred and ennobled hearse,

Would offer a burnt sacrifice of verse
          And melody.   10

          How heavenward thou soundedst
            Live temple of sweet noise;
          And discord unconfoundedst –
            Giving delight new joys,
          And pleasure nobler pinions –
          O where are thy dominions?
                Lend thine ear
To a young delian oath – aye by thy soul,
By all that from thy mortal lips did roll,
And by the kernel of thine earthly love,   20
Beauty, in things on earth and things above;
          When every childish fashion
            Has vanish'd from my rhyme,
          Will I, grey-gone in passion,
            Leave to an after time
          Hymning and harmony
Of thee, and of thy works, and of thy life;
But vain is now the burning and the strife,
Pangs are in vain – until I grow high-rife
                With old philosophy;   30
And mad with glimpses at futurity!

For many years my offerings must be hush'd.
  When I do speak, I'll think upon this hour,
Because I feel my forehead hot and flush'd –
  Even at the simplest vassal of thy power –
A lock of thy bright hair – sudden it came,
And I was startled, when I caught thy name
          Coupled so unaware –
Yet at the moment, temperate was my blood.
Methought I had beheld it from the flood.   40

On sitting down to read King Lear once again

O golden-tongued romance, with serene lute!
  Fair plumed syren, queen of far-away!
  Leave melodizing on this wintry day,
Shut up thine olden pages, and be mute.
Adieu! for, once again, the fierce dispute   5
  Betwixt damnation and impassion'd clay
  Must I burn through; once more humbly assay
The bitter-sweet of this Shaksperean fruit.
Chief poet! and ye clouds of Albion,
  Begetters of our deep eternal theme!   10
When through the old oak forest I am gone,
  Let me not wander in a barren dream:
But, when I am consumed in the fire,
Give me new phœnix wings to fly at my desire.

'When I have fears that I may cease to be'

When I have fears that I may cease to be
  Before my pen has glean'd my teeming brain,
Before high piled books, in charact'ry,
  Hold like rich garners the full-ripen'd grain;
When I behold, upon the night's starr'd face,   5
  Huge cloudy symbols of a high romance,
And think that I may never live to trace
  Their shadows, with the magic hand of chance;
And when I feel, fair creature of an hour!
  That I shall never look upon thee more,   10
Never have relish in the faery power
  Of unreflecting love! – then on the shore
Of the wide world I stand alone, and think
Till love and fame to nothingness do sink.

Robin Hood. To a Friend

No! those days are gone away,
And their hours are old and gray,
And their minutes buried all
Under the down-trodden pall
Of the leaves of many years:
Many times have winter's shears,
Frozen North, and chilling East,
Sounded tempests to the feast
Of the forest's whispering fleeces,
Since men knew nor rent nor leases.   10

No, the bugle sounds no more,
And the twanging bow no more;
Silent is the ivory shrill
Past the heath and up the hill;
There is no mid-forest laugh,
Where lone Echo gives the half
To some wight, amaz'd to hear
Jesting, deep in forest drear.

On the fairest time of June
You may go, with sun or moon,   20
Or the seven stars to light you,
Or the polar ray to right you;
But you never may behold
Little John, or Robin bold;
Never one, of all the clan,
Thrumming on an empty can
Some old hunting ditty, while
He doth his green way beguile
To fair hostess Merriment,
Down beside the pasture Trent;   30
For he left the merry tale
Messenger for spicy ale.

Gone, the merry morris din;
Gone, the song of Gamelyn;
Gone, the tough-belted outlaw
Idling in the 'grenè shawe';

All are gone away and past!
And if Robin should be cast
Sudden from his turfed grave,
And if Marian should have　　　　　　　　40
Once again her forest days,
She would weep, and he would craze:
He would swear, for all his oaks,
Fall'n beneath the dockyard strokes,
Have rotted on the briny seas;
She would weep that her wild bees
Sang not to her — strange! that honey
Can't be got without hard money!

    So it is: yet let us sing,
Honour to the old bow-string!　　　　　　50
Honour to the bugle-horn!
Honour to the woods unshorn!
Honour to the Lincoln green!
Honour to the archer keen!
Honour to tight little John,
And the horse he rode upon!
Honour to bold Robin Hood,
Sleeping in the underwood!
Honour to maid Marian,
And to all the Sherwood-clan!　　　　　　60
Though their days have hurried by
Let us two a burden try.

Lines on the Mermaid Tavern

Souls of Poets dead and gone,
What Elysium have ye known,
Happy field or mossy cavern,
Choicer than the Mermaid Tavern?
Have ye tippled drink more fine
Than mine host's Canary wine?
Or are fruits of Paradise
Sweeter than those dainty pies
Of venison? O generous food!

Drest as though bold Robin Hood   10
Would, with his maid Marian,
Sup and bowse from horn and can.

   I have heard that on a day
Mine host's sign-board flew away,
Nobody knew whither, till
An astrologer's old quill
To a sheepskin gave the story,
Said he saw you in your glory,
Underneath a new old-sign
Sipping beverage divine,   20
And pledging with contented smack
The Mermaid in the Zodiac.

   Souls of Poets dead and gone,
What Elysium have ye known,
Happy field or mossy cavern,
Choicer than the Mermaid Tavern?

To — ['Time's sea']

Time's sea hath been five years at its slow ebb;
   Long hours have to and fro let creep the sand,
Since I was tangled in thy beauty's web,
   And snared by the ungloving of thine hand.
And yet I never look on midnight sky,   5
   But I behold thine eyes' well-memoried light;
I cannot look upon the rose's dye,
   But to thy cheek my soul doth take its flight;
I cannot look on any budding flower,
   But my fond ear, in fancy at thy lips,   10
And harkening for a love-sound, doth devour
   Its sweets in the wrong sense: – Thou dost
     eclipse
Every delight with sweet remembering,
And grief unto my darling joys dost bring.

'Dear Reynolds, as last night I lay in bed'

Dear Reynolds, as last night I lay in bed,
There came before my eyes that wonted thread
Of shapes, and shadows and remembrances,
That every other minute vex and please:
Things all disjointed come from north and south,
Two witch's eyes above a cherub's mouth,
Voltaire with casque and shield and habergeon,
And Alexander with his night-cap on –
Old Socrates a tying his cravat;
And Hazlitt playing with Miss Edgworth's cat;   10
And Junius Brutus pretty well so so,
Making the best of 's way towards Soho.

   Few are there who escape these visitings –
Perhaps one or two, whose lives have patient wings;
And through whose curtains peeps no hellish nose.
No wild boar tushes, and no mermaid's toes:
But flowers bursting out with lusty pride,
And young Æolian harps personified,
Some, Titian colours touch'd into real life. –
The sacrifice goes on; the pontif knife   20
Gleams in the sun, the milk-white heifer lows,
The pipes go shrilly, the libation flows:
A white sail shews above the green-head cliff
Moves round the point, and throws her anchor stiff.
The mariners join hymn with those on land. –
You know the Enchanted Castle – it doth stand
Upon a rock on the border of a lake
Nested in trees, which all do seem to shake
From some old magic like Urganda's sword.
O Phœbus, that I had thy sacred word   30
To shew this castle in fair dreaming wise
Unto my friend, while sick and ill he lies.

   You know it well enough, where it doth seem
A mossy place, a Merlin's Hall, a dream.
You know the clear lake, and the little isles,
The mountains blue, and cold near neighbour rills –
All which elsewhere are but half animate

Here do they look alive to love and hate;
To smiles and frowns; they seem a lifted mound
Above some giant, pulsing underground.   40

    Part of the building was a chosen see
Built by a banish'd santon of Chaldee:
The other part two thousand years from him
Was built by Cuthbert de Saint Aldebrim;
Then there's a little wing, far from the sun,
Built by a Lapland witch turn'd maudlin nun –
And many other juts of aged stone
Founded with many a mason-devil's groan.

    The doors all look as if they oped themselves,
The windows as if latch'd by fays and elves –   50
And from them comes a silver flash of light
As from the westward of a summer's night;
Or like a beauteous woman's large blue eyes
Gone mad through olden songs and poesies.

    See what is coming from the distance dim!
A golden galley all in silken trim!
Three rows of oars are lightening moment-whiles
Into the verdurous bosoms of those Isles.
Towards the shade under the castle wall
It comes in silence – now 'tis hidden all.   60
The clarion sounds; and from a postern grate
An echo of sweet music doth create
A fear in the poor herdsman who doth bring
His beasts to trouble the enchanted spring:
He tells of the sweet music and the spot
To all his friends, and they believe him not.

    O that our dreamings all of sleep or wake
Would all their colours from the sunset take:
From something of material sublime,
Rather than shadow our own soul's daytime   70
In the dark void of night. For in the world
We jostle – but my flag is not unfurl'd
On the admiral staff – and to philosophize
I dare not yet! – Oh never will the prize,

High reason, and the lore of good and ill,
Be my award. Things cannot to the will
Be settled, but they tease us out of thought.
Or is it that imagination brought
Beyond its proper bound, yet still confined, –
Lost in a sort of purgatory blind,   80
Cannot refer to any standard law
Of either earth or heaven? – It is a flaw
In happiness to see beyond our bourn –
It forces us in summer skies to mourn:
It spoils the singing of the nightingale.

Dear Reynolds, I have a mysterious tale
And cannot speak it. The first page I read
Upon a lampit rock of green sea weed
Among the breakers. – 'Twas a quiet eve;
The rocks were silent – the wide sea did weave   90
An untumultuous fringe of silver foam
Along the flat brown sand. I was at home,
And should have been most happy – but I saw
Too far into the sea; where every maw
The greater on the less feeds evermore: –
But I saw too distinct into the core
Of an eternal fierce destruction,
And so from happiness I far was gone.
Still am I sick of it: and though to-day
I've gathered young spring-leaves, and flowers gay   100
Of periwinkle and wild strawberry,
Still do I that most fierce destruction see,
The shark at savage prey – the hawk at pounce,
The gentle robin, like a pard or ounce,
Ravening a worm. – Away ye horrid moods,
Moods of one's mind! You know I hate them well,
You know I'd sooner be a clapping bell
To some Kamschatkan missionary church,
Than with these horrid moods be left in lurch –
Do you get health – and Tom the same – I'll dance,   110
And from detested moods in new romance
Take refuge. – Of bad lines a centaine dose
Is sure enough – and so 'here follows prose'.

Isabella; or, the Pot of Basil

A STORY FROM BOCCACCIO

I

Fair Isabel, poor simple Isabel!
   Lorenzo, a young palmer in Love's eye!
They could not in the self-same mansion dwell
   Without some stir of heart, some malady;
They could not sit at meals but feel how well
   It soothed each to be the other by;
They could not, sure, beneath the same roof sleep
But to each other dream, and nightly weep.

2

With every morn their love grew tenderer,
   With every eve deeper and tenderer still;   10
He might not in house, field, or garden stir,
   But her full shape would all his seeing fill;
And his continual voice was pleasanter
   To her, than noise of trees or hidden rill;
Her lute-string gave an echo of his name,
She spoilt her half-done broidery with the same.

3

He knew whose gentle hand was at the latch,
   Before the door had given her to his eyes;
And from her chamber-window he would catch
   Her beauty farther than the falcon spies;   20
And constant as her vespers would he watch,
   Because her face was turn'd to the same skies;
And with sick longing all the night outwear,
To hear her morning-step upon the stair.

4

A whole long month of May in this sad plight
   Made their cheeks paler by the break of June:
'To-morrow will I bow to my delight,

To-morrow will I ask my lady's boon.' –
'O may I never see another night,
   Lorenzo, if thy lips breathe not love's tune.' –   30
So spake they to their pillows; but, alas,
Honeyless days and days did he let pass;

5

Until sweet Isabella's untouch'd cheek
   Fell sick within the rose's just domain,
Fell thin as a young mother's, who doth seek
   By every lull to cool her infant's pain:
'How ill she is,' said he, 'I may not speak,
   And yet I will, and tell my love all plain:
If looks speak love-laws, I will drink her tears,
And at the least 'twill startle off her cares.'   40

6

So said he one fair morning, and all day
   His heart beat awfully against his side;
And to his heart he inwardly did pray
   For power to speak; but still the ruddy tide
Stifled his voice, and puls'd resolve away –
   Fever'd his high conceit of such a bride,
Yet brought him to the meekness of a child:
Alas! when passion is both meek and wild!

7

So once more he had wak'd and anguished
   A dreary night of love and misery,   50
If Isabel's quick eye had not been wed
   To every symbol on his forehead high;
She saw it waxing very pale and dead,
   And straight all flush'd; so, lisped tenderly,
'Lorenzo!' – here she ceas'd her timid quest,
But in her tone and look he read the rest.

8

'O Isabella, I can half perceive
   That I may speak my grief into thine ear;

If thou didst ever any thing believe,
　Believe how I love thee, believe how near   60
My soul is to its doom: I would not grieve
　Thy hand by unwelcome pressing, would not fear
Thine eyes by gazing; but I cannot live
Another night, and not my passion shrive.

9

'Love! thou art leading me from wintry cold,
　Lady! thou leadest me to summer clime,
And I must taste the blossoms that unfold
　In its ripe warmth this gracious morning time.'
So said, his erewhile timid lips grew bold,
　And poesied with hers in dewy rhyme: 70
Great bliss was with them, and great happiness
Grew, like a lusty flower in June's caress.

10

Parting they seem'd to tread upon the air,
　Twin roses by the zephyr blown apart
Only to meet again more close, and share
　The inward fragrance of each other's heart.
She, to her chamber gone, a ditty fair
　Sang, of delicious love and honey'd dart;
He with light steps went up a western hill.
And bade the sun farewell, and joy'd his fill.   80

11

All close they met again, before the dusk
　Had taken from the stars its pleasant veil,
All close they met, all eves, before the dusk
　Had taken from the stars its pleasant veil,
Close in a bower of hyacinth and musk,
　Unknown of any, free from whispering tale.
Ah! better had it been for ever so,
Than idle ears should pleasure in their woe.

12

Were they unhappy then? — It cannot be —
　Too many tears for lovers have been shed,   90

Too many sighs give we to them in fee,
    Too much of pity after they are dead,
Too many doleful stories do we see,
    Whose matter in bright gold were best be read;
Except in such a page where Theseus' spouse
Over the pathless waves towards him bows.

13

But, for the general award of love,
    The little sweet doth kill much bitterness;
Though Dido silent is in under-grove,
    And Isabella's was a great distress,   100
Though young Lorenzo in warm Indian clove
    Was not embalm'd, this truth is not the less —
Even bees, the little almsmen of spring-bowers,
Know there is richest juice in poison-flowers.

14

With her two brothers this fair lady dwelt,
    Enriched from ancestral merchandize,
And for them many a weary hand did swelt
    In torched mines and noisy factories,
And many once proud-quiver'd loins did melt
    In blood from stinging whip; — with hollow eyes   110
Many all day in dazzling river stood,
To take the rich-ored driftings of the flood.

15

For them the Ceylon diver held his breath,
    And went all naked to the hungry shark;
For them his ears gush'd blood; for them in death
    The seal on the cold ice with piteous bark
Lay full of darts; for them alone did seethe
    A thousand men in troubles wide and dark:
Half-ignorant, they turn'd an easy wheel,
That set sharp racks at work, to pinch and peel.   120

16

Why were they proud? Because their marble founts
  Gush'd with more pride than do a wretch's tears? –
Why were they proud? Because fair orange-mounts
  Were of more soft ascent than lazar stairs? –
Why were they proud? Because red-lin'd accounts
  Were richer than the songs of Grecian years? –
Why were they proud? again we ask aloud,
Why in the name of Glory were they proud?

17

Yet were these Florentines as self-retired
  In hungry pride and gainful cowardice,   130
As two close Hebrews in that land inspired,
  Paled in and vineyarded from beggar-spies;
The hawks of ship-mast forests – the untired
  And pannier'd mules for ducats and old lies –
Quick cat's-paws on the generous stray-away, –
Great wits in Spanish, Tuscan, and Malay.

18

How was it these same ledger-men could spy
  Fair Isabella in her downy nest?
How could they find out in Lorenzo's eye
  A straying from his toil? Hot Egypt's pest   140
Into their vision covetous and sly!
  How could these money-bags see east and west? –
Yet so they did – and every dealer fair
Must see behind, as doth the hunted hare.

19

O eloquent and famed Boccaccio!
  Of thee we now should ask forgiving boon,
And of thy spicy myrtles as they blow,
  And of thy roses amorous of the moon,
And of thy lilies, that do paler grow
  Now they can no more hear thy ghittern's tune,   150
For venturing syllables that ill beseem
The quiet glooms of such a piteous theme.

20

Grant thou a pardon here, and then the tale
    Shall move on soberly, as it is meet;
There is no other crime, no mad assail
    To make old prose in modern rhyme more sweet:
But it is done – succeed the verse or fail –
    To honour thee, and thy gone spirit greet;
To stead thee as a verse in English tongue,
An echo of thee in the north-wind sung.   160

21

These brethren having found by many signs
    What love Lorenzo for their sister had,
And how she lov'd him too, each unconfines
    His bitter thoughts to other, well nigh mad
That he, the servant of their trade designs,
    Should in their sister's love be blithe and glad,
When 'twas their plan to coax her by degrees
To some high noble and his olive-trees.

22

And many a jealous conference had they,
    And many times they bit their lips alone,   170
Before they fix'd upon a surest way
    To make the youngster for his crime atone;
And at the last, these men of cruel clay
    Cut Mercy with a sharp knife to the bone;
For they resolved in some forest dim
To kill Lorenzo, and there bury him.

23

So on a pleasant morning, as he leant
    Into the sun-rise, o'er the balustrade
Of the garden-terrace, towards him they bent
    Their footing through the dews; and to him said,   180
'You seem there in the quiet of content,
    Lorenzo, and we are most loth to invade
Calm speculation; but if you are wise,
Bestride your steed while cold is in the skies.

24

'To-day we purpose, ay, this hour we mount
　To spur three leagues towards the Apennine;
Come down, we pray thee, ere the hot sun count
　His dewy rosary on the eglantine.'
Lorenzo, courteously as he was wont,
　Bow'd a fair greeting to these serpents' whine;   190
And went in haste, to get in readiness,
With belt, and spur, and bracing huntsman's dress.

25

And as he to the court-yard pass'd along,
　Each third step did he pause, and listen'd oft
If he could hear his lady's matin-song,
　Or the light whisper of her footstep soft;
And as he thus over his passion hung,
　He heard a laugh full musical aloft;
When, looking up, he saw her features bright
Smile through an in-door lattice, all delight.   200

26

'Love, Isabel!' said he, 'I was in pain
　Lest I should miss to bid thee a good morrow:
Ah! what if I should lose thee, when so fain
　I am to stifle all the heavy sorrow
Of a poor three hours' absence? but we'll gain
　Out of the amorous dark what day doth borrow.
Goodbye! I'll soon be back.' – 'Goodbye!' said she: –
And as he went she chanted merrily.

27

So the two brothers and their murder'd man
　Rode past fair Florence, to where Arno's stream   210
Gurgles through straiten'd banks, and still doth fan
　Itself with dancing bulrush, and the bream
Keeps head against the freshets. Sick and wan
　The brothers' faces in the ford did seem,
Lorenzo's flush with love. – They pass'd the water
Into a forest quiet for the slaughter.

28

There was Lorenzo slain and buried in,
   There in that forest did his great love cease;
Ah! when a soul doth thus its freedom win,
   It aches in loneliness – is ill at peace   220
As the break-covert blood-hounds of such sin:
   They dipp'd their swords in the water, and did tease
Their horses homeward, with convulsed spur,
Each richer by his being a murderer.

29

They told their sister how, with sudden speed,
   Lorenzo had ta'en ship for foreign lands,
Because of some great urgency and need
   In their affairs, requiring trusty hands.
Poor Girl! put on thy stifling widow's weed,
   And 'scape at once from Hope's accursed bands;   230
To-day thou wilt not see him, nor to-morrow,
And the next day will be a day of sorrow.

30

She weeps alone for pleasures not to be;
   Sorely she wept until the night came on,
And then, instead of love, O misery!
   She brooded o'er the luxury alone:
His image in the dusk she seem'd to see,
   And to the silence made a gentle moan,
Spreading her perfect arms upon the air,
And on her couch low murmuring 'Where? O where?'   240

31

But Selfishness, Love's cousin, held not long
   Its fiery vigil in her single breast;
She fretted for the golden hour, and hung
   Upon the time with feverish unrest –
Not long – for soon into her heart a throng
   Of higher occupants, a richer zest,
Came tragic; passion not to be subdued,
And sorrow for her love in travels rude.

32

In the mid days of autumn, on their eves
   The breath of Winter comes from far away,   250
And the sick west continually bereaves
   Of some gold tinge, and plays a roundelay
Of death among the bushes and the leaves,
   To make all bare before he dares to stray
From his north cavern. So sweet Isabel
By gradual decay from beauty fell,

33

Because Lorenzo came not. Oftentimes
   She ask'd her brothers, with an eye all pale,
Striving to be itself, what dungeon climes
   Could keep him off so long? They spake a tale   260
Time after time, to quiet her. Their crimes
   Came on them, like a smoke from Hinnom's vale;
And every night in dreams they groan'd aloud,
To see their sister in her snowy shroud.

34

And she had died in drowsy ignorance,
   But for a thing more deadly dark than all;
It came like a fierce potion, drunk by chance,
   Which saves a sick man from the feather'd pall
For some few gasping moments; like a lance,
   Waking an Indian from his cloudy hall   270
With cruel pierce, and bringing him again
Sense of the gnawing fire at heart and brain.

35

It was a vision. – In the drowsy gloom,
   The dull of midnight, at her couch's foot
Lorenzo stood, and wept: the forest tomb
   Had marr'd his glossy hair which once could shoot
Lustre into the sun, and put cold doom
   Upon his lips, and taken the soft lute
From his lorn voice, and past his loamed ears
Had made a miry channel for his tears.   280

36

Strange sound it was, when the pale shadow spake;
   For there was striving, in its piteous tongue,
To speak as when on earth it was awake,
   And Isabella on its music hung:
Languor there was in it, and tremulous shake,
   As in a palsied Druid's harp unstrung;
And through it moan'd a ghostly under-song,
Like hoarse night-gusts sepulchral briars among.

37

Its eyes, though wild, were still all dewy bright
   With love, and kept all phantom fear aloof   290
From the poor girl by magic of their light,
   The while it did unthread the horrid woof
Of the late darken'd time, — the murderous spite
   Of pride and avarice, — the dark pine roof
In the forest, — and the sodden turfed dell,
Where, without any word, from stabs he fell.

38

Saying moreover, 'Isabel, my sweet!
   Red whortle-berries droop above my head,
And a large flint-stone weighs upon my feet;
   Around me beeches and high chestnuts shed   300
Their leaves and prickly nuts; a sheep-fold bleat
   Comes from beyond the river to my bed:
Go, shed one tear upon my heather-bloom,
And it shall comfort me within the tomb.

39

'I am a shadow now, alas! alas!
   Upon the skirts of human-nature dwelling
Alone: I chant alone the holy mass,
   While little sounds of life are round me knelling,
And glossy bees at noon do fieldward pass,
   And many a chapel bell the hour is telling,   310
Paining me through: those sounds grow strange to me,
And thou art distant in Humanity.

40

'I know what was, I feel full well what is,
    And I should rage, if spirits could go mad;
Though I forget the taste of earthly bliss,
    That paleness warms my grave, as though I had
A Seraph chosen from the bright abyss
    To be my spouse: thy paleness makes me glad;
Thy beauty grows upon me, and I feel
A greater love through all my essence steal.'   320

41

The Spirit mourn'd 'Adieu!' – dissolv'd, and left
    The atom darkness in a slow turmoil;
As when of healthful midnight sleep bereft,
    Thinking on rugged hours and fruitless toil,
We put our eyes into a pillowy cleft,
    And see the spangly gloom froth up and boil:
It made sad Isabella's eyelids ache,
And in the dawn she started up awake;

42

'Ha! ha!' said she, 'I knew not this hard life,
    I thought the worst was simple misery;   330
I thought some Fate with pleasure or with strife
    Portion'd us – happy days, or else to die;
But there is crime – a brother's bloody knife!
    Sweet Spirit, thou hast school'd my infancy:
I'll visit thee for this, and kiss thine eyes,
And greet thee morn and even in the skies.'

43

When the full morning came, she had devised
    How she might secret to the forest hie;
How she might find the clay, so dearly prized,
    And sing to it one latest lullaby;   340
How her short absence might be unsurmised,
    While she the inmost of the dream would try.
Resolv'd, she took with her an aged nurse,
And went into that dismal forest-hearse.

44

See, as they creep along the river side,
　　How she doth whisper to that aged Dame,
And, after looking round the champaign wide,
　　Shows her a knife. – 'What feverous hectic flame
Burns in thee, child? – What good can thee betide,
　　That thou should'st smile again?' – The evening
　　　　　　came,　　　　　　　　　　　　　　350
And they had found Lorenzo's earthy bed;
The flint was there, the berries at his head.

45

Who hath not loiter'd in a green church-yard,
　　And let his spirit, like a demon-mole,
Work through the clayey soil and gravel hard,
　　To see scull, coffin'd bones, and funeral stole;
Pitying each form that hungry Death hath marr'd,
　　And filling it once more with human soul?
Ah! this is holiday to what was felt
When Isabella by Lorenzo knelt.　　　　　　360

46

She gaz'd into the fresh-thrown mould, as though
　　One glance did fully all its secrets tell;
Clearly she saw, as other eyes would know
　　Pale limbs at bottom of a crystal well;
Upon the murderous spot she seem'd to grow,
　　Like to a native lily of the dell:
Then with her knife, all sudden, she began
To dig more fervently than misers can.

47

Soon she turn'd up a soiled glove, whereon
　　Her silk had play'd in purple phantasies,　　370
She kiss'd it with a lip more chill than stone,
　　And put it in her bosom, where it dries
And freezes utterly unto the bone
　　Those dainties made to still an infant's cries:
Then 'gan she work again; nor stay'd her care,
But to throw back at times her veiling hair.

48

That old nurse stood beside her wondering,
   Until her heart felt pity to the core
At sight of such a dismal labouring,
   And so she kneeled, with her locks all hoar,   380
And put her lean hands to the horrid thing:
   Three hours they labour'd at this travail sore;
At last they felt the kernel of the grave,
And Isabella did not stamp and rave.

49

Ah! wherefore all this wormy circumstance?
   Why linger at the yawning tomb so long?
O for the gentleness of old Romance,
   The simple plaining of a minstrel's song!
Fair reader, at the old tale take a glance,
   For here, in truth, it doth not well belong   390
To speak: — O turn thee to the very tale,
And taste the music of that vision pale.

50

With duller steel than the Perséan sword
   They cut away no formless monster's head,
But one, whose gentleness did well accord
   With death, as life. The ancient harps have said,
Love never dies, but lives, immortal Lord:
   If Love impersonate was ever dead,
Pale Isabella kiss'd it, and low moan'd.
'Twas love; cold, — dead indeed, but not dethroned.   400

51

In anxious secrecy they took it home,
   And then the prize was all for Isabel:
She calm'd its wild hair with a golden comb,
   And all around each eye's sepulchral cell
Pointed each fringed lash; the smeared loam
   With tears, as chilly as a dripping well,
She drench'd away: — and still she comb'd, and kept
Sighing all day — and still she kiss'd, and wept.

52

Then in a silken scarf, — sweet with the dews
   Of precious flowers pluck'd in Araby,   410
And divine liquids come with odorous ooze
   Through the cold serpent-pipe refreshfully, —
She wrapp'd it up; and for its tomb did choose
   A garden-pot, wherein she laid it by,
And cover'd it with mould, and o'er it set
Sweet Basil, which her tears kept ever wet.

53

And she forgot the stars, the moon, and sun,
   And she forgot the blue above the trees,
And she forgot the dells where waters run,
   And she forgot the chilly autumn breeze;   420
She had no knowledge when the day was done,
   And the new morn she saw not: but in peace
Hung over her sweet Basil evermore,
And moisten'd it with tears unto the core.

54

And so she ever fed it with thin tears,
   Whence thick, and green, and beautiful it grew,
So that it smelt more balmy than its peers
   Of Basil-tufts in Florence; for it drew
Nurture besides, and life, from human fears,
   From the fast mouldering head there shut from view: 430
So that the jewel, safely casketed,
Came forth, and in perfumed leafits spread.

55

O Melancholy, linger here awhile!
   O Music, Music, breathe despondingly!
O Echo, Echo, from some sombre isle,
   Unknown, Lethean, sigh to us — O sigh!
Spirits in grief, lift up your heads, and smile;
   Lift up your heads, sweet Spirits, heavily,
And make a pale light in your cypress glooms,
Tinting with silver wan your marble tombs.   440

56

Moan hither, all ye syllables of woe,
  From the deep throat of sad Melpomene!
Through bronzed lyre in tragic order go,
  And touch the strings into a mystery;
Sound mournfully upon the winds and low;
  For simple Isabel is soon to be
Among the dead: She withers, like a palm
Cut by an Indian for its juicy balm.

57

O leave the palm to wither by itself;
  Let not quick Winter chill its dying hour! –   450
It may not be – those Baälites of pelf,
  Her brethren, noted the continual shower
From her dead eyes; and many a curious elf,
  Among her kindred, wonder'd that such dower
Of youth and beauty should be thrown aside
By one mark'd out to be a noble's bride.

58

And, furthermore, her brethren wonder'd much
  Why she sat drooping by the Basil green,
And why it flourish'd, as by magic touch;
  Greatly they wonder'd what the thing might mean: 460
They could not surely give belief, that such
  A very nothing would have power to wean
Her from her own fair youth, and pleasures gay,
And even remembrance of her love's delay.

59

Therefore they watch'd a time when they might sift
  This hidden whim; and long they watch'd in vain;
For seldom did she go to chapel-shrift,
  And seldom felt she any hunger-pain;
And when she left, she hurried back, as swift
  As bird on wing to breast its eggs again;   470
And, patient as a hen-bird, sat her there
Beside her Basil, weeping through her hair.

60

Yet they contriv'd to steal the Basil-pot,
    And to examine it in secret place:
The thing was vile with green and livid spot,
    And yet they knew it was Lorenzo's face:
The guerdon of their murder they had got,
    And so left Florence in a moment's space,
Never to turn again. — Away they went,
With blood upon their heads, to banishment.   480

61

O Melancholy, turn thine eyes away!
    O Music, Music, breathe despondingly!
O Echo, Echo, on some other day,
    From isles Lethean, sigh to us — O sigh!
Spirits of grief, sing not your 'Well-a-way!'
    For Isabel, sweet Isabel, will die;
Will die a death too lone and incomplete,
Now they have ta'en away her Basil sweet.

62

Piteous she look'd on dead and senseless things,
    Asking for her lost Basil amorously;   490
And with melodious chuckle in the strings
    Of her lorn voice, she oftentimes would cry
After the Pilgrim in his wanderings,
    To ask him where her Basil was; and why
'Twas hid from her: 'For cruel 'tis,' said she,
'To steal my Basil-pot away from me.'

63

And so she pined, and so she died forlorn,
    Imploring for her Basil to the last.
No heart was there in Florence but did mourn
    In pity of her love, so overcast.   500
And a sad ditty of this story born
    From mouth to mouth through all the country pass'd:
Still is the burthen sung — 'O cruelty,
To steal my Basil-pot away from me!'

Mother of Hermes! and still youthful Maia!
    May I sing to thee
As thou wast hymned on the shores of Baiæ?
    Or may I woo thee
In earlier Sicilian? or thy smiles
Seek as they once were sought, in Grecian isles,
By bards who died content in pleasant sward,
    Leaving great verse unto a little clan?
O give me their old vigour, and unheard,
    Save of the quiet primrose, and the span   10
      Of heaven, and few ears,
Rounded by thee my song should die away,
      Content as theirs,
Rich in the simple worship of a day.

On Visiting the Tomb of Burns

The town, the churchyard, and the setting sun,
    The clouds, the trees, the rounded hills all seem
    Though beautiful, cold – strange – as in a dream
I dreamed long ago. Now new begun,
The short-lived, paly summer is but won
    From winter's ague for one hour's gleam;
    Through sapphire warm their stars do never beam;
All is cold beauty; pain is never done
For who has mind to relish, Minos-wise,
    The real of beauty, free from that dead hue   10
      Fickly imagination and sick pride
    Cast wan upon it! Burns! with honour due
    I have oft honoured thee. Great shadow, hide
Thy face, I sin against thy native skies.

To Ailsa Rock

Hearken, thou craggy ocean pyramid,
  Give answer by thy voice, the sea fowls' screams!
  When were thy shoulders mantled in huge streams?
When from the sun was thy broad forehead hid?
How long is't since the mighty power bid
  Thee heave to airy sleep from fathom dreams —
  Sleep in the lap of thunder or sunbeams,
Or when grey clouds are thy cold coverlid?
Thou answer'st not, for thou art dead asleep.
  Thy life is but two dead eternities,
The last in air, the former in the deep —
  First with the whales, last with the eagle skies —
Drown'd wast thou till an earthquake made thee steep —
  Another cannot wake thy giant size!

10

'Read me a lesson, Muse'

Read me a lesson, Muse, and speak it loud
  Upon the top of Nevis blind in mist!
I look into the chasms and a shroud
  Vaprous doth hide them; just so much I wist
Mankind do know of hell: I look o'erhead
  And there is sullen mist; even so much
Mankind can tell of heaven: mist is spread
  Before the earth beneath me — even such,
Even so vague is man's sight of himself.
  Here are the craggy stones beneath my feet;
Thus much I know, that a poor witless elf
  I tread on them; that all my eye doth meet
Is mist and crag — not only on this height,
But in the world of thought and mental might.

10

Hyperion. A Fragment

BOOK I

Deep in the shady sadness of a vale
Far sunken from the healthy breath of morn,
Far from the fiery noon, and eve's one star,
Sat gray-hair'd Saturn, quiet as a stone,
Still as the silence round about his lair;
Forest on forest hung above his head
Like cloud on cloud. No stir of air was there,
Not so much life as on a summer's day
Robs not one light seed from the feather'd grass,
But where the dead leaf fell, there did it rest.   10
A stream went voiceless by, still deadened more
By reason of his fallen divinity
Spreading a shade: the Naiad 'mid her reeds
Press'd her cold finger closer to her lips.

Along the margin-sand large foot-marks went,
No further than to where his feet had stray'd,
And slept there since. Upon the sodden ground
His old right hand lay nerveless, listless, dead,
Unsceptred; and his realmless eyes were closed;
While his bow'd head seem'd list'ning to the Earth,   20
His ancient mother, for some comfort yet.

It seem'd no force could wake him from his place;
But there came one, who with a kindred hand
Touch'd his wide shoulders, after bending low
With reverence, though to one who knew it not.
She was a Goddess of the infant world;
By her in stature the tall Amazon
Had stood a pigmy's height: she would have ta'en
Achilles by the hair and bent his neck;
Or with a finger stay'd Ixion's wheel.   30
Her face was large as that of Memphian sphinx,
Pedestal'd haply in a palace court,
When sages look'd to Egypt for their lore.
But oh! how unlike marble was that face:
How beautiful, if sorrow had not made

Sorrow more beautiful than Beauty's self.
There was a listening fear in her regard,
As if calamity had but begun;
As if the vanward clouds of evil days
Had spent their malice, and the sullen rear   40
Was with its stored thunder labouring up.
One hand she press'd upon that aching spot
Where beats the human heart, as if just there,
Though an immortal, she felt cruel pain:
The other upon Saturn's bended neck
She laid, and to the level of his ear
Leaning with parted lips, some words she spake
In solemn tenour and deep organ tone:
Some mourning words, which in our feeble tongue
Would come in these like accents; O how frail   50
To that large utterance of the early Gods!
'Saturn, look up! – though wherefore, poor old King?
I have no comfort for thee, no not one:
I cannot say, "O wherefore sleepest thou?"
For heaven is parted from thee, and the earth
Knows thee not, thus afflicted, for a God;
And ocean too, with all its solemn noise,
Has from thy sceptre pass'd; and all the air
Is emptied of thine hoary majesty.
Thy thunder, conscious of the new command,   60
Rumbles reluctant o'er our fallen house;
And thy sharp lightning in unpractised hands
Scorches and burns our once serene domain.
O aching time! O moments big as years!
All as ye pass swell out the monstrous truth,
And press it so upon our weary griefs
That unbelief has not a space to breathe.
Saturn, sleep on: – O thoughtless, why did I
Thus violate thy slumbrous solitude?
Why should I ope thy melancholy eyes?   70
Saturn, sleep on! while at thy feet I weep.'

    As when, upon a tranced summer-night,
Those green-rob'd senators of mighty woods,
Tall oaks, branch-charmed by the earnest stars,
Dream, and so dream all night without a stir,

Save from one gradual solitary gust
Which comes upon the silence, and dies off,
As if the ebbing air had but one wave;
So came these words and went; the while in tears
She touch'd her fair large forehead to the ground,   80
Just where her falling hair might be outspread
A soft and silken mat for Saturn's feet.
One moon, with alteration slow, had shed
Her silver seasons four upon the night,
And still these two were postured motionless,
Like natural sculpture in cathedral cavern;
The frozen God still couchant on the earth,
And the sad Goddess weeping at his feet:
Until at length old Saturn lifted up
His faded eyes, and saw his kingdom gone,   90
And all the gloom and sorrow of the place,
And that fair kneeling Goddess; and then spake,
As with a palsied tongue, and while his beard
Shook horrid with such aspen-malady:
'O tender spouse of gold Hyperion,
Thea, I feel thee ere I see thy face;
Look up, and let me see our doom in it;
Look up, and tell me if this feeble shape
Is Saturn's; tell me, if thou hear'st the voice
Of Saturn; tell me, if this wrinkling brow,   100
Naked and bare of its great diadem,
Peers like the front of Saturn. Who had power
To make me desolate? whence came the strength?
How was it nurtur'd to such bursting forth,
While Fate seem'd strangled in my nervous grasp?
But it is so; and I am smother'd up,
And buried from all godlike exercise
Of influence benign on planets pale,
Of admonitions to the winds and seas,
Of peaceful sway above man's harvesting,   110
And all those acts which Deity supreme
Doth ease its heart of love in. – I am gone
Away from my own bosom: I have left
My strong identity, my real self,
Somewhere between the throne, and where I sit
Here on this spot of earth. Search, Thea, search!

Open thine eyes eterne, and sphere them round
Upon all space: space starr'd, and lorn of light;
Space region'd with life-air; and barren void;
Spaces of fire, and all the yawn of hell. –   120
Search, Thea, search! and tell me, if thou seest
A certain shape or shadow, making way
With wings or chariot fierce to repossess
A heaven he lost erewhile: it must – it must
Be of ripe progress – Saturn must be King.
Yes, there must be a golden victory;
There must be Gods thrown down, and trumpets blown
Of triumph calm, and hymns of festival
Upon the gold clouds metropolitan,
Voices of soft proclaim, and silver stir   130
Of strings in hollow shells; and there shall be
Beautiful things made new, for the surprise
Of the sky-children; I will give command:
Thea! Thea! Thea! where is Saturn?'

   This passion lifted him upon his feet,
And made his hands to struggle in the air,
His Druid locks to shake and ooze with sweat,
His eyes to fever out, his voice to cease.
He stood, and heard not Thea's sobbing deep;
A little time, and then again he snatch'd   140
Utterance thus. – 'But cannot I create?
Cannot I form? Cannot I fashion forth
Another world, another universe,
To overbear and crumble this to nought?
Where is another Chaos? Where?' – That word
Found way unto Olympus, and made quake
The rebel three. – Thea was startled up,
And in her bearing was a sort of hope,
As thus she quick-voic'd spake, yet full of awe.

   'This cheers our fallen house: come to our friends,   150
O Saturn! come away, and give them heart;
I know the covert, for thence came I hither.'
Thus brief; then with beseeching eyes she went
With backward footing through the shade a space:
He follow'd, and she turn'd to lead the way

Through aged boughs, that yielded like the mist
Which eagles cleave upmounting from their nest.

Meanwhile in other realms big tears were shed,
More sorrow like to this, and such like woe,
Too huge for mortal tongue or pen of scribe: 160
The Titans fierce, self-hid, or prison-bound,
Groan'd for the old allegiance once more,
And listen'd in sharp pain for Saturn's voice.
But one of the whole mammoth-brood still kept
His sov'reignty, and rule, and majesty; —
Blazing Hyperion on his orbed fire
Still sat, still snuff'd the incense, teeming up
From man to the sun's God; yet unsecure:
For as among us mortals omens drear
Fright and perplex, so also shuddered he —   170
Not at dog's howl, or gloom-bird's hated screech,
Or the familiar visiting of one
Upon the first toll of his passing-bell,
Or prophesyings of the midnight lamp;
But horrors, portion'd to a giant nerve,
Oft made Hyperion ache. His palace bright
Bastion'd with pyramids of glowing gold,
And touch'd with shade of bronzed obelisks,
Glar'd a blood-red through all its thousand courts,
Arches, and domes, and fiery galleries;   180
And all its curtains of Aurorian clouds
Flush'd angerly: while sometimes eagle's wings,
Unseen before by Gods or wondering men,
Darken'd the place; and neighing steeds were heard,
Not heard before by Gods or wondering men.
Also, when he would taste the spicy wreaths
Of incense, breath'd aloft from sacred hills,
Instead of sweets, his ample palate took
Savour of poisonous brass and metal sick:
And so, when harbour'd in the sleepy west,   190
After the full completion of fair day, —
For rest divine upon exalted couch
And slumber in the arms of melody,
He pac'd away the pleasant hours of ease
With stride colossal, on from hall to hall;

While far within each aisle and deep recess,
His winged minions in close clusters stood,
Amaz'd and full of fear; like anxious men
Who on wide plains gather in panting troops,
When earthquakes jar their battlements and towers.   200
Even now, while Saturn, rous'd from icy trance,
Went step for step with Thea through the woods,
Hyperion, leaving twilight in the rear,
Came slope upon the threshold of the west;
Then, as was wont, his palace-door flew ope
In smoothest silence, save what solemn tubes,
Blown by the serious Zephyrs, gave of sweet
And wandering sounds, slow-breathed melodies;
And like a rose in vermeil tint and shape,
In fragrance soft, and coolness to the eye,   210
That inlet to severe magnificence
Stood full blown, for the God to enter in.

He enter'd, but he enter'd full of wrath;
His flaming robes stream'd out beyond his heels,
And gave a roar, as if of earthly fire,
That scar'd away the meek ethereal Hours
And made their dove-wings tremble. On he flared,
From stately nave to nave, from vault to vault,
Through bowers of fragrant and enwreathed light,
And diamond-paved lustrous long arcades,   220
Until he reach'd the great main cupola;
There standing fierce beneath, he stampt his foot,
And from the basements deep to the high towers
Jarr'd his own golden region; and before
The quavering thunder thereupon had ceas'd,
His voice leapt out, despite of godlike curb,
To this result: 'O dreams of day and night!
O monstrous forms! O effigies of pain!
O spectres busy in a cold, cold gloom!
O lank-eared Phantoms of black-weeded pools!   230
Why do I know ye? why have I seen ye? why
Is my eternal essence thus distraught
To see and to behold these horrors new?
Saturn is fallen, am I too to fall?
Am I to leave this haven of my rest,

This cradle of my glory, this soft clime,
This calm luxuriance of blissful light,
These crystalline pavilions, and pure fanes,
Of all my lucent empire? It is left
Deserted, void, nor any haunt of mine.   240
The blaze, the splendor, and the symmetry,
I cannot see — but darkness, death and darkness.
Even here, into my centre of repose,
The shady visions come to domineer,
Insult, and blind, and stifle up my pomp. —
Fall! — No, by Tellus and her briny robes!
Over the fiery frontier of my realms
I will advance a terrible right arm
Shall scare that infant thunderer, rebel Jove,
And bid old Saturn take his throne again.' —   250
He spake, and ceas'd, the while a heavier threat
Held struggle with his throat but came not forth;
For as in theatres of crowded men
Hubbub increases more they call out 'Hush!'
So at Hyperion's words the Phantoms pale
Bestirr'd themselves, thrice horrible and cold;
And from the mirror'd level where he stood
A mist arose, as from a scummy marsh.
At this, through all his bulk an agony
Crept gradual, from the feet unto the crown,   260
Like a lithe serpent vast and muscular
Making slow way, with head and neck convuls'd
From over-strained might. Releas'd, he fled
To the eastern gates, and full six dewy hours
Before the dawn in season due should blush,
He breath'd fierce breath against the sleepy portals,
Clear'd them of heavy vapours, burst them wide
Suddenly on the ocean's chilly streams.
The planet orb of fire, whereon he rode
Each day from east to west the heavens through,   270
Spun round in sable curtaining of clouds;
Not therefore veiled quite, blindfold, and hid,
But ever and anon the glancing spheres,
Circles, and arcs, and broad-belting colure,
Glow'd through, and wrought upon the muffling dark
Sweet-shaped lightnings from the nadir deep

Up to the zenith, – hieroglyphics old,
Which sages and keen-eyed astrologers
Then living on the earth, with labouring thought
Won from the gaze of many centuries: 280
Now lost, save what we find on remnants huge
Of stone, or marble swart; their import gone,
Their wisdom long since fled. – Two wings this orb
Possess'd for glory, two fair argent wings,
Ever exalted at the God's approach:
And now, from forth the gloom their plumes immense
Rose, one by one, till all outspreaded were;
While still the dazzling globe maintain'd eclipse,
Awaiting for Hyperion's command.
Fain would he have commanded, fain took throne   290
And bid the day begin, if but for change.
He might not: – No, though a primeval God:
The sacred seasons might not be disturb'd.
Therefore the operations of the dawn
Stay'd in their birth, even as here 'tis told.
Those silver wings expanded sisterly,
Eager to sail their orb; the porches wide
Open'd upon the dusk demesnes of night;
And the bright Titan, phrenzied with new woes,
Unus'd to bend, by hard compulsion bent   300
His spirit to the sorrow of the time;
And all along a dismal rack of clouds,
Upon the boundaries of day and night,
He stretch'd himself in grief and radiance faint.
There as he lay, the Heaven with its stars
Look'd down on him with pity, and the voice
Of Cœlus, from the universal space,
Thus whisper'd low and solemn in his ear.
'O brightest of my children dear, earth-born
And sky-engendered, Son of Mysteries   310
All unrevealed even to the powers
Which met at thy creating; at whose joys
And palpitations sweet, and pleasures soft,
I, Cœlus, wonder, how they came and whence;
And at the fruits thereof what shapes they be,
Distinct, and visible; symbols divine,
Manifestations of that beauteous life

Diffus'd unseen throughout eternal space:
Of these new-form'd art thou, oh brightest child!
Of these, thy brethren and the Goddesses!   320
There is sad feud among ye, and rebellion
Of son against his sire. I saw him fall,
I saw my first-born tumbled from his throne!
To me his arms were spread, to me his voice
Found way from forth the thunders round his head!
Pale wox I, and in vapours hid my face.
Art thou, too, near such doom? vague fear there is:
For I have seen my sons most unlike Gods.
Divine ye were created, and divine
In sad demeanour, solemn, undisturb'd,   330
Unruffled, like high Gods, ye liv'd and ruled:
Now I behold in you fear, hope, and wrath;
Actions of rage and passion; even as
I see them, on the mortal world beneath,
In men who die. – This is the grief, O Son!
Sad sign of ruin, sudden dismay, and fall!
Yet do thou strive; as thou art capable,
As thou canst move about, an evident God;
And canst oppose to each malignant hour
Ethereal presence: – I am but a voice;   340
My life is but the life of winds and tides,
No more than winds and tides can I avail: –
But thou canst. – Be thou therefore in the van
Of circumstance; yea, seize the arrow's barb
Before the tense string murmur. – To the earth!
For there thou wilt find Saturn, and his woes.
Meantime I will keep watch on thy bright sun,
And of thy seasons be a careful nurse.' –
Ere half this region-whisper had come down,
Hyperion arose, and on the stars   350
Lifted his curved lids, and kept them wide
Until it ceas'd; and still he kept them wide:
And still they were the same bright, patient stars.
Then with a slow incline of his broad breast,
Like to a diver in the pearly seas,
Forward he stoop'd over the airy shore,
And plung'd all noiseless into the deep night.

BOOK II

Just at the self-same beat of Time's wide wings
Hyperion slid into the rustled air,
And Saturn gain'd with Thea that sad place
Where Cybele and the bruised Titans mourn'd.
It was a den where no insulting light
Could glimmer on their tears; where their own groans
They felt, but heard not, for the solid roar
Of thunderous waterfalls and torrents hoarse,
Pouring a constant bulk, uncertain where.
Crag jutting forth to crag, and rocks that seem'd   10
Ever as if just rising from a sleep,
Forehead to forehead held their monstrous horns;
And thus in thousand hugest phantasies
Made a fit roofing to this nest of woe.
Instead of thrones, hard flint they sat upon,
Couches of rugged stone, and slaty ridge
Stubborn'd with iron. All were not assembled:
Some chain'd in torture, and some wandering.
Cœus, and Gyges, and Briareüs,
Typhon, and Dolor, and Porphyrion,   20
With many more, the brawniest in assault,
Were pent in regions of laborious breath;
Dungeon'd in opaque element, to keep
Their clenched teeth still clench'd, and all their limbs
Lock'd up like veins of metal, crampt and screw'd;
Without a motion, save of their big hearts
Heaving in pain, and horribly convuls'd
With sanguine feverous boiling gurge of pulse.
Mnemosyne was straying in the world;
Far from her moon had Phœbe wandered;   30
And many else were free to roam abroad,
But for the main, here found they covert drear.
Scarce images of life, one here, one there,
Lay vast and edgeways; like a dismal cirque
Of Druid stones, upon a forlorn moor,
When the chill rain begins at shut of eve,
In dull November, and their chancel vault,
The Heaven itself, is blinded throughout night.
Each one kept shroud, nor to his neighbour gave

Or word, or look, or action of despair.   40
Creüs was one; his ponderous iron mace
Lay by him, and a shatter'd rib of rock
Told of his rage, ere he thus sank and pined.
Iäpetus another; in his grasp,
A serpent's plashy neck; its barbed tongue
Squeez'd from the gorge, and all its uncurl'd length
Dead; and because the creature could not spit
Its poison in the eyes of conquering Jove.
Next Cottus: prone he lay, chin uppermost,
As though in pain; for still upon the flint   50
He ground severe his skull, with open mouth
And eyes at horrid working. Nearest him
Asia, born of most enormous Caf,
Who cost her mother Tellus keener pangs,
Though feminine, than any of her sons:
More thought than woe was in her dusky face,
For she was prophesying of her glory;
And in her wide imagination stood
Palm-shaded temples, and high rival fanes,
By Oxus or in Ganges' sacred isles.   60
Even as Hope upon her anchor leans,
So lent she, not so fair, upon a tusk
Shed from the broadest of her elephants.
Above her, on a crag's uneasy shelve,
Upon his elbow rais'd, all prostrate else,
Shadow'd Enceladus; once tame and mild
As grazing ox unworried in the meads;
Now tiger-passion'd, lion-thoughted, wroth,
He meditated, plotted, and even now
Was hurling mountains in that second war,   70
Not long delay'd, that scar'd the younger Gods
To hide themselves in forms of beast and bird.
Not far hence Atlas; and beside him prone
Phorcus, the sire of Gorgons. Neighbour'd close
Oceanus, and Tethys, in whose lap
Sobb'd Clymene among her tangled hair.
In midst of all lay Themis, at the feet
Of Ops the queen all clouded round from sight;
No shape distinguishable, more than when
Thick night confounds the pine-tops with the clouds: 80

And many else whose names may not be told.
For when the Muse's wings are air-ward spread,
Who shall delay her flight? And she must chaunt
Of Saturn, and his guide, who now had climb'd
With damp and slippery footing from a depth
More horrid still. Above a sombre cliff
Their heads appear'd, and up their stature grew
Till on the level height their steps found ease:
Then Thea spread abroad her trembling arms
Upon the precincts of this nest of pain,   90
And sidelong fix'd her eye on Saturn's face:
There saw she direct strife; the supreme God
At war with all the frailty of grief,
Of rage, of fear, anxiety, revenge,
Remorse, spleen, hope, but most of all despair.
Against these plagues he strove in vain; for Fate
Had pour'd a mortal oil upon his head,
A disanointing poison: so that Thea,
Affrighted, kept her still, and let him pass
First onwards in, among the fallen tribe.   100

    As with us mortal men, the laden heart
Is persecuted more, and fever'd more,
When it is nighing to the mournful house
Where other hearts are sick of the same bruise;
So Saturn, as he walk'd into the midst,
Felt faint, and would have sunk among the rest,
But that he met Enceladus's eye,
Whose mightiness, and awe of him, at once
Came like an inspiration; and he shouted,
'Titans, behold your God!' at which some groan'd;   110
Some started on their feet; some also shouted;
Some wept, some wail'd, all bow'd with reverence;
And Ops, uplifting her black folded veil,
Show'd her pale cheeks, and all her forehead wan,
Her eye-brows thin and jet, and hollow eyes.
There is a roaring in the bleak-grown pines
When Winter lifts his voice; there is a noise
Among immortals when a God gives sign,
With hushing finger, how he means to load
His tongue with the full weight of utterless thought,   120

With thunder, and with music, and with pomp:
Such noise is like the roar of bleak-grown pines;
Which, when it ceases in this mountain'd world,
No other sound succeeds; but ceasing here,
Among these fallen, Saturn's voice therefrom
Grew up like organ, that begins anew
Its strain, when other harmonies, stopt short,
Leave the dinn'd air vibrating silverly.
Thus grew it up – 'Not in my own sad breast,
Which is its own great judge and searcher out,   130
Can I find reason why ye should be thus:
Not in the legends of the first of days,
Studied from that old spirit-leaved book
Which starry Uranus with finger bright
Sav'd from the shores of darkness, when the waves
Low-ebb'd still hid it up in shallow gloom; –
And the which book ye know I ever kept
For my firm-based footstool: – Ah, infirm!
Not there, nor in sign, symbol, or portent
Of element, earth, water, air, and fire, –   140
At war, at peace, or inter-quarreling
One against one, or two, or three, or all
Each several one against the other three,
As fire with air loud warring when rain-floods
Drown both, and press them both against earth's face,
Where, finding sulphur, a quadruple wrath
Unhinges the poor world; – not in that strife,
Wherefrom I take strange lore, and read it deep,
Can I find reason why ye should be thus:
No, no-where can unriddle, though I search,   150
And pore on Nature's universal scroll
Even to swooning, why ye Divinities,
The first-born of all shap'd and palpable Gods,
Should cower beneath what, in comparison,
Is untremendous might. Yet ye are here,
O'erwhelm'd, and spurn'd, and batter'd, ye are here!
O Titans shall I say "Arise!" – Ye groan:
Shall I say "Crouch!" – Ye groan. What can I then?
O Heaven wide! O unseen parent dear!
What can I? Tell me, all ye brethren Gods,   160
How we can war, how engine our great wrath!

O speak your counsel now, for Saturn's ear
Is all a-hunger'd. Thou, Oceanus,
Ponderest high and deep; and in thy face
I see, astonied, that severe content
Which comes of thought and musing: give us help!'

So ended Saturn; and the God of the Sea,
Sophist and sage, from no Athenian grove,
But cogitation in his watery shades,
Arose, with locks not oozy, and began,   170
In murmurs, which his first-endeavouring tongue
Caught infant-like from the far-foamed sands.
'O ye, whom wrath consumes! who, passion-stung,
Writhe at defeat, and nurse your agonies!
Shut up your senses, stifle up your ears,
My voice is not a bellows unto ire.
Yet listen, ye who will, whilst I bring proof
How ye, perforce, must be content to stoop:
And in the proof much comfort will I give,
If ye will take that comfort in its truth.   180
We fall by course of Nature's law, not force
Of thunder, or of Jove. Great Saturn, thou
Hast sifted well the atom-universe;
But for this reason, that thou art the King,
And only blind from sheer supremacy,
One avenue was shaded from thine eyes,
Through which I wandered to eternal truth.
And first, as thou wast not the first of powers,
So art thou not the last; it cannot be:
Thou art not the beginning nor the end.   190
From Chaos and parental darkness came
Light, the first fruits of that intestine broil,
That sullen ferment, which for wondrous ends
Was ripening in itself. The ripe hour came,
And with it light, and light, engendering
Upon its own producer, forthwith touch'd
The whole enormous matter into life.
Upon that very hour, our parentage,
The Heavens and the Earth, were manifest:
Then thou first-born, and we the giant-race,   200
Found ourselves ruling new and beauteous realms.

Now comes the pain of truth, to whom 'tis pain;
O folly! for to bear all naked truths,
And to envisage circumstance, all calm,
That is the top of sovereignty. Mark well!
As Heaven and Earth are fairer, fairer far
Than Chaos and blank Darkness, though once chiefs;
And as we show beyond that Heaven and Earth
In form and shape compact and beautiful,
In will, in action free, companionship,   210
And thousand other signs of purer life;
So on our heels a fresh perfection treads,
A power more strong in beauty, born of us
And fated to excel us, as we pass
In glory that old Darkness: nor are we
Thereby more conquer'd, than by us the rule
Of shapeless Chaos. Say, doth the dull soil
Quarrel with the proud forests it hath fed,
And feedeth still, more comely than itself?
Can it deny the chiefdom of green groves?   220
Or shall the tree be envious of the dove
Because it cooeth, and hath snowy wings
To wander wherewithal and find its joys?
We are such forest-trees, and our fair boughs
Have bred forth, not pale solitary doves,
But eagles golden-feather'd, who do tower
Above us in their beauty, and must reign
In right thereof; for 'tis the eternal law
That first in beauty should be first in might:
Yea, by that law, another race may drive   230
Our conquerors to mourn as we do now.
Have ye beheld the young God of the Seas,
My dispossessor? Have ye seen his face?
Have ye beheld his chariot, foam'd along
By noble winged creatures he hath made?
I saw him on the calmed waters scud,
With such a glow of beauty in his eyes,
That it enforc'd me to bid sad farewel
To all my empire: farewell sad I took,
And hither came, to see how dolorous fate   240
Had wrought upon ye; and how I might best

Give consolation in this woe extreme.
Receive the truth, and let it be your balm.'

Whether through poz'd conviction, or disdain,
They guarded silence, when Oceanus
Left murmuring, what deepest thought can tell?
But so it was, none answer'd for a space,
Save one whom none regarded, Clymene;
And yet she answer'd not, only complain'd,
With hectic lips, and eyes up-looking mild,   250
Thus wording timidly among the fierce:
'O Father, I am here the simplest voice,
And all my knowledge is that joy is gone,
And this thing woe crept in among our hearts,
There to remain for ever, as I fear:
I would not bode of evil, if I thought
So weak a creature could turn off the help
Which by just right should come of mighty Gods;
Yet let me tell my sorrow, let me tell
Of what I heard, and how it made me weep,   260
And know that we had parted from all hope.
I stood upon a shore, a pleasant shore,
Where a sweet clime was breathed from a land
Of fragrance, quietness, and trees, and flowers.
Full of calm joy it was, as I of grief;
Too full of joy and soft delicious warmth;
So that I felt a movement in my heart
To chide, and to reproach that solitude
With songs of misery, music of our woes;
And sat me down, and took a mouthed shell   270
And murmur'd into it, and made melody –
O melody no more! for while I sang,
And with poor skill let pass into the breeze
The dull shell's echo, from a bowery strand
Just opposite, an island of the sea,
There came enchantment with the shifting wind,
That did both drown and keep alive my ears.
I threw my shell away upon the sand,
And a wave fill'd it, as my sense was fill'd
With that new blissful golden melody.   280
A living death was in each gush of sounds,
Each family of rapturous hurried notes,

That fell, one after one, yet all at once,
Like pearl beads dropping sudden from their string:
And then another, then another strain,
Each like a dove leaving its olive perch,
With music wing'd instead of silent plumes,
To hover round my head, and make me sick
Of joy and grief at once. Grief overcame,
And I was stopping up my frantic ears, 290
When, past all hindrance of my trembling hands,
A voice came sweeter, sweeter than all tune,
And still it cried, "Apollo! young Apollo!
The morning-bright Apollo! young Apollo!"
I fled, it follow'd me, and cried "Apollo!"
O Father, and O Brethren, had ye felt
Those pains of mine; O Saturn, hadst thou felt,
Ye would not call this too indulged tongue
Presumptuous, in thus venturing to be heard.'

So far her voice flow'd on, like timorous brook 300
That, lingering along a pebbled coast,
Doth fear to meet the sea: but sea it met,
And shudder'd; for the overwhelming voice
Of huge Enceladus swallow'd it in wrath:
The ponderous syllables, like sullen waves
In the half-glutted hollows of reef-rocks,
Came booming thus, while still upon his arm
He lean'd; not rising, from supreme contempt.
'Or shall we listen to the over-wise,
Or to the over-foolish, Giant-Gods? 310
Not thunderbolt on thunderbolt, till all
That rebel Jove's whole armoury were spent,
Not world on world upon these shoulders piled,
Could agonize me more than baby-words
In midst of this dethronement horrible.
Speak! roar! shout! yell! ye sleepy Titans all.
Do ye forget the blows, the buffets vile?
Are ye not smitten by a youngling arm?
Dost thou forget, sham Monarch of the Waves,
Thy scalding in the seas? What, have I rous'd 320
Your spleens with so few simple words as these?
O joy! for now I see ye are not lost:

O joy! for now I see a thousand eyes
Wide glaring for revenge!' – As this he said,
He lifted up his stature vast, and stood,
Still without intermission speaking thus:
'Now ye are flames, I'll tell you how to burn,
And purge the ether of our enemies;
How to feed fierce the crooked stings of fire,
And singe away the swollen clouds of Jove,   330
Stifling that puny essence in its tent.
O let him feel the evil he hath done;
For though I scorn Oceanus's lore,
Much pain have I for more than loss of realms:
The days of peace and slumberous calm are fled;
Those days, all innocent of scathing war,
When all the fair Existences of heaven
Came open-eyed to guess what we would speak: –
That was before our brows were taught to frown,
Before our lips knew else but solemn sounds;   340
That was before we knew the winged thing,
Victory, might be lost, or might be won.
And be ye mindful that Hyperion,
Our brightest brother, still is undisgraced –
Hyperion, lo! his radiance is here!'

        All eyes were on Enceladus's face,
And they beheld, while still Hyperion's name
Flew from his lips up to the vaulted rocks,
A pallid gleam across his features stern:
Not savage, for he saw full many a God   350
Wroth as himself. He look'd upon them all,
And in each face he saw a gleam of light,
But splendider in Saturn's, whose hoar locks
Shone like the bubbling foam about a keel
When the prow sweeps into a midnight cove.
In pale and silver silence they remain'd,
Till suddenly a splendour, like the morn,
Pervaded all the beetling gloomy steeps,
All the sad spaces of oblivion,
And every gulf, and every chasm old,   360
And every height, and every sullen depth,
Voiceless, or hoarse with loud tormented streams:

And all the everlasting cataracts,
And all the headlong torrents far and near,
Mantled before in darkness and huge shade,
Now saw the light and made it terrible.
It was Hyperion: – a granite peak
His bright feet touch'd, and there he stay'd to view
The misery his brilliance had betray'd
To the most hateful seeing of itself.   370
Golden his hair of short Numidian curl,
Regal his shape majestic, a vast shade
In midst of his own brightness, like the bulk
Of Memnon's image at the set of sun
To one who travels from the dusking East:
Sighs, too, as mournful as that Memnon's harp
He utter'd, while his hands contemplative
He press'd together, and in silence stood.
Despondence seiz'd again the fallen Gods
At sight of the dejected King of Day,   380
And many hid their faces from the light:
But fierce Enceladus sent forth his eyes
Among the brotherhood; and, at their glare,
Uprose Iäpetus, and Creüs too,
And Phorcus, sea-born, and together strode
To where he towered on his eminence.
There those four shouted forth old Saturn's name;
Hyperion from the peak loud answered, 'Saturn!'
Saturn sat near the Mother of the Gods,
In whose face was no joy, though all the Gods   390
Gave from their hollow throats the name of 'Saturn!'

BOOK III

Thus in alternate uproar and sad peace,
Amazed were those Titans utterly.
O leave them, Muse! O leave them to their woes;
For thou art weak to sing such tumults dire:
A solitary sorrow best befits
Thy lips, and antheming a lonely grief.
Leave them, O Muse! for thou anon wilt find
Many a fallen old Divinity

Wandering in vain about bewildered shores.
Meantime touch piously the Delphic harp,   10
And not a wind of heaven but will breathe
In aid soft warble from the Dorian flute;
For lo! 'tis for the Father of all verse.
Flush every thing that hath a vermeil hue,
Let the rose glow intense and warm the air,
And let the clouds of even and of morn
Float in voluptuous fleeces o'er the hills;
Let the red wine within the goblet boil,
Cold as a bubbling well; let faint-lipp'd shells,
On sands, or in great deeps, vermilion turn   20
Through all their labyrinths; and let the maid
Blush keenly, as with some warm kiss surpris'd.
Chief isle of the embowered Cyclades,
Rejoice, O Delos, with thine olives green,
And poplars, and lawn-shading palms, and beech,
In which the Zephyr breathes the loudest song,
And hazels thick, dark-stemm'd beneath the shade:
Apollo is once more the golden theme!
Where was he, when the Giant of the Sun
Stood bright, amid the sorrow of his peers?   30
Together had he left his mother fair
And his twin-sister sleeping in their bower,
And in the morning twilight wandered forth
Beside the osiers of a rivulet,
Full ankle-deep in lilies of the vale.
The nightingale had ceas'd, and a few stars
Were lingering in the heavens, while the thrush
Began calm-throated. Throughout all the isle
There was no covert, no retired cave
Unhaunted by the murmurous noise of waves,   40
Though scarcely heard in many a green recess.
He listen'd, and he wept, and his bright tears
Went trickling down the golden bow he held.
Thus with half-shut suffused eyes he stood,
While from beneath some cumbrous boughs hard by
With solemn step an awful Goddess came,
And there was purport in her looks for him,
Which he with eager guess began to read
Perplex'd, the while melodiously he said:

'How cam'st thou over the unfooted sea?   50
Or hath that antique mien and robed form
Mov'd in these vales invisible till now?
Sure I have heard those vestments sweeping o'er
The fallen leaves, when I have sat alone
In cool mid-forest. Surely I have traced
The rustle of those ample skirts about
These grassy solitudes, and seen the flowers
Lift up their heads, as still the whisper pass'd.
Goddess! I have beheld those eyes before,
And their eternal calm, and all that face,   60
Or I have dream'd.' – 'Yes,' said the supreme shape,
'Thou hast dream'd of me; and awaking up
Didst find a lyre all golden by thy side,
Whose strings touch'd by thy fingers, all the vast
Unwearied ear of the whole universe
Listen'd in pain and pleasure at the birth
Of such new tuneful wonder. Is't not strange
That thou shouldst weep, so gifted? Tell me, youth,
What sorrow thou canst feel; for I am sad
When thou dost shed a tear: explain thy griefs   70
To one who in this lonely isle hath been
The watcher of thy sleep and hours of life,
From the young day when first thy infant hand
Pluck'd witless the weak flowers, till thine arm
Could bend that bow heroic to all times.
Show thy heart's secret to an ancient Power
Who hath forsaken old and sacred thrones
For prophecies of thee, and for the sake
Of loveliness new born.' – Apollo then,
With sudden scrutiny and gloomless eyes,   80
Thus answer'd, while his white melodious throat
Throbb'd with the syllables. – 'Mnemosyne!
Thy name is on my tongue, I know not how;
Why should I tell thee what thou so well seest?
Why should I strive to show what from thy lips
Would come no mystery? For me, dark, dark,
And painful vile oblivion seals my eyes:
I strive to search wherefore I am so sad,
Until a melancholy numbs my limbs;
And then upon the grass I sit, and moan,   90

Like one who once had wings. – O why should I
Feel curs'd and thwarted, when the liegeless air
Yields to my step aspirant? why should I
Spurn the green turf as hateful to my feet?
Goddess benign, point forth some unknown thing:
Are there not other regions than this isle?
What are the stars? There is the sun, the sun!
And the most patient brilliance of the moon!
And stars by thousands! Point me out the way
To any one particular beauteous star,   100
And I will flit into it with my lyre,
And make its silvery splendour pant with bliss.
I have heard the cloudy thunder: Where is power?
Whose hand, whose essence, what divinity
Makes this alarum in the elements,
While I here idle listen on the shores
In fearless yet in aching ignorance?
O tell me, lonely Goddess, by thy harp,
That waileth every morn and eventide,
Tell me why thus I rave, about these groves!   110
Mute thou remainest – Mute! yet I can read
A wondrous lesson in thy silent face:
Knowledge enormous makes a God of me.
Names, deeds, gray legends, dire events, rebellions,
Majesties, sovran voices, agonies,
Creations and destroyings, all at once
Pour into the wide hollows of my brain,
And deify me, as if some blithe wine
Or bright elixir peerless I had drunk,
And so become immortal.' – Thus the God,   120
While his enkindled eyes, with level glance
Beneath his white soft temples, stedfast kept
Trembling with light upon Mnemosyne.
Soon wild commotions shook him, and made flush
All the immortal fairness of his limbs;
Most like the struggle at the gate of death;
Or liker still to one who should take leave
Of pale immortal death, and with a pang
As hot as death's is chill, with fierce convulse
Die into life: so young Apollo anguish'd: 130
His very hair, his golden tresses famed

Kept undulation round his eager neck.
During the pain Mnemosyne upheld
Her arms as one who prophesied. – At length
Apollo shriek'd; – and lo! from all his limbs
Celestial * * * * * *
* * * * * * * *

THE END

Fancy

Ever let the Fancy roam,
Pleasure never is at home:
At a touch sweet Pleasure melteth,
Like to bubbles when rain pelteth;
Then let winged Fancy wander
Through the thought still spread beyond her:
Open wide the mind's cage-door,
She'll dart forth, and cloudward soar.
O sweet Fancy! let her loose;
Summer's joys are spoilt by use,   10
And the enjoying of the Spring
Fades as does its blossoming;
Autumn's red-lipp'd fruitage too,
Blushing through the mist and dew,
Cloys with tasting: What do then?
Sit thee by the ingle, when
The sear faggot blazes bright,
Spirit of a winter's night;
When the soundless earth is muffled,
And the caked snow is shuffled   20
From the ploughboy's heavy shoon;
When the Night doth meet the Noon
In a dark conspiracy
To banish Even from her sky.
Sit thee there, and send abroad,
With a mind self-overaw'd,
Fancy, high-commission'd: – send her!
She has vassals to attend her:
She will bring, in spite of frost,
Beauties that the earth hath lost;   30
She will bring thee, all together,
All delights of summer weather;
All the buds and bells of May,
From dewy sward or thorny spray;
All the heaped Autumn's wealth,
With a still, mysterious stealth:
She will mix these pleasures up
Like three fit wines in a cup,
And thou shalt quaff it: – thou shalt hear

Distant harvest-carols clear;   40
Rustle of the reaped corn;
Sweet birds antheming the morn:
And, in the same moment — hark!
'Tis the early April lark,
Or the rooks, with busy caw,
Foraging for sticks and straw.
Thou shalt, at one glance, behold
The daisy and the marigold;
White-plum'd lilies, and the first
Hedge-grown primrose that hath burst;   50
Shaded hyacinth, alway
Sapphire queen of the mid-May;
And every leaf, and every flower
Pearled with the self-same shower.
Thou shalt see the field-mouse peep
Meagre from its celled sleep;
And the snake all winter-thin
Cast on sunny bank its skin;
Freckled nest-eggs thou shalt see
Hatching in the hawthorn-tree,   60
When the hen-bird's wing doth rest
Quiet on her mossy nest;
Then the hurry and alarm
When the bee-hive casts its swarm;
Acorns ripe down-pattering,
While the autumn breezes sing.

    Oh, sweet Fancy! let her loose;
Every thing is spoilt by use:
Where's the cheek that doth not fade,
Too much gaz'd at? Where's the maid   70
Whose lip mature is ever new?
Where's the eye, however blue,
Doth not weary? Where's the face
One would meet in every place?
Where's the voice, however soft,
One would hear so very oft?
At a touch sweet Pleasure melteth
Like to bubbles when rain pelteth.
Let, then, winged Fancy find

Thee a mistress to thy mind: 80
Dulcet-eyed as Ceres' daughter,
Ere the God of Torment taught her
How to frown and how to chide;
With a waist and with a side
White as Hebe's, when her zone
Slipt its golden clasp, and down
Fell her kirtle to her feet,
While she held the goblet sweet,
And Jove grew languid. – Break the mesh
Of the Fancy's silken leash;   90
Quickly break her prison-string
And such joys as these she'll bring. –
Let the winged Fancy roam,
Pleasure never is at home.

Ode

['Bards of Passion']

Bards of Passion and of Mirth,
Ye have left your souls on earth!
Have ye souls in heaven too,
Double-lived in regions new?
Yes, and those of heaven commune
With the spheres of sun and moon;
With the noise of fountains wond'rous,
And the parle of voices thund'rous;
With the whisper of heaven's trees
And one another, in soft ease   10
Seated on Elysian lawns
Brows'd by none but Dian's fawns;
Underneath large blue-bells tented,
Where the daisies are rose-scented,
And the rose herself has got
Perfume which on earth is not;
Where the nightingale doth sing

Not a senseless, tranced thing,
But divine melodious truth;
Philosophic numbers smooth; 20
Tales and golden histories
Of heaven and its mysteries.

Thus ye live on high, and then
On the earth ye live again;
And the souls ye left behind you
Teach us, here, the way to find you,
Where your other souls are joying,
Never slumber'd, never cloying.
Here, your earth-born souls still speak
To mortals, of their little week; 30
Of their sorrows and delights;
Of their passions and their spites;
Of their glory and their shame;
What doth strengthen and what maim.
Thus ye teach us, every day,
Wisdom, though fled far away.

Bards of Passion and of Mirth,
Ye have left your souls on earth!
Ye have souls in heaven too,
Double-lived in regions new! 40

The Eve of St Agnes

1

St Agnes' Eve – Ah, bitter chill it was!
The owl, for all his feathers, was a-cold;
The hare limp'd trembling through the frozen grass,
And silent was the flock in woolly fold:
Numb were the Beadsman's fingers, while he told
His rosary, and while his frosted breath,
Like pious incense from a censer old,
Seem'd taking flight for heaven, without a death,
Past the sweet Virgin's picture, while his prayer he saith.

2

His prayer he saith, this patient, holy man; 10
Then takes his lamp, and riseth from his knees,
And back returneth, meagre, barefoot, wan,
Along the chapel aisle by slow degrees:
The sculptur'd dead, on each side, seem to freeze,
Emprison'd in black, purgatorial rails:
Knights, ladies, praying in dumb orat'ries,
He passeth by; and his weak spirit fails
To think how they may ache in icy hoods and mails.

3

Northward he turneth through a little door,
And scarce three steps, ere Music's golden tongue 20
Flatter'd to tears this aged man and poor;
But no – already had his deathbell rung;
The joys of all his life were said and sung:
His was harsh penance on St Agnes' Eve:
Another way he went, and soon among
Rough ashes sat he for his soul's reprieve,
And all night kept awake, for sinners' sake to grieve.

4

That ancient Beadsman heard the prelude soft;
And so it chanc'd, for many a door was wide,

From hurry to and fro. Soon, up aloft,   30
The silver, snarling trumpets 'gan to chide:
The level chambers, ready with their pride,
Were glowing to receive a thousand guests:
The carved angels, ever eager-eyed,
Star'd, where upon their heads the cornice rests,
With hair blown back, and wings put cross-wise on their
       breasts.

5

At length burst in the argent revelry,
With plume, tiara, and all rich array,
Numerous as shadows haunting fairily
The brain, new stuff'd, in youth, with triumphs gay   40
Of old romance. These let us wish away,
And turn, sole-thoughted, to one Lady there,
Whose heart had brooded, all that wintry day,
On love, and wing'd St Agnes' saintly care,
As she had heard old dames full many times declare.

6

They told her how, upon St Agnes' Eve,
Young virgins might have visions of delight,
And soft adorings from their loves receive
Upon the honey'd middle of the night,
If ceremonies due they did aright;   50
As, supperless to bed they must retire,
And couch supine their beauties, lily white;
Nor look behind, nor sideways, but require
Of Heaven with upward eyes for all that they desire.

7

Full of this whim was thoughtful Madeline:
The music, yearning like a God in pain,
She scarcely heard: her maiden eyes divine,
Fix'd on the floor, saw many a sweeping train
Pass by – she heeded not at all: in vain
Came many a tiptoe, amorous cavalier,   60
And back retir'd; not cool'd by high disdain,

But she saw not: her heart was otherwhere:
She sigh'd for Agnes' dreams, the sweetest of the year.

8

She danc'd along with vague, regardless eyes,
Anxious her lips, her breathing quick and short:
The hallow'd hour was near at hand: she sighs
Amid the timbrels, and the throng'd resort
Of whisperers in anger, or in sport;
'Mid looks of love, defiance, hate, and scorn,
Hoodwink'd with faery fancy; all amort,   70
Save to St Agnes and her lambs unshorn,
And all the bliss to be before to-morrow morn.

9

So, purposing each moment to retire,
She linger'd still. Meantime, across the moors,
Had come young Porphyro, with heart on fire
For Madeline. Beside the portal doors,
Buttress'd from moonlight, stands he, and implores
All saints to give him sight of Madeline,
But for one moment in the tedious hours,
That he might gaze and worship all unseen;   80
Perchance speak, kneel, touch, kiss — in sooth such things
          have been.

10

He ventures in: let no buzz'd whisper tell:
All eyes be muffled, or a hundred swords
Will storm his heart, Love's fev'rous citadel:
For him, those chambers held barbarian hordes,
Hyena foemen, and hot-blooded lords,
Whose very dogs would execrations howl
Against his lineage: not one breast affords
Him any mercy, in that mansion foul,
Save one old beldame, weak in body and in soul.   90

11

Ah, happy chance! the aged creature came,

Shuffling along with ivory-headed wand,
To where he stood, hid from the torch's flame,
Behind a broad hall-pillar, far beyond
The sound of merriment and chorus bland:
He startled her; but soon she knew his face,
And grasp'd his fingers in her palsied hand,
Saying, 'Mercy, Porphyro! hie thee from this place;
They are all here to-night, the whole blood-thirsty race!

12

'Get hence! get hence! there's dwarfish Hildebrand;   100
He had a fever late, and in the fit
He cursed thee and thine, both house and land:
Then there's that old Lord Maurice, not a whit
More tame for his gray hairs – Alas me! flit!
Flit like a ghost away.' – 'Ah, Gossip dear,
We're safe enough; here in this arm-chair sit,
And tell me how' – 'Good Saints! not here, not here;
Follow me, child, or else these stones will be thy bier.'

13

He follow'd through a lowly arched way,
Brushing the cobwebs with his lofty plume,   110
And as she mutter'd 'Well-a – well-a-day!'
He found him in a little moonlight room,
Pale, lattic'd, chill, and silent as a tomb.
'Now tell me where is Madeline,' said he,
'O tell me, Angela, by the holy loom
Which none but secret sisterhood may see,
When they St Agnes' wool are weaving piously.'

14

'St Agnes! Ah! it is St Agnes' Eve –
Yet men will murder upon holy days:
Thou must hold water in a witch's sieve,
And be liege-lord of all the Elves and Fays,   120
To venture so: it fills me with amaze
To see thee, Porphyro! – St Agnes' Eve!
God's help! my lady fair the conjuror plays

This very night: good angels her deceive!
But let me laugh awhile, I've mickle time to grieve.'

15

Feebly she laugheth in the languid moon,
While Porphyro upon her face doth look,
Like puzzled urchin on an aged crone
Who keepeth clos'd a wond'rous riddle-book,   130
As spectacled she sits in chimney nook.
But soon his eyes grew brilliant, when she told
His lady's purpose; and he scarce could brook
Tears, at the thought of those enchantments cold,
And Madeline asleep in lap of legends old.

16

Sudden a thought came like a full-blown rose,
Flushing his brow, and in his pained heart
Made purple riot: then doth he propose
A stratagem, that makes the beldame start:
'A cruel man and impious thou art: 140
Sweet lady, let her pray, and sleep, and dream
Alone with her good angels, far apart
From wicked men like thee. Go, go! – I deem
Thou canst not surely be the same that thou didst seem.'

17

'I will not harm her, by all saints I swear,'
Quoth Porphyro: 'O may I ne'er find grace
When my weak voice shall whisper its last prayer,
If one of her soft ringlets I displace,
Or look with ruffian passion in her face:
Good Angela, believe me by these tears;   150
Or I will, even in a moment's space,
Awake, with horrid shout, my foemen's ears,
And beard them, though they be more fang'd than wolves
        and bears.'

18

'Ah! why wilt thou affright a feeble soul?
A poor, weak, palsy-stricken, churchyard thing,
Whose passing-bell may ere the midnight toll;
Whose prayers for thee, each morn and evening,
Were never miss'd.' – Thus plaining, doth she bring
A gentler speech from burning Porphyro;
So woful, and of such deep sorrowing,   160
That Angela gives promise she will do
Whatever he shall wish, betide her weal or woe.

19

Which was, to lead him, in close secrecy,
Even to Madeline's chamber, and there hide
Him in a closet, of such privacy
That he might see her beauty unespied,
And win perhaps that night a peerless bride,
While legion'd fairies pac'd the coverlet,
And pale enchantment held her sleepy-eyed.
Never on such a night have lovers met,   170
Since Merlin paid his Demon all the monstrous debt.

20

'It shall be as thou wishest,' said the Dame:
'All cates and dainties shall be stored there
Quickly on this feast-night: by the tambour frame
Her own lute thou wilt see: no time to spare,
For I am slow and feeble, and scarce dare
On such a catering trust my dizzy head.
Wait here, my child, with patience; kneel in prayer
The while: Ah! thou must needs the lady wed,
Or may I never leave my grave among the dead.'   180

21

So saying, she hobbled off with busy fear.
The lover's endless minutes slowly pass'd;
The dame return'd, and whisper'd in his ear
To follow her; with aged eyes aghast
From fright of dim espial. Safe at last,

Through many a dusky gallery, they gain
The maiden's chamber, silken, hush'd, and chaste;
Where Porphyro took covert, pleas'd amain.
His poor guide hurried back with agues in her brain.

22

Her falt'ring hand upon the balustrade,   190
Old Angela was feeling for the stair,
When Madeline, St Agnes' charmed maid,
Rose, like a mission'd spirit, unaware:
With silver taper's light, and pious care,
She turn'd, and down the aged gossip led
To a safe level matting. Now prepare,
Young Porphyro, for gazing on that bed;
She comes, she comes again, like ring-dove fray'd and fled.

23

Out went the taper as she hurried in;
Its little smoke, in pallid moonshine, died: 200
She clos'd the door, she panted, all akin
To spirits of the air, and visions wide:
No uttered syllable, or, woe betide!
But to her heart, her heart was voluble,
Paining with eloquence her balmy side;
As though a tongueless nightingale should swell
Her throat in vain, and die, heart-stifled, in her dell.

24

A casement high and triple-arch'd there was,
All garlanded with carven imag'ries
Of fruits, and flowers, and bunches of knot-grass,   210
And diamonded with panes of quaint device,
Innumerable of stains and splendid dyes,
As are the tiger-moth's deep-damask'd wings;
And in the midst, 'mong thousand heraldries,
And twilight saints, and dim emblazonings,
A shielded scutcheon blush'd with blood of queens and
        kings.

25

Full on this casement shone the wintry moon,
And threw warm gules on Madeline's fair breast,
As down she knelt for heaven's grace and boon;
Rose-bloom fell on her hands, together prest,   220
And on her silver cross soft amethyst,
And on her hair a glory, like a saint:
She seem'd a splendid angel, newly drest,
Save wings, for heaven: – Porphyro grew faint:
She knelt, so pure a thing, so free from mortal taint.

26

Anon his heart revives: her vespers done,
Of all its wreathed pearls her hair she frees;
Unclasps her warmed jewels one by one;
Loosens her fragrant boddice; by degrees
Her rich attire creeps rustling to her knees: 230
Half-hidden, like a mermaid in sea-weed,
Pensive awhile she dreams awake, and sees,
In fancy, fair St Agnes in her bed,
But dares not look behind, or all the charm is fled.

27

Soon, trembling in her soft and chilly nest,
In sort of wakeful swoon, perplex'd she lay,
Until the poppied warmth of sleep oppress'd
Her soothed limbs, and soul fatigued away;
Flown, like a thought, until the morrow-day;
Blissfully haven'd both from joy and pain;   240
Clasp'd like a missal where swart Paynims pray;
Blinded alike from sunshine and from rain,
As though a rose should shut, and be a bud again.

28

Stol'n to this paradise, and so entranced,
Porphyro gazed upon her empty dress,
And listen'd to her breathing, if it chanced
To wake into a slumberous tenderness;
Which when he heard, that minute did he bless,

And breath'd himself: then from the closet crept,
Noiseless as fear in a wide wilderness,   250
And over the hush'd carpet, silent, stept,
And 'tween the curtains peep'd, where, lo! – how fast she
     slept.

29

Then by the bed-side, where the faded moon
Made a dim, silver twilight, soft he set
A table, and, half anguish'd, threw thereon
A cloth of woven crimson, gold, and jet: –
O for some drowsy Morphean amulet!
The boisterous, midnight, festive clarion,
The kettle-drum, and far-heard clarionet,
Affray his ears, though but in dying tone: –   260
The hall door shuts again, and all the noise is gone.

30

And still she slept an azure-lidded sleep,
In blanched linen, smooth, and lavender'd,
While he from forth the closet brought a heap
Of candied apple, quince, and plum, and gourd;
With jellies soother than the creamy curd,
And lucent syrops, tinct with cinnamon;
Manna and dates, in argosy transferr'd
From Fez; and spiced dainties, every one,
From silken Samarcand to cedar'd Lebanon.   270

31

These delicates he heap'd with glowing hand
On golden dishes and in baskets bright
Of wreathed silver: sumptuous they stand
In the retired quiet of the night,
Filling the chilly room with perfume light. –
'And now, my love, my seraph fair, awake!
Thou art my heaven, and I thine eremite:
Open thine eyes, for meek St Agnes' sake,
Or I shall drowse beside thee, so my soul doth ache.'

32

Thus whispering, his warm, unnerved arm   280
Sank in her pillow. Shaded was her dream
By the dusk curtains: — 'twas a midnight charm
Impossible to melt as iced stream:
The lustrous salvers in the moonlight gleam;
Broad golden fringe upon the carpet lies:
It seem'd he never, never could redeem
From such a stedfast spell his lady's eyes;
So mus'd awhile, entoil'd in woofed phantasies.

33

Awakening up, he took her hollow lute, —
Tumultuous, — and, in chords that tenderest be,   290
He play'd an ancient ditty, long since mute,
In Provence call'd, 'La belle dame sans mercy':
Close to her ear touching the melody; —
Wherewith disturb'd, she utter'd a soft moan:
He ceased — she panted quick — and suddenly
Her blue affrayed eyes wide open shone:
Upon his knees he sank, pale as smooth-sculptured stone.

34

Her eyes were open, but she still beheld,
Now wide awake, the vision of her sleep:
There was a painful change, that nigh expell'd   300
The blisses of her dream so pure and deep
At which fair Madeline began to weep,
And moan forth witless words with many a sigh;
While still her gaze on Porphyro would keep;
Who knelt, with joined hands and piteous eye,
Fearing to move or speak, she look'd so dreamingly.

35

'Ah, Porphyro! said she, 'but even now
Thy voice was at sweet tremble in mine ear,
Made tuneable with every sweetest vow;
And those sad eyes were spiritual and clear: 310
How chang'd thou art! how pallid, chill, and drear!

Give me that voice again, my Porphyro,
Those looks immortal, those complainings dear!
Oh leave me not in this eternal woe,
For if thou diest, my Love, I know not where to go.'

36

Beyond a mortal man impassion'd far
At these voluptuous accents, he arose,
Ethereal, flush'd, and like a throbbing star
Seen mid the sapphire heaven's deep repose;
Into her dream he melted, as the rose   320
Blendeth its odour with the violet, –
Solution sweet: meantime the frost-wind blows
Like Love's alarum pattering the sharp sleet
Against the window-panes; St Agnes' moon hath set.

37

'Tis dark: quick pattereth the flaw-blown sleet:
'This is no dream, my bride, my Madeline!'
'Tis dark: the iced gusts still rave and beat:
'No dream, alas! alas! and woe is mine!
Porphyro will leave me here to fade and pine. –
Cruel! what traitor could thee hither bring?   330
I curse not, for my heart is lost in thine,
Though thou forsakest a deceived thing; –
A dove forlorn and lost with sick unpruned wing.'

38

'My Madeline! sweet dreamer! lovely bride!
Say, may I be for aye thy vassal blest?
Thy beauty's shield, heart-shap'd and vermeil dyed?
Ah, silver shrine, here will I take my rest
After so many hours of toil and quest,
A famish'd pilgrim, – saved by miracle.
Though I have found, I will not rob thy nest   340
Saving of thy sweet self; if thou think'st well
To trust, fair Madeline, to no rude infidel.'

39

'Hark! 'tis an elfin-storm from faery land,
Of haggard seeming, but a boon indeed:
Arise – arise! the morning is at hand; –
The bloated wassaillers will never heed: –
Let us away, my love, with happy speed;
There are no ears to hear, or eyes to see, –
Drown'd all in Rhenish and the sleepy mead:
Awake! arise! my love, and fearless be,   350
For o'er the southern moors I have a home for thee.'

40

She hurried at his words, beset with fears,
For there were sleeping dragons all around,
At glaring watch, perhaps, with ready spears –
Down the wide stairs a darkling way they found. –
In all the house was heard no human sound.
A chain-droop'd lamp was flickering by each door;
The arras, rich with horseman, hawk, and hound,
Flutter'd in the besieging wind's uproar;
And the long carpets rose along the gusty floor.   360

41

They glide, like phantoms, into the wide hall;
Like phantoms, to the iron porch, they glide;
Where lay the Porter, in uneasy sprawl,
With a huge empty flaggon by his side:
The wakeful bloodhound rose, and shook his hide,
But his sagacious eye an inmate owns:
By one, and one, the bolts full easy slide: –
The chains lie silent on the footworn stones; –
The key turns, and the door upon its hinges groans.   370

42

And they are gone: ay, ages long ago
These lovers fled away into the storm.
That night the Baron dreamt of many a woe,
And all his warrior-guests, with shade and form

Of witch, and demon, and large coffin-worm,
Were long be-nightmar'd. Angela the old
Died palsy-twitch'd, with meagre face deform;
The Beadsman, after thousand aves told,
For aye unsought for slept among his ashes cold.

The Eve of St Mark

Upon a Sabbath day it fell;
Thrice holy was the sabbath bell
That call'd the folk to evening prayer.
The city streets were clean and fair
From wholesome drench of April rains,
And on the western window panes
The chilly sunset faintly told
Of immatur'd, green vallies cold,
Of the green, thorny, bloomless hedge,
Of rivers new with springtide sedge,   10
Of primroses by shelter'd rills,
And daisies on the aguish hills.
Thrice holy was the sabbath bell:
The silent streets were crowded well
With staid and pious companies,
Warm from their fireside oratries,
And moving with demurest air
To even song and vesper prayer.
Each arched porch and entry low
Was fill'd with patient crowd and slow,   20
With whispers hush and shuffling feet,
While play'd the organs loud and sweet.

    The bells had ceas'd, the prayers begun,
And Bertha had not yet half done
A curious volume, patch'd and torn,
That all day long, from earliest morn,
Had taken captive her fair eyes
Among its golden broideries: –
Perplex'd her with a thousand things –
The stars of heaven, and angels' wings;   30
Martyrs in a fiery blaze;
Azure saints 'mid silver rays;
Aaron's breastplate, and the seven
Candlesticks John saw in heaven;
The winged Lion of St Mark,
And the Covenantal Ark
With its many mysteries,
Cherubim and golden mice.

Bertha was a maiden fair,
Dwelling in the old Minster Square: 40
From her fireside she could see
Sidelong its rich antiquity,
Far as the Bishop's garden wall,
Where sycamores and elm trees tall
Full leav'd the forest had outstript,
By no sharp north wind ever nipt,
So sheltered by the mighty pile.

Bertha arose and read awhile
With forehead 'gainst the window pane, –
Again she tried, and then again,   50
Until the dusk eve left her dark
Upon the legend of St Mark:
From pleated lawn-frill fine and thin
She lifted up her soft warm chin,
With aching neck and swimming eyes
All daz'd with saintly imageries.

All was gloom, and silent all,
Save now and then the still foot fall
Of one returning homewards late
Past the echoing minster gate.   60
The clamorous daws that all the day
Above tree tops and towers play,
Pair by pair had gone to rest,
Each in their ancient belfry nest
Where asleep they fall betimes
To music of the drowsy chimes.

All was silent, all was gloom
Abroad and in the homely room; –
Down she sat, poor cheated soul,
And struck a swart lamp from the coal,   70
Leaned forward with bright drooping hair
And slant book full against the glare.
Her shadow, in uneasy guise,
Hover'd about, a giant size,
On ceiling, beam, and old oak chair,

The parrot's cage and pannel square,
And the warm-angled winter screne,
On which were many monsters seen,
Call'd, Doves of Siam, Lima Mice,
And legless birds of Paradise,   80
Macaw, and tender Av'davat,
And silken-furr'd Angora Cat.

    Untir'd she read – her shadow still
Glowerd about as it would fill
The room with ghastly forms and shades –
As though some ghostly Queen of Spades
Had come to mock behind her back,
And dance, and ruffle her garments black.

    Untir'd she read the legend page
Of holy Mark from youth to age,   90
On land, on sea, in pagan-chains,
Rejoicing for his many pains.
Sometimes the learned eremite
With golden star, or dagger bright,
Refer'd to pious poesies
Written in smallest crow quill size
Beneath the text, and thus the rhyme
Was parcell'd out from time to time:
' – Als writeth he of swevenis
Men han beforne they waken in blis,   100
When that hir friendes thinke hem bounde
In crimpide shroude farre under grounde:
And how a litling childe mot be
A scainte er its natavitie,
Gif that the modre (God her blesse)
Kepen in solitarinesse,
And kissen devoute the holy croce.
Of Goddis love and Sathan's force
He writithe; and things many moe,
Of swiche thinges I may not show,   110
Bot I must tellen verilie
Somedele of Saintè Cicilie,
And chieflie what he auctoreth
Of Saintè Markis life and dethe.'

'Why did I laugh tonight'

Why did I laugh tonight? No voice will tell:
  No god, no demon of severe response
Deigns to reply from heaven or from hell.
  Then to my human heart I turn at once –
Heart! thou and I are here sad and alone;
  Say, wherefore did I laugh? O mortal pain!
O darkness! darkness! ever must I moan
  To question heaven and hell and heart in vain!
Why did I laugh? I know this being's lease
  My fancy to its utmost blisses spreads: 10
Yet could I on this very midnight cease,
  And the world's gaudy ensigns see in shreds.
Verse, fame, and beauty are intense indeed
But death intenser – death is life's high meed.

La belle dame sans merci

O what can ail thee knight at arms,
   Alone and palely loitering?
The sedge has withered from the lake
   And no birds sing!

O what can ail thee knight at arms,
   So haggard and so woe begone?
The squirrel's granary is full
   And the harvest's done.

I see a lilly on thy brow
   With anguish moist and fever dew,   10
And on thy cheeks a fading rose
   Fast Withereth too –

I met a Lady in the Meads
   Full beautiful, a faery's child;
Her hair was long, her foot was light
   And her eyes were wild –

I made a Garland for her head,
   And bracelets too, and fragrant Zone
She look'd at me as she did love
   And made sweet moan –   20

I set her on my pacing steed
   And nothing else saw all day long,
For sidelong would she bend, and sing
   A faery's song –

She found me roots of relish sweet
   And honey wild and manna dew,
And sure in language strange she said
   I love thee true –

La Belle Dame sans Mercy

[*INDICATOR* version]

Ah, what can ail thee, wretched wight,
   Alone and palely loitering;
The sedge is wither'd from the lake,
     And no birds sing.

Ah, what can ail thee, wretched wight,
   So haggard and so woe-begone?
The squirrel's granary is full,
     And the harvest's done.

I see a lily on thy brow,
   With anguish moist and fever dew;   10
And on thy cheek a fading rose
     Fast withereth too.

I met a Lady in the meads
   Full beautiful, a fairy's child;
Her hair was long, her foot was light,
     And her eyes were wild.

I set her on my pacing steed,
   And nothing else saw all day long;
For sideways would she lean, and sing
     A fairy's song.   20

I made a garland for her head,
   And bracelets too, and fragrant zone:
She look'd at me as she did love,
     And made sweet moan.

She found me roots of relish sweet,
   And honey wild, and manna dew;
And sure in language strange she said,
     I love thee true.

She took me to her elfin grot
  And there she wept and sigh'd full sore,   30
And there I shut her wild wild eyes
  With kisses four.

And there she lulled me asleep
  And there I dream'd Ah Woe betide!
The latest dream I ever dreamt
  On the cold hill side.

I saw pale kings and Princes too,
  Pale warriors, death pale were they all;
They cried 'La belle dame sans merci
  Thee hath in thrall.'   40

I saw their starv'd lips in the gloam
  With horrid warning gaped wide,
And I awoke and found me here
  On the cold hill's side.

And this is why I sojourn here
  Alone and palely loitering;
Though the sedge is wither'd from the Lake
  And no birds sing.

She took me to her elfin grot,
   And there she gaz'd and sighed deep,   30
And there I shut her wild sad eyes –
     So kiss'd to sleep.

And there we slumber'd on the moss,
   And there I dream'd, ah woe betide,
The latest dream I ever dream'd
     On the cold hill side.

I saw pale kings, and princes too,
   Pale warriors, death-pale were they all;
Who cried, 'La belle Dame sans mercy
     Hath thee in thrall!'   40

I saw their starv'd lips in the gloom
   With horrid warning gaped wide,
And I awoke, and found me here
     On the cold hill side.

And this is why I sojourn here
   Alone and palely loitering,
Though the sedge is wither'd from the lake,
     And no birds sing.

                    CAVIARE

To Sleep

O soft embalmer of the still midnight,
  Shutting with careful fingers and benign
Our gloom-pleas'd eyes embowered from the light,
  Enshaded in forgetfulness divine –
O soothest sleep, if so it please thee close   5
  In midst of this thine hymn my willing eyes,
Or wait the amen, ere thy poppy throws
  Around my bed its dewy charities –
Then save me or the passed day will shine
Upon my pillow breeding many woes.   10
Save me from curious conscience that still lords
Its strength for darkness, burrowing like a mole –
Turn the key deftly in the oiled wards
And seal the hushed casket of my soul.

Ode to Psyche

O Goddess! hear these tuneless numbers, wrung
  By sweet enforcement and remembrance dear,
And pardon that thy secrets should be sung
  Even into thine own soft-conched ear:
Surely I dreamt to-day, or did I see
  The winged Psyche with awaken'd eyes?
I wander'd in a forest thoughtlessly,
  And, on the sudden, fainting with surprise,
Saw two fair creatures, couched side by side
  In deepest grass, beneath the whisp'ring roof   10
  Of leaves and trembled blossoms, where there ran
    A brooklet, scarce espied:

'Mid hush'd, cool-rooted flowers, fragrant-eyed,
  Blue, silver-white, and budded Tyrian,
They lay calm-breathing on the bedded grass;
  Their arms embraced, and their pinions too;
Their lips touch'd not, but had not bade adieu
As if disjoined by soft-handed slumber,
And ready still past kisses to outnumber

At tender eye-dawn of aurorean love: 20
  The winged boy I knew;
But who wast thou, O happy, happy dove?
  His Psyche true!

O latest born and loveliest vision far
 Of all Olympus' faded hierarchy!
Fairer than Phœbe's sapphire-region'd star,
 Or Vesper, amorous glow-worm of the sky;
Fairer than these, though temple thou hast none,
  Nor altar heap'd with flowers;
Nor virgin-choir to make delicious moan   30
  Upon the midnight hours;
No voice, no lute, no pipe, no incense sweet
 From chain-swung censer teeming;
No shrine, no grove, no oracle, no heat
 Of pale-mouth'd prophet dreaming.

O brightest! though too late for antique vows,
 Too, too late for the fond believing lyre,
When holy were the haunted forest boughs,
 Holy the air, the water, and the fire;
Yet even in these days so far retir'd   40
 From happy pieties, thy lucent fans,
 Fluttering among the faint Olympians,
I see, and sing, by my own eyes inspired.
So let me be thy choir, and make a moan
  Upon the midnight hours;
Thy voice, thy lute, thy pipe, thy incense sweet
 From swinged censer teeming;
Thy shrine, thy grove, thy oracle, thy heat
 Of pale-mouth'd prophet dreaming.

Yes, I will be thy priest, and build a fane   50
 In some untrodden region of my mind,
Where branched thoughts, new grown with pleasant pain,
 Instead of pines shall murmur in the wind:
Far, far around shall those dark-cluster'd trees
 Fledge the wild-ridged mountains steep by steep;
And there by zephyrs, streams, and birds, and bees,
 The moss-lain Dryads shall be lull'd to sleep;

And in the midst of this wide quietness
A rosy sanctuary will I dress
With the wreath'd trellis of a working brain,   60
   With buds, and bells, and stars without a name,
With all the gardener Fancy e'er could feign,
   Who breeding flowers, will never breed the same:
And there shall be for thee all soft delight
   That shadowy thought can win,
A bright torch, and a casement ope at night,
   To let the warm Love in!

'If by dull rhymes our English must be chain'd'

If by dull rhymes our English must be chain'd
And, like Andromeda, the sonnet sweet
Fetter'd in spite of pained loveliness;
Let us find out, if we must be constrain'd,
Sandals more interwoven and complete   5
To fit the naked foot of Poesy;
Let us inspect the lyre and weigh the stress
Of every chord and see what may be gained
By ear industrious and attention meet;
Misers of sound and syllable, no less   10
Than Midas of his coinage, let us be
Jealous of dead leaves in the bay wreath crown;
So if we may not let the Muse be free,
She will be bound with garlands of her own.

Ode to a Nightingale

I

My heart aches, and a drowsy numbness pains
   My sense, as though of hemlock I had drunk,
Or emptied some dull opiate to the drains
   One minute past, and Lethe-wards had sunk:

'Tis not through envy of thy happy lot,
　　But being too happy in thine happiness, –
　　　　That thou, light-winged Dryad of the trees,
　　　　　　In some melodious plot
　　Of beechen green, and shadows numberless,
　　　　Singest of summer in full-throated ease.　　　　　　10

2

O, for a draught of vintage! that hath been
　　Cool'd a long age in the deep-delvèd earth,
Tasting of Flora and the country green,
　　Dance, and Provençal song, and sunburnt mirth!
O for a beaker full of the warm South,
　　Full of the true, the blushful Hippocrene,
　　　　With beaded bubbles winking at the brim,
　　　　　　And purple-stainèd mouth;
　　That I might drink, and leave the world unseen,
　　　　And with thee fade away into the forest dim:　　　　20

3

Fade far away, dissolve, and quite forget
　　What thou among the leaves hast never known,
The weariness, the fever, and the fret
　　Here, where men sit and hear each other groan;
Where palsy shakes a few, sad, last gray hairs,
　　Where youth grows pale, and spectre-thin, and dies;
　　　　Where but to think is to be full of sorrow
　　　　　　And leaden-eyed despairs,
　　Where Beauty cannot keep her lustrous eyes,
　　　　Or new Love pine at them beyond to-morrow.　　　　30

4

Away! away! for I will fly to thee,
　　Not charioted by Bacchus and his pards,
But on the viewless wings of Poesy,
　　Though the dull brain perplexes and retards:
Already with thee! tender is the night,
　　And haply the Queen-Moon is on her throne,
　　　　Cluster'd around by all her starry Fays;
　　　　　　But here there is no light,

Save what from heaven is with the breezes blown
  Through verdurous glooms and winding mossy ways.   40

5

I cannot see what flowers are at my feet,
  Nor what soft incense hangs upon the boughs,
But, in embalmed darkness, guess each sweet
  Wherewith the seasonable month endows
The grass, the thicket, and the fruit-tree wild;
  White hawthorn, and the pastoral eglantine;
    Fast fading violets cover'd up in leaves;
      And mid-May's eldest child,
  The coming musk-rose, full of dewy wine,
    The murmurous haunt of flies on summer eves.   50

6

Darkling I listen; and, for many a time
  I have been half in love with easeful Death,
Call'd him soft names in many a mused rhyme,
  To take into the air my quiet breath;
Now more than ever seems it rich to die,
  To cease upon the midnight with no pain,
    While thou art pouring forth thy soul abroad
      In such an ecstasy!
  Still wouldst thou sing, and I have ears in vain —
    To thy high requiem become a sod.   60

7

Thou wast not born for death, immortal Bird!
  No hungry generations tread thee down;
The voice I hear this passing night was heard
  In ancient days by emperor and clown:
Perhaps the self-same song that found a path
  Through the sad heart of Ruth, when, sick for home,
    She stood in tears amid the alien corn;
      The same that oft-times hath
  Charm'd magic casements, opening on the foam
    Of perilous seas, in faery lands forlorn.   70

8

Forlorn! the very word is like a bell
   To toll me back from thee to my sole self!
Adieu! the fancy cannot cheat so well
   As she is fam'd to do, deceiving elf.
Adieu! adieu! thy plaintive anthem fades
   Past the near meadows, over the still stream,
      Up the hill-side; and now 'tis buried deep
        In the next valley-glades:
   Was it a vision, or a waking dream?
      Fled is that music: – Do I wake or sleep?   80

Ode on a Grecian Urn

1

Thou still unravish'd bride of quietness,
   Thou foster-child of silence and slow time,
Sylvan historian, who canst thus express
   A flowery tale more sweetly than our rhyme:
What leaf-fring'd legend haunts about thy shape
   Of deities or mortals, or of both,
      In Tempe or the dales of Arcady?
   What men or gods are these? What maidens loth?
What mad pursuit? What struggle to escape?
      What pipes and timbrels? What wild ecstasy?   10

2

Heard melodies are sweet, but those unheard
   Are sweeter; therefore, ye soft pipes, play on;
Not to the sensual ear, but, more endear'd,
   Pipe to the spirit ditties of no tone:
Fair youth, beneath the trees, thou canst not leave
   Thy song, nor ever can those trees be bare;
      Bold lover, never, never canst thou kiss,
Though winning near the goal – yet, do not grieve;
   She cannot fade, though thou hast not thy bliss,
      For ever wilt thou love, and she be fair!   20

3

Ah, happy, happy boughs! that cannot shed
    Your leaves, nor ever bid the spring adieu;
And, happy melodist, unwearied,
    For ever piping songs for ever new;
More happy love! more happy, happy love!
    For ever warm and still to be enjoy'd,
      For ever panting, and for ever young;
All breathing human passion far above,
    That leaves a heart high-sorrowful and cloy'd,
      A burning forehead, and a parching tongue.   30

4

Who are these coming to the sacrifice?
    To what green altar, O mysterious priest,
Lead'st thou that heifer lowing at the skies,
    And all her silken flanks with garlands drest?
What little town by river or sea shore,
    Or mountain-built with peaceful citadel,
      Is emptied of this folk, this pious morn?
And, little town, thy streets for evermore
    Will silent be; and not a soul to tell
      Why thou art desolate, can e'er return.   40

5

O Attic shape! Fair attitude! with brede
    Of marble men and maidens overwrought,
With forest branches and the trodden weed;
    Thou, silent form, dost tease us out of thought
As doth eternity: Cold Pastoral!
    When old age shall this generation waste,
      Thou shalt remain, in midst of other woe
Than ours, a friend to man, to whom thou say'st,
    'Beauty is truth, truth beauty,' – that is all
      Ye know on earth, and all ye need to know.   50

Ode on Melancholy

1

No, no, go not to Lethe, neither twist
  Wolf's-bane, tight-rooted, for its poisonous wine;
Nor suffer thy pale forehead to be kiss'd
  By nightshade, ruby grape of Proserpine;
Make not your rosary of yew-berries,
  Nor let the beetle, nor the death-moth be
    Your mournful Psyche, nor the downy owl
A partner in your sorrow's mysteries;
  For shade to shade will come too drowsily,
    And drown the wakeful anguish of the soul.   10

2

But when the melancholy fit shall fall
  Sudden from heaven like a weeping cloud,
That fosters the droop-headed flowers all,
  And hides the green hill in an April shroud;
Then glut thy sorrow on a morning rose,
  Or on the rainbow of the salt sand-wave,
    Or on the wealth of globed peonies;
Or if thy mistress some rich anger shows,
  Emprison her soft hand, and let her rave,
    And feed deep, deep upon her peerless eyes.   20

3

She dwells with Beauty – Beauty that must die;
  And Joy, whose hand is ever at his lips
Bidding adieu; and aching Pleasure nigh,
  Turning to poison while the bee-mouth sips:
Ay, in the very temple of Delight
  Veil'd Melancholy has her sovran shrine,
    Though seen of none save him whose strenuous tongue
Can burst Joy's grape against his palate fine;
  His soul shall taste the sadness of her might,
    And be among her cloudy trophies hung.   30

Ode on Indolence

'They toil not, neither do they spin.'

1

One morn before me were three figures seen,
    With bowed necks, and joined hands, side-faced;
And one behind the other stepp'd serene,
    In placid sandals, and in white robes graced;
They pass'd, like figures on a marble urn,
    When shifted round to see the other side;
        They came again; as when the urn once more
Is shifted round, the first seen shades return;
    And they were strange to me, as may betide
        With vases, to one deep in Phidian lore.   10

2

How is it, Shadows, that I knew ye not?
    How came ye muffled in so hush a mask?
Was it a silent deep-disguised plot
    To steal away, and leave without a task
My idle days? Ripe was the drowsy hour;
    The blissful cloud of summer-indolence
        Benumb'd my eyes: my pulse grew less and less;
Pain had no sting, and pleasure's wreath no flower:
    O, why did ye not melt, and leave my sense
        Unhaunted quite of all but – nothingness?   20

3

A third time pass'd they by, and, passing, turn'd
    Each one the face a moment whiles to me;
Then faded, and to follow them I burn'd
    And ached for wings, because I knew the three;
The first was a fair maid, and Love her name;
    The second was Ambition, pale of cheek,
        And ever watchful with fatigued eye;
The last, whom I love more, the more of blame
    Is heap'd upon her, maiden most unmeek, –
        I knew to be my demon Poesy.   30

4

They faded, and, forsooth! I wanted wings:
   O folly! What is Love? and where is it?
And for that poor Ambition – it springs
   From a man's little heart's short fever-fit;
For Poesy! – no, – she has not a joy, –
   At least for me, – so sweet as drowsy noons,
      And evenings steep'd in honied indolence;
O, for an age so shelter'd from annoy,
   That I may never know how change the moons,
      Or hear the voice of busy common-sense!   40

5

A third time came they by; – alas! wherefore?
   My sleep had been embroider'd with dim dreams;
My soul had been a lawn besprinkled o'er
   With flowers, and stirring shades, and baffled beams:
The morn was clouded, but no shower fell,
   Though in her lids hung the sweet tears of May;
      The open casement press'd a new-leaved vine,
   Let in the budding warmth and throstle's lay;
O shadows! 'twas a time to bid farewell!
      Upon your skirts had fallen no tears of mine.   50

6

So, ye three ghosts, adieu! Ye cannot raise
   My head cool-bedded in the flowery grass;
For I would not be dieted with praise,
   A pet-lamb in a sentimental farce!
Fade softly from my eyes, and be once more
   In masque-like figures on the dreamy urn;
      Farewell! I yet have visions for the night,
And for the day faint visions there is store;
      Vanish, ye Phantoms, from my idle spright,
Into the clouds, and never more return!   60

Lamia

PART I

Upon a time, before the faery broods
Drove Nymph and Satyr from the prosperous woods,
Before King Oberon's bright diadem,
Sceptre, and mantle, clasp'd with dewy gem,
Frighted away the Dryads and the Fauns
From rushes green, and brakes, and cowslip'd lawns,
The ever-smitten Hermes empty left
His golden throne, bent warm on amorous theft:
From high Olympus had he stolen light,
On this side of Jove's clouds, to escape the sight   10
Of his great summoner, and made retreat
Into a forest on the shores of Crete.
For somewhere in that sacred island dwelt
A nymph, to whom all hoofed Satyrs knelt;
At whose white feet the languid Tritons poured
Pearls, while on land they wither'd and adored.
Fast by the springs where she to bathe was wont,
And in those meads where sometime she might haunt,
Were strewn rich gifts, unknown to any Muse,
Though Fancy's casket were unlock'd to choose.   20
Ah, what a world of love was at her feet!
So Hermes thought, and a celestial heat
Burnt from his winged heels to either ear,
That from a whiteness, as the lily clear,
Blush'd into roses 'mid his golden hair,
Fallen in jealous curls about his shoulders bare.

From vale to vale, from wood to wood, he flew,
Breathing upon the flowers his passion new,
And wound with many a river to its head,
To find where this sweet nymph prepar'd her secret bed: 30
In vain; the sweet nymph might nowhere be found,
And so he rested, on the lonely ground,
Pensive, and full of painful jealousies
Of the Wood-Gods, and even the very trees.
There as he stood, he heard a mournful voice,
Such as once heard, in gentle heart, destroys

All pain but pity: thus the lone voice spake:
'When from this wreathed tomb shall I awake!
When move in a sweet body fit for life,
And love, and pleasure, and the ruddy strife   40
Of hearts and lips! Ah, miserable me!'
The God, dove-footed, glided silently
Round bush and tree, soft-brushing, in his speed,
The taller grasses and full-flowering weed,
Until he found a palpitating snake,
Bright, and cirque-couchant in a dusky brake.

   She was a gordian shape of dazzling hue,
Vermilion-spotted, golden, green, and blue;
Striped like a zebra, freckled like a pard,
Eyed like a peacock, and all crimson barr'd;   50
And full of silver moons, that, as she breathed,
Dissolv'd, or brighter shone, or interwreathed
Their lustres with the gloomier tapestries –
So rainbow-sided, touch'd with miseries,
She seem'd, at once, some penanced lady elf,
Some demon's mistress, or the demon's self.
Upon her crest she wore a wannish fire
Sprinkled with stars, like Ariadne's tiar:
Her head was serpent, but ah, bitter-sweet!
She had a woman's mouth with all its pearls complete: 60
And for her eyes: what could such eyes do there
But weep, and weep, that they were born so fair?
As Proserpine still weeps for her Sicilian air.
Her throat was serpent, but the words she spake
Came, as through bubbling honey, for Love's sake,
And thus; while Hermes on his pinions lay,
Like a stoop'd falcon ere he takes his prey.

   'Fair Hermes, crown'd with feathers, fluttering light,
I had a splendid dream of thee last night:
I saw thee sitting, on a throne of gold,   70
Among the Gods, upon Olympus old,
The only sad one; for thou didst not hear
The soft, lute-finger'd Muses chaunting clear,
Nor even Apollo when he sang alone,
Deaf to his throbbing throat's long, long melodious moan.

I dreamt I saw thee, robed in purple flakes,
Break amorous through the clouds, as morning breaks,
And, swiftly as a bright Phœbean dart,
Strike for the Cretan isle; and here thou art!
Too gentle Hermes, hast thou found the maid?'   80
Whereat the star of Lethe not delay'd
His rosy eloquence, and thus inquired:
'Thou smooth-lipp'd serpent, surely high inspired!
Thou beauteous wreath, with melancholy eyes,
Possess whatever bliss thou canst devise,
Telling me only where my nymph is fled, —
Where she doth breathe!' 'Bright planet, thou hast said,'
Return'd the snake, 'but seal with oaths, fair God!'
'I swear,' said Hermes, 'by my serpent rod,
And by thine eyes, and by thy starry crown!'   90
Light flew his earnest words, among the blossoms blown.
Then thus again the brilliance feminine:
'Too frail of heart! for this lost nymph of thine,
Free as the air, invisibly, she strays
About these thornless wilds; her pleasant days
She tastes unseen; unseen her nimble feet
Leave traces in the grass and flowers sweet;
From weary tendrils, and bow'd branches green,
She plucks the fruit unseen, she bathes unseen:
And by my power is her beauty veil'd   100
To keep it unaffronted, unassail'd
By the love-glances of unlovely eyes,
Of Satyrs, Fauns, and blear'd Silenus' sighs.
Pale grew her immortality, for woe
Of all these lovers, and she grieved so
I took compassion on her, bade her steep
Her hair in weïrd syrops, that would keep
Her loveliness invisible, yet free
To wander as she loves, in liberty.
Thou shalt behold her, Hermes, thou alone,   110
If thou wilt, as thou swearest, grant my boon!'
Then, once again, the charmed God began
An oath, and through the serpent's ears it ran
Warm, tremulous, devout, psalterian.
Ravish'd, she lifted her Circean head,
Blush'd a live damask, and swift-lisping said,

'I was a woman, let me have once more
A woman's shape, and charming as before.
I love a youth of Corinth — O the bliss!
Give me my woman's form, and place me where he is.   120
Stoop, Hermes, let me breathe upon thy brow,
And thou shalt see thy sweet nymph even now.'
The God on half-shut feathers sank serene,
She breath'd upon his eyes, and swift was seen
Of both the guarded nymph near-smiling on the green.
It was no dream; or say a dream it was,
Real are the dreams of Gods, and smoothly pass
Their pleasures in a long immortal dream.
One warm, flush'd moment, hovering, it might seem
Dash'd by the wood-nymph's beauty, so he burn'd;   130
Then, lighting on the printless verdure, turn'd
To the swoon'd serpent, and with languid arm,
Delicate, put to proof the lythe Caducean charm.
So done, upon the nymph his eyes he bent
Full of adoring tears and blandishment,
And towards her stept: she, like a moon in wane,
Faded before him, cower'd, nor could restrain
Her fearful sobs, self-folding like a flower
That faints into itself at evening hour:
But the God fostering her chilled hand,   140
She felt the warmth, her eyelids open'd bland,
And, like new flowers at morning song of bees,
Bloom'd, and gave up her honey to the lees.
Into the green-recessed woods they flew;
Nor grew they pale, as mortal lovers do.

    Left to herself, the serpent now began
To change; her elfin blood in madness ran,
Her mouth foam'd, and the grass, therewith besprent,
Wither'd at dew so sweet and virulent;
Her eyes in torture fix'd, and anguish drear,   150
Hot, glaz'd, and wide, with lid-lashes all sear,
Flash'd phosphor and sharp sparks, without one cooling tear.
The colours all inflam'd throughout her train,
She writh'd about, convuls'd with scarlet pain:
A deep volcanian yellow took the place
Of all her milder-mooned body's grace;

And, as the lava ravishes the mead,
Spoilt all her silver mail, and golden brede;
Made gloom of all her frecklings, streaks and bars,
Eclips'd her crescents, and lick'd up her stars: 160
So that, in moments few, she was undrest
Of all her sapphires, greens, and amethyst,
And rubious-argent: of all these bereft,
Nothing but pain and ugliness were left.
Still shone her crown; that vanish'd, also she
Melted and disappear'd as suddenly;
And in the air, her new voice luting soft,
Cried, 'Lycius! gentle Lycius!' – Borne aloft
With the bright mists about the mountains hoar
These words dissolv'd: Crete's forests heard no more.   170

    Whither fled Lamia, now a lady bright,
A full-born beauty new and exquisite?
She fled into that valley they pass o'er
Who go to Corinth from Cenchreas' shore;
And rested at the foot of those wild hills,
The rugged founts of the Peræan rills,
And of that other ridge whose barren back
Stretches, with all its mist and cloudy rack,
South-westward to Cleone. There she stood
About a young bird's flutter from a wood,   180
Fair, on a sloping green of mossy tread,
By a clear pool, wherein she passioned
To see herself escap'd from so sore ills,
While her robes flaunted with the daffodils.

    Ah, happy Lycius! – for she was a maid
More beautiful than ever twisted braid,
Or sigh'd, or blush'd, or on spring-flowered lea
Spread a green kirtle to the minstrelsy:
A virgin purest lipp'd, yet in the lore
Of love deep learned to the red heart's core: 190
Not one hour old, yet of sciential brain
To unperplex bliss from its neighbour pain;
Define their pettish limits, and estrange
Their points of contact, and swift counterchange;
Intrigue with the specious chaos, and dispart

Its most ambiguous atoms with sure art;
As though in Cupid's college she had spent
Sweet days a lovely graduate, still unshent,
And kept his rosy terms in idle languishment.

   Why this fair creature chose so fairily   200
By the wayside to linger, we shall see;
But first 'tis fit to tell how she could muse
And dream, when in the serpent prison-house,
Of all she list, strange or magnificent:
How, ever, where she will'd, her spirit went;
Whether to faint Elysium, or where
Down through tress-lifting waves the Nereids fair
Wind into Thetis' bower by many a pearly stair;
Or where God Bacchus drains his cups divine,
Stretch'd out, at ease, beneath a glutinous pine;   210
Or where in Pluto's gardens palatine
Mulciber's columns gleam in far piazzian line.
And sometimes into cities she would send
Her dream, with feast and rioting to blend;
And once, while among mortals dreaming thus,
She saw the young Corinthian Lycius
Charioting foremost in the envious race,
Like a young Jove with calm uneager face,
And fell into a swooning love of him.
Now on the moth-time of that evening dim   220
He would return that way, as well she knew,
To Corinth from the shore; for freshly blew
The eastern soft wind, and his galley now
Grated the quaystones with her brazen prow
In port Cenchreas, from Egina isle
Fresh anchor'd; whither he had been awhile
To sacrifice to Jove, whose temple there
Waits with high marble doors for blood and incense rare.
Jove heard his vows, and better'd his desire;
For by some freakful chance he made retire   230
From his companions, and set forth to walk,
Perhaps grown wearied of their Corinth talk:
Over the solitary hills he fared,
Thoughtless at first, but ere eve's star appeared
His phantasy was lost, where reason fades,

In the calm'd twilight of Platonic shades.
Lamia beheld him coming, near, more near —
Close to her passing, in indifference drear,
His silent sandals swept the mossy green;
So neighbour'd to him, and yet so unseen   240
She stood: he pass'd, shut up in mysteries,
His mind wrapp'd like his mantle, while her eyes
Follow'd his steps, and her neck regal white
Turn'd — syllabling thus, 'Ah, Lycius bright,
And will you leave me on the hills alone?
Lycius, look back! and be some pity shown.'
He did; not with cold wonder fearingly,
But Orpheus-like at an Eurydice;
For so delicious were the words she sung,
It seem'd he had lov'd them a whole summer long: 250
And soon his eyes had drunk her beauty up,
Leaving no drop in the bewildering cup,
And still the cup was full, — while he, afraid
Lest she should vanish ere his lip had paid
Due adoration, thus began to adore;
Her soft look growing coy, she saw his chain so sure:
'Leave thee alone! Look back! Ah, Goddess, see
Whether my eyes can ever turn from thee!
For pity do not this sad heart belie —
Even as thou vanishest so I shall die.   260
Stay! though a Naiad of the rivers, stay!
To thy far wishes will thy streams obey:
Stay! though the greenest woods be thy domain,
Alone they can drink up the morning rain:
Though a descended Pleiad, will not one
Of thine harmonious sisters keep in tune
Thy spheres, and as thy silver proxy shine?
So sweetly to these ravish'd ears of mine
Came thy sweet greeting, that if thou shouldst fade
Thy memory will waste me to a shade: —   270
For pity do not melt!' — 'If I should stay,'
Said Lamia, 'here, upon this floor of clay,
And pain my steps upon these flowers too rough,
What canst thou say or do of charm enough
To dull the nice remembrance of my home?
Thou canst not ask me with thee here to roam

Over these hills and vales, where no joy is, –
Empty of immortality and bliss!
Thou art a scholar, Lycius, and must know
That finer spirits cannot breathe below   280
In human climes, and live: Alas! poor youth,
What taste of purer air hast thou to soothe
My essence? What serener palaces,
Where I may all my many senses please,
And by mysterious sleights a hundred thirsts appease?
It cannot be – Adieu!' So said, she rose
Tiptoe with white arms spread. He, sick to lose
The amorous promise of her lone complain,
Swoon'd, murmuring of love, and pale with pain.
The cruel lady, without any show   290
Of sorrow for her tender favourite's woe,
But rather, if her eyes could brighter be,
With brighter eyes and slow amenity,
Put her new lips to his, and gave afresh
The life she had so tangled in her mesh:
And as he from one trance was wakening
Into another, she began to sing,
Happy in beauty, life, and love, and every thing,
A song of love, too sweet for earthly lyres,
While, like held breath, the stars drew in their panting fires.   300
And then she whisper'd in such trembling tone,
As those who, safe together met alone
For the first time through many anguish'd days,
Use other speech than looks; bidding him raise
His drooping head, and clear his soul of doubt,
For that she was a woman, and without
Any more subtle fluid in her veins
Than throbbing blood, and that the self-same pains
Inhabited her frail-strung heart as his.
And next she wonder'd how his eyes could miss   310
Her face so long in Corinth, where, she said,
She dwelt but half retir'd, and there had led
Days happy as the gold coin could invent
Without the aid of love; yet in content
Till she saw him, as once she pass'd him by,
Where 'gainst a column he leant thoughtfully
At Venus' temple porch, 'mid baskets heap'd

Of amorous herbs and flowers, newly reap'd
Late on that eve, as 'twas the night before
The Adonian feast; whereof she saw no more,   320
But wept alone those days, for why should she adore?
Lycius from death awoke into amaze,
To see her still, and singing so sweet lays;
Then from amaze into delight he fell
To hear her whisper woman's lore so well;
And every word she spake entic'd him on
To unperplex'd delight and pleasure known.
Let the mad poets say whate'er they please
Of the sweets of Fairies, Peris, Goddesses,
There is not such a treat among them all,   330
Haunters of cavern, lake, and waterfall,
As a real woman, lineal indeed
From Pyrrha's pebbles or old Adam's seed.
Thus gentle Lamia judg'd, and judg'd aright,
That Lycius could not love in half a fright,
So threw the goddess off, and won his heart
More pleasantly by playing woman's part,
With no more awe than what her beauty gave,
That, while it smote, still guaranteed to save.
Lycius to all made eloquent reply,   340
Marrying to every word a twinborn sigh;
And last, pointing to Corinth, ask'd her sweet,
If 'twas too far that night for her soft feet.
The way was short, for Lamia's eagerness
Made, by a spell, the triple league decrease
To a few paces; not at all surmised
By blinded Lycius, so in her comprized.
They pass'd the city gates, he knew not how,
So noiseless, and he never thought to know.

      As men talk in a dream, so Corinth all,   350
Throughout her palaces imperial,
And all her populous streets and temples lewd,
Mutter'd, like tempest in the distance brew'd,
To the wide-spreaded night above her towers.
Men, women, rich and poor, in the cool hours,
Shuffled their sandals o'er the pavement white,
Companion'd or alone; while many a light

Flared, here and there, from wealthy festivals,
And threw their moving shadows on the walls,
Or found them cluster'd in the corniced shade   360
Of some arch'd temple door, or dusky colonnade.

    Muffling his face, of greeting friends in fear,
Her fingers he press'd hard, as one came near
With curl'd gray beard, sharp eyes, and smooth bald crown,
Slow-stepp'd, and robed in philosophic gown:
Lycius shrank closer, as they met and past,
Into his mantle, adding wings to haste,
While hurried Lamia trembled: 'Ah,' said he,
'Why do you shudder, love, so ruefully?
Why does your tender palm dissolve in dew?' —   370
'I'm wearied,' said fair Lamia: 'tell me who
Is that old man? I cannot bring to mind
His features: — Lycius! wherefore did you blind
Yourself from his quick eyes?' Lycius replied,
' 'Tis Apollonius sage, my trusty guide
And good instructor; but to-night he seems
The ghost of folly haunting my sweet dreams.'

    While yet he spake they had arrived before
A pillar'd porch, with lofty portal door,
Where hung a silver lamp, whose phosphor glow   380
Reflected in the slabbed steps below,
Mild as a star in water; for so new,
And so unsullied was the marble hue,
So through the crystal polish, liquid fine,
Ran the dark veins, that none but feet divine
Could e'er have touch'd there. Sounds Æolian
Breath'd from the hinges, as the ample span
Of the wide doors disclos'd a place unknown
Some time to any, but those two alone,
And a few Persian mutes, who that same year   390
Were seen about the markets: none knew where
They could inhabit; the most curious
Were foil'd, who watch'd to trace them to their house:
And but the flitter-winged verse must tell,
For truth's sake, what woe afterwards befel,
'Twould humour many a heart to leave them thus,
Shut from the busy world of more incredulous.

PART II

Love in a hut, with water and a crust,
Is — Love, forgive us! — cinders, ashes, dust;
Love in a palace is perhaps at last
More grievous torment than a hermit's fast: —
That is a doubtful tale from faery land,
Hard for the non-elect to understand.
Had Lycius liv'd to hand his story down,
He might have given the moral a fresh frown,
Or clench'd it quite: but too short was their bliss
To breed distrust and hate, that make the soft voice hiss.   10
Besides, there, nightly, with terrific glare,
Love, jealous grown of so complete a pair,
Hover'd and buzz'd his wings, with fearful roar,
Above the lintel of their chamber door,
And down the passage cast a glow upon the floor.

　　For all this came a ruin: side by side
They were enthroned, in the even tide,
Upon a couch, near to a curtaining
Whose airy texture, from a golden string,
Floated into the room, and let appear   20
Unveil'd the summer heaven, blue and clear,
Betwixt two marble shafts: — there they reposed,
Where use had made it sweet, with eyelids closed,
Saving a tythe which love still open kept,
That they might see each other while they almost slept;
When from the slope side of a suburb hill,
Deafening the swallow's twitter, came a thrill
Of trumpets — Lycius started — the sounds fled,
But left a thought, a buzzing in his head.
For the first time, since first he harbour'd in   30
That purple-lined palace of sweet sin,
His spirit pass'd beyond its golden bourn
Into the noisy world almost forsworn.
The lady, ever watchful, penetrant,
Saw this with pain, so arguing a want
Of something more, more than her empery
Of joys; and she began to moan and sigh
Because he mused beyond her, knowing well
That but a moment's thought is passion's passing bell.

'Why do you sigh, fair creature?' whisper'd he: 40
'Why do you think?' return'd she tenderly:
'You have deserted me; – where am I now?
Not in your heart while care weighs on your brow:
No, no, you have dismiss'd me; and I go
From your breast houseless: ay, it must be so.'
He answer'd, bending to her open eyes,
Where he was mirror'd small in paradise,
'My silver planet, both of eve and morn!
Why will you plead yourself so sad forlorn,
While I am striving how to fill my heart   50
With deeper crimson, and a double smart?
How to entangle, trammel up and snare
Your soul in mine, and labyrinth you there
Like the hid scent in an unbudded rose?
Ay, a sweet kiss – you see your mighty woes.
My thoughts! shall I unveil them? Listen then!
What mortal hath a prize, that other men
May be confounded and abash'd withal,
But lets it sometimes pace abroad majestical,
And triumph, as in thee I should rejoice   60
Amid the hoarse alarm of Corinth's voice.
Let my foes choke, and my friends shout afar,
While through the thronged streets your bridal car
Wheels round its dazzling spokes.' – The lady's cheek
Trembled; she nothing said, but, pale and meek,
Arose and knelt before him, wept a rain
Of sorrows at his words; at last with pain
Beseeching him, the while his hand she wrung,
To change his purpose. He thereat was stung,
Perverse, with stronger fancy to reclaim   70
Her wild and timid nature to his aim:
Besides, for all his love, in self despite,
Against his better self, he took delight
Luxurious in her sorrows, soft and new.
His passion, cruel grown, took on a hue
Fierce and sanguineous as 'twas possible
In one whose brow had no dark veins to swell.
Fine was the mitigated fury, like
Apollo's presence when in act to strike
The serpent – Ha, the serpent! certes, she   80

Was none. She burnt, she lov'd the tyranny,
And, all subdued, consented to the hour
When to the bridal he should lead his paramour.
Whispering in midnight silence, said the youth,
'Sure some sweet name thou hast, though, by my truth,
I have not ask'd it, ever thinking thee
Not mortal, but of heavenly progeny,
As still I do. Hast any mortal name,
Fit appellation for this dazzling frame?
Or friends or kinsfolk on the citied earth,   90
To share our marriage feast and nuptial mirth?'
'I have no friends,' said Lamia, 'no, not one;
My presence in wide Corinth hardly known:
My parents' bones are in their dusty urns
Sepulchred, where no kindled incense burns,
Seeing all their luckless race are dead, save me,
And I neglect the holy rite for thee.
Even as you list invite your many guests;
But if, as now it seems, your vision rests
With any pleasure on me, do not bid   100
Old Apollonius – from him keep me hid.'
Lycius, perplex'd at words so blind and blank,
Made close inquiry; from whose touch she shrank,
Feigning a sleep; and he to the dull shade
Of deep sleep in a moment was betray'd.

It was the custom then to bring away
The bride from home at blushing shut of day,
Veil'd, in a chariot, heralded along
By strewn flowers, torches, and a marriage song,
With other pageants: but this fair unknown   110
Had not a friend. So being left alone,
(Lycius was gone to summon all his kin)
And knowing surely she could never win
His foolish heart from its mad pompousness,
She set herself, high-thoughted, how to dress
The misery in fit magnificence.
She did so, but 'tis doubtful how and whence
Came, and who were her subtle servitors.
About the halls, and to and from the doors,
There was a noise of wings, till in short space   120

The glowing banquet-room shone with wide-arched grace.
A haunting music, sole perhaps and lone
Supportress of the faery-roof, made moan
Throughout, as fearful the whole charm might fade.
Fresh carved cedar, mimicking a glade
Of palm and plantain, met from either side,
High in the midst, in honour of the bride:
Two palms and then two plantains, and so on,
From either side their stems branch'd one to one
All down the aisled place; and beneath all   130
There ran a stream of lamps straight on from wall to wall.
So canopied, lay an untasted feast
Teeming with odours. Lamia, regal drest,
Silently paced about, and as she went,
In pale contented sort of discontent,
Mission'd her viewless servants to enrich
The fretted splendour of each nook and niche.
Between the tree-stems, marbled plain at first,
Came jasper pannels; then, anon, there burst
Forth creeping imagery of slighter trees,   140
And with the larger wove in small intricacies.
Approving all, she faded at self-will,
And shut the chamber up, close, hush'd and still,
Complete and ready for the revels rude,
When dreadful guests would come to spoil her solitude.

    The day appear'd, and all the gossip rout.
O senseless Lycius! Madman! wherefore flout
The silent-blessing fate, warm cloister'd hours,
And show to common eyes these secret bowers?
The herd approach'd; each guest, with busy brain,   150
Arriving at the portal, gaz'd amain,
And enter'd marveling: for they knew the street,
Remember'd it from childhood all complete
Without a gap, yet ne'er before had seen
That royal porch, that high-built fair demesne;
So in they hurried all, maz'd, curious and keen:
Save one, who look'd thereon with eye severe,
And with calm-planted steps walk'd in austere;
'Twas Apollonius: something too he laugh'd,

As though some knotty problem, that had daft   160
His patient thought, had now begun to thaw,
And solve and melt: — 'twas just as he foresaw.

He met within the murmurous vestibule
His young disciple. ' 'Tis no common rule,
Lycius,' said he, 'for uninvited guest
To force himself upon you, and infest
With an unbidden presence the bright throng
Of younger friends; yet must I do this wrong,
And you forgive me.' Lycius blush'd, and led
The old man through the inner doors broad-spread;   170
With reconciling words and courteous mien
Turning into sweet milk the sophist's spleen.

Of wealthy lustre was the banquet-room,
Fill'd with pervading brilliance and perfume:
Before each lucid pannel fuming stood
A censer fed with myrrh and spiced wood,
Each by a sacred tripod held aloft,
Whose slender feet wide-swerv'd upon the soft
Wool-woofed carpets: fifty wreaths of smoke
From fifty censers their light voyage took   180
To the high roof, still mimick'd as they rose
Along the mirror'd walls by twin-clouds odorous.
Twelve sphered tables, by silk seats insphered,
High as the level of a man's breast rear'd
On libbard's paws, upheld the heavy gold
Of cups and goblets, and the store thrice told
Of Ceres' horn, and, in huge vessels, wine
Come from the gloomy tun with merry shine.
Thus loaded with a feast the tables stood,
Each shrining in the midst the image of a God.   190

When in an antichamber every guest
Had felt the cold full sponge to pleasure press'd,
By minist'ring slaves, upon his hands and feet,
And fragrant oils with ceremony meet
Pour'd on his hair, they all mov'd to the feast
In white robes, and themselves in order placed
Around the silken couches, wondering

Whence all this mighty cost and blaze of wealth could
    spring.

    Soft went the music the soft air along,
While fluent Greek a vowel'd undersong   200
Kept up among the guests, discoursing low
At first, for scarcely was the wine at flow;
But when the happy vintage touch'd their brains,
Louder they talk, and louder come the strains
Of powerful instruments: — the gorgeous dyes,
The space, the splendour of the draperies,
The roof of awful richness, nectarous cheer,
Beautiful slaves, and Lamia's self, appear,
Now, when the wine has done its rosy deed,
And every soul from human trammels freed,   210
No more so strange; for merry wine, sweet wine,
Will make Elysian shades not too fair, too divine.

    Soon was God Bacchus at meridian height;
Flush'd were their cheeks, and bright eyes double bright:
Garlands of every green, and every scent
From vales deflower'd, or forest-trees branch-rent,
In baskets of bright osier'd gold were brought
High as the handles heap'd, to suit the thought
Of every guest; that each, as he did please,
Might fancy-fit his brows, silk-pillow'd at his ease.   220

    What wreath for Lamia? What for Lycius?
What for the sage, old Apollonius?
Upon her aching forehead be there hung
The leaves of willow and of adder's tongue;
And for the youth, quick, let us strip for him
The thyrsus, that his watching eyes may swim
Into forgetfulness; and, for the sage,
Let spear-grass and the spiteful thistle wage
War on his temples. Do not all charms fly
At the mere touch of cold philosophy?   230
There was an awful rainbow once in heaven:
We know her woof, her texture; she is given
In the dull catalogue of common things.
Philosophy will clip an Angel's wings,

Conquer all mysteries by rule and line,
Empty the haunted air, and gnomed mine –
Unweave a rainbow, as it erewhile made
The tender-person'd Lamia melt into a shade.

  By her glad Lycius sitting, in chief place,
Scarce saw in all the room another face,   240
Till, checking his love trance, a cup he took
Full brimm'd, and opposite sent forth a look
'Cross the broad table, to beseech a glance
From his old teacher's wrinkled countenance,
And pledge him. The bald-head philosopher
Had fix'd his eye, without a twinkle or stir
Full on the alarmed beauty of the bride,
Brow-beating her fair form, and troubling her sweet pride.
Lycius then press'd her hand, with devout touch,
As pale it lay upon the rosy couch: 250
'Twas icy, and the cold ran through his veins;
Then sudden it grew hot, and all the pains
Of an unnatural heat shot to his heart.
'Lamia, what means this? Wherefore dost thou start?
Know'st thou that man?' Poor Lamia answer'd not.
He gaz'd into her eyes, and not a jot
Own'd they the lovelorn piteous appeal:
More, more he gaz'd: his human senses reel:
Some hungry spell that loveliness absorbs;
There was no recognition in those orbs.   260
'Lamia!' he cried – and no soft-toned reply.
The many heard, and the loud revelry
Grew hush; the stately music no more breathes;
The myrtle sicken'd in a thousand wreaths.
By faint degrees, voice, lute, and pleasure ceased;
A deadly silence step by step increased,
Until it seem'd a horrid presence there,
And not a man but felt the terror in his hair.
'Lamia!' he shriek'd; and nothing but the shriek
With its sad echo did the silence break.   270
'Begone, foul dream!' he cried, gazing again
In the bride's face, where now no azure vein
Wander'd on fair-spaced temples; no soft bloom
Misted the cheek; no passion to illume

The deep-recessed vision: — all was blight;
Lamia, no longer fair, there sat a deadly white.
'Shut, shut those juggling eyes, thou ruthless man!
Turn them aside, wretch! or the righteous ban
Of all the Gods, whose dreadful images
Here represent their shadowy presences,   280
May pierce them on the sudden with the thorn
Of painful blindness; leaving thee forlorn,
In trembling dotage to the feeblest fright
Of conscience, for their long offended might,
For all thine impious proud-heart sophistries,
Unlawful magic, and enticing lies.
Corinthians! look upon that gray-beard wretch!
Mark how, possess'd, his lashless eyelids stretch
Around his demon eyes! Corinthians, see!
My sweet bride withers at their potency.'   290
'Fool!' said the sophist, in an under-tone
Gruff with contempt; which a death-nighing moan
From Lycius answer'd, as heart-struck and lost,
He sank supine beside the aching ghost.
'Fool! Fool!' repeated he, while his eyes still
Relented not, nor mov'd; 'from every ill
Of life have I preserv'd thee to this day,
And shall I see thee made a serpent's prey?'
Then Lamia breath'd death breath; the sophist's eye,
Like a sharp spear, went through her utterly,   300
Keen, cruel, perceant, stinging: she, as well
As her weak hand could any meaning tell,
Motion'd him to be silent; vainly so,
He look'd and look'd again a level — No!
'A Serpent!' echoed he; no sooner said,
Than with a frightful scream she vanished:
And Lycius' arms were empty of delight,
As were his limbs of life, from that same night.
On the high couch he lay! — his friends came round —
Supported him — no pulse, or breath they found,   310
And, in its marriage robe, the heavy body wound.

To Autumn

1

Season of mists and mellow fruitfulness,
   Close bosom-friend of the maturing sun;
Conspiring with him how to load and bless
   With fruit the vines that round the thatch-eves run;
To bend with apples the moss'd cottage-trees,
   And fill all fruit with ripeness to the core;
     To swell the gourd, and plump the hazel shells
With a sweet kernel; to set budding more,
   And still more, later flowers for the bees,
   Until they think warm days will never cease,   10
     For Summer has o'er-brimm'd their clammy cells.

2

Who hath not seen thee oft amid thy store?
   Sometimes whoever seeks abroad may find
Thee sitting careless on a granary floor,
   Thy hair soft-lifted by the winnowing wind;
Or on a half-reap'd furrow sound asleep,
   Drows'd with the fume of poppies, while thy hook
     Spares the next swath and all its twined flowers:
And sometimes like a gleaner thou dost keep
   Steady thy laden head across a brook;   20
   Or by a cyder-press, with patient look,
     Thou watchest the last oozings hours by hours.

3

Where are the songs of Spring? Ay, where are they?
   Think not of them, thou hast thy music too, –
While barred clouds bloom the soft-dying day,
   And touch the stubble-plains with rosy hue;
Then in a wailful choir the small gnats mourn
   Among the river sallows, borne aloft
     Or sinking as the light wind lives or dies;
And full-grown lambs loud bleat from hilly bourn;   30
   Hedge-crickets sing; and now with treble soft
   The red-breast whistles from a garden-croft;
     And gathering swallows twitter in the skies.

The Fall of Hyperion: A Dream

Fanatics have their dreams wherewith they weave
A paradise for a sect; the savage too
From forth the loftiest fashion of his sleep
Guesses at heaven: pity these have not
Trac'd upon vellum, or wild Indian leaf
The shadows of melodious utterance:
But bare of laurel they live, dream, and die,
For Poesy alone can tell her dreams,
With the fine spell of words alone can save
Imagination from the sable charm   10
And dumb enchantment. Who alive can say
'Thou art no poet; may'st not tell thy dreams'?
Since every man whose soul is not a clod
Hath visions, and would speak, if he had lov'd
And been well nurtured in his mother tongue.
Whether the dream now purposed to rehearse
Be poet's or fanatic's will be known
When this warm scribe my hand is in the grave.

   Methought I stood where trees of every clime,
Palm, myrtle, oak, and sycamore, and beech,   20
With plantane, and spice blossoms, made a screen;
In neighbourhood of fountains, by the noise
Soft showering in mine ears, and, by the touch
Of scent, not far from roses. Turning round,
I saw an arbour with a drooping roof
Of trellis vines, and bells, and larger blooms,
Like floral-censers swinging light in air;
Before its wreathed doorway, on a mound
Of moss, was spread a feast of summer fruits,
Which, nearer seen, seem'd refuse of a meal   30
By angel tasted, or our mother Eve;
For empty shells were scattered on the grass,
And grape stalks but half bare, and remnants more,
Sweet smelling, whose pure kinds I could not know.
Still was more plenty than the fabled horn

Thrice emptied could pour forth, at banqueting
For Proserpine return'd to her own fields,
Where the white heifers low. And appetite
More yearning than on earth I ever felt
Growing within, I ate deliciously;   40
And, after not long, thirsted, for thereby
Stood a cool vessel of transparent juice,
Sipp'd by the wander'd bee, the which I took,
And, pledging all the mortals of the world,
And all the dead whose names are in our lips,
Drank. That full draught is parent of my theme.
No Asian poppy, nor elixir fine
Of the soon fading jealous caliphat;
No poison gender'd in close monkish cell
To thin the scarlet conclave of old men,   50
Could so have rapt unwilling life away.
Among the fragrant husks and berries crush'd,
Upon the grass I struggled hard against
The domineering potion; but in vain:
The cloudy swoon came on, and down I sunk
Like a Silenus on an antique vase.
How long I slumber'd 'tis a chance to guess.
When sense of life return'd, I started up
As if with wings; but the fair trees were gone,
The mossy mound and arbour were no more;   60
I look'd around upon the carved sides
Of an old sanctuary, with roof august
Builded so high, it seem'd that filmed clouds
Might sail beneath, as o'er the stars of heaven.
So old the place was, I remembered none
The like upon the earth; what I had seen
Of grey cathedrals, buttress'd walls, rent towers,
The superannuations of sunk realms,
Or nature's rocks hard toil'd in winds and waves,
Seem'd but the failing of decrepit things   70
To that eternal domed monument.
Upon the marble, at my feet, there lay
Store of strange vessels and large draperies
Which needs had been of dyed asbestus wove,
Or in that place the moth could not corrupt,
So white the linen; so, in some, distinct

Ran imageries from a sombre loom.
All in a mingled heap confus'd there lay
Robes, golden tongs, censer, and chafing dish.
Girdles, and chains, and holy jewelries.   80

   Turning from these, with awe once more I rais'd
My eyes to fathom the space every way;
The embossed roof, the silent massive range
Of columns north and south, ending in mist
Of nothing; then to eastward, where black gates
Were shut against the sunrise evermore.
Then to the west I look'd, and saw far off
An image, huge of feature as a cloud,
At level of whose feet an altar slept,
To be approach'd on either side by steps,   90
And marble balustrade, and patient travail
To count with toil the innumerable degrees.
Towards the altar sober-pac'd I went,
Repressing haste, as too unholy there;
And, coming nearer, saw beside the shrine
One minist'ring; and there arose a flame.
When in mid-May the sickening east wind
Shifts sudden to the south, the small warm rain
Melts out the frozen incense from all flowers,
And fills the air with so much pleasant health   100
That even the dying man forgets his shroud;
Even so that lofty sacrificial fire,
Sending forth Maian incense, spread around
Forgetfulness of every thing but bliss,
And clouded all the altar with soft smoke,
From whose white fragrant curtains thus I heard
Language pronounc'd. 'If thou canst not ascend
These steps, die on that marble where thou art.
Thy flesh, near cousin to the common dust,
Will parch for lack of nutriment – thy bones   110
Will wither in few years, and vanish so
That not the quickest eye could find a grain
Of what thou now art on that pavement cold.
The sands of thy short life are spent this hour,
And no hand in the universe can turn
Thy hour glass, if these gummed leaves be burnt

Ere thou canst mount up these immortal steps.'
I heard, I look'd: two senses both at once
So fine, so subtle, felt the tyranny
Of that fierce threat, and the hard task proposed.   120
Prodigious seem'd the toil; the leaves were yet
Burning, — when suddenly a palsied chill
Struck from the paved level up my limbs,
And was ascending quick to put cold grasp
Upon those streams that pulse beside the throat:
I shriek'd; and the sharp anguish of my shriek
Stung my own ears — I strove hard to escape
The numbness; strove to gain the lowest step.
Slow, heavy, deadly was my pace: the cold
Grew stifling, suffocating, at the heart;   130
And when I clasp'd my hands I felt them not.
One minute before death, my iced foot touch'd
The lowest stair; and as it touch'd, life seem'd
To pour in at the toes: I mounted up,
As once fair angels on a ladder flew
From the green turf to heaven. — 'Holy Power,'
Cried I, approaching near the horned shrine,
'What am I that should so be sav'd from death?
What am I that another death come not
To choak my utterance sacrilegious here?'   140
Then said the veiled shadow — 'Thou hast felt
What 'tis to die and live again before
Thy fated hour. That thou hadst power to do so
Is thy own safety; thou hast dated on
Thy doom.' — 'High Prophetess,' said I, 'purge off
Benign, if so it please thee, my mind's film.'
'None can usurp this height,' return'd that shade,
'But those to whom the miseries of the world
Are misery, and will not let them rest.
All else who find a haven in the world,   150
Where they may thoughtless sleep away their days,
If by a chance into this fane they come,
Rot on the pavement where thou rotted'st half.' —
'Are there not thousands in the world,' said I,
Encourag'd by the sooth voice of the shade,
'Who love their fellows even to the death;
Who feel the giant agony of the world;

And more, like slaves to poor humanity,
Labour for mortal good? I sure should see
Other men here: but I am here alone.'   160
'They whom thou spak'st of are no vision'ries,'
Rejoin'd that voice – 'They are no dreamers weak,
They seek no wonder but the human face;
No music but a happy-noted voice –
They come not here, they have no thought to come –
And thou art here, for thou art less than they.
What benefit canst thou do, or all thy tribe,
To the great world? Thou art a dreaming thing;
A fever of thyself – think of the earth;
What bliss even in hope is there for thee?   170
What haven? Every creature hath its home;
Every sole man hath days of joy and pain,
Whether his labours be sublime or low –
The pain alone; the joy alone; distinct:
Only the dreamer venoms all his days,
Bearing more woe than all his sins deserve.
Therefore, that happiness be somewhat shar'd,
Such things as thou art are admitted oft
Into like gardens thou didst pass erewhile,
And suffer'd in these temples; for that cause   180
Thou standest safe beneath this statue's knees.'
'That I am favored for unworthiness,
By such propitious parley medicin'd
In sickness not ignoble, I rejoice,
Aye, and could weep for love of such award.'
So answer'd I, continuing, 'If it please,
Majestic shadow, tell me: sure not all
Those melodies sung into the world's ear
Are useless: sure a poet is a sage;
A humanist, physician to all men.   190
That I am none I feel, as vultures feel
They are no birds when eagles are abroad.
What am I then? Thou spakest of my tribe:
What tribe?' – The tall shade veil'd in drooping white
Then spake, so much more earnest, that the breath
Mov'd the thin linen folds that drooping hung
About a golden censer from the hand
Pendent. – 'Art thou not of the dreamer tribe?

The poet and the dreamer are distinct,
Diverse, sheer opposite, antipodes.   200
The one pours out a balm upon the world,
The other vexes it.' Then shouted I
Spite of myself, and with a Pythia's spleen,
'Apollo! faded, far flown Apollo!
Where is thy misty pestilence to creep
Into the dwellings, through the door crannies,
Of all mock lyrists, large self worshipers,
And careless hectorers in proud bad verse.
Though I breathe death with them it will be life
To see them sprawl before me into graves.   210
Majestic shadow, tell me where I am:
Whose altar this; for whom this incense curls:
What image this, whose face I cannot see,
For the broad marble knees; and who thou art,
Of accent feminine, so courteous.'
Then the tall shade in drooping linens veil'd
Spake out, so much more earnest, that her breath
Stirr'd the thin folds of gauze that drooping hung
About a golden censer from her hand
Pendent; and by her voice I knew she shed   220
Long treasured tears. 'This temple sad and lone
Is all spar'd from the thunder of a war
Foughten long since by giant hierarchy
Against rebellion: this old image here,
Whose carved features wrinkled as he fell,
Is Saturn's; I, Moneta, left supreme
Sole priestess of his desolation.' –
I had no words to answer; for my tongue,
Useless, could find about its roofed home
No syllable of a fit majesty   230
To make rejoinder to Moneta's mourn.
There was a silence while the altar's blaze
Was fainting for sweet food: I look'd thereon
And on the paved floor, where nigh were pil'd
Faggots of cinnamon, and many heaps
Of other crisped spice-wood – then again
I look'd upon the altar and its horns
Whiten'd with ashes, and its lang'rous flame,
And then upon the offerings again;

And so by turns – till sad Moneta cried,   240
'The sacrifice is done, but not the less
Will I be kind to thee for thy good will.
My power, which to me is still a curse,
Shall be to thee a wonder; for the scenes
Still swooning vivid through my globed brain
With an electral changing misery
Thou shalt with those dull mortal eyes behold,
Free from all pain, if wonder pain thee not.'
As near as an immortal's sphered words
Could to a mother's soften, were these last: 250
But yet I had a terror of her robes,
And chiefly of the veils, that from her brow
Hung pale, and curtain'd her in mysteries
That made my heart too small to hold its blood.
This saw that Goddess, and with sacred hand
Parted the veils. Then saw I a wan face,
Not pin'd by human sorrows, but bright blanch'd
By an immortal sickness which kills not;
It works a constant change, which happy death
Can put no end to; deathwards progressing   260
To no death was that visage; it had pass'd
The lily and the snow; and beyond these
I must not think now, though I saw that face –
But for her eyes I should have fled away.
They held me back, with a benignant light,
Soft mitigated by divinest lids
Half closed, and visionless entire they seem'd
Of all external things – they saw me not,
But in blank splendor beam'd like the mild moon,
Who comforts those she sees not, who knows not   270
What eyes are upward cast. As I had found
A grain of gold upon a mountain's side,
And twing'd with avarice strain'd out my eyes
To search its sullen entrails rich with ore,
So at the view of sad Moneta's brow,
I ached to see what things the hollow brain
Behind enwombed: what high tragedy
In the dark secret chambers of her skull
Was acting, that could give so dread a stress
To her cold lips, and fill with such a light   280

Her planetary eyes; and touch her voice
With such a sorrow. 'Shade of Memory!'
Cried I, with act adorant at her feet,
'By all the gloom hung round thy fallen house,
By this last temple, by the golden age,
By great Apollo, thy dear foster child,
And by thy self, forlorn divinity,
The pale Omega of a wither'd race,
Let me behold, according as thou said'st,
What in thy brain so ferments to and fro.' –   290
No sooner had this conjuration pass'd
My devout lips, than side by side we stood,
(Like a stunt bramble by a solemn pine)
Deep in the shady sadness of a vale,
Far sunken from the healthy breath of morn,
Far from the fiery noon, and eve's one star.
Onward I look'd beneath the gloomy boughs,
And saw, what first I thought an image huge,
Like to the image pedestal'd so high
In Saturn's temple. Then Moneta's voice   300
Came brief upon mine ear, – 'So Saturn sat
When he had lost his realms.' – Whereon there grew
A power within me of enormous ken,
To see as a God sees, and take the depth
Of things as nimbly as the outward eye
Can size and shape pervade. The lofty theme
At those few words hung vast before my mind,
With half unravel'd web. I set myself
Upon an eagle's watch, that I might see,
And seeing ne'er forget. No stir of life   310
Was in this shrouded vale, not so much air
As in the zoning of a summer's day
Robs not one light seed from the feather'd grass,
But where the dead leaf fell there did it rest:
A stream went voiceless by, still deaden'd more
By reason of the fallen divinity
Spreading more shade: the Naiad mid her reeds
Press'd her cold finger closer to her lips.
Along the margin sand large footmarks went
No farther than to where old Saturn's feet   320
Had rested, and there slept, how long a sleep!

Degraded, cold, upon the sodden ground
His old right hand lay nerveless, listless, dead,
Unsceptred; and his realmless eyes were clos'd,
While his bow'd head seem'd listening to the Earth,
His antient mother, for some comfort yet.

   It seem'd no force could wake him from his place;
But there came one who with a kindred hand
Touch'd his wide shoulders, after bending low
With reverence, though to one who knew it not.   330
Then came the griev'd voice of Mnemosyne,
And griev'd I hearken'd. 'That divinity
Whom thou saw'st step from yon forlornest wood,
And with slow pace approach our fallen King,
Is Thea, softest-natur'd of our brood.'
I mark'd the goddess in fair statuary
Surpassing wan Moneta by the head,
And in her sorrow nearer woman's tears.
There was a listening fear in her regard,
As if calamity had but begun;   340
As if the vanward clouds of evil days
Had spent their malice, and the sullen rear
Was with its stored thunder labouring up.
One hand she press'd upon that aching spot
Where beats the human heart; as if just there,
Though an immortal, she felt cruel pain;
The other upon Saturn's bended neck
She laid, and to the level of his hollow ear
Leaning, with parted lips, some words she spake
In solemn tenor and deep organ tune;   350
Some mourning words, which in our feeble tongue
Would come in this-like accenting; how frail
To that large utterance of the early Gods! –
'Saturn! look up – and for what, poor lost King?
I have no comfort for thee, no – not one:
I cannot cry, *Wherefore thus sleepest thou?*
For heaven is parted from thee, and the earth
Knows thee not, so afflicted, for a God;
And ocean too, with all its solemn noise,
Has from thy sceptre pass'd, and all the air   360
Is emptied of thine hoary majesty.

Thy thunder, captious at the new command,
Rumbles reluctant o'er our fallen house;
And thy sharp lightning in unpracticed hands
Scorches and burns our once serene domain.
With such remorseless speed still come new woes
That unbelief has not a space to breathe.
Saturn, sleep on: – Me thoughtless, why should I
Thus violate thy slumbrous solitude?
Why should I ope thy melancholy eyes?   370
Saturn, sleep on, while at thy feet I weep.'

    As when, upon a tranced summer night,
Forests, branch-charmed by the earnest stars,
Dream, and so dream all night, without a noise,
Save from one gradual solitary gust,
Swelling upon the silence; dying off;
As if the ebbing air had but one wave;
So came these words, and went; the while in tears
She press'd her fair large forehead to the earth,
Just where her fallen hair might spread in curls,   380
A soft and silken mat for Saturn's feet.
Long, long, those two were postured motionless,
Like sculpture builded up upon the grave
Of their own power. A long awful time
I look'd upon them; still they were the same;
The frozen God still bending to the earth,
And the sad Goddess weeping at his feet;
Moneta silent. Without stay or prop
But my own weak mortality, I bore
The load of this eternal quietude,   390
The unchanging gloom, and the three fixed shapes
Ponderous upon my senses a whole moon.
For by my burning brain I measured sure
Her silver seasons shedded on the night,
And every day by day methought I grew
More gaunt and ghostly. Oftentimes I pray'd
Intense, that death would take me from the vale
And all its burthens. Gasping with despair
Of change, hour after hour I curs'd myself:
Until old Saturn rais'd his faded eyes,   400
And look'd around, and saw his kingdom gone,

And all the gloom and sorrow of the place,
And that fair kneeling Goddess at his feet.
As the moist scent of flowers, and grass, and leaves
Fills forest dells with a pervading air
Known to the woodland nostril, so the words
Of Saturn fill'd the mossy glooms around,
Even to the hollows of time-eaten oaks,
And to the windings in the foxes' hole,
With sad low tones, while thus he spake, and sent   410
Strange musings to the solitary Pan.

   'Moan, brethren, moan; for we are swallow'd up
And buried from all godlike exercise
Of influence benign on planets pale,
And peaceful sway above man's harvesting,
And all those acts which deity supreme
Doth ease its heart of love in. Moan and wail.
Moan, brethren, moan; for lo! the rebel spheres
Spin round, the stars their antient courses keep,
Clouds still with shadowy moisture haunt the earth,   420
Still suck their fill of light from sun and moon,
Still buds the tree, and still the sea-shores murmur.
There is no death in all the universe,
No smell of death – there shall be death – Moan, moan,
Moan, Cybele, moan, for thy pernicious babes
Have chang'd a God into a shaking palsy.
Moan, brethren, moan; for I have no strength left,
Weak as the reed – weak – feeble as my voice –
O, O, the pain, the pain of feebleness.
Moan, moan; for still I thaw – or give me help: 430
Throw down those imps and give me victory.
Let me hear other groans, and trumpets blown
Of triumph calm, and hymns of festival
From the gold peaks of heaven's high piled clouds;
Voices of soft proclaim, and silver stir
Of strings in hollow shells; and let there be
Beautiful things made new for the surprize
Of the sky children.' – So he feebly ceas'd,
With such a poor and sickly sounding pause,
Methought I heard some old man of the earth   440
Bewailing earthly loss; nor could my eyes

And ears act with that pleasant unison of sense
Which marries sweet sound with the grace of form,
And dolorous accent from a tragic harp
With large limb'd visions. More I scrutinized:
Still fix'd he sat beneath the sable trees,
Whose arms spread straggling in wild serpent forms,
With leaves all hush'd: his awful presence there
(Now all was silent) gave a deadly lie
To what I erewhile heard: only his lips   450
Trembled amid the white curls of his beard.
They told the truth, though, round, the snowy locks
Hung nobly, as upon the face of heaven
A midday fleece of clouds. Thea arose
And stretch'd her white arm through the hollow dark,
Pointing some whither: whereat he too rose
Like a vast giant seen by men at sea
To grow pale from the waves at dull midnight.
They melted from my sight into the woods:
Ere I could turn, Moneta cried – 'These twain   460
Are speeding to the families of grief,
Where roof'd in by black rocks they waste in pain
And darkness for no hope.' – And she spake on,
As ye may read who can unwearied pass
Onward from the antichamber of this dream,
Where even at the open doors awhile
I must delay, and glean my memory
Of her high phrase: perhaps no further dare.

CANTO II

'Mortal! that thou may'st understand aright
I humanize my sayings to thine ear,
Making comparisons of earthly things;
Or thou might'st better listen to the wind
Whose language is to thee a barren noise,
Though it blows legend-laden through the trees.
In melancholy realms big tears are shed,
More sorrow like to this, and such-like woe,
Too huge for mortal tongue, or pen of scribe.
The Titans fierce, self-hid, or prison-bound,   10
Groan for the old allegiance once more,

Listening in their doom for Saturn's voice.
But one of our whole eagle-brood still keeps
His sov'reignty, and rule, and majesty;
Blazing Hyperion on his orbed fire
Still sits, still snuffs the incense teeming up
From man to the Sun's God: yet unsecure;
For as upon the earth dire prodigies
Fright and perplex, so also shudders he:
Nor at dog's howl, or gloom-bird's even screech,   20
Or the familiar visitings of one
Upon the first toll of his passing bell:
But horrors portion'd to a giant nerve
Make great Hyperion ache. His palace bright,
Bastion'd with pyramids of glowing gold,
And touch'd with shade of bronzed obelisks,
Glares a blood red through all the thousand courts,
Arches, and domes, and fiery galeries:
And all its curtains of Aurorian clouds
Flush angerly: when he would taste the wreaths   30
Of incense breath'd aloft from sacred hills,
Instead of sweets, his ample palate takes
Savour of poisonous brass and metals sick.
Wherefore when harbour'd in the sleepy west,
After the full completion of fair day,
For rest divine upon exalted couch
And slumber in the arms of melody,
He paces through the pleasant hours of ease,
With strides colossal, on from hall to hall;
While, far within each aisle and deep recess,   40
His winged minions in close clusters stand
Amaz'd, and full of fear; like anxious men
Who on a wide plain gather in sad troops,
When earthquakes jar their battlements and towers.
Even now, while Saturn, rous'd from icy trance,
Goes, step for step, with Thea from yon woods,
Hyperion, leaving twilight in the rear,
Is sloping to the threshold of the west.
Thither we tend.' – Now in clear light I stood,
Reliev'd from the dusk vale. Mnemosyne   50
Was sitting on a square edg'd polish'd stone,
That in its lucid depth reflected pure

Her priestess-garments. My quick eyes ran on
From stately nave to nave, from vault to vault,
Through bowers of fragrant and enwreathed light,
And diamond paved lustrous long arcades.
Anon rush'd by the bright Hyperion;
His flaming robes stream'd out beyond his heels,
And gave a roar, as if of earthly fire,
That scar'd away the meek ethereal hours   60
And made their dove-wings tremble: on he flared

*   *   *   *   *   *   *   *   *

'Bright Star, would I were stedfast as thou art'

Bright Star, would I were stedfast as thou art –
　　Not in lone splendor hung aloft the night
And watching, with eternal lids apart,
　　Like nature's patient, sleepless Eremite,
The moving waters at their priestlike task　　　　　5
　　Of pure ablution round earth's human shores,
Or gazing on the new soft-fallen masque
　　Of snow upon the mountains and the moors.
No – yet still stedfast, still unchangeable,
　　Pillow'd upon my fair love's ripening breast,　　　10
To feel for ever its soft swell and fall,
　　Awake for ever in a sweet unrest,
Still, still to hear her tender-taken breath,
And so live ever – or else swoon to death.

'In after-time a sage of mickle lore'

In after-time a sage of mickle lore
Yclep'd Typographus, the Giant took
And did refit his limbs as heretofore,
And made him read in many a learned book,
And into many a lively legend look;　　　　　5
Thereby in goodly themes so training him,
That all his brutishness he quite forsook,
When, meeting Artegall and Talus grim,
The one he struck stone-blind, the other's eyes wox dim

NOTES

Quotations from Milton's poems are taken from *The Poems of John Milton*, ed. John Carey and Alastair Fowler (1968). Quotations from Shakespeare are taken from the appropriate volume in the Arden Shakespeare series; Shakespeare's sonnets are quoted from *The Sonnets and A Lover's Complaint*, ed. John Kerrigan (1986). Wordsworth's poems are quoted from *William Wordsworth. Selected Poetry*, ed. Nicholas Roe (1992); *The Excursion* is quoted from the first edition of 1814.

On Peace (p. 3)
Written probably Apr. 1814, not published by K. First published by Ernest de Selincourt, *Notes & Queries* (4 Feb. 1905), 82.

K uses an irregular Shakespearean sonnet to commemorate the surrender of Napoleon (11 Apr.) and his exile to Elba, apparently bringing the war with France to an end. K echoes the sentiments of Leigh Hunt's leaders in the *Examiner* newspaper at this moment, and also recalls the manner of Wordsworth's *Sonnets Dedicated to Liberty* in *Poems in Two Volumes* (1807). For further reading see Gittings, 70–71; Newey (1989), 266–7; David Pirie, 'Keats', *The Penguin History of Literature. The Romantic Period*, ed. D. Pirie (1994), 343–6.

8   **sweet mountain nymph**: liberty. Cf. Milton, *l'Allegro*, 36: 'The mountain nymph, sweet Liberty'.

9   Gittings, 71, points out that this line is 'practically a translation' of the inscription which decorated Somerset House in celebration of the victory: '*Europa Instaurata, Auspice Britanniae / Tyrannide Subversa, Vindice Libertatis*'.

10–14   cf. Hunt's remarks on the prospect of the restoration of Louis XVIII, May 1814, *The Examiner* (1 May 1814), 273: '[Louis] will not have the power to play the tyrant like some of his predecessors, his subjects will take care, if they remain true to their new charter'. The new French constitution had been agreed, Apr. 1814.

Lines Written on 29 May, the Anniversary of Charles's Restoration, on Hearing the Bells Ringing (p. 3)

Written probably 1814, possibly 1815 not published by K. First published Amy Lowell, *John Keats* (1925), I. 66.

In response to loyal commemoration of Charles II's Restoration in 1660, K recalls three patriotic republicans executed for treason against the king. K's anti-monarchist sentiments echo those of *On Peace*. For further reading, see Barnard, 5–7; Newey (1989), 266–7; David Pirie, 'Keats', *The Penguin History of Literature. The Romantic Period*, ed. D. Pirie (1994), 343–6; Newey (1995), 166–7.

5   Algernon Sydney (1622–83), Lord William Russell (1639–83), executed for conspiracy in the Rye House Plot, and Sir Henry Vane (1613–62), executed for treason during the English Commonwealth. All three were heroes for English liberals and republicans; cf. K's admiration for the seventeenth-century republicans in his letter of 14–31 Oct. 1818 (*Letters*, 164).

Written on the day that Mr Leigh Hunt left Prison (p. 3)
Written 2 Feb. 1815. First published in *1817*, the text reproduced here.

Leigh Hunt (1784–1859), poet and editor of the radical *Examiner* newspaper, was jailed for two years after libelling the Prince Regent in an *Examiner* article, 22 March 1812. The *Examiner* had been a strong influence on K's political and imaginative life since his schooldays at Enfield, although he did not meet Hunt until Oct. 1816. See *Recollections*, 124, 127, 133.

For further reading, see Bate, 40–2; Newey (1989), 265–89; David Pirie, 'Keats', *The Penguin History of Literature. The Romantic Period*, ed. D. Pirie (1994), 354–9; Newey (1995), 167–8.

5   **Minion of grandeur:** an underling dependent on the favour of aristocracy or royal family.
9–11   Edmund Spenser (1552?–99) and John Milton (1608–74): early and enduring influences on K's poetry, and admired by Leigh Hunt.
14   **wretched crew:** cf. the 'horrid crew' of devils in *Paradise Lost*, I. 51.

To Charles Cowden Clarke (p. 4)
Written at Margate, Kent, Sept. 1816. First published in *1817*, the text reproduced here.

CCC (1787–1877) was the son of John Clarke, schoolmaster at Enfield; he befriended K and encouraged his reading and earliest poetic compositions (see Introduction). In Oct. 1816, he introduced K to Leigh Hunt. The poem is a tribute to CCC's friendship and influence, reflecting on K's hopes and difficulties as a poet. For CCC and K see in particular Gittings, 121–3, *Recollections*, 120–57, and for new documentary evidence of CCC's literary and political interests, John Barnard, 'Charles Cowden Clarke's "Cockney" Commonplace Book', *K&H*, 65–87.

6   **Naiad Zephyr:** a composite god invented by K: a naiad was a minor (feminine) deity presiding over rivers, streams, springs (cf. *Endymion*, II. 98–100). A zephyr was a (masculine) god of the wind.

27   **Helicon:** synecdoche: Helicon was the mountain in Boeotia, Greece, from which the 'sparkling' Hippocrene flowed; both were sacred to the Muses.

29–31   CCC introduced K to the works of the Italian poet Torquato Tasso (1544–95). **Baiæ:** the bay of Naples, Tasso's home; **Armida:** heroine of Tasso's *Gerusalemme Liberata* (1581).

33–7   A cluster of allusions of Spenser. CCC introduced K to Spenser's poetry, see *Recollections*, 125–6. **Mulla's stream:** the river near Spenser's home, Kilcolman Castle, Co. Cork, Ireland. **breasts of cream:** cf. Spenser's *Epithalamion*, 175, 'Her brest like to a bowl of cream'. **Belphœbe, Una, Archimago,** characters in Spenser's *Faerie Queene*.

40   **Titania:** queen of the fairies in *A Midsummer Night's Dream*.

41   **Urania:** L: 'one of the Muses . . . who presided over astronomy'; also identified with Venus. Milton invokes Urania as his muse at the opening of *Paradise Lost*, VII.

44   **Libertas:** Leigh Hunt, a political and literary hero for K at this time. CCC introduced K to Hunt shortly after this poem was written (see above).

45   **laurel chaplets:** garlands of laurel, emblems of poetic achievement ('Apollo's glories'); cf. *On receiving a laurel crown from Leigh Hunt*.

46–7   Alluding to Hunt's *The Story of Rimini*, 1. 147 ff., published in Feb. 1816.

52–3   K had known CCC since entering Enfield School in 1803.

59   Referring to *Paradise Lost*.

63   **Atlas:** one of the Titans, in various legends listed by L he was reputed to 'bear the heavens on his shoulders'.

67   K's interest in astronomy dated from his years at Enfield School. The school's founder John Ryland (1723–92) was acquainted with the astronomer William Herschel (1738–1822) who discovered the planet Uranus; see *On first looking into Chapman's Homer*, 9 n. Astronomy was one of the subjects taught at Enfield School, and K won John Bonnycastle's *Introduction to Astronomy* (1807 edn) as a school prize.

68   **Clio:** Muse of History.

69–72   King Alfred, William Tell, and Brutus were all 'patriotic' heroes celebrated in liberal opinion of the day. John Ryland, founder of K's school (see 67 n. above), published *The Life and Character of Alfred the Great* (1784), hailing Alfred as founder of the true constitutional liberties of England.

76   **benefits forget:** cf. 'benefits forgot' in Amiens' song 'Blow, blow, thou winter wind', *As You Like It*, 2.7.186.

84   K had been visiting Margate with his brother Tom since Aug. 1816.

98   **measures:** the metres of poetry.

101   At Margate K had written a sonnet and verse epistle, both entitled *To my Brother George* (not included in this selection).

109–130   Recalling K's friendship with CCC at Enfield and subsequently during his apprenticeship as surgeon at Edmonton. See *Recollections*, 122–5.

110–11   Eighteenth-century composers whose music CCC admired and played. For K's memory of musical evenings at Enfield, see *The Eve of St Agnes*, 261, and *Recollections*, 143. For K and Mozart, see *Letters*, 162, 180.

112   **Erin:** Ireland. K may recall CCC singing Irish folk-songs; possibly he refers to Thomas Moore's *Irish Melodies* (1807).

122   **bland:** gentle.

On first looking into Chapman's Homer (p. 7)
Written Oct. 1816. First published in the *Examiner*, 1 Dec. 1816; subsequently in *1817*, the text reproduced here.

For K's reading in George Chapman's translation of Homer (1616), and his composition of this sonnet, see *Recollections*, 128–31, and Gittings, 127–31. To evoke K's momentous encounter with Chapman's Homer, the sonnet draws on discovery narratives in William Robertson's *History of America* (1777), read by K at school, and the astronomical discoveries of William Herschel as described in K's prize copy of John Bonnycastle's *Introduction to Astronomy* (1807 edn).

For detailed discussion of sources for the poem see J. M. Murry, *Studies in Keats* (1930), and B. Ifor Evans, 'Keats's Approach to the Chapman Sonnet', *Essays and Studies*, 16 (1931). Recent discussion of the sonnet has focused on its historical and political dimensions. See Marjorie Levinson, *Keats's Life of Allegory* (1988), 11–15; Watkins, 26–31; Newey (1995), 165–93.

1–3   A geography of the imagination, associated with discoveries of fabulous wealth in South America as narrated in William Robertson's *History of America*; see above and 11–14 n. below.

4   Poets are the feudal vassals of Apollo, god of poetry.

6   **demesne:** the territory (of poetry) ruled by Homer.

7   Cf. S. T. Coleridge, *A Hymn before Sunrise in the vale of Chamouni*, 72: 'glittering through the pure serene'.

9–10   Recalling William Herschel's discovery of Uranus, described in John Bonnycastle's *Introduction to Astronomy*; see above and *To Charles Cowden Clarke*, 67n.

11–14   Two notable sources have been suggested for these lines: Balboa's rapt contemplation of the Pacific from the isthmus of Darien in Robertson's *History of America* (1792 edn) I. 289–90; and 'the distant, vast Pacific' mentioned in a note to William Gilbert's *The*

Hurricane (1796), quoted in Wordsworth's *Excursion* (1814), 427. As Watkins, 28–31, suggests, Robertson's 'virtually identical' discovery narratives of Cortez and Balboa may explain K's merging them here.

14 **Darien:** the narrow isthmus connecting North and South America, to the north of Colombia.

'Keen, fitful gusts are whisp'ring' (p. 8)
Written Oct. or Nov. 1816. First published *1817*, the text reproduced here.

CCC had introduced K to Leigh Hunt in Oct. 1816, 'a "red-letter day" in the young poet's life' (*Recollections*, 133). This sonnet was composed after an evening visit to Hunt's cottage in the Vale of Health, Hampstead; K faced a walk of over five miles back to London, where he lodged in Dean Street, Southwark. For more on K's early friendship with Hunt, see Bate, 78–94, and Gittings, 131–45.

1–2 Cf. Wordsworth's 'A whirl-blast from behind the hill'.
9–10 A 'characteristic appreciation of the spirit in which he had been received' at Hunt's home (*Recollections*, 134).
11–14 Literary topics discussed with Hunt.
12 **Lycid:** Milton's name for Edward King in his elegy *Lycidas*.
13–14 The Italian poet Petrarch (1304–74) celebrated his love for Laura in his *Canzoniere*. Hunt possessed a picture of Petrarch's meeting with Laura; cf. *Sleep and Poetry*, 389–91.

Addressed to the same ['Great spirits'] (p. 8)
Written 20 Nov. 1816. Published *1817*, the text reproduced here.

This sonnet, the second of three that K addressed to the historical painter Benjamin Robert Haydon (1786–1846), was sent to him in a letter of 20 Nov. 1816 (*Letters*, 2). K had passed the evening of 19 Nov. with Haydon, whom he had first met at Hunt's home the previous month. Haydon's energy, enthusiasm, and gusto 'wrought up' K, as he says in his letter; his sonnet celebrates the artistic achievements of the present age, and looks forward to those of future years. For more on K and Haydon, and the composition of this sonnet, see Bate, 94–7, Gittings, 153–5, and Jack, 23–45.

1 Cf. Wordsworth's sonnet 'Great men have been among us'. Wordsworth's poem was turned towards the past; K's sonnet looks in hope to the present and the future.
2 William Wordsworth (1770–1850), whose *Excursion* (1814) greatly impressed K.
3 **Helvellyn:** a mountain about five miles from Wordsworth's home at Rydal Mount, frequently mentioned in his poems. Mist prevented K from climbing Helvellyn while on his walking tour in July 1818

(*Letters*, 107). In 1842 Haydon painted a celebrated portrait 'Wordsworth on Helvellyn'.

5–6   Characterising Leigh Hunt's poetry, social manner, and political liberalism.

7–8   An elliptical but complimentary comparison of Haydon with the great Renaissance painter Raphael.

9–10   K was perhaps thinking of Shelley, and almost certainly of his own ambitions as a poet.

13   K had originally written 'Of mighty Workings in a distant Mart?', but on Haydon's suggestion had altered the line.

To Kosciusko (p. 9)

Written Dec. 1816. First published in the *Examiner*, 16 Feb. 1817; subsequently in *1817*, the text reproduced here.

Thaddeus Kosciusko (1746–1817), Polish patriot, soldier and revolutionary had been a hero for British liberals since the 1790s. Hunt had a bust of Kosciusko in his cottage at the Vale of Health, see *Sleep and Poetry*, 387 n.

3–5   The music of the spheres, constant and harmonious.

11   King Alfred was a patriotic hero for K; cf. *To Charles Cowden Clarke*, 69–72 and n.

Sleep and Poetry (p. 10)

Written Oct.–Dec. 1816. First published as the concluding poem in *1817*, the text reproduced here.

CCC gives the circumstances of composition: 'It was in the library at Hunt's cottage, where an extemporary bed had been made up for him on the sofa, that [K] composed the frame-work and many lines of the poem . . . the last sixty or seventy being an inventory of the art garniture of the room' (*Recollections*, 133–4). The poem is K's first sustained verse meditation on poetry and the poet's calling, exploring his self-doubt and ambitions as a writer. For further reading, see Bate, 124–30; Gittings, 159–63; Jack, 130–9; Harold Bloom, *The Visionary Company* (rev. edn, 1971), 363–8; Dickstein, 48–52; Sperry 79–89; Barnard, 15–34.

Motto: From *The Floure and the Leafe*, 17–21; this poem is no longer attributed to Chaucer.

5   **blowing:** blooming.

9   Cordelia is Lear's third daughter in *King Lear*.

14   **poppy buds:** associated with Morpheus, god of sleep; cf. 348 below.

33   **shapes of light, aerial lymning:** spirits of light, delicately tinted (recalling Ariel in *The Tempest*).

41   Cf. Wordsworth's *Ode* ('Intimations'), 16: 'The sunshine is a glorious birth'.

48 denizen: a citizen or inhabitant, specifically an alien admitted to citizenship.

58 bays: laurels, used to make a poet's wreath or garland; cf. 216 below.

62–71 K at this time followed Hunt in associating 'sweets', 'bowers' and 'nymphs' with poetic creativity; cf. 101–121 below.

64 elysium: L: 'a place or island in the infernal regions, where, according to the mythology of the antients, the souls of the virtuous were placed after death. There happiness was complete'. Hence, any place of ideal happiness.

69–70 Cf. Wordsworth, *To the Daisy* ('In youth . . .), 70–1: 'A happy, genial influence, / Coming one knows not how, nor whence'.

74 meander: sinuous windings of a stream.

76 awfuller: more awe-inspiring.

79 tablets: notebook.

85–7 Recalling Hamlet's melancholy wish, 'O, that this too too sullied flesh would melt, / Thaw, and resolve itself into a dew!', *Hamlet*, 1.2.129–30.

89 Montmorenci: the falls of Montmorenci in Quebec.

96–154 An early declaration of the seriousness and scope of K's poetic ambition; he projects the various stages of his poetic career, foreshadowing his account of 'human life as far as I now perceive it' in his letter to John Hamilton Reynolds, 3 May 1818 (*Letters*, 95). See also 289–90 n. below.

102 Flora (goddess of flowers and gardens) and Pan (god of shepherds and the country) are associated here with the 'luxuries' of sensual poetry.

122–5 In quitting fanciful pleasures, K anticipates his 'nobler' existence as a poet aware of the reality of human suffering; cf. *Hyperion*, III. 114–6, and *The Fall of Hyperion*, I. 157–9.

125–54 The celestial charioteer (resembling Apollo) represents the sublimity of K's poetic ambition. Jack, 136–8, identifies Poussin's painting 'The Realm of Flora' as a source for this figure.

155 The visions all are fled: cf. *Ode to a Nightingale*, 80: 'Fled is that music'.

162–229 K's anxiety about poetry of the present day is succeeded by a survey of English poetry, from the great writers of the Elizabethan era (171–80), through a decline during the eighteenth century (181–206), to the comparatively 'fairer season' of the present (221–9).

170 Jove: Jupiter, 'most powerful of all the gods of the antients' (L).

172 paragon: surpass.

173–7 Elizabethan poetry is compared to the music of the spheres. K's striking image of a huge orbiting planet reflects his early interest in astronomy. Cf. *On first looking into Chapman's Homer*.

185–7 Referring to the heroic couplet in some eighteenth-century (or 'Augustan') poetry.

185 **puling:** whining.
187 **Pegasus:** the winged horse, a favourite of the Muses. K almost certainly recalls Hazlitt's essay 'On Milton's Versification' in the *Examiner*, 20 Aug. 1815: 'Dr Johnson and Pope would have converted [Milton's] vaulting Pegasus into a rocking-horse'. See Howe, IV. 40.
189–90 Cf. Wordsworth, 'The world is too much with us', 5: 'This Sea that bares her bosom to the moon'.
195–6 Alluding to the strict formal rules of the heroic couplet.
198 See Genesis, 30. 25–43.
202 **bright Lyrist:** Apollo, 'god of all the fine arts, of medicine, music, poetry, and eloquence, of which he was deemed the inventor' (L).
206 Nicolas Boileau (1636–1711), French poet and critic whose *l'Art poétique* (1674) was influential in formulating neoclassical principles.
206 **O ye:** the English poets.
214 The River Avon flows through Shakespeare's native town Stratford.
218–9 Poets who died in their youth, e.g. Thomas Chatterton (1752–70) and Henry Kirke White (1785–1806).
221–9 Evoking Wordsworth's poetry. In the background, perhaps, is *Ode* ('Intimations'), 26–35.
226 **ebon:** black.
234 **Polyphemes:** in strength and clumsiness some contemporary poets resemble the savage one-eyed giant Polyphemus in Homer's *Odyssey*, IX. K may have been referring to Wordsworth and Byron here.
237 Recalled by Coleridge in the lines added to *The Eolian Harp* in the 'errata' of *Sibylline Leaves* (1817): 'the mute still Air / Is Music slumbering on its instrument!'.
238 **her:** 'Poesy'.
245–7 One of K's earliest claims for the meliorative purpose of poetry. Cf. 'I stood tip-toe', 138–40.
249 **Paphos:** a 'famous city of the island of Cyprus' (L); the birthplace of Venus, to whom the myrtle was sacred.
257 **Yeaned:** born.
258 **sward:** turf or grass.
273 Cf. *As You Like It*, 2.7.145: 'the whining school-day with his satchel'.
276 **fane:** a temple.
285 **spanning:** widely extending.
289–90 Cf. K's letter to J. H. Reynolds, 3 May 1818, on the 'dark passages' of human life leading from the 'Chamber of Maiden Thought' (*Letters*, 95).
302–4 Daedalus made wings for himself and his son Icarus to escape from exile in Crete; K here likens himself to Icarus, who flew too close to the sun and melted the wax which held together his wings.

311   'I could unsay those [vows I have made].'

335-6   Ariadne, daughter of King Minos, was abandoned by her lover Theseus on the island of Naxos, where Bacchus (god of wine and revelry) found her. See Jack, 130-1, for a source in Titian's painting 'Bacchus and Ariadne'.

339   harbingers: forerunners.

348   Cf. 14 and n. above.

354-91   K's 'inventory of the art garniture' in Hunt's library begins here (see headnote). For paintings and engravings that may have influenced these lines, see Jack, 132-3.

372-3   Jack, 133, cites Titian's 'Diana and Actaeon' as a source for these lines.

379   unshent: disentangled.

381   Sappho: a bust of the Greek poetess of Lesbos.

385   Great Alfred: King Alfred, one of K's patriotic heroes. Cf. *To Charles Cowden Clarke*, 69-72 and n.

387   Kosciusko: Thaddeus Kosciusko (1746-1817), Polish patriot, soldier and revolutionary. Cf. K's sonnet *To Kosciusko*.

389-90   Cf. 'Keen, fitful gusts', 13-14 and n.

396-400   Cf. the ambiguous state of consciousness at the conclusion of *Ode to a Nightingale*.

'I stood tip-toe upon a little hill' (p. 21)
Written spring/summer 1816-Dec. 1816. Published *1817* as the first poem in the volume, the text reproduced here.

For details of composition and for the biographical context, see Bate, 122-4; Gittings, 112-14. K's working title for the poem was *Endymion*, and the episode at 193-210 outlines the myth that was the basis for *Endymion*, begun Apr. 1817. For further reading, see Dickstein, 39-48; Sperry, 79-89; McGann, KHM, 28-31; Barnard, 15-34.

Motto: Leigh Hunt's *The Story of Rimini* (1816), III. 430.

7   The morning dew.

35-46   Cf. the 'ravage' of a hazel grove in Wordsworth's *Nutting*.

48   ardent: glowing.

59-60   The curling tendrils of sweet peas.

61-80   CCC remarks: 'the following lovely passage [K] himself told me was the recollection of our having frequently loitered over the rail of a foot-bridge that spanned ... a little brook in the last field upon entering Edmonton' (*Recollections*, 138).

67   sallows: willows.

70-71   Cf. *As You Like It*, 2.1.16-17: 'tongues in trees, books in the running brooks, / Sermons in stones'.

114   swim: *OED* cites this line as the first recorded use of 'swim' as a noun meaning 'A swimming motion; *colloq.* or *dial.* a swimming or dizzy sensation'. Cf. *Endymion*, I. 571.

125–204   This passage explores poetic creativity through reflecting on the origins of classical myths (Psyche and Cupid; Pan and Syrinx; Narcissus and Echo; Endymion and Cynthia) in humanity's imaginative response to nature. In the background is Wordsworth's *Excursion*, IV, much admired by K; see esp. IV. 694–762; 847–87.

129   **staid**: grave, serious.

138–40   The consoling effects of poetry; cf. *Sleep and Poetry*, 245–7.

141–50   Describing the apotheosis of Psyche, 'a nymph whom Cupid married and carried into a place of bliss. Venus put her to death because she had robbed the world of her son; but Jupiter, at the request of Cupid, granted immortality to Psyche. The word signifies *the soul*' (L). K returned to this story in *Ode to Psyche*.

153   Wood nymphs and satyrs.

157–62   The nymph Syrinx, pursued by Pan, was transformed into reeds. See also *Endymion*, I. 242–3 and n.

164–80   Echo was a nymph who pined away out of love for Narcissus, until only her voice remained. Narcissus was punished by Aphrodite, who made him fall in love with his own reflection in a pool, mistakenly thinking it was a nymph of the place; he killed himself, and was transformed into the flower which bears his name.

175   **Zephyrus**: breezes (literally, the west wind).

180   **bale**: woe.

189   **speculation**: gaze, contemplation.

193–210   See headnote. Cynthia was 'a surname of Diana' (L); she was goddess of hunting, and was also identified with the moon. She fell in love with the shepherd Endymion and visited him on Mount Latmos in Caria (south-west Turkey). See also *Endymion*, II. 170 n.

212   **Phœbus**: the sun; Apollo.

221–26   Ward, 59–60, links this passage to Keats's experiences as a medical student at Guy's Hospital.

On receiving a laurel crown from Leigh Hunt (p. 28)
Written c. Dec. 1816–1 Mar. 1817. Not published by K. Text here based on the single extant ms, a fair copy of the poem written in a copy of *1817* presented by K to J. H. Reynolds; see *JK*, 46–7.

The sonnet was a contribution to one of Hunt's poetry-writing competitions, recording a playful incident subsequently described by Richard Woodhouse: 'As [K] and Leigh Hunt were taking their wine together, after a dinner at the house of the latter, the whim seized them to crown themselves, after the fashion of the elder poets, with a wreath of laurel' (Bate, 139). For related poems on this occasion by Hunt, see 'To John Keats', 'On receiving a crown of ivy from the Same', 'To the Same'. Bate, 137–9, explores K's subsequent remorse for having mocked an emblem of the poet's art. The sonnet was first published in *The Times* (18 May 1914). See also Newey (1995), 167–8.

3   **delphic labyrinth:** the oracle of Apollo was at Delphi; associated here with the mysterious source of poetic inspiration.

7–8   Cf. the reference to Hunt ('Libertas') in *To Charles Cowden Clarke*, 44–5 and n.

12   Cf. the political invective in *Endymion*, III. 1–22.

13–14   Cf. *On first looking into Chapman's Homer*, 13–14.

To Leigh Hunt, Esq. (p. 28)
Written Feb. 1817. Published *1817* as the 'Dedication' to the volume, the text reproduced here.

CCC recalled that K composed this sonnet extempore: 'when the last proof-sheet [of *1817*] was brought from the printer, it was accompanied by the information that if a "dedication to the book was intended it must be sent forthwith." Whereupon [K] withdrew to a side-table, and in the buzz of a mixed conversation (for there were several friends in the room) he composed . . . the Dedication Sonnet to Leigh Hunt' (*Recollections*, 137–8). Bate, 142–3, conjectures K already had a dedication to Hunt in mind. For more on Hunt, see headnote to *Written on the day that Mr Leigh Hunt left Prison*.

1   Cf. Wordsworth, *Ode* ('Intimations'), 18: 'there hath passed away a glory from the earth'.

5–8   Jack, 117, suggests a print of Poussin's 'Triumph of Flora' as source for the imagery here.

14   **offerings:** the poems in *1817*.

On seeing the Elgin Marbles (p. 29)
Written 1 or 2 Mar. 1817. First published in the *Champion* (9 Mar. 1817), the *Examiner* (9 Mar. 1817), then *Annals of the Fine Arts*, 3 (Apr. 1818) and in *L&L*, I. 27. Text here based on K's fair copy in the copy of *1817* presented to J. H. Reynolds; see *JK*, 48–9.

The Elgin Marbles (sculptures from the frieze around the Parthenon, Athens) had been transported to England between 1803 and 1812. The historical painter Benjamin Robert Haydon (1786–1846) championed the authenticity and unique value of the sculptures as the work of the sculptor Phidias. Haydon met K Oct. 1816, and took him to see the marbles at the British Museum on 1 or 2 Mar. 1817. In a letter of 3 Mar. Haydon thanked K for sending him 'two noble sonnets' – the present poem and another, *To B. R. Haydon, with a Sonnet Written on Seeing the Elgin Marbles* (not included in this selection); see *Benjamin Robert Haydon: Correspondence and Table-Talk*, ed. F. W. Haydon (2 vols, 1876), II. 2. For more on Haydon, K and the Marbles, see Bate, 146–8; Gittings, 139–40; Jack, 31–6; Theresa M. Kelley, 'Keats, Ekphrasis, and History', *K&H*, 212–37.

12 **rude:** violent, harsh.
13 **main:** the sea.
14 **a magnitude:** the brilliancy of a star, here evoking a vastness of possibility similar to *On first looking into Chapman's Homer*, 9–14. See also John Bonnycastle, *An Introduction to Astronomy* (1786), 421: 'the stars are divided into six sizes, or classes; of which the brightest are called stars of the first magnitude; the next in brightness to these stars of the second magnitude; and so on'. K had been presented with Bonnycastle's *Introduction* as a school prize; cf. *To Charles Cowden Clarke*, 67 and n.

On the Sea (p. 29)
Written c. 17 Apr. 1817, the date on which K included the sonnet in a letter of 17–18 Apr. to J. H. Reynolds (*Letters*, 6–7). First published in *The Champion* (17 Aug. 1817) and subsequently in *L&L*, II. 291. Text here based on *Letters*, 6–7.

K was staying at Carisbrooke, Isle of Wight, hoping to begin work on *Endymion* and, as he said in the letter to Reynolds, 'rather *narvus* – and the passage in *Lear* – "Do you not hear the Sea?" has haunted me intensely' ['Hark! do you hear the sea?' *King Lear*, 4.6.4]. He then copies out his sonnet. In the continuation of his letter to Reynolds, 18 Apr., K adds: 'I had become all in a Tremble from not having written any thing of late – the Sonnet over leaf did me some good'. Further reading, see Bate, 160–1; Jones, 197–8; Sperry, 75–6; Jonathan Bate, *Shakespeare and the English Romantic Imagination* (1986), 80–2; R. S. White, *Keats as a Reader of Shakespeare* (1987), 189–90.

3–4 **the spell / Of Hecate:** Hecate was goddess of the moon, and identified with Diana; she also presided over magic and enchantment. K refers to the moon's power over the tides.

Endymion: A Poetic Romance (p. 30)
Begun c. 18 Apr. 1817 at Carisbrooke, Ise of Wight; finished in draft by 28 Nov. 1817 at Burford Bridge, Surrey. First published as a volume late Apr. 1818, the text reproduced here. For the preface published with the poem, see Appendix 1.

K knew the legend of Endymion from his schoolboy reading: CCC recalled, 'his constantly recurrent sources of attraction were Tooke's "Pantheon", Lemprière's "Classical Dictionary", which he appeared to *learn*, and Spence's "Polymetis". This was the store whence he acquired his intimacy with the Greek mythology' (*Recollections*, 124). To these may be added Ovid's *Metamorphoses* in the original Latin and in George Sandys' translation (1626); John Lyly's *Endymion* (1588); Michael Drayton's *Man in the Moone* (1606); Mary Tighe's *Psyche* (1811); Southey's *Curse of Kehama* (1810), and Shelley's *Alastor* (1816). K had outlined the myth of Endymion in 'I stood tip-toe' (see ll. 193–210); in returning to it, he thought of *Endymion* as ' "a test, a trial of my Powers of Imagination and chiefly of my invention which is a rare thing indeed – by which I must make 4000 Lines of one bare circumstance and fill them with Poetry . . . Do not the Lovers of Poetry like to have a little Region to wander in where they may pick and choose, and in which the images are so numerous that many are forgotten and found new in a second Reading . . . ? Besides a Long Poem is a test of Invention which I take to be the Polar Star of Poetry, as Fancy is the Sails, and Imagination the Rudder. Did our great Poets ever write short Pieces?" ' (to Benjamin Bailey, 8 Oct. 1817, *Letters*, 27).

For further discussion, see Jack, 143–60; Dickstein, 53–129; Sperry, 90–116; John Bayley, *The Uses of Division. Unity and Disharmony in Literature* (1976), 107–156; Barnard, 35–55; Watkins, 35–53; Newey (1989), 265–89; Nicholas Roe, 'Keats's Lisping Sedition', *Essays in Criticism* (Jan. 1992), 36–55; David Pirie, 'Keats', *The Penguin History of Literature. The Romantic Period*, ed. D. Pirie (1994), 359–80; Newey (1995), 166–93.

Motto: From Shakespeare's sonnet 17, l. 12.

Dedication: Thomas Chatterton (1752–70), poet and forger, author of pseudo-mediaeval verses supposed to have been translated from the manuscripts of Thomas Rowley, a fifteenth-century priest. Chatterton committed suicide at the age of 17, initiating the myth of youthful genius destroyed by public neglect which held a potent appeal for subsequent generations. For K, Chatterton was 'the purest writer in the English Language' (*Letters*, 293, 325).

Preface: K's original preface, dated 19 Mar. 1818, had been hostile and self-protective. It was criticised by K's publishers, Taylor and Hessey, and by his friend John Hamilton Reynolds (see K's response in *Letters*, 84–5). On 10 Apr. he wrote the preface published with *Endymion* later that month (See Appendix 1).

Book 1 Begun c. 18 Apr. 1817; date of completion unknown.

1. 14   **boon:** gift or favour.
1. 18   **brake:** thicket.
1. 40   **city's din:** cf. *Tintern Abbey*, 26–7: 'the din / Of towns and cities'.
1. 41   **early budders:** flowers of early spring, cf. 1. 138 below.
1. 46–8   For K's idea of imagination as the 'rudder' of poetic invention, see headnote.
1. 50   **vermeil:** bright red.
1. 55–7   K did indeed finish a draft of his poem in autumn 1817. See headnote.
1. 62   **thorough:** through.
1. 63   **Latmos:** a mountain in Caria (south-west Turkey), the residence of Endymion.

l. 76   **pard:** leopard.

l. 78   **ay:** always.

l. 109–13   Recalling the May festival in Wordsworth's *Ode* ('Intimations'), 29–50.

l. 121   Cf. Coleridge, 'The stilly murmur of the distant Sea / Tells us of Silence'; *Effusion* XXXV, 11–12, retitled *The Eolian Harp* in *Sibylline Leaves*, published July 1817. When K was writing this section of *Endymion* in the Isle of Wight, he was haunted by the sound of the sea; cf. headnote to *On the Sea*.

l. 26   **alley:** a walk in a garden, park, woodland. Cf. 'I stood tip-toe', 20.

l. 32   **unmew:** set free.

l. 140   **Arcadian books:** books of pastoral poetry.

l. 141–4   Apollo was exiled for nine years in Thessaly where he lived as a shepherd, 'from which circumstance he was called the god of shepherds' (L).

l. 158   **Leda's love:** Jupiter, in the form of a swan.

l. 170   **Ganymede:** 'A beautiful youth of Phrygia . . . taken up to heaven by Jupiter . . . he became the cup-bearer of the gods' (L).

l. 174   **nervy:** muscular.

l. 177   **groves Elysian:** where the souls of the virtuous were placed after death: 'There happiness was complete' (L).

l. 190   Without an equal in the whole forest.

l. 192   **chase:** unenclosed land for hunting.

l. 206   **Triton's horn:** Triton was 'a sea deity . . . generally represented as blowing a shell, his body above the waist is like that of a man, and below, a dolphin' (L). Cf. Wordsworth, 'The world is too much with us', 14: 'Or hear old Triton blow his wreathed horn'.

l. 208   **scrip, with needments:** satchel containing food. Cf. l. 392 below.

l. 220   **earth is glad:** Cf. Wordsworth, *Ode* ('Intimations'), 29: 'All the earth is gay'.

l. 232–306   Shelley thought that this stanzaic 'Hymn to Pan' offered the ' "surest promise of ultimate excellence" ' (*L&L*, I. 86), and in some respects it represents an important development towards the great odes of 1819. Haydon reports that Wordsworth, on hearing Keats recite the hymn, dismissed it as 'a very pretty piece of Paganism'; this was 'unfeeling, & unworthy', as Haydon says, and not least because K admired Wordsworth's account of the origin of classical myth in his *Excursion*, IV (see *KC*, II. 143–4, and 'I stood tip-toe', 125–204 n.).

l. 236   **hamadryads:** L: 'nymphs who lived in the country, and presided over trees, with which they were said to live and die'.

l. 242–3   'Syrinx, a nymph of Arcadia. . . . Pan became enamoured of her . . . but Syrinx escaped, and at her own request was changed by the gods into a reed called Syrinx by the Greeks. The god made himself a pipe with the reeds, into which his favourite nymph had been changed' (L). Cf. 'I stood tip-toe', 157–62.

l. 247   **turtles:** turtle-doves.

l. 258   **pent up butterflies:** butterflies still in chrysalis form.

l. 263   **faun and satyr:** L: 'deities of the country . . . having the legs, feet and ears of goats, and the rest of the body human. They were called satyrs by the Greeks'. See also IV. 228 n. below.

l. 267   **maw:** throat, stomach.

l. 272   For naiads, see *To Charles Cowden Clarke*, 6 n.

l. 288–9 Cf. K's letter to Reynolds, 3 May 1818, on the 'doors' and 'dark passages' of human life (*Letters*, 95).

l. 290   **Dryope:** a nymph of Arcadia, mother of Pan by Mercury.

l. 298   **ethereal:** celestial, heavenly (in contrast to the 'clodded earth' at l. 297 above). On K's uses of 'ethereal', see R. T. Davies, 'Some Ideas and Uses', *John Keats. A Reassessment*, ed. K. Muir (1969), 136: 'When applied to physical things and actions it can mean "having the insubstantiality and rarity of *ether*, delicate, refined, volatile". It seems to be derived from Keats's medical studies in which he would have found ether contrasted with heavy spirits'.

l. 305   **Pæan:** hymn of praise.

l. 306   **mount Lycean:** 'Lycaeus, a mountain of Arcadia, sacred to Jupiter . . . also sacred to Pan, whose festivals, called *Lycæa*, were celebrated there' (L).

l. 310   **Ionian:** the Mediterranean sea, at the south of the Adriatic.

l. 318   **Thermopylæ:** a mountain pass between northern and southern Greece, the site of a battle in 480 BC between three hundred Spartans and a massive army led by Xerxes.

l. 320   **genitors:** progenitors.

l. 326–9 K follows L's account of how Hyacinthus, playing at quoits with his tutor Apollo, was killed when the breeze (Zephyr) blew the quoit so that it struck Hyacinthus on the head. Apollo changed Hyacinthus's blood into the flower that bears his name.

l. 334   **raft:** torn off.

l. 337–43 Apollo slaughtered Niobe's children, because of her arrogance; 'Niobe, struck at the suddenness of her misfortunes, was changed into a stone' (L).

l. 347–54 The Argonauts sailed with Jason in the *Argo*, in search of the golden fleece.

l. 358   **eld:** old age.

l. 363   **Vesper:** Venus, the evening star.

l. 367   **fire-tailed exhalations:** comets.

l. 380   **eye-earnestly:** with earnest eyes.

l. 384   **Mercury:** the Roman name for Hermes, messenger of the gods. See also l. 563 n.

l. 405–6 See 'The Story of the Young King of the Black Islands' in *The Arabian Nights*. The young king had been transformed to stone from the waist downwards by his unfaithful wife.

l. 408 **Peona:** Peona's name may have been derived from Paeon, physician to the gods, and possibly from Spenser's Poeana, *The Faerie Queene*, 4.9.3–16.

l. 423 **shallop:** a dinghy.

l. 432 **fingering:** elaborate interweaving (of the overhanging plants).

l. 452 **sere:** dry.

l. 453–5 Sleep is likened to the halcyon, a mythical bird which was believed to charm the sea into calmness.

l. 481 **poll:** lop branches off.

l. 495 **Dryope:** a girl who was transformed into a tree as she nursed her child. See Ovid's *Metamorphoses*, IX.

l. 499 **Delphic:** mysterious and inspired; cf. *On receiving a laurel crown from Leigh Hunt*, 3 n.

l. 510 **Paphian:** from Paphos (now Cyprus), which was sacred to the goddess Venus; cf. the 'Paphian army' of lovers at III. 853.

l. 531 **Lucifer:** the morning star; Venus when it precedes the rising of the sun. Cf. Hesperus, at I. 685 n.

l. 541 Cf. *King John*, 5.2.45–6, 'this honourable dew, / That silverly doth progress on thy cheeks'.

l. 552 **snorting four:** four horses drew Apollo's chariot. Cf. III. 364 and n.

l. 553 **zodiac-lion:** the constellation Leo.

l. 555 **ditamy . . . poppies:** plants sacred to Diana. The herb ditamy, or dittany, had powerful healing qualities.

l. 559–60 Morpheus, god of sleep, was traditionally associated with poppies. Cf. *Sleep and Poetry*, 14 n. **pinions:** wings; cf I. 586 below.

l. 563 **his rod:** Mercury's magic wand caduceus, 'entwined at one end by two serpents, in the form of two equal semicircles . . . With it Mercury conducted to the infernal regions the souls of the dead, and could lull to sleep, and even raise to life a dead person' (L).

l. 571 **gulph'd:** 'Swallowed like a gulf, or as in a gulf; engulfed' (*OED*); cf. III. 351. **swim:** cf. 'I stood tip-toe', 114.

l. 581 **travelling:** here used transitively.

l. 605 **Olympus:** 'A mountain of Macedonia and Thessaly . . . The ancients supposed that it touched the heavens with its top; and, from that circumstance, they have placed the residence of the gods there, and have made it the court of Jupiter' (L).

l. 614 **gordian'd up:** tied up in knots.

l. 621–2 The painful return from the vision of Diana to the reality of earthly life; cf. I. 681–705 below.

l. 624–7 Venus 'sprung from the froth of the sea' (L). Jack, 154, points out that although this passage is 'remarkably reminiscent' of

Botticelli's 'Birth of Venus', the painting 'was unknown in England at this time'. K's depiction of Venus conforms to a traditional representation of the goddess in eighteenth-century sources. See following note.

l. 627-8   Perhaps recalling the engraving of Diana and Endymion in Spence's *Polymetis*, a book well-known to Keats; see Jack, 146-7.

l. 635   **waning**: losing colour, but also recalling the waxing and waning of the moon. Cf. *Lamia*, l. 136-7.

l. 666   **alp**: mountain pasture.

l. 671   **arch**: mischievous. **Oread**: a mountain nymph.

l. 679   **a gentle creep**: here and elsewhere in the poem K follows Leigh Hunt's manner of using verbs as nouns; cf. for example l. 933 'silver ramble'.

l. 683   **ouzel**: blackbird.

l. 685   **Hesperus**: the evening star; Venus, when it follows the setting of the sun.

l. 696   **vermeil**: see l. 50 n. above.

l. 701   **knit**: unite.

l. 702   **under darkness**: the darkness of the underworld.

l. 714   **enchased crocodile**: the crocodile's scales are adorned with decoration like a suit of armour.

l. 723   **middle earth**: the earth, placed between heaven and the underworld.

l. 732   **sprig of yew**: emblem of mourning.

l. 747-9   Cf. *The Tempest*, 4.1.156-7: 'We are such stuff / As dreams are made on . . .'. For Morphean, see l. 559-60 n. above.

l. 759   **high-fronted**: noble in bearing.

l. 761   **ruth**: regret.

l. 762   **plaited brow**: furrowed with concentration.

l. 764   **fans**: wings.

l. 766   **manna-dew**: cf. *La belle dame sans merci*, 26, and Coleridge's *Kubla Khan* (1816), 53: 'For he on honey-dew hath fed'. Manna was a miraculous food gathered by the Israelites in the wilderness, Exodus, 16. 14-21. K apparently thought manna was a fruit picked from trees; see *Endymion*, II. 452 and *The Eve of St Agnes*, 268-9.

l. 770   **base**: mean.

l. 772-4   Cf. *To Charles Cowden Clarke*, 17: 'With shatter'd boat, oar snapt, and canvass rent'.

l. 777-842   Lines 777-81 were included as a revision in K's letter to his publisher John Taylor, 30 Jan. 1818, with an important comment on the whole passage to l. 842: 'You must indulge me by putting this in for . . . such a preface is necessary to the Subject. The whole thing must I think have appeared to you, who are a consequitive Man, as a thing almost of mere words – but I assure you that when I wrote it, it was a regular stepping of the Imagination towards a Truth. My having written that Argument will perhaps be of the greatest Service to me of any thing I ever did – It set before me at once the gradations of happiness even like a kind of Pleasure Thermometer – and is my first Step towards the chief Attempt in the Drama – the playing of different Natures with Joy and Sorrow' (*Letters*, 59–60). The 'gradations' of K's 'Pleasure Thermometer' are, in ascending order, enjoyment of the natural world represented by the 'rose leaf' (I. 782); the pleasure of music (I. 783–94); friendship and love (I. 800–805); and, finally, passionate love (I. 805–42), which makes 'Men's being mortal, immortal' (I. 844). For a recent discussion, see Sperry, 48–9.

I. 779   **fellowship with essence:** there has been much argument about whether this is to be understood as a transcendental state, or identified with sensual beauty; for a summary, see N. F. Ford, 'The Meaning of "Fellowship with Essence" in *Endymion*', PMLA, 62 (1947), 1061–76.

I. 791   **bruit:** sound.

I. 792   **a giant battle:** between the Titans and the Olympians, one of K's themes in *Hyperion* and *The Fall of Hyperion*.

I. 794   **infant Orpheus:** 'All nature seemed charmed and animated' by young Orpheus's skill in playing the lyre (L.)

I. 799   **self-destroying:** subduing self-consciousness.

I. 808   **genders:** engenders.

I. 815   **pelican brood:** the pelican was thought to feed its offspring with its own blood.

I. 816   **unsating:** never satisfying, never cloying.

I. 817   **van:** vanguard.

I. 818–20   cf. *Troilus and Cressida*, 1.3.27–8: 'Distinction, with a broad and powerful fan / Puffing at all, winnows the light away'.

I. 820–1   Cf. K's use of animal imagery in *Endymion*, III. 3–18.

I. 837   **mail:** scales like armour.

I. 845   **brim:** fill to the brim.

I. 851   **atomies:** mites; cf. *Romeo and Juliet*, 1.4.57: 'a team of little atomi'.

I. 862   **Latona:** mother of Apollo and Diana; see also I. 966 n. below.

I. 865   **athwart:** across.

I. 907   **gnawing sloth:** A species of Indian bear (not the sluggish mammal that hangs upside-down in trees).

I. 939   Cf. *Romeo and Juliet*, 2.2.184: 'Parting is such sweet sorrow'.

I. 944   **Proserpine:** daughter of Ceres and Jupiter: 'Pluto carried her away into the infernal regions, of which she became the queen ... Jupiter, to appease the resentment of Ceres ... permitted that Proserpine should remain six months with Pluto ... and that she should spend the rest of the year with her mother on earth' (L). Proserpine was also known by the name Hecate: both of these, according to L, were also identified with Diana.

I. 947   **Echo:** see 'I stood tip-toe', 164–80 n.

l. **966 Delos:** an island of the Cyclades, famous 'for the nativity of Apollo and Diana; and the solemnity with which the festivals of these deities were celebrated there' (L).

l. **968 cloys:** suggesting the movement of the hand through 'labyrinthine' hair.

l. **971 Whither are they fled?:** cf. Wordsworth, *Ode* ('Intimations'), 56: 'Whither is fled the visionary gleam?'

l. **989 car:** chariot, cf. l. 165 above.

Book II Written at Hampstead, summer 1817; completed c. 28 Aug. 1817. Gittings, 211–12 suggests that the panegyric on love (II.1–130) was written June 1817, after K's return from Hastings and his romantic encounter with Isabella Jones.

II. **1–43** K's affirmation of love's 'sovereign power', in comparison to which the heroic events of 'pageant history' are a 'cheat', is an *apologia* for *Endymion* as a whole. Cf. love as 'the chief intensity', l. 800.

II. **7** Cf. Coleridge's *Kubla Khan* (1816), 53, and l. 766 n.

II. **12 amain:** with vigour.

II. **13 close:** embrace.

II. **15 Swart:** dark.

II. **22–3 What care:** this elliptical reference probably derives from K's reading in John Potter's *Archæologia Græca: or, the Antiquities of Greece* (1697): '*Plutarch* reports, that when *Themistocles* was consulting with the other Officers, upon the uppermost Deck of the Ship, and most of them opposed him, being unwilling to hazard a Battle, an Owl coming upon the Right-side of the Ship, and lighting upon the Mast, so animated them, that they unanimously concurred with him, and prepared themselves for the Fight' (9th edn, 2 vols, London, 1775, I. 326).

II. **24–5** Alexander the Great crossed the river Indus with his army in 326 BC.

II. **26–7** Odysseus blinded the sleeping Cyclops; see *The Odyssey* IX, and cf. *Sleep and Poetry*, 233–5 and n.

II. **27–30** See *Romeo and Juliet*, 2.2.

II. **31–2** Hero, Imogen, and Pastorella were the heroines, respectively, of Marlowe's *Hero and Leander*, Shakespeare's *Cymbeline*, and Spenser's *Faerie Queene*, VI. 11.

II. **60 pight:** settled, poised.

II. **81–2** Pilgrims sailing to the oracle of Apollo at Delphi; cf. *On receiving a laurel crown from Leigh Hunt*, 3 and n.

II. **90 smutch:** smear, stain; cf. *The Winter's Tale*, 1.2.121: 'What! hast smutch'd thy nose?'

II. **91 mealy gold:** the coloured dust on a butterfly's wings. Cf. *Troilus and Cressida*, 3.3.79, 'mealy wings'.

II. **109 Amphitrite:** L: 'daughter of Oceanus and Tethys, married

Neptune . . . She had by him Triton, one of the sea deities. She . . . is often taken for the sea itself'. See also III. 1004 below.

II. 110   **rainbow-sided**: cf. *Lamia*, I. 54.

II. 118   **Meander**: in classical geography, a river in Asia Minor that flowed into the Aegean Sea, famous for its winding course.

II. 138   **burr**: suggesting mental haziness or confusion; derived from its seventeenth-century use to describe a nebulous halo around the moon (*OED*).

II. 145   **travelling**: travailing, toiling.

II. 153–6   Cf. *Sleep and Poetry*, 122–5 and n.

II. 162–3   Cf. *On first looking into Chapman's Homer*, 12–14, and II. 166–7 below.

II. 164–5   For Orpheus and Eurydice, see Ovid's *Metamorphoses*, IX.

II. 168   **thrice-seen love**: Diana, although Endymion does not yet realise this.

II. 170   **Cynthia**: 'A surname of Diana, from mount Cythnus [on the island of Delos], where she was born' (L). See also 'I stood tip-toe', 193–210 and n.

II. 180   **Cupids shun thee**: because of Diana's reputation for chastity.

II. 183   **propitious**: gracious, well-disposed.

II. 197–8   Deucalion waited on the peak of Mount Parnassus for the deluge sent by Jupiter to subside. Orion, blinded, recovered his eyesight on facing towards the rising sun. For K's knowledge of Poussin's 'Landscape with Orion' (in which Diana is also represented), see Jack, 156.

II. 204   **sparry**: sparkling, crystalline.

II. 205–10   Alluding to Endymion's mountain home.

II. 230–1   **antre**: a cavern; cf. *Othello* 1.3.140: 'of antres vast, and deserts idle'. **metal woof . . . Vulcan**: a rainbow, fashioned with interwoven metal by Vulcan, blacksmith of the gods, who presides over metal workers and their craft.

II. 240   **vast**: used here as a noun. Cf. III. 120 n.

II. 245   **fray**: frighten.

II. 247   **stun**: stunning or stupefying effect.

II. 251   **planet's sphering time**: earth's orbiting of the sun, which will cease when the world ends.

II. 253   **mighty ones**: the greatest of the poets.

II. 262   **quiver'd Dian**: Diana as goddess of hunting, with a quiver of arrows. **awfully**: full of awe.

II. 275–6   **self . . . self**: cf. 'self-destroying', I. 799 and n., and II. 282–3 below.

II. 277   **fog-born elf**: a Will-o'-the-Wisp, or *ignis fatuus*. Cf. *King Lear*, 3.4.50–52. An elf was a malicious dwarf or fairy. Spenser frequently used the word to describe his knights in *The Faerie Queene*, hence perhaps K's liking for the word. See, for example, 'fond elf', II. 461 below.

II. 282   **raught**: reached; an archaic word used by Spenser.

II. 288   **cloudy rack**: a mass of cloud.

II. 298   **temple's chief**: the upper end of a temple.

II. 301   **plain**: complain.

II. 308   **disparted**: separated.

II. 309   **crescent**: the crescent moon was one of Diana's emblems.

II. 341   **sallows**: willows.

II. 360   **Arion**: L: 'famous lyric poet and musician . . . in the island of Lesbos'.

II. 362   The rhyme for 'lyre' was lost in K's revision of his draft.

II. 363   **Tyrian**: perhaps suggesting 'seas of Tyre', i.e. the eastern Mediterranean.

II. 373   **the Carian**: Endymion, who was from Caria.

II. 376   **swart abysm**: cf. *The Tempest*, 1.2.50: 'the dark backward and abysm of time', quoted by K in his letter to Reynolds, Apr. 1817 (*Letters*, 7).

II. 389–427   K's Bower of Adonis draws some details from Spenser's Garden of Adonis in *The Faerie Queene*, 3.6.39–45.

II. 392–410   K's Adonis may recall Poussin's 'Echo and Narcissus'; see Jack, 156–7, and plate 17.

II. 405   **damask**: cf. *Lamia*, 1. 116: 'Blush'd a live damask'.

II. 407   **disparts**: opens.

II. 421   **the pathos**: the tender sound of the lyre.

II. 441–5   Cf. *Ode to a Nightingale*, 11–18.

II. 443   **Ariadne**: See *Sleep and Poetry*, 335–6 and n.

II. 445–6   **Vertumnus**: 'a deity among the Romans, who presided over the spring and over orchards' (L). He wooed but was at first rejected by Pomona, a nymph who presided over gardens and 'all sorts of fruit-trees' (L).

II. 448–9   **Amalthea**: L: 'daughter of Melissus king of Crete, fed Jupiter with goat's milk'.

II. 452   See 1. 766 and n. above.

II. 453   **the three Hesperides**: three nymphs who guarded the golden apples Juno gave to Jupiter on their marriage; their home was traditionally held to be Africa (not Syria).

II. 457–80   For Venus and Adonis, K draws on Shakespeare's *Venus and Adonis*, *The Faerie Queene*, 3.1.34–8 and 3.6.46–9, and Ovid's *Metamorphoses*, x.

II. 458   **sea-born goddess**: cf. 1. 624–7 and n.

II. 474–8   Venus pleading with Jupiter apparently derives from K's reading in Edward Baldwin [i.e. William Godwin], *The Pantheon: or, Ancient History of the Gods of Greece and Rome* (London, 1806).

II. 490   **scuds:** cf. Adonis's horse in *Venus and Adonis*, 301: 'Sometime he scuds far off'. See also Neptune's chariot, *Hyperion*, II. 236.

II. 492   **Cytherea:** Venus.

II. 494   **clamant:** clamorous, noisy.

II. 497   **Pigeons and doves:** birds sacred to Venus.

II. 517   **disparted:** separated; cf. II. 308 above.

II. 518   **car:** chariot; cf. I. 989 above.

II. 532   **unchariest:** least bashful.

II. 535   **Love's self:** Cupid. **superb:** grand, stately, majestic (*OED*).

II. 537   **quell:** the power to destroy, a rare archaism: this is the last recorded use cited in *OED*.

II. 548   **My child:** Cupid was Venus's son.

II. 569   **zoned:** encircled.

II. 578–87   Cf. CCC's 'Biographical Notes on Keats, 16 March 1846', prepared for Milnes's *L&L*: 'I have often thought of that Sunday afternoon, when he read to Mr Severn and myself the description of the "Bower of Adonis"; and the conscious pleasure with which he looked up when he came to the passage that tells the ascent of the car of Venus' (*KC*, II. 151).

II. 601–4   Cf. the sublime scenery in Coleridge's *Kubla Khan* (1816), 17–19, and Shelley's *Alastor* (1816), 374–84: both poems were well-known to K.

II. 611   **float:** a boat. **Thetis:** a sea goddess, the mother of Achilles by Peleus, King of Thessaly.

II. 625   **aloof:** at a distance, here meaning far in the future.

II. 627   **Protean:** varying in shape: the sea god Proteus could assume any shape he wished.

II. 636   **wolds:** rolling uplands.

II. 640   **Cybele:** L: 'a goddess ... generally represented as a robust woman, far advanced in her pregnancy, to intimate the fecundity of the earth. She held keys in her hand, and her head was crowned with rising turrets, and sometimes with the leaves of an oak. She sometimes appears riding in a chariot drawn by two tame lions'.

II. 641   **foldings:** enfolding clothes.

II. 642   **death-pale:** cf. *La belle dame sans merci*, 38: 'Pale warriors, death-pale were they all'.

II. 658   **eagle:** the eagle was an emblem of Jupiter.

II. 663   **asphodel:** in Greek mythology, a flower which grows in the Elysian fields, the heavenly resort of the virtuous.

II. 672   **ethereal:** refined, finely tuned. See also I. 298 and n. above.

II. 674   **Hesperean:** Westward, of the land of the west; from Hesperus, the western or evening star.

II. 687–94   Endymion does not yet realise that his beloved is the goddess Diana. Here he conjectures that she may be one of the Horae, who tended the gates of heaven (II. 687-8); one of the Pleiades (II. 689-90); a sea-nymph (II. 690-1); a nymph attending on Diana (II. 692-4).

II. 691   **Triton:** see I. 206 and n. above.

II. 693   **scions:** shoots or twigs.

II. 696   **Aurora:** goddess of the dawn.

II. 716   **Helicon:** The mountain in Boeotia, Greece, from which the Hippocrene sprang; both were sacred to the Muses. Cf. *To Charles Cowden Clarke*, 27 and n.

II. 740-2   Cf. 'Bright star' esp. 10-11, and III. 173-4 below.

II. 761   **Ida:** 'A celebrated mountain . . . in the neighbourhood of Troy [where] the shepherd Paris adjudged the prize of beauty to the goddess Venus' (L); here perhaps an invocation of Venus herself.

II. 773   **O bliss! O pain!:** the coincidence of pleasure and pain appears frequently in K's poems; cf. for example *Ode to a Nightingale*, 1-2, *Ode on Melancholy*, 25-6, and II. 822-4 below.

II. 778   **shame:** because of her chaste reputation hitherto; cf. II. 789-94 and n. below.

II. 789-94   Diana is horrified at the prospect of her lost reputation for chastity.

II. 791   **Minerva:** goddess of wisdom, famous for her celibacy (hence her 'start' at Diana's loss of 'purity').

II. 793   **veiled:** 'vailed' or lowered as a token of respect; K's spelling was acceptable in his day. Cf. IV. 263 below.

II. 795-6   Cf. *On first looking into Chapman's Homer*, 10: 'swims into his ken'.

II. 799   **Pallas:** Minerva, see II. 791 n. above.

II. 815   **melt into thee:** cf. *The Eve of St Agnes*, 320: 'Into her dream he melted'.

II. 819   **empyrean:** heavenly.

II. 827-53   Shelley's draft letter to the *Quarterly Review*, c. 20 Oct. 1820, praised this passage, and III. 113-20, 193 ff., as demonstrating 'promise of ultimate excellence'. See *KCH*, 124.

II. 829-39   On K's interest in the origins of myths, cf. 'I stood tip-toe', 125-204 and n.

II. 854   **former chroniclers:** those in the past who have told the story of Endymion and Diana.

II. 866   **Eolian tuned:** finely tuned like the strings of an aeolian harp, which creates harmonious music from the movements of the breeze.

II. 875   **Alecto:** one of the Furies; her head was covered with serpents.

II. 875-7   Hermes' music had lulled to sleep the hundred-eyed monster Argus.

II. 899   **maw:** see I. 267 n. above.

II. 905-6   **essences . . . spiritual:** things which once seemed trancendent. **lees:** dregs, sediments.

II. 909–11 Light bright enough to dazzle Jupiter's eagle. See II. 658 and n. above.

II. 936–1009 The story of the passion of the river god Alpheus for the nymph Arethusa, one of Diana's attendants, is based on Ovid's *Metamorphoses*, V.

II. 961 **Oread-Queen:** Diana.

II. 990 L.: 'Alpheus . . . a famous river of Peloponnesus . . . rises in Arcadia, and after passing through Elis and Achaia, falls into the sea'. See also II. 1008–9 below.

II. 994 **Saturn in his exile:** Saturn was defeated in battle by the Olympians; he appears in exile at the opening of *Hyperion*, I.

II. 996 **mealy:** powdery; cf. II. 91 n. above.

II. 1008–1017 L: 'Diana opened a secret passage under the earth and under the sea, where the waters of Arethusa disappeared, and rose in the island of Ortygia, near Syracuse in Sicily. The river Alpheus followed her also under the sea, and rose also in Ortygia; so that, as mythologists relate, whatever is thrown into the Alpheus in Elis, rises again, after some time, in the fountain of Arethusa near Syracuse'.

Book III Written Sept. 1817, while K was staying with Benjamin Bailey at Magdalen Hall, Oxford. In a letter to R. M. Milnes, 7 May 1849, Bailey recalled K's habits of composition: 'He wrote, & I read, sometimes at the same table, & sometimes at separate desks or tables, from breakfast to the time of our going out for exercise, – generally two or three o'clock. He sat down to his task, – which was about 50 lines a day, – with his paper before him, & wrote with as much regularity, & apparently with as much ease, as he wrote his letters. Indeed he quite acted up to the principle he lays down in the letter of axioms to his publisher . . . "That if poetry comes not as naturally as the leaves of a tree, it had better not come at all" [27 Feb. 1818, *Letters*, 70]. This axiom he fulfilled to the letter by his own practice, *me teste*, while he composed the third Book of Endymion . . . until he completed it. Sometimes he fell short of his allotted task, – but not often: & he would make it up another day. But he never forced himself. When he had finished his writing for the day, he usually read it over to me; & he read or wrote letters until we went out for a walk. This was our habit day by day. The rough manuscript was written off daily, & with few erasures' (*KC*, II. 270). Bailey also mentions that K was reading *Paradise Lost* while at Oxford, producing traces of Miltonic phrasing and syntax in Book III (see for example, III. 615–6, 695–6).

III. 1–21 An attack on oppressive, aristocratic governments and on the Church of England, in which K echoes the sentiments of Leigh Hunt's *Examiner* newspaper, which he had read since his schooldays. Bailey suggested in 1849 (see headnote) that K 'had written the few first introductory lines . . . before he became my guest' (*KC*, II. 269). But

K's animus against the church (III. 11 below) may in part reflect Bailey's disappointed hopes of preferment to a curacy in the diocese of Lincoln. See K's letter to Bailey, 3 Nov. 1817: 'That a mitre should cover a man guilty of the most coxcombical, tyranical and indolent impertinence! . . . Yet doth he sit in his palace. Such is this world . . .' (*Letters*, 32).

III. 7   **Fire-branded foxes**: see Judges, 15.4–5: 'And Samson went and caught three hundred foxes, and took firebrands, and turned tail to tail, and put a firebrand in the midst between two tails. And when he had set the brands on fire, he let them go into the corn of the Philistines, and burnt up both the shocks, and also the standing corn, with the vineyards and olives'.

III. 11   See III. 1–21 n. above.

III. 12   Cf. *On receiving a laurel crown from Leigh Hunt*, 10–12.

III. 13   **blown**: inflated, conceited.

III. 25   **ethereal**: see I. 298 n. above.

III. 38   **Ceres**: goddess of corn and harvests, mother of Proserpine; see I. 944 n. above.

III. 42   The sun god Apollo's sister was Diana, the moon. See I. 862 n. and I. 966 n. above.

III. 57   **kine**: cattle.

III. 70–1   **spooming**: foaming. **Tellus**: Earth, who feels the tides moving under Diana's influence.

III. 72   **Cynthia**: see II. 170 n. above.

III. 78   **Vesper**: see I. 363 n. above.

III. 80   Cf. *The Eve of St Agnes*, 311: 'How chang'd thou art! how pallid, chill, and drear!'

III. 82–3   **stress . . . spangles**: sparkling moonlight on the water.

III. 97–9   Leander, Orpheus, and Pluto braved respectively the sea, the underworld, and the air for love.

III. 113–20   This passage much impressed Shelley; see II. 827–53 n. above.

III. 120–136   Probably recalling Clarence's dream in *Richard III*, I.4.21–33:

> O Lord, Methought what pain it was to drown:
> What dreadful noise of waters in my ears;
> What sights of ugly death within my eyes!
> Methoughts I saw a thousand fearful wrecks;
> Ten thousand men that fishes gnaw'd upon;
> Wedges of gold, great anchors, heaps of pearl,
> Inestimable stones, unvalu'd jewels,
> All scatter'd in the bottom of the sea.
> Some lay in dead men's skulls, and in the holes
> Where eyes did once inhabit, there were crept –

As 'twere in scorn of eyes – reflecting gems,
That woo'd the slimy bottom of the deep,
And mock'd the dead bones that lay scatter'd by.

III. 120 **vast:** the sea; cf. II. 240 and n.

III. 124 **brazen beaks:** the bronze beaks, or prows, of wrecked war-ships. **targe:** shield.

III. 129 **Saturn's vintage:** distant antiquity. Saturn was one of the oldest of the gods; see *Hyperion*, I.

III. 133 **ancient Nox:** cf. 'ancient Night', *Paradise Lost*, II. 970.

III. 134 **behemoth … leviathan:** biblical monsters, respectively of the land and sea: see Job, 40. 15 and Isaiah, 27. 1. Probably noticed by K in his reading of *Paradise Lost*, VII. 412–16, 471–2 (see headnote to Book III).

III. 157 **mesh:** interweave.

III. 158 **like a passing spright:** lively as a passing fairy or spirit.

III. 173–4 Cf. 'Bright star', 10–12, and II. 740 above.

III. 175–6 Endymion's 'strange love' is in fact the moon, although he does not yet realise this. Cf. 'Dearest love' at III. 183.

III. 176 **Felicity's abyss:** profound pleasure.

III. 182 **do not blind:** the influence of the moon was traditionally held to confuse the reason ('moon-mad'), or to cause actual blindness.

III. 192 **old man:** Glaucus, a sea deity; for his story see III. 318–638 and n.

III. 193–5 Jack, 158–9, suggests Salvator Rosa's engraving 'Glaucus and Scylla' (Jack, plate 18) as a source for K's description. Also in the background is Wordsworth's 'Old Man', the leech-gatherer in *Resolution and Independence*, esp. 55–63. Shelley particularly admired this description of Glaucus, see II. 827–53 n.

III. 196 **winding-sheet:** for a corpse.

III. 202 **woof:** woven fabric.

III. 205 **gulphing:** see I. 571 n.; possibly also with the sense 'To rush along like a gulf or whirlpool; to eddy, swirl' (*OED*).

III. 211 **Neptune:** 'Neptune, as being god of the sea, was entitled to more power than any of the other gods, except Jupiter. Not only the ocean, rivers, and fountains, were subjected to him, but he also could cause earthquakes at his pleasure, and raise islands from the bottom of the sea with a blow of his trident' (L).

III. 215 **denizen:** see *Sleep and Poetry*, 48 n.

III. 218–25 See Bailey's letter to Milnes, 7 May 1849: 'Most vivid in my recollection of … the fine & affecting story of the old man, Glaucus, which he read to me immediately after its composition [Bailey quotes these lines] … I remember his upward look when he read of the "magic ploughs", which in his hands have turned up so much of the rich soil of Fairyland' (*KC*, II. 270–1).

III. 230   stole: robe.

III. 234   Thou art the man!: see 2 Samuel, 12.7.

III. 240   serpent-skin: Glaucus's lower body was the scaly tail of a fish.

III. 243   that giant: Typhœs, 'a famous giant … who had 100 heads like those of a serpent or dragon' (L). Jupiter crushed him under Mount Etna in Sicily. Cf. *Hyperion*, II. 22–8 and n.

III. 251   Sisters three: the Fates, but see also Macbeth's three witches at III. 254 and n. below.

III. 254   wither, droop, and pine: see *Macbeth*, 1.3.22–3: 'Weary sev'n-nights nine times nine, / Shall he dwindle, peak, and pine'.

III. 265   magian: magical; *OED* cites this line as the sole instance of the word in this sense.

III. 269   Tartarus: L: 'one of the regions of hell, where, according to the antients, the most impious and guilty among mankind were punished'.

III. 274   garner'd: gathered up and stored. Cf. 'When I have fears', 3–4.

III. 285   contumelious: contemptuous.

III. 305   case: body.

III. 318–638   The tale of Glaucus and Scylla is freely adapted from Ovid's *Metamorphoses*, XIII.

III. 338   trod no measures: did not dance.

III. 342   Plaining: complaining (as in the cry of a sea-gull). discrepant: 'Apart or separate in space', *OED*, citing this line as the last recorded use of the word in this sense.

III. 351   gulph'd: see I. 571n.

III. 364   Æthon: one of Apollo's horses; see also I. 552 and n.

III. 366   brim of day-tide: noon.

III. 372–92   In *Metamorphoses*, Glaucus becomes a sea god by eating a magical herb found on the seashore.

III. 376   ocean's sire: the god Neptune.

III. 380–7   Possibly an illustration of K's idea of self-loss in achieving 'fellowship with essence' (I. 779 and n.); cf. also K's description of the sea in *Sleep and Poetry*, 375–80.

III. 399   Scylla: daughter 'of the giant Typhon, or, as some say, of Phorcys, who was greatly loved by Glaucus' (L).

III. 402   white of truth: the 'white' is the centre of a target; hence, here, 'complete truth'.

III. 406   The ends of the earth; the 'Pillars of Hercules' were rocks at the entrance of the Mediterranean between Spain and Africa, originally separated by Hercules.

III. 415   Ææa's isle: where Circe lived, off the coast of Italy.

III. 428   flower'd Elysium: See II. 663 n. above.

III. 449–72   In *Metamorphoses*, Glaucus resists Circe's advances;

in revenge, Circe changes Scylla's lower body into a pack of wild dogs.

III. 454 **ambrosia**: 'The food of the gods ... sweeter than honey, and of a most odoriferous smell' (L).

III. 459 **arbitrary**: despotic; cf. III. 507 below.

III. 461 **Amphion**: said to have been the inventor of music, and 'to have built the walls of Thebes at the sound of his lyre' (L).

III. 467 Glaucus was at liberty to wander through Circe's enchanted bower.

III. 474 **Pluto**: god 'of the infernal regions, of death and funerals' (L); cf. I. 944 n. above.

III. 476 **specious**: without genuine substance.

III. 488 **complain**: complaint.

III. 493 **brake**: see I. 18 n.

III. 494 **gordian**: entwined, knotted. Cf. I. 614 and n.

III. 500 **wizard**: bewitched.

III. 503–4 Charon 'conducted the souls of the dead in a boat over the rivers Styx and Acheron to the infernal regions, for an obolus' (L).

III. 528 **wildering**: perplexing.

III. 529 **writhen**: twisted.

III. 530–1 Python was a celebrated serpent that emerged from mud after Deucalion's flood; cf. II. 197–8 n. Boreas was the north wind.

III. 545–6 Cf. Brutus to Portia, *Julius Caesar*, 2.1.288–90: 'You are my true and honourable wife, / As dear to me as are the ruddy drops / That visit my sad heart'.

III. 552 **mesh**: entanglement; cf. 'dull mortality's harsh net', III. 907.

III. 567 **Dis**: Pluto.

III. 568 Cf. *La belle dame sans merci*, 9–10.

III. 588 **thews**: bodily powers.

III. 615–6 The inverted syntax here probably reflects K's recent reading of *Paradise Lost*; see headnote to Book III.

III. 619–35 Scylla's deathly sleep is K's invention; in *Metamorphoses* Circe turned her into a monster.

III. 624–5 Cf. *Sleep and Poetry*, 376–80.

III. 653 **Eolus**: Aeolus was god of the winds.

III. 656–60 Cf. *The Tempest*, 1.2.3–9:

> The sky, it seems, would pour down stinking pitch,
> But that the sea, mounting to th' welkin's cheek,
> Dashes the fire out. O, I have suffered
> With those that I saw suffer! a brave vessel,
> (Who had, no doubt, some noble creature in her,)
> Dash'd all to pieces. O, the cry did knock
> Against my very heart! Poor souls, they perish'd!

III. 656 **shrouds:** the ship's rigging.

III. 659 **gulphing:** cf. I. 571 n.

III. 661 **eld:** old age.

III. 684–5 Each line as powerful as Atlas in alleviating pain. See *To Charles Cowden Clarke*, 63 n.

III. 695–6 The inverted syntax here reflects K's recent reading of *Paradise Lost*; see headnote to Book III.

III. 700 Cf. I. 779 n.

III. 706 **Time's creeping:** cf. *Macbeth*, 5.5.19–20: 'To-morrow, and tomorrow, and to-morrow, / Creeps in this petty pace from day to day'.

III. 728 **haughty Mars:** god of war.

III. 737–44 This passage may well owe something to the preparation of the dead K had witnessed at Guy's Hospital.

III. 756 **clue:** a ball of thread.

III. 762 **charactery:** cf. 'When I have fears', 3 n.

III. 766–806 Probably written on 20 Sept. 1817; see Bailey's letter to Reynolds, 21 Sept. 1817: 'There is one passage of Keats's 3d Book which beats all he has written. It is on *death*. He wrote it last night' (*KC*, I. 7).

III. 786 **Apollo's touch:** the warmth of the sun.

III. 802 **ooz'd out:** cf. *To Autumn*, 21–2.

III. 816 Cf. *To Autumn*, 33.

III. 819 **spar:** see II. 204 n.

III. 830 **sea-mark:** a buoy or other object serving as a guide at sea.

III. 835 **shoulder'd:** cf. CCC on K's early reading of Spenser. 'He *hoisted* himself up, and looked burly and dominant, as he said, "what an image that is – *'sea-shouldering whales!'*"' (*Recollections*, 126). See *The Faerie Queene*, 2.12.23: 'sea-shouldring Whales'.

III. 845–9 The syntax and punctuation are confusing. The sense of the passage is: What poor mortals treasure up in fragments pure as marble was there used lavishly, in a palace whose size far surpassed that of the greatest cities of antiquity.

III. 850–1 Iris, goddess of rainbows.

III. 853 **Paphian army:** an army of lovers. Cf. I. 510 n.

III. 856 **raught:** reached. Cf. II. 282.

III. 862–5 Jack, 159, suggests this scene may recall 'the portrayal of Neptune and Venus in Tooke's *Pantheon* and Poussin's "The Triumph of Neptune and Amphitrite" as well as the section "Of the Deities of the Waters" in Spence's *Polymetis*'. Jack also suggests that these images influenced the 'Hymn to Neptune', III. 943–90.

III. 882–7 The syntax here is confusing: 'The lake might appear to be air, but for the clouds and sky reflected in it. So too the palace floor might be taken for air, but for the wonders glimpsed in its depths – the blazing dome and its reflection together forming a "golden sphere".'

III. 888–9 Triton: see I. 206 n. Nereids ... Syrens: L: 'nymphs of the sea'.

III. 893 ooze-born Goddess: Venus; cf. I. 624–7.

III. 899 Nais: mother of Glaucus by Neptune.

III. 908–15 Venus knows of Diana's love for Endymion.

III. 918 Cytherea: an island in the Aegean sea, sacred to Venus.

III. 923 halcyon: see I. 453–5 n.

III. 927 pleach'd: intertwined. Cf. *Much Ado About Nothing*, 3.1.7–9: 'the pleached bower / Where honeysuckles, ripen'd by the sun, / Forbid the sun to enter'. See also III. 930 n. below.

III. 930 coverture: shelter; cf. *Much Ado About Nothing*, 3.1.30: 'couched in the woodbine coverture'.

III. 943–90 For the imagery in the Hymn to Neptune, see III. 862–5 n. above.

III. 951 Eolus: See III. 653 n.

III. 956 gulphs: rushes forward.

III. 973 Eolian twang: the sound of an Aeolian Harp.

III. 975 Cytherea: Venus; cf. II. 492 n., and III. 918 n.

III. 994 Oceanus: L: 'a powerful deity of the sea ... According to Homer, Oceanus was the father of all the gods ... He is generally represented as an old man with a long flowing beard, and sitting upon the waves of the sea'. For K's later interest in Oceanus, see *Hyperion*, II. 163–243.

III. 1000 Doris was a 'goddess of the sea, daughter of Oceanus and Tethys' (L). She married her brother Nereus, also a sea god – hence K's 'Egean seer': 'He had the gift of prophecy, and informed those that consulted him [of] the different fates that attended them' (L.).

III. 1002–5 For Amphion, see III. 461 n.; for Amphitrite see II. 109 n.; for Thetis, see II. 611 n.

III. 1008–9 dizzier pain: cf. *On seeing the Elgin Marbles*, 11: 'a most dizzy pain'.

Book IV Written at Hampstead and at Burford Bridge, Surrey, Oct.–Nov. 1817. By 30 Oct. he had 'written 300 Lines' of Book IV (*Letters*, 30). In his letter to Bailey, 22 Nov. 1817, K explains: 'I am just arrived at Dorking to change the Scene – change the Air and give me a spur to wind up my Poem, of which there are wanting 500 Lines' (*Letters*, 38). Completed 28 Nov. 1817 at Burford Bridge (*TKP*, 146). He must have written the second half of Book IV at the rate of some 80 lines a day (cf. Bailey's account of K's habits of composition in headnote to Book III).

IV. 1–29 This invocation, outlining the development of poetry, recalls Milton's manner in *Paradise Lost*, recently read by K (see headnote to Book III). K copied out this passage in his letter to Bailey, 28–30 Oct. 1817, with the comment: 'you will see from the Manner I had not an opportunity of mentioning any Poets, for fear of spoiling the effect of the passage by particularising them!' (*Letters*, 29–30).

IV. 1   **my native land**: possibly echoing Byron's *Childe Harold*, I. 125 (1812); see IV. 30–1 n. and IV. 354 below.

IV. 10   Referring to the Bible.

IV. 11–14   The classical poets.

IV. 15   **Ausonia**: an ancient name for Italy; the two voices are Virgil and Dante.

IV. 18–20   **done ... undone ... barren souls**: recalling the repetition of 'done' following the murder of Duncan in *Macbeth*, 2.2.9–14 (see also IV. 21 n. and IV. 28 n. below). K emphasises the magnitude of past poetic achievements in contrast to the poverty of the present. Cf. II. 723–9 above.

IV. 21   **curbs ... frets**: cf. *Macbeth*, 3.4.23: 'cabin'd, cribb'd, confin'd, bound in'.

IV. 22   **despondency besets**: cf. I. 8 above, and Wordsworth's *Resolution and Independence*, 49: 'thereof comes in the end despondency and madness'.

IV. 26   **shrives**: confesses (to the 'Great Muse' in IV. 20). Cf. *Isabella*, 64.

IV. 27   **I thought on poets gone**: echoing Wordsworth's meditation on dead poets in *Resolution and Independence*, 43: 'I thought of Chatterton . . .'.

IV. 28   **could not pray**: cf. *Macbeth*, 2.2.28: 'I could not say, "Amen"'.

IV. 29   **lowliness of heart**: cf. the conclusion of Wordsworth's *Lines Left Upon a Seat in a Yew-Tree* (1797–8):

> True dignity abides with him alone
> Who, in the silent hour of inward thought,
> Can still suspect, and still revere himself,
> In lowliness of heart.   (57–60)

IV. 30–1   Cf. *Childe Harold* (1812), I. 124–5: 'Farewell awhile to him and thee, / My native land – Good Night'.

IV. 34   **freshet**: a small stream of fresh water.

IV. 39   **hecatomb**: a large number.

IV. 56   **Phœbe**: L: 'a name given to Diana or the moon, on account of the brightness of that luminary'.

IV. 66   **Hermes' wand**: see I. 563 n. Hermes was the Greek name for Mercury.

IV. 68–9   **Hyacinthus**: see I. 326–9 and n.

IV. 95   **triple soul**: Endymion has a 'triple soul' because of his love for the moon, his unknown goddess, and for the Indian maid.

IV. 110   **sith**: since.

IV. 111   **Thou art my executioner**: Cf. Phebe's words to Silvius in *As You Like It*, 3.5.8: 'I would not be thy executioner'.

IV. 118 **that lily hand**: a detail which lends support to Sir Sidney Colvin's suggestion that K's Indian Maid was derived from his reading of the old French *Lai d' Aristote* in G. L. Way's *Fabliaux or Tales* (1800); see Sidney Colvin, *John Keats. His Life and Poetry, His Friends, Critics and After-Fame* (1917), 33 and n., 551–3.

IV. 121 **Erebus**: hell, named after the god Erebus 'son of Chaos and Darkness' (L).

IV. 129 **gorgon**: terrible.

IV. 145 **roundelay**: a short simple song with a refrain (*OED*).

IV. 146–181 K copied out this 'little song' (with variations) in his letter to Bailey 3 Nov. 1817 (*Letters*, 34–5); in his letter to Bailey, 22 Nov. 1817, he commented:

I am certain of nothing but of the holiness of the Heart's affections and the truth of Imagination – What the imagination seizes as Beauty must be truth – whether it existed before or not – for I have the same Idea of all our Passions as of Love they are all in their sublime, creative of essential Beauty – In a Word, you may know my favorite Speculation by my first Book [*Endymion*, I. 777 ff.] and the little song I sent in my last – which is a representation from the fancy of the probable mode of operating in these Matters – The Imagination may be compared to Adam's dream – he awoke and found it truth. I am the more zealous in this affair, because I have never yet been able to perceive how any thing can be known for truth by consequitive reading – and yet it must be – Can it be that even the greatest Philosopher ever arrived at his goal without putting aside numerous objections – However it may be, O for a Life of Sensations rather than of Thoughts! It is "a Vision in the form of Youth" a Shadow of reality to come (*Letters*, 36–7).

IV. 148 **vermeil**: see I. 50 n.

IV. 157 **spry**: spray.

IV. 186 Echoing Milton's *Lycidas*, 150: 'And daffadillies fill their cups with tears'.

IV. 193–272 K's triumphal progress of Bacchus, god of wine and of drinkers, may have been influenced by Poussin's 'Indian Triumph of Bacchus', and by Titian's 'Bacchus and Ariadne'; see Jack, 159–60, and plate 19. See also L: 'His expedition into the east is celebrated. He marched, at the head of an army composed of men, as well as of women, all inspired with divine fury, and armed with thyrsuses, cymbals, and other musical instruments. The leader was drawn in a chariot by a lion and a tyger, and was accompanied by Pan and Silenus, and all the Satyrs. His conquests were easy, and without bloodshed: the people easily submitted, and gratefully elevated to the rank of a god the hero who taught them the use of the vine, the cultivation of the earth, and the manner of making honey'.

IV. 195 **purple**: with wine.

IV. 210 **ivy-dart**: ivy was sacred to Bacchus; cf. IV. 240 below.

IV. 212   **imbrued:** stained.

IV. 215–17   L: 'Silenus is generally represented as a fat and jolly old man, riding on an ass, crowned with flowers, and always intoxicated'. A portly Silenus appears in Poussin's 'Indian Triumph of Bacchus' propped up on an ass's back by two attendants; see Jack, plate 19.

IV. 228   **Satyrs:** L: 'They are represented like men, but with the feet and the legs of goats, short horns on the head, and the whole body covered with thick hair. They chiefly attended upon Bacchus, and rendered themselves known in his orgies by their riot and lasciviousness'.

IV. 241–2   Bacchus's chariot is drawn by leopards in Poussin's 'Indian Triumph of Bacchus', and in the background are two elephants; see Jack, plate 19.

IV. 247   **coil:** bustle and noise.

IV. 251   **panthers' furs:** L: 'The panther is sacred to [Bacchus], because he went in his expedition covered with the skin of that beast'.

IV. 256   **spleenful unicorn:** unicorns were not traditionally associated with Bacchus's expedition. A grumpy-looking unicorn does appear, however, in the background of Poussin's 'Indian Triumph of Bacchus'; see Jack, plate 19.

IV. 257   **Osirian Egypt:** Osiris was 'a great deity of the Egyptians, son of Jupiter and Niobe' (L).

IV. 263   **vail:** lower as a gesture of respect. Cf. II. 793 and n.

IV. 265   **Great Brahma:** in Hinduism, the Absolute, or God conceived as an impersonal abstraction.

IV. 295–7   Cf. 'In drear nighted December', 1–6.

IV. 318   **let me sip that tear:** cf. *Isabella*, 39 and n.

IV. 331   **Mercury:** cf. I. 384, 563 and nn.

IV. 333   **slanted hail-storm:** cf. *The Eve of St Agnes*, 322–3, 325.

IV. 336   **his wand:** cf. I. 563 and n.

IV. 346   **in spleen:** fiery-tempered and resolute.

IV. 349–50   Anticipating *The Eve of St Agnes*, 370: 'And they are gone: ay, ages long ago'.

IV. 370   **pillow:** cf. IV. 385 n., and IV. 389 below.

IV. 375   **Cimmerian:** dark, obscure; from the people reputed by the ancients to live in perpetual darkness.

IV. 380   **Jove's daughter:** Diana (Phoebe) was daughter of Latona by Jupiter.

IV. 385   **litter:** the vehicle in which Sleep journeys, reclining on a couch. Cf. Milton's *Comus*, 553: 'the litter of close-curtained sleep'.

IV. 392   **sallows:** willows; cf. II. 341 and n. above.

IV. 394   **old Skiddaw:** the mountain above Keswick in the north of the Lake District. K knew the mountain from his reading of Wordsworth's poems, and saw it during his walk through the Lake District in June 1818.

IV. 399 **splenetic:** cf. IV. 346 and n. above.

IV. 400 **blood wide:** distended.

IV. 407 **the mournful wanderer:** Endymion.

IV. 410 Peacocks were associated with Juno.

IV. 413 **Pallas:** Pallas Athene (Minerva), 'goddess of wisdom, war, and all the liberal arts. ... In one hand she held a spear, and in the other a shield' (L). See II. 791, 799 and nn. above.

IV. 415 **Hebe:** L: 'goddess of youth ... cup-bearer to all the gods', displaced by Jupiter's favourite Ganymede. See I. 170 n. above.

IV. 422 **Green-kyrtled:** wrapped in a green gown.

IV. 424 **Hours:** nymphs that attend upon the sun; cf. *Hyperion*, I. 216.

IV. 426 **floating morris:** dancing in the air.

IV. 427 **Dis:** see III. 567 n.

IV. 429–31 **Dian's ... goddess:** Diana and Endymion's unknown goddess are revealed as identical.

IV. 430 **crescented:** see II. 309 n.

IV. 440–2 Referring to Icarus; see *Sleep and Poetry*, 302–4 n.

IV. 456 Cf. K's remark in his letter to Bailey, 22 Nov. 1817: 'The Imagination may be compared to Adam's dream – he awoke and found it truth' (*Letters*, 37).

IV. 459 **dædale:** cunning, here possibly also with the sense 'changeful' (*OED*).

IV. 461 **bourne:** boundary.

IV. 479 **Nemesis:** L: 'one of the infernal deities ... goddess of vengeance, always prepared to punish impiety, and at the same time liberally to reward the good and virtuous'.

IV. 485 **Vesper:** see I. 363 n.

IV. 512–54 The 'Cave of Quietude' (see IV. 548), a retreat in which K develops his theme of the interconnection between suffering and creativity. For more, see J. M. Murry, *The Mystery of Keats* (1949), 118–50.

IV. 531 **death-watch ... stifled:** The ticking of the death-watch beetle is superstitiously held to portend death; it is 'stifled' when death has occurred. See *A Dictionary of Superstitions*, ed. I. Opie and M. Tatem (1992), 117–18.

IV. 536 **Semele:** mother of Bacchus by Jupiter.

IV. 558 **mask:** the masque was an elaborate entertainment, popular in aristocratic circles during the seventeenth century, with which K was familiar from his reading in the Elizabethans, Jacobeans, and Milton. Here he refers to the procession that was often part of the masque; K's spelling was an acceptable form in his time.

IV. 569 **lucid:** shining.

IV. 570 For Zephyrus see 'I stood tip-toe', 175 n.; for Flora, see *Sleep and Poetry*, 102 n.

IV. 575   **pines**: pineapples.

IV. 576   **latter-mint**: K's own coinage, meaning late-growing mint.

IV. 581–605   Figures from the zodiac (the 'belt of heaven', IV. 581) and from the constellations of the stars join in a procession to celebrate Diana's wedding. K copied out IV. 581–90 in his letter to Reynolds, 22 Nov. 1817; see *Letters*, 41.

IV. 582   **Aquarius**: the water-carrier; L points out that Ganymede was 'changed to this sign', and here K follows this tradition.

IV. 589   **Star-Queen**: Diana.

IV. 591–2   Castor and Pollux were twin brothers, sons of Jupiter by Leda; they were transformed by Jupiter into the constellation Gemini. Here they defeat two other constellations, the 'Lion' (Leo) and the 'Bear' (Ursa Major).

IV. 597   **Centaur**: the constellation Sagittarius.

IV. 599   **shent**: disgraced.

IV. 602–9   The constellations Andromeda and Perseus ('Danae's Son', IV. 606), representing two lovers whose story in some respects parallels that of Endymion and Diana; see *Metamorphoses*, IV.

IV. 611   Daphne was rescued from Apollo's lustful pursuit when she was turned into a tree; see *Metamorphoses*, I.

IV. 623   Diana has now resumed her disguise as the Indian Maid.

IV. 646–55   Here Endymion seems deliberately to reject the visionary idealism of Shelley's *Alastor* (1816).

IV. 669–70   Echoing the conclusion of *Paradise Lost*, XII, where Adam and Eve leave Paradise: 'The world was all before them, where to choose / Their place of rest . . .' (646–7).

IV. 686   Alluding to the legend of Pan and Syrinx; see I. 242–3 and n.

IV. 697–8   **eglantine . . . bee wine**: cf. *Ode to a Nightingale*, 46, 49.

IV. 701   **Vesta**: L: 'mother of the gods . . . the patroness of the vestal virgins and the goddess of fire . . . a fire was continually kept lighted by a certain number of virgins, who had dedicated themselves to the service of the goddess'.

IV. 704–709   For Vesper, see I. 363 n. above; for Flora, see *Sleep and Poetry*, 102 n.; for Naiad, see *To Charles Cowden Clarke*, 6 n.

IV. 713   **my Delphos**: my oracle. Cf. *On receiving a laurel crown from Leigh Hunt*, 3 n.

IV. 730–48   Addressed to Cupid, the 'feather'd tyrant' of IV. 730.

IV. 759   Cf. *Ode to a Nightingale*, 55: 'Now more than ever seems it rich to die'.

IV. 760–1   Addressed to the 'voluptuous thought' of IV. 759.

IV. 769   **cirque**: circle.

IV. 774   **lute-voic'd brother**: Apollo, Diana's brother (and therefore Endymion's), about whom K was already projecting a poem. He began *Hyperion* in autumn 1818.

IV. 780–2   Anticipating the opening lines of *Hyperion*, esp. I. 10.

IV. 783   **amaranth:** a mythical flower that never fades.
IV. 784   The Eden-like world of early childhood.
IV. 792   **fear'd:** frightened.
IV. 808   Cf. Balthasar's song in *Much Ado About Nothing*, 2.3.62: 'Sigh no more, ladies, sigh no more'.
IV. 877–8   See Matthew, 10. 29–31: 'Are not two sparrows sold for a farthing? and one of them shall not fall on the ground without your Father. But the very hairs of your head are all numbered. Fear ye not therefore, ye are of more value than many sparrows'.
IV. 884   **monitor:** guide, instruct.
IV. 906   **maw:** see I. 267 n.
IV. 929   **serene father:** Apollo, the summer sun.
IV. 936   **sward:** see *Sleep and Poetry*, 258 n.
IV. 943   **Titan's foe:** Jupiter.
IV. 950   **seemlihed:** seemliness, an archaic word deriving from K's reading in Spenser's *Faerie Queene*.
IV. 953   **Rhadamanthus:** L: 'one of the judges of hell . . . employed in the infernal regions in obliging the dead to confess their crimes, and in punishing them for their offences'.
IV. 955   'According to Apollodorus, Prometheus made the first man and woman that ever were upon the earth, with clay, which he animated by means of the fire which he had stolen from heaven' (L).
IV. 956–7   Cf. the description of Saturn in *Hyperion*, I. 89–90, 92–4.
IV. 959   **lorn:** forlorn.
IV. 988   **lucid:** see IV. 569 n. above.
IV. 1000–3   See Benjamin Bailey's letter to John Taylor, 20 May 1818: 'I have read over the Poem two or three times with *great* attention . . . The 4th book, which I at first thought inferior, I *now* think as fine, & perhaps finer than any. . . . Nor do I think the abrupt conclusion so bad – it is *rather*, but not *much* too abrupt. It is like the conclusion of Paradise Regained' (*KC*, I. 25).
IV. 1002–3   Cf. 'I stood tip-toe', 141–2: 'Psyche went / On the smooth wind to realms of wonderment'.

'In drear nighted December' (p. 134)
Written Dec. 1817. First published in the *Literary Gazette*, 19 Sept. 1829. Text based on K's manuscript fair copy in Bristol University Library, reproduced and discussed in relation to other mss and printed texts of the poem by Alvin Whitley, 'The Autograph of Keats's "In Drear Nighted December"', *Harvard Library Bulletin*, 5 (1951), 116–22. The poem is related to K's idea of 'negative capability' in his letter to George and Tom Keats, 21, 27 Dec. 1817, *Letters*, 42–3. For further discussion, see in particular Dickstein, 7–14; Jones, 35–41.

1–6   Cf. *Endymion*, IV. 295–7.

8 **prime:** springtime.
15 **petting:** sulking.
21 See Richard Woodhouse's letter to John Taylor, 23 Nov. 1818: 'I plead guilty, even before I am accused, of an utter abhorrence of the word "feel" for feeling (substantively) – But Keats seems fond of it and will ingraft it "in aeternum" on our language' (*KC*, 1. 64). Cf. K's similar use of 'feel' as a noun in *Endymion*, 11. 284, 111. 139, 496.

Lines on seeing a Lock of Milton's Hair (p. 134)
Written 21 Jan. 1818. First published in *Plymouth and Devonport Weekly Journal*, 15 Nov. 1838. See K's letter to Bailey, 23 Jan. 1818: 'I was at Hunt's the other day, and he surprised me with a real authenticated Lock of *Milton's Hair*. I know you would like what I wrote thereon – so here it is [K transcribes his poem] . . . This I did at Hunt's at his request – perhaps I should have done something better alone and at home' (*Letters*, 53–5). The poem reflects K's new admiration for Milton, dating from his visit to Bailey at Oxford in Sept. 1817: see headnote to *Endymion*, 111. For further reading, see Bate, 285–7; Dickstein, 136–8; Lucy Newlyn, *'Paradise Lost' and the Romantic Reader* (1993), 26–7. Text based on K's fair copy, written on the last page of his reprint of Shakespeare's First Folio at Keats House, Hampstead.

1 **organic numbers:** poetry which resembles the tones of an organ. Cf. *Hyperion*, 1. 48.
2 **spheres:** the music of the spheres.
18 **young delian oath:** the oath of a young poet (like K himself). The island of Delos was the birthplace of Apollo, god of poetry; see *Endymion*, 1. 966.

On sitting down to read King Lear *once again* (p. 136)
Written 22 Jan. 1818. See K's letter to Bailey, 23 Jan. 1818: 'I sat down to read King Lear yesterday, and felt the greatness of the thing up to the writing of a Sonnet preparatory thereto'; see also K's letter to George and Tom Keats, 23 Jan. 1818: 'I sat down yesterday to read King Lear once again and the thing appeared to demand the prologue of a Sonnet, I wrote it & began to read' (*Letters*, 55, 57). The sonnet concludes with a couplet, registering K's attraction to the Shakespearean rhyme-scheme from Jan. 1818 onwards. First published in *Plymouth and Devonport Weekly Journal*, 8 Nov. 1838. Text based on K's fair copy written opposite the first page of *King Lear*, in his reprint of Shakespeare's First Folio at Keats House, Hampstead. For further discussion, see Dickstein, 138–42; J. Bate, *Shakespeare and the English Romantic Imagination* (1986), 166–9; R. S. White, *Keats as a Reader of Shakespeare* (1987), 23–30.

1 **romance:** K was preparing his 'Poetic Romance' *Endymion* for the

press during Jan. 1818, and this emphasised the contrast between
'Romantic' poetry and Shakespeare's writing; see K's letter to Bailey,
23 Jan. 1818 (*Letters*, 55).

2   **Fair plumed syren**: 'Romance' is imagined as a Spenserian heroine.

5   **once again**: for K's earlier reading of *King Lear*, see headnote to *On the Sea*.

7   **assay**: test.

13–14   K will be reborn through the fiery experience of reading *King Lear*. The phoenix was a mythical bird reputed to live five or six hundred years, 'after which it burnt itself to ashes on a funeral pyre of aromatic twigs ignited by the sun and fanned by its own wings, but only to emerge from its ashes with renewed youth, to live through another cycle of years' (*OED*).

'When I have fears that I may cease to be' (p. 136)
Written between 22 and 31 Jan. 1818; first published *L&L*, II. 293, from which the text here is drawn. This sonnet shows K's attraction from this moment to the Shakespearean form (see also headnote to previous poem). Cf. K's later break with this form of the sonnet; see *To Sleep* and 'If by dull rhymes', and headnotes.

1   Cf. Shakespeare's sonnet 12, 'When I do count the clock that tells the time', and sonnet 107, 'Not mine own fears . . .'. K also echoes Coleridge's poem 'Human Life, on the Denial of Immortality', published in *Sibylline Leaves* (1817): 'If dead, we cease to be; if total gloom / Swallow up life's brief flash for aye . . .' (1–2).

3   **charact'ry**: writing, handwritten or printed.

4   **garners**: granaries.

5–6   Cf. K to J. H. Reynolds, 19 Feb. 1818: 'man should . . . weave a tapestry empyrean – full of Symbols for his spiritual eye' (*Letters*, 66).

7–8   Richard Woodhouse remarked: 'These lines give some insight into K's mode of writing Poetry. He had repeatedly said that he never sits down to write, unless he is full of ideas – and then thoughts come about him in troops, as tho' soliciting to be acc[epte]d & he selects – one of his Maxims is that if P[oetry] does not come naturally, it had better not come at all' (*KC*, I. 128).

Robin Hood. To a Friend (p. 137)
Written early Feb. 1818 and transcribed in a letter to J. H. Reynolds, 3 Feb. 1818, the 'friend' in the title (*Letters*, 61–2). First published *1820*, the basis of the text here.

K's poem responds to Reynolds's 'Robin Hood Sonnets' (*To a Friend, on Robin Hood* and *To the Same*) recently read by K and subsequently printed in the *Yellow Dwarf*, 21 Feb. 1818. In his letter to Reynolds, K attacks the egotism and 'palpable design' of contemporary poetry –

especially Wordsworth's and Hunt's – and compares the 'great & unobtrusive' poetry of the past: 'Let us have the old Poets, & robin Hood' (*Letters*, 60–1). In poem and letter K compares the diminished present and a lost English past, associating the great Elizabethan poets and the folk-hero Robin Hood with English liberties and antipathy to capitalist values (cf. *Isabella*, stanzas 14–16). For further reading see Dickstein, 159–61; John Barnard, 'Keats's "Robin Hood", John Hamilton Reynolds, and the "Old Poets"', *Proceedings of the British Academy*, 75 (1989), 181–200.

6–9 The trees are 'sheared' of their leaves by winter, like sheep of their fleeces; cf. 52 below.

10 **rent or leases:** as an outlaw, Robin Hood lived freely in Sherwood Forest. K told Reynolds that this poem, and *Lines on the Mermaid Tavern* were 'written in the Spirit of Outlawry' (*Letters*, 62).

13 **ivory shrill:** the sound of a hunting horn.

18 **forest drear:** cf. Milton, *Il Penseroso*, 119: 'Of forests, and enchantments drear'.

21–2 **seven stars ... polar ray:** the Pleiades and the North Star.

26 **can:** a drinking vessel. See *Lines on the Mermaid Tavern*, 12 and n.

30 **pasture:** pastoral.

33 **morris din:** the music and noise of morris-dancing.

34 **song of Gamelyn:** *The Tale of Gamelyn*, a mediaeval romance once attributed to Chaucer. Gamelyn rebels against his tyrannical elder brother and, like Robin Hood, becomes leader of outlaws in the forests.

36 **'grenè shawe':** see Chaucer's 'Friar's Tale', 88.

55 **tight:** skilful, smart, compact: ironically applied to 'Little John', so named because of his great height.

62 **us two:** K and Reynolds; see headnote. **burden:** the refrain of a song.

Lines on the Mermaid Tavern (p. 138)
Written early Feb. 1818, and transcribed after *Robin Hood* in K's letter to Reynolds, 3 Feb. 1818 (*Letters*, 62). First published in *1820*, the basis of the text here.

K may have written the poem after a visit to the Mermaid Tavern, Cheapside, formerly the meeting-place of Elizabethan and Jacobean poets and dramatists such as Shakespeare, Jonson, Beaumont and Fletcher (see Gittings, 281). Like his letter to Reynolds and *Robin Hood*, this poem expresses K's admiration for 'the old Poets' of the Elizabethan era. For further reading see Dickstein, 130–1; John Barnard, 'Keats's "Robin Hood", John Hamilton Reynolds, and the "Old Poets"', *Proceedings of the British Academy*, 75 (1989), 181–200.

2 **Elysium:** where the souls of the virtuous were placed after death: 'There happiness was complete' (L).

10–11 For Robin Hood, politics, and poetry, see headnote to previous poem and Barnard's essay, cited above.

12 **bowse:** drink with relish. **horn and can:** drinking vessels, which K associated with the distant past.

17 **sheepskin:** a parchment made of sheepskin.

To — ['*Time's sea*'] (p. 139)
Written 4 Feb. 1818; first published in *Hood's Magazine* (Sept. 1844) and subsequently in *L&L*, II. 297. Text here based on *L&L*. The sonnet is addressed to a woman K had glimpsed in Vauxhall Gardens in summer 1814. For further reading, see Gittings, 280–1, and Jones, 197–200.

1–2 The imagery and phrasing recall Shakespeare's sonnets 60 and 104.

14 The antithesis is Shakespearean. **darling joys:** also recalls Shakespeare; cf. sonnet 18, 3: 'the darling buds of May'.

'*Dear Reynolds, as last night I lay in bed*' (p. 140)
Written 25 Mar. 1818 at Teignmouth. First published (without last four lines) *L&L*, I. 113–16. Text here based on *Letters*, 79–82.

K's verse epistle was accompanied by a short letter to Reynolds, who was ill at the time: 'In hopes of cheering you through a Minute or two I was determined nill he will he to send you some lines so you will excuse the unconnected subject, and careless verse – You know, I am sure, Claude's Enchanted Castle and I wish you may be pleased with my remembrance of it' (*Letters*, 82). Jack, 127–30, discusses K's response to Claude, suggesting that he knew the 'Enchanted Castle' from William Woollett's famous engraving of 1782 (reproduced in Jack, plate 12). The poem's light-hearted mood turns, at line 67, to a more serious considera-tion of life's contradictions, suffering, and the role of the imagination, in a way that looks forward to the odes of 1819 and to *The Fall of Hyperion*. For further discussion, see Bate, 306–9; Dickstein, 149–56; Sperry, 117–31; Barnard, 54–5.

1–12 K's account of 'disjointed' dreams, and the effects of daytime life on dreaming (see 70–1 below), may be indebted to his reading of Hunt's essays 'On the Night-Mare' in *The Round Table* (1817), esp. 226–7; two figures listed by Keats appear in Hunt's essay, Socrates and 'Alexander in bed after one of his triumphant feasts'.

7 K had been reading Voltaire in Feb. 1818 (*Letters*, 68). **casque:** helmet. **habergeon:** a jacket of chain mail.

8 See 1–12 n. above.

10 K's joke turns on the fact that Maria Edgeworth (1767–1849) was fond of cats, and she was disliked by Hazlitt; see for example, 'On the English Novelists', Howe, VI. 123–4.

11   Junius Brutus Booth (1796–1852), actor. **so so**: drunk.

16   **tushes**: tusks.

18   **Æolian harps**: see *Endymion*, II. 866 n.

19   **Titian colours**: richly coloured, like Titian's paintings.

20–2   Details here suggest K was thinking of Claude's 'Landscape with the Father of Psyche sacrificing at the Milesian Temple of Apollo', see Jack, 130, and plate 35. Cf. also *Ode on a Grecian Urn*, 31–4 and n.

20   **pontif**: pontiff, or high priest.

26–66   K's description of Claude's 'Enchanted Castle' incorporates some details from the same artist's 'Landscape with the Father of Psyche . . .'. See headnote and 20–2 n. above.

29   **Urganda**: enchantress in the fifteenth-century romance *Amadis of Gaul*.

30   **Phœbus**: see 'I stood tip-toe', 212 n.

32   **my friend**: Reynolds, see headnote.

34   **Merlin's Hall**: the castle appears to have been built by a magician such as Merlin.

36   **rills**: streams.

39–40   Perhaps recalling the Titans Enceladus or Typhoeus, buried underground by Jupiter. It is just possible that K refers to the mounds of prehistoric earthworks ('giants' graves') on Salisbury Plain, seen on his coach-journey from London to Teignmouth, 4–6 Mar. 1818.

41   **see**: dwelling-place.

42   **santon**: 'A European designation for a kind of monk or hermit among the Muslims' (*OED*).

44   **Cuthbert de Saint Aldebrim**: invented by K.

46   **Lapland witch**: associated with black magic. Cf. *Paradise Lost*, II. 664–5: 'Lured with the smell of infant blood, to dance / With Lapland witches'. K's intensive reading of *Paradise Lost* dated from Sept. 1817; see headnote to *Endymion*, III.

50   Cf. *Ode to a Nightingale*, 69–70: 'magic casements, opening on the foam / Of perilous seas . . .'.

57   **lightening**: flashing with light.

58   Cf. *Ode to a Nightingale*, 40: 'verdurous glooms'.

68–9   Cf. Wordsworth's *Tintern Abbey*, 96–8: 'a sense sublime / Of something far more deeply interfused, / Whose dwelling is the light of setting suns'.

70–1   Evoking the disjointed aspects of daytime life as they appear in dreams; cf. the opening passage of the poem, 1–12 and n.

72–3   K recalls 'The Life of Alcibiades' in *Plutarch's Lives*, tr. Thomas North (1676), 178: Alcibiades, intervening to help the Athenians in a sea-battle with the Lacedæmonians, identified himself by 'setting up a Flag in the top of his Admiral Galley, to shew what he was'.

73–4   Cf. *Lines on seeing* a Lock of Milton's Hair, 29–30, and see also K's letter to John Taylor, 24 Apr. 1818: 'I find that I can have no enjoyment in the World but continual drinking of Knowledge . . . the road lies th[r]ough application study and thought. . . . I have been hovering for some time between an exquisite sense of the luxurious and a love of Philosophy . . . I shall turn all my soul to the latter' (*Letters*, 88).

77   Cf. *Ode on a Grecian Urn*, 44: 'Thou, silent form, dost tease us out of thought'.

88   **lampit**: limpet.

90   **rocks were silent**: cf. *Hyperion*, I. 4: 'quiet as a stone'.

93–105   K's meditation on the predatory cruelty of nature may recall schoolboy reading about fishes in William Mavor's *Youth's Miscellany* (1798), 109: 'To obtain food is their ruling passion, and this never deserts them but with life. Their digestive faculties are immense: a single pike has been known to devour three hundred roaches in three days. This amazing concoctive power in the cold maws of fishes, has justly excited the curiosity of philosophers . . .'. See also *Isabella*, 113–15 and n., and for K's reading of Mavor at Enfield School, *Recollections*, 124. For K's later reflections on the affinity of humanity and 'wild nature' see his letter of 14 Feb. – 3 May 1819 (*Letters*, 229).

94–5   Cf. *Pericles*, 2.1.26–9: 'I marvel how the fishes live in the sea . . . Why, as men do a-land: the great ones eat up the little ones'.

106   **Moods of one's mind!**: Wordsworth had titled a group of poems 'Moods of my own mind' in his *Poems* (1807).

108   For K's knowledge of the Kamchatka peninsula, in the far north-east of Russia, and the Christian mission there, see A. D. Atkinson, 'Keats and Kamchatka', *Notes & Queries*, 196 (Aug. 1951), 340–6.

111   **new romance**: K was already at work on *Isabella*; see headnote to next poem.

112   **centaine dose**: a 'dose' of one hundred lines.

113   **'here follows prose'**: see *Twelfth Night*, 2.5.142.

Isabella; or, the Pot of Basil (p. 143)

Written Feb.–Apr. 1818. K had begun the poem before quitting Hampstead for Teignmouth on 4 Mar.; see his letter to Reynolds, 27 Apr. 1818: 'I have written for my folio Shakespeare, in which there is the first few stanzas of my "Pot of Basil": I have the rest here finish'd' (*Letters*, 90). First published 1820, the basis of the text here.

K's source was the fifth novel of the fourth day in Boccaccio's *Decameron*, and the poem was intended as a contribution to a volume of verse tales based on Boccaccio which K had projected with Reynolds. K had attended Hazlitt's lecture 'On Dryden and Pope', 3 Feb. 1818, and may have been encouraged by Hazlitt's observation that 'I should think that a translation of some of the other serious tales in Boccaccio . . . as that of Isabella . . . if executed with taste and spirit, could not fail to succeed in the present day' (*Lectures on the English Poets* (1818), in Howe, v. 82). K adopts the ottava rima stanza, familiar from his own copy of Fairfax's translation of Tasso's *Gerusalemme Liberata* (1600) and recently given fashionable currency in Frere's *Whistlecraft* (1817) and Byron's *Beppo* (published 24 Feb. 1818). The poem also shows the decline of Hunt's influence on K's verse, in favour of a more vigorous, consonantal verbal texture.

K had ambivalent feelings about his poem, writing on 22 Sept. 1819 to Richard Woodhouse: 'I will give you a few reasons why I shall persist in not publishing The Pot of Basil – It is too smokeable ... There is too much inexperience of life, and simplicity of knowledge in it ... It is possible to write fine things which cannot be laugh'd at in any way. Isabella is what I should call were I a reviewer "A weak-sided Poem" with an amusing sober-sadness about it' (*Letters*, 298). Cf. K's sense that *Lamia* did not share these weaknesses; see headnote to that poem.

Charles Lamb, reviewing *1820* in *New Times* (19 July 1820), thought the poem the 'finest thing in the volume' (*KCH*, 157), and (like *The Eve of St Agnes*) it subsequently appealed strongly to the Pre-Raphaelites (see William Holman Hunt's painting on the cover of this volume). There has recently been an intensification of interest in the poem's social and political dimensions.

For further reading, see M. R. Ridley, *Keats's Craftsmanship* (1933), 18–56; Bate, 310–15; Miriam Allott, 'Isabella, The Eve of St Agnes, and Lamia', *John Keats. A Reassessment*, ed. K. Muir (1969), 40–63; Christopher Ricks, *Keats and Embarrassment* (1974), 97–9; Watkins, 54–63; Kelvin Everest, 'Isabella in the Market-Place: Keats and Feminism', *K&H*, 107–26.

2   **palmer**: pilgrim.
21 **vespers**: evening prayers.
28 **boon**: favour; cf. 146 below.
36 **lull**: lulling sound.
46 **conceit**: conception or thought, but also with the sense of 'fanciful notion'.
52 **symbol on his forehead**: expression or mark of feeling.
62 **fear**: make afraid.
64 **shrive**: confess. Cf. *Endymion*, IV. 26 and n.
74 **zephyr**: breeze.
81 **close**: close together, but also in secret; cf. 86 below.
95 **Theseus' spouse**: Ariadne; see *Sleep and Poetry*, 335–6 n.
99 Referring to Virgil's *Aeneid*, VI: 'Here there are secluded paths and a surrounding myrtle-wood which hides all those who have pined and wilted under the harsh cruelties of love. Even in death their sorrows never leave them ... Among them was Phoenician Dido ...'. Tr. W. Jackson Knight (1956).
103 **almsmen**: like almsmen depending on the charity of others, the bees receive nectar as a gift from 'spring-bowers'.

104   Cf. *Ode on Melancholy*, 23–4: 'aching Pleasure nigh, / Turning to poison while the bee-mouth sips'.

105–44   K gives Isabella two brothers, not three as in Boccaccio's story, and he differs from his source in emphasising their greedy and exploitative capitalism.

107   **swelt:** swelter, because of intense heat. K probably derived the word from *The Faerie Queene*; see for example 1.7.6: 'a fever fit through all his body swelt'.

113–15   Possibly recalling the 'miserable employment' of pearl divers described in William Mavor's *Youth's Miscellany* (1798): 'The wretched negroes, or others who are employed in diving for this marine spoil, are not only exposed to the dangers of the deep, to suffocation, and to being devoured by sharks, or a species of ray; but by the pressure of the air on their lungs in descending, they universally labour under a spitting of blood'. Cf. 'Dear Reynolds', 93–105 and n.

123   **orange-mounts:** hills terraced with orange groves.

124   **lazar stairs:** stairs in a house or hospital for lepers.

131   **that land:** Palestine.

140–1   Alluding to the plague of 'thick darkness' visited on Egypt; Exodus, 10.21–3.

150   **ghittern:** a form of guitar.

159   **stead:** render service to.

165–8   K, not Boccaccio, supplied these motives for the brothers' murder of Lorenzo; their animosity is in keeping with their characters outlined at 105–44 above.

175   **forest dim:** cf. *Ode to a Nightingale*, 20.

189   **as he was wont:** in his customary manner.

200   **in-door lattice:** a door with a lattice window set in it.

209   Charles Lamb remarked: The anticipation of the assassination is wonderfully conceived in one epithet' (*KCH*, 158). Cf. 361–84 n. below.

213   **freshet:** a small stream of fresh water; cf. *Endymion*, IV. 34.

219–21   The soul of a murdered man is as restless as the murderers' consciences. Cf. 261–2 and n. below.

251   **sick west:** the west wind.

252   **roundelay:** a short simple song with a refrain (*OED*); cf. *Endymion*, IV. 145.

262   **Hinnom's vale:** here Ahaz 'burnt his children in the fire, after the abominations of the heathen' (2 Chronicles, 28.3). The brothers' guilt torments them with comparable pain.

268   **feather'd pall:** death.

269–72   K recalls William Robertson's description of the painful test of 'fortitude' undergone by American warriors to demonstrate their 'capacity to suffer': the warrior is 'suspended in his hammoc, and covered with leaves of the palmetto. A fire of stinking herbs is kindled underneath, so as he may feel its heat, and be involved in its smoke. Though scorched and almost suffocated, he must continue to endure with the same patient insensibility'. See *The History of America* (1792 edn), II. 162.

292   **woof:** woven fabric; cf. *Endymion*, III. 202.

319–20   K quoted these lines in his letter to Fanny Brawne, Feb. (?) 1820: 'In my present state of Health I feel too much separated from you and could almost speak to you in the words of Lorenzo's Ghost to Isabella' (*Letters*, 356).

339   **clay:** Lorenzo's dead body.

356   **stole:** robe; cf. *Endymion*, III. 230.

361–84   Highly praised by Lamb: 'there is nothing more awfully simple in diction, more nakedly grand and moving in sentiment, in Dante, in Chaucer, or in Spenser' (*KCH*, 158). Cf. next note.

385–8   K contrasts the elaborate manner of his own poem with the more direct and simple idiom of 'old Romance'.

393   **Perséan sword:** the sword with which Perseus beheaded the Gorgon. See Ovid's *Metamorphoses*, IV.

409   **dews:** perfumes.

412   **cold serpent-pipe:** the coiled pipe used to distil perfume.

416   **Basil:** an aromatic herb.

417–20   Possibly recalling Wordsworth's *The Thorn* (1798), 69–74.

429   Cf. Wordsworth's 'A slumber did my spirit seal' (1800), 2: 'I had no human fears'.

436   **Lethean:** forgotten; from Lethe – 'one of the rivers of hell, whose waters . . . had the power of making [the dead] forget whatever they had done, seen or heard before' (L).

442   **Melpomene:** Muse of Tragedy.

451   **Baälites of pelf:** worshippers of the false god, money.

453   **elf:** cf. *Endymion*, II. 277 and n.

467   **chapel-shrift:** confession. Cf. 'shrive' at 64 and n. above.

477   **guerdon:** reward.

'Mother of Hermes! and still youthful Maia' (p. 159)

Written at Teignmouth, 1 May 1818, and transcribed in K's letter to Reynolds, 3 May 1818 (*Letters*, 92–3), the basis of the text here. First published *L&L*, I. 135.

Intended as an ode to May, K's poem was never completed. The fourteen-line stanza reflects his recent interest in the sonnet form, and looks forward to his endeavour in spring 1819 'to discover a better sonnet stanza than we have' (*Letters*, 255).

1   **Mother of Hermes!:** Maia was 'mother of Mercury by Jupiter. She was one of the Pleiades, the most luminous of the seven sisters' (L).

3   **shores of Baiæ:** the bay of Naples.

9–14 Cf. K's idea of poetry in his letter to Reynolds, 3 Feb. 1818: 'Poetry should be great & unobtrusive, a thing which enters into one's soul, and does not startle it or amaze it with itself but with its subject. – How beautiful are the retired flowers! how would they lose their beauty were they to throng into the highway crying out, "admire me I am a violet! dote upon me I am a primrose!"' (*Letters*, 61).

On Visiting the Tomb of Burns (p. 159)
Written 1 July 1818, the day that K visited Burns's tomb at Dumfries. K included the sonnet in a letter to Tom Keats, 1 July 1818 (now lost), explaining: 'This sonnet I have written in a strange mood, half asleep. I know not how it is, the Clouds, the sky, the Houses, all seem anti Grecian & anti Charlemagnish – I will endeavour to get rid of my prejudices, & tell you fairly about the Scotch' (*Letters*, 109–10). First published *L&L*, I. 156–7, from a copy taken of the single extant ms. in a transcript of K's letter by John Jeffrey. For further reading, see Carol Kyros Walker, *Walking North with Keats* (1992); for discussion of the textual and interpretive difficulties of this sonnet, see *TKP*, 189, and J. C. Maxwell, 'Keats's Sonnet on the Tomb of Burns', *Keats-Shelley Journal*, 4 (Winter 1955), 77–80. Text here based on Maxwell's transcript of Jeffrey's ms.

9 Minos-wise: the wisdom of King Minos was legendary; 'he was rewarded for his equity, after death, with the office of supreme and absolute judge in the infernal regions' (L).
11 Fickly: 'In a fickle manner . . . inconstantly, deceitfully' (*OED*).

To Ailsa Rock (p. 160)
Written 10 July 1818 at 'our inn in Girvan' (Charles Brown, *KC*, II. 62), and copied out that day in K's letter to Tom Keats, 10–14 July 1818 (*Letters*, 126), the basis of the text here. First published in Leigh Hunt's *Literary Pocket-Book* (1819).

K and Brown had walked up the coast from Stranraer: 'we had a gradual ascent and got among the tops of the Mountains whence in a little time I descried in the Sea Ailsa Rock . . . it was 15 Miles distant and seemed close upon us – The effect of ailsa with the peculiar perspective of the Sea in connection with the ground we stood on, and the misty rain then falling gave me a complete Idea of a deluge – Ailsa struck me very suddenly – really I was a little alarmed . . . This is the only Sonnet of any worth I have of late written' (*Letters*, 125–6). For further reading, see Carol Kyros Walker, *Walking North with Keats* (1992).

8 coverlid: coverlet, the covering of a bed.

'Read me a lesson, Muse' (p. 160)
Written on the top of Ben Nevis, 2 Aug. 1818, and copied in K's letter to

Tom Keats 3, 6 Aug. 1818 (*Letters*, 148), the basis of the text here. First published in *Plymouth and Devonport Weekly Journal*, 6 Sept. 1838.

K writes at length about climbing Ben Nevis in his letter (see *Letters*, 145–7, and notes below); Charles Brown recalled composition of the sonnet more particularly: 'When on the summit of this mountain, we were enveloped in a cloud, and, waiting till it was slowly wafted away, [K] sat on the stones, a few feet from the edge of that fearful precipice, fifteen hundred feet perpendicular from the valley below, and wrote this sonnet' (*KC*, II. 63). For further reading, see Carol Kyros Walker, *Walking North with Keats* (1992), 22–3.

1–4   See K's letter to Tom Keats: 'we gained the first tolerable level after the valley to the height of what in the Valley we had thought the top and saw still above us another huge crag which still the Guide said was not the top – to that we made with an obstinate fag and having gained it there came on a Mist, so that from that part to the very top we walked in a Mist. ... Talking of chasms they are the finest wonder of the whole – they appear great rents in the very heart of the mountain though they are not, being at the side of it, but other huge crags arising round it give the appearance to Nevis of a shattered heart or Core in itself – These Chasms are 1500 feet in depth and are the most tremendous places I have ever seen – they turn one giddy if you choose to give way to it – We tumbled in large stones and set the echoes at work in fine style' (*Letters*, 146).

10   'The whole immense head of the Mountain is composed of large loose stones' (*Letters*, 146).

11   elf: suggesting how diminutive the human figure is amid the sublime scenery of the mountain. Cf. also *Endymion*, II. 277 and n.

Hyperion. A Fragment (p. 161)
Written autumn 1818 (probably begun by 27 Oct., *Letters*, 157); abandoned during or before Apr. 1819; see Bate, 459–60; Gittings, 447. First published, *1820*, the basis for the text here.

K had announced his wish to 'sing' of Apollo in *Endymion*, IV. 774; other anticipations of *Hyperion* also appears in *Endymion*, III. 993–7, and in the 'Preface' to that poem, where K looks forward to writing of 'the beautiful mythology of Greece . . . once more'. K adopts Miltonic blank verse for his epic narrative describing the Titans' overthrow by their offspring, the Olympians, who are led by Jupiter. The poem opens with Saturn and the Titans already defeated, except for the sun god Hyperion who is, nevertheless, 'unsecure' in his divinity. In Book II the Titans make speeches offering different interpretations of their fall (like Satan's followers in *Paradise Lost*, II). The fragmentary third book shows Hyperion's successor Apollo in process of deification as god of the sun, poetry, music and medicine – at which point the poem breaks off. The 'transcendental cosmopolitics' of *Hyperion* (Leigh Hunt's phrase) include the themes of historical progress and revolution (see especially Oceanus's speech, II. 173–243), which K seeks to relate, via the symbolic figure of Apollo, to the poet's function in his own revolutionary era. In this way the poem offers a sublime projection of K's own ambitions as a poet of human suffering, first announced in *Sleep and Poetry*, 123–5, although he seems to have been uncertain how to proceed beyond Apollo's attainment of divinity (but see III. 136 and n.). K had difficulty in making progress with his poem in the early months of 1819; see his letters to Haydon, 8 Mar.; to Fanny Keats, 12 Apr.; to the George Keatses, 15 Apr. (*Letters*, 201, 206, 233). For K's later reconstruction of the poem as a dream-vision, see headnote to *The Fall of Hyperion*.

The poem was highly praised by K's contemporaries; for Shelley's and Byron's responses, see *KCH*, 124–5, 131. For further reading, see H. W. Garrod, *Keats* (1926), 68–71; M. R. Ridley, *Keats's Craftsmanship* (1933), 57–95; K. Muir, 'The Meaning of *Hyperion*' in *John Keats. A Reassessment*, ed. K. Muir (1969), 103–123; Jones, 74–91; Sperry, 155–197; John Bayley, *The Uses of Division* (1976), 122–3; Jack, 161–175; Marilyn Butler, *Romantics, Rebels and Reactionaries* (1981); David Bromwich, 'Keats's Radicalism', KP, 197–210; Alan Bewell, 'The Political Implications of Keats's Classicist Aesthetics', KP, 220–29; Barnard, 56–67; Marjorie Levinson, *Keats's Life of Allegory* (1988), 191–226; Watkins, 85–103; Newey (1989), 265–89; J. Bate, 'Keats's two *Hyperions* and the Problem of Milton', *Romantic Revisions*, ed. Brinkley and Hanley (1992), 321–38; Michael O'Neill, ' "When this warm scribe my hand": Writing and History in *Hyperion* and *The Fall of Hyperion*', *K&H*, 143–164.

Book I

1. 1–7 K's Oxford friend Benjamin Bailey quoted these lines to demonstrate K's theory of melody in verse: 'the vowels should be so managed as not to clash one with another so as to mar the melody, – & yet that they should be interchanged, like differing notes of music to prevent monotony' (*KC*, II. 277).

1. 1 vale: cf. K's marginal note on *Paradise Lost*, I. 321: 'There is a cool pleasure in the very sound of vale. The English word is of the very happiest chance. Milton has put vales in heaven and hell with the very utter affection and learning of a great Poet. It is a sort of Delphic Abstraction – a beautiful thing made more beautiful by being reflected and put in a mist'.

1. 4 Saturn: one of the oldest deities in classical mythology, Saturn was leader of the Titans until Jupiter, his son, rebelled and overthrew him.

1. 13 Naiad: see *To Charles Cowden Clarke*, 6 n.

1. 20–1 Tellus (Terra), 'the same as the Earth', was 'the most antient

of all the gods after Chaos. She was mother by Coelus [her son, an ancient deity identified with Heavens] of Oceanus, Hyperion, Ceus, Rhea, Japetus, Themis, Saturn, Phoebe, Tethys, &c.' (L).

l. 23 **one ... kindred hand**: Thea, wife of Saturn's brother Hyperion. Cf. l. 95 below.

l. 29 **Achilles**: L: 'bravest of all the Greeks in the Trojan war'.

l. 30 **Ixion's wheel**: Jupiter, displeased with Ixion's insolence, ordered him to be tied to a wheel in hell. 'The wheel was perpetually in motion, therefore the punishment ... was eternal' (L).

l. 31–3 Napoleon's Egyptian campaign of 1798 had encouraged contemporary interest in Egyptian antiquity, and the British Museum had acquired some sculptures in 1818. K may not have seen these until spring 1819; see his letter of 14 Feb.–3 May: 'Severn & I took a turn round the [British] Museum. There is a Sphinx there of a giant size, & most voluptuous Egyptian expression. I had not seen it before' (*Letters*, 219). K's interest in ancient Egyptian sculpture is discussed by Jack and Bewell; see headnote to this poem.

l. 31 **Memphian**: L: 'a celebrated town of Egypt ... It once contained many beautiful temples'.

l. 34–6 cf. the description of Moneta in *The Fall of Hyperion*, 1. 256–63.

l. 48 **organ tone**: cf. *Lines on Seeing* a Lock of Milton's Hair, 1 and n.

l. 60–2 After Saturn's overthrow, his weapons are now commanded by Jupiter.

l. 61 **Rumbles reluctant**: a Miltonic construction, illustrating the influence of *Paradise Lost* on the verbal texture of K's poem. **fallen house**: referring to the Titans as a whole; cf. l. 150–1 below.

l. 72–9 Cf. *The Fall of Hyperion*, 1. 372–8.

l. 85–6 K draws on memories of coastal rocks, eroded into sculptural forms by the sea, which he had seen on his Scottish tour in summer 1818.

l. 87 **couchant**: a heraldic word meaning 'lying down'. Cf. Satan's 'couchant watch' in *Paradise Lost*, IV. 406.

l. 90 **faded eyes**: cf. Satan's 'faded cheek', *Paradise Lost*, I. 602.

l. 94 **horrid ... aspen-malady**: 'horrid' here has its Latin sense, meaning 'bristling'; cf. 'horrid hair', *Paradise Lost*, II. 710. The leaves of the aspen tree quiver in the lightest breeze, like someone trembling with a fever.

l. 98–103 Saturn's confusion after his fall echoes *King Lear*, 1.4.223–7:

> Does any here know me? This is not Lear:
> Does Lear walk thus? speak thus? Where are his eyes?
> Either his notion weakens, his discernings
> Are lethargied – Ha! waking? 'tis not so.
> Who is it that can tell me who I am?

l. 102 **front:** forehead.

l. 105 **nervous:** vigorous; cf. l. 18 above: 'nerveless, listless, dead'.

l. 112-16 The Titans had embodied strong identity and power; their successors, the Olympians, have no comparable presence and – like Apollo – represent the poetical character which 'has no self' and exists through 'negative capability'; see *Letters*, 43 and 157; II. 203-5 and n. below, and the apotheosis of Apollo at III. 113-20 and n. below.

l. 122-33 Saturn imagines the 'certain shape' of his former self carrying on the battle against the Olympians.

l. 129 **gold clouds metropolitan:** the clouds are the gods' golden metropolis; the word-order is Miltonic.

l. 137 **Druid locks:** cf. Thomas Gray's *The Bard*, 18-20: 'With haggard eyes the poet stood; (Loose his beard and hoary hair / Streamed, like a meteor, to the troubled air)'. Cf also II. 34-5 and n. below.

l. 138 **fever out:** become swollen, as with a fever.

l. 146 **Olympus:** see *Endymion*, I. 605 and n.

l. 147 **rebel three:** Jupiter, Neptune and Pluto, Saturn's sons who, after his overthrow, divided his kingdom and ruled heaven, sea, and the underworld respectively.

l. 152 **covert:** hiding-place.

l. 166 L: 'a son of Coelus and Terra ... Hyperion is often taken by the poets for the sun itself'. Unlike his successor Apollo, Hyperion was not identified with poetry, music, or medicine.

l. 171 **gloom-bird:** the owl, traditionally a bird of ill-omen. See *Macbeth*, 2.2.3-4: 'It was the owl that shriek'd, the fatal bellman, / Which gives the stern'st good-night'.

l. 172-3 **Ambiguous:** K may refer to family attendance at a relative's death-bed or, more likely, to the apparition of a dead man visiting his relatives at the moment of his passing.

l. 176-82 Hyperion's palace is described as dawn lights up the eastern sky. Jack, 170-2, points to the Egyptian aspects of K's architecture, and to the possible influence of John Martin's 'The Fall of Babylon'. Important literary precedents include *Paradise Lost*, I. 710-30; the 'mighty city' of cloud at the close of Wordsworth's *Excursion*, II; the 'stately palace' in the air in Southey's *Thalaba*, I; and William Beckford's *Vathek*.

l. 181 **Aurorian clouds:** clouds lit up by the dawn.

l. 182 **angerly:** angrily.

l. 182-5 Omens of ill-fortune.

l. 189 Cf. K. to Fanny Brawne, Aug. 1820: 'The last two years taste like brass upon my Palate' (*Letters*, 385).

l. 196-200 Cf. the fallen angels described in *Paradise Lost*, I. 767-71.

l. 206-8 Probably suggested by the ancient Egyptian statue of

Memnon, which was reputed to utter musical sounds when touched by the sun's light. Cf. II. 373–6 below, and Jack, 168–70.

I. 216   **Hours:** nymphs attending the sun. Cf. *Endymion*, IV. 424.

I. 227–30   portents of disaster.

I. 236–9   Echoing John of Gaunt's speech in *Richard* II, 2.1.40–2: 'This royal throne of kings, this scept'red isle, / This earth of majesty, this seat of Mars, / This other Eden'. Cf. also Satan's speech in *Paradise Lost*, I. 242–5.

I. 239   **lucent:** shining.

I. 246   **Tellus:** see I. 20–1 and n. above.

I. 258–63   Recalling Satan entering the serpent in *Paradise Lost*, IX. 179–90, and probably, as Jack 173–4 suggests, engravings and reproductions of Laocoön.

I. 274   **colure:** 'Each of two great circles which intersect each other in right angles at the poles, and divide the equinoctial and the ecliptic into four equal parts' (*OED*); Milton uses the word at *Paradise Lost*, IX. 66.

I. 277   **hieroglyphics old:** the signs of the zodiac.

I. 282   **swart:** black.

I. 296   **sisterly:** like twin sisters.

I. 302   **rack:** a mass of cloud; cf. *Endymion*, II. 288 and n.

I. 305–8   In making Coelus express sympathy for his son Hyperion (see I. 20–1 n. above), K breaks with the tradition of savage hostility between them.

I. 311   **the powers:** Tellus and Coelus, Hyperion's parents; see I. 20–1 and n. above.

I. 321–2   Cf. Gloucester's speech in *King Lear*, 1.2.107: 'there's son against father'.

I. 323   **first-born:** Saturn.

I. 326   **wox:** grew; from 'waxed', an archaic word used by Spenser.

I. 349   **region-whisper:** a voice from the skies.

Book II

II. 4   **Cybele:** daughter of Coelus and Tellus, wife of Saturn; she was also known as Ops, see II. 78 and n. below. For more, see *Endymion*, II. 640 n.

II. 5–17   Jack, 173, suggests this landscape is indebted to John Martin's painting 'Sadak in Search of the Waters of Oblivion'. K was certainly also recalling scenes from his walk through the Lake District and Scotland, summer 1818. Cf. II. 122–3, 358–66 below, and 'Read me a lesson, Muse'.

II. 19–81   The gathering of the Titans is indebted to Milton's account of the fallen angels in hell, *Paradise Lost*, I. 376–522. K's naming of the Titans reflects his reading in a number of sources, but cf. in particular L: 'a name given to the sons of Coelus and Terra . . . The most known of the Titans are Saturn, Hyperion, Oceanus, Japetus, Cottus, and Briareus, to whom Horace adds Typhoeus, Mimus, Porphyrion, Rhoetus, and Enceladus, who are by other mythologists reckoned among the giants. They were all of a gigantic stature, and with proportionable strength'.

II. 22–8 Typhoeus (Typhon) was imprisoned by Jupiter under Mount Etna; his struggles caused the volcano to erupt. Cf. *Endymion*, III. 243 and n.

II. 29 **Mnemosyne:** L: 'a daughter of Coelus and Terra, mother of the nine Muses, by Jupiter'. Sometimes identified with the Titans, here she is seeking Apollo (see III. 46 and n.); in *The Fall of Hyperion*, Mnemosyne is identified with Moneta.

II. 30 **Phœbe:** see *Endymion*, IV. 56 and n.

II. 34–7 See K's account of visiting Castlerigg stone circle in his letter to Tom Keats, 29 June 1818: 'we ordered dinner, & set forth about a mile & a half on the Penrith road, to see the Druid temple. We had a fag up hill, rather too near dinner time, which was rendered void, by the gratification of seeing those aged stones, on a gentle rise in the midst of Mountains, which at that time darkened all around' (*Letters*, 107–8).

II. 52 **horrid working:** moving in anguish.

II. 53 **Caf:** K invented this parent for Asia, drawing on his reading in oriental romances where Caf (or Kaf) is a mountain.

II. 66 **Enceladus:** L: 'the most powerful of all the giants who conspired against Jupiter. He was struck with Jupiter's thunders, and overwhelmed under mount Ætna'. Cf. II. 107–9 below. Sometimes identified with Typhoeus, see II. 22–8 n. above.

II. 73–4 For Atlas, see *To Charles Cowden Clarke*, 63 n.; Phorcus was 'a sea deity, son of Pontus and Terra [Sea and Earth], who married his sister Ceto, by whom he had the Gorgons . . . and other monsters' (L).

II. 75–8 For Oceanus, see II. 19–81 n. above. Tethys was 'the greatest of the sea deities . . . wife to Oceanus' (L), and Clymene was their daughter. Themis was 'a daughter of Coelus and Terra' (L), as was Ops (also known as Cybele) 'who married Saturn, and became mother of Jupiter' (L).

II. 92–5 Cf. Milton's description of Satan in *Paradise Lost*, IV. 114–15: 'each passion dimmed his face / Thrice changed with pale, ire, envy and despair'.

II. 97–8 The 'mortal oil' disanoints Saturn of his majesty and his immortality as a God.

II. 120 **utterless:** unutterable.

II. 129–345 The Titans' speeches strongly recall the council of the fallen angels in *Paradise Lost*, II.

II. 134 Uranus was another name for Coelus; see I. 20–1 n. above.

II. **157** Cf. *Paradise Lost*, I. 330: 'Awake, arise, or be forever fallen'.

II. **163** **Oceanus:** L: 'a powerful deity of the sea ... generally represented as an old man with a long flowing beard, and sitting upon the waves of the sea'. See also I. 20–1 n., and II. 19–81 n. above.

II. **168–9** For Oceanus's wisdom, see also *Endymion*, III. 993–7.

II. **173–243** Oceanus's speech in the midst of defeat nevertheless affirms a law of progress, and in this respect it reflects K's thinking about personal (poetic) development and, more broadly, about human history. Cf. *Sleep and Poetry*, 96–154, and K's remarks about life and the 'grand march of intellect' in his letter to Reynolds, 3 May 1818 (*Letters*, 95–6). See also K's remarks about 'changes ... in progress' in politics and European history in his letter to the George Keatses, 17–27 Sept. 1819 (*Letters*, 311–312).

II. **190** Cf. Revelation, I. 8: 'I am Alpha and Omega, the beginning and the ending, saith the Lord'.

II. **191** Cf. *Paradise Lost*, II. 968–70: 'Ye powers / And spirits of this nethermost abyss, / Chaos and ancient Night'.

II. **192** **intestine broil:** civil war; from Chaos's speech in *Paradise Lost*, II. 1001–2: 'our intestine broils / Weakening the sceptre of old Night'.

II. **196** **its own producer:** the darkness of chaos.

II. **199** **Heavens ... Earth:** Coelus and Tellus.

II. **203–5** Oceanus recommends an equanimity that recalls K's ideas of 'negative capability' and the poetic self (see *Letters*, 43, 157).

II. **209–10** Cf. Edmund's speech in *King Lear*, 1.2.7–8: 'my dimensions are as well compact, / My mind as generous, and my shape as true ...'. Cf. also *Hamlet*, 2.2.303–6.

II. **232–5** Neptune, 'generally represented sitting in a chariot made of a shell, and drawn by sea horses or dolphins. Sometimes he is drawn by winged horses, and holds his trident in his hand, and stands up as his chariot flies over the surface of the sea' (L).

II. **244** **poz'd:** pretended or assumed.

II. **248** **Clymene:** see II. 75–8 and n. above.

II. **281** Cf. *The Eve of St Agnes*, 56: 'The music, yearning like a God in pain'.

II. **304** For Enceladus, see II. 66 n. above.

II. **305–6** Cf. *On the Sea*, 1–3.

II. **309–45** Enceladus's speech is in a vein similar to that by Moloch, 'the strongest and the fiercest spirit', in *Paradise Lost*, II. 51–105.

II. **329** **crooked stings of fire:** lightning.

II. **341** **the winged thing:** victory was 'represented with wings' (L).

II. **358–66** Cf. II. 5–17 n. above.

II. **374–80** For the ancient Egyptian statue of Memnon, see I. 196–

8 and n. above. K may here have been thinking of the (different) statue of Ramases II in the British Museum, known in K's day as the 'young Memnon'. See Jack, 168–9. The implication of these lines is that the 'dejected' sun-god Hyperion gives way to his successor Apollo, god of the sun, music, poetry, and healing – hence the Titan's 'despondence'.

Book III

III. 2 **Amazed:** here pronounced 'amazèd': stunned, bewildered, terrified.

III. 10 **Delphic:** inspired; cf. *On receiving a laurel crown from Leigh Hunt*, 3 and n., and *Endymion*, 1. 499 and n.

III. 12 **Dorian flute:** 'Dorian' was one of the ancient Grecian modes of music, 'characterized by simplicity and solemnity' (*OED*). Cf. *Paradise Lost*, 1. 550–1: 'the Dorian mood / Of flutes and soft recorders'.

III. 14–28 The sunrise, contrasted with the 'fiery' dawn in 1. 176–82.

III. 23–4 For the Cyclades and Delos, see *Endymion*, 1. 966 n.

III. 29 **Giant of the Sun:** Hyperion.

III. 31–2 Apollo's mother was Latona, his twin sister Diana. See *Endymion*, 1. 862.

III. 46 **awful Goddess:** Mnemosyne; see II. 29 and n. above.

III. 77 **forsaken:** Mnemosyne has abandoned the Titans for Apollo.

III. 81–120 Richard Woodhouse recorded K's thoughts about the phrase 'white melodious throat', and Apollo's speech following: 'He has wondered how he came to hit upon it . . . It seemed to come by chance or magic – to be as it were something given to him' (*KC*, 1. 129).

III. 86–7 Cf. *Samson Agonistes*, 80–1: 'O dark, dark, dark, amid the blaze of noon, / Irrecoverably dark'.

III. 92 **liegeless:** not subjected; free.

III. 113–20 Apollo attains godhead through his knowledge of suffering, affirming the relationship between suffering and poetic achievement – a theme to which K will return in *The Fall of Hyperion*. For K's earlier poetic aspiration to 'the agonies, the strife / Of human hearts' see *Sleep and Poetry*, 122–5; see also his letter to Reynolds, 3 May 1818: 'Until we are sick, we understand not; – in fine, as Byron says, "Knowledge is Sorrow"; and I go on to say that "Sorrow is Wisdom"' (*Letters*, 93).

III. 136 Richard Woodhouse commented: 'The poem, if completed, would have treated of the dethronement of Hyperion, the former God of the Sun, by Apollo – and incidentally, of those of Oceanus by Neptune, of Saturn by Jupiter, etc. – and of the war of the Giants for Saturn's re-establishment, with other events, of which we have but very dark hints in the mythological poets of Greece and Rome.

In fact, the incidents would have been pure creations of the poet's brain'. See Barnard, 65.

Fancy (p. 184)

Written probably Dec. 1818, and copied out on 2 Jan. 1819 with *Ode*, ['Bards of Passion'] in K's journal letter to the George Keatses, 16 Dec. 1818–4 Jan. 1819 (*Letters*, 189–94). K comments in his letter, 'These are specimens of a sort of rondeau which I think I shall become partial to – because you have one idea amplified with greater ease and more delight and freedom than in the sonnet' (*Letters*, 194). In both poems K uses four-stressed lines in rhyming couplets, as he had done in *Robin Hood* and *Lines on the Mermaid Tavern*. First published 1820, the basis of the text here.

16 **ingle:** a house-fire or hearth.

17 **sear:** dry.

21 **shoon:** shoes.

22–4 Evoking the shortness of a winter day.

80–1 Ceres' daughter Proserpine was carried away by Pluto to be queen of the underworld; cf. *Endymion*, 1. 944 n.

85 **Hebe:** L: 'goddess of youth . . . cup-bearer to all the gods'.

89–92 Fancy is imagined as a bird tethered by a 'silken leash'.

Ode ['Bards of Passion'] (p. 186)

Written probably Dec. 1818; see headnote to *Fancy*. In his journal letter, 2 Jan. 1819, K remarks that this poem 'is on the double immortality of poets' (*Letters*, 193).

8 **parle:** speech.

19–20 K's idea of the heavenly union of poetry and philosophy recalls *Comus*, 475–7: 'How charming is divine philosophy! / Not harsh, and crabbed as dull fools suppose, / But musical as is Apollo's lute'.

The Eve of St Agnes (p. 188)

Written 18 Jan.–2 Feb. 1819 at Bedhampton and Chichester. See K's spring journal letter to the George Keatses, 14 Feb.–3 May 1819, under 14 Feb.: 'I took down some of the thin paper and wrote on it a little Poem call'd "St Agnes Eve"' (*Letters*, 211). See Gittings (1954), 61–3, for the poem's subject suggested to K by Mrs Isabella Jones. Revised at Winchester, Sept. 1819; see K's letter to John Taylor, 5 Sept.: 'am now occupied in revising St Agnes' Eve' (*Letters*, 288), and for K's uncertainty about the poem at this time, see his letter to Richard Woodhouse, 21, 22 Sept. (*Letters*, 298). For discussion of K's revisions and the complicated background to publication of this poem, see *TKP*, 214–220. First published 1820, the basis of the text here.

The romantic and erotic atmosphere of the poem probably owes much to K's love for Fanny Brawne; he had met her in autumn 1818 and they had come to an 'understanding' on 25 Dec. 1819. The poem is written in Spenserian stanzas. K's sources for the legend of St Agnes' Eve (see esp. stanza 6) included current superstition, Robert Burton's *Anatomy of Melancholy*, and John Brand's *Popular Antiquities*: 'On the eve of [St Agnes'] day many kinds of divination were practised by virgins to discover their future husbands . . . Burton, in his *Anatomy of Melancholy* . . . speaks of *Maids fasting on St Agnes's Eve*, to know who shall be their first husband' (1849 edn, 1. 34-5). Other significant influences on the poem include *The Faerie Queene*; *Romeo and Juliet*; *Paradise Lost*; Mrs Radcliffe's novels; Scott's *Lay of the Last Minstrel* (1805); Coleridge's *Christabel* (1816).

For further reading see Leigh Hunt's perceptive criticism in *Imagination and Fancy* (1844), rpt *KCH*, 275-80; M. R. Ridley, *Keats's Craftsmanship* (1933), 96-190; Gittings (1954), 64-82; Bate, 438-51; Jack Stillinger, 'The Hoodwinking of Madeline' in *Keats. A Collection of Critical Essays*, ed. W. J. Bate (1964), 71-90; Jack, 191-4; Miriam Allott, '*Isabella, The Eve of St Agnes,* and *Lamia*', *John Keats. A Reassessment*, ed. K. Muir (1969), 40-63; Harold Bloom, *The Visionary Company* (rev. edn, 1971), 378-84; John Bayley, *The Uses of Division* (1976), 115-56; John Kerrigan, 'Keats and *Lucrece*', *Shakespeare Survey* (1988), 103-18; Marjorie Levinson, *Keats's Life of Allegory* (1988), 96-190; Watkins, 63-84; Greg Kucich, *Keats, Shelley, and Romantic Spenserianism* (1991), 202-18; Lucy Newlyn, '*Paradise Lost*' *and the Romantic Reader* (1993), 174-82.

1   **chill**: St Agnes' Eve is 20 January. Cf. also Coleridge's *Christabel* (1816), 15: 'The night is chilly'.

5   **Beadsman**: one 'paid or endowed to pray for others' (*OED*).

8   The beadsman's breath rises in the chill air like a spirit departing after death.

13-18   As Jack, 192-3, points out, K may be recalling the monuments he had seen in Chichester Cathedral, Jan. 1819.

21   **Flatter'd**: Leigh Hunt: 'In this word . . . is the whole theory of the secret of tears; which are the tributes . . . of self-pity to self-love'. See *Imagination and Fancy* (1844), Keats and his Critics, pp. 342-3 below.

37   **argent**: silver; silver used in a coat of arms.

51   **supperless**: for fasting on St Agnes' Eve, see headnote, and Burton's *Anatomy of Melancholy* (1652 edn), 3. II. 4. i.: 'fasting on S. *Annes* Eve or night, to know who shall be their first husband'.

55   **Madeline**: see K's letter to Reynolds, 14 Mar. 1818: 'beautiful name, that Magdalen' (*Letters*, 76).

56   Cf. *Hyperion*, II. 281.

58   **sweeping train**: see K's letter to John Taylor, 11 June 1820: 'I do not

use *train* for *concourse of passers by* but for *Skirts* sweeping along the floor' (*Letters*, 380).

67   **timbrels:** tambourines.

70   **amort:** lifeless, spiritless, dejected.

71   **lambs unshorn:** After St Agnes' martyrdom, her parents saw a vision of her with a lamb standing beside her. See Brand, *Popular Antiquities*, I. 34.

75   **Porphyro:** from the Greek 'purple', whence also 'porphyry', 'a beautiful and very hard rock' often used by poets 'in the sense of a beautiful and valuable purple stone taking a high polish' (*OED*). Cf. 'purple riot' at 138 below.

82   **buzz'd:** told in a low voice, murmured.

88–9   Like the Capulets and Montagues in *Romeo and Juliet*, Porphyro's family has quarrelled with Madeline's. Cf. also the 'insult' between Roland and Sir Leoline in *Christabel*.

90   **beldame:** an aged woman or nurse: K's treatment of Angela, and her part in the story, recall the nurse in *Romeo and Juliet*.

98   **hie:** hasten.

112–13   Gittings (1954), 71, suggests that the room may have arisen from the '*pulpitum*, or stone pulpit' in the Vicars' Hall at Chichester.

115–17   See 71 n. above.

126   **mickle:** much.

138   **purple riot:** see 75 n. above.

153   **beard:** set at defiance, affront.

163–6   Angela's stratagem to conceal Porphyro in Madeline's room is a stock device. Cf. for example Iachimo in Imogen's bedroom in *Cymbeline*, 2.2; Satan spying on Adam and Eve in *Paradise Lost*, IV; Mr B hidden in the closet of Pamela's bedroom in *Pamela* (1740): in all three instances the voyeur is ill-intentioned.

171   The allusion is puzzling; K may refer to Merlin's love for the Lady of the Lake, an enchantress who imprisoned him perpetually in a rock. K's source may have been *The Faerie Queene*, 3.3.10–11.

173   **cates:** delicacies; see 264–75 below.

174   **tambour frame:** a frame for embroidery.

188   **amain:** exceedingly, greatly.

198   **fray'd:** frightened.

208–16   Gittings (1954), 79–80, suggests K took some of the details here from buildings at Chichester and Stansted Chapel; cf. *The Eve of St Mark*, 30–8 and n. See also Scott's *Lay of the Last Minstrel* (1805), 2.11 for a possible literary source.

215   **emblazonings:** heraldic devices.

216   **scutcheon:** a coat-of-arms, showing Madeline's family and their royal connections.

218   **warm gules:** warm red colours.

222   **glory:** a halo, or aura.

241 Ambiguous: either clasped in the hand of a believer among pagans, or shut up with clasps as a missal would be in a mosque.

244 **this paradise:** evoking the pleasures of passionate love; cf. Satan, spying jealously on Adam and Eve 'Imparadised in one another's arms / The happier Eden', *Paradise Lost*, IV. 506–7.

257 **Morphean amulet:** a charm to induce sleep; Morpheus was god of sleep, cf. *Endymion*, I. 559–60 n.

261 CCC recalled K reading this line and commenting, ' "that line", said he, "came into my head when I remembered how I used to listen in bed to your music at school" ' (*Recollections*, 143).

262–75 Cf. the feast in *Endymion*, II. 440–53.

268 **argosy:** a large merchant ship.

268–9 Cf. *Endymion*, I. 766 and n.

269–70 The city of Fez is in Morocco; Samarcand was an ancient Persian city famous for its silk.

277 **eremite:** a recluse or hermit. Cf. *Eve of St Mark*, 93.

288 **woofed:** woven.

292 'La Belle Dame Sans Mercy' was a poem by Alain Chartier dating from 1424; see also headnote to *La belle dame sans merci*.

296 **affrayed:** frightened.

323 **alarum:** the wind sounds as if it were a warning of danger threatening the lovers.

325 **flaw-blown:** blown in a squall of wind.

333 **unpruned:** unpreened.

335 Cf. K to Fanny Brawne, 25 July 1819: 'the very first week I knew you I wrote myself your vassal' (*Letters*, 271).

336 **vermeil:** scarlet.

344 **haggard:** wild, fierce. **boon:** a gift or favour.

349 **Rhenish:** wine from the Rhine valley.

350 Cf. Satan's exhortation to his followers in *Paradise Lost*, I. 330: 'Awake, arise, or be forever fallen'. For more on *Paradise Lost* and the poem, see Newlyn cited in headnote.

355 **darkling:** in darkness; cf. *Ode to a Nightingale*, 51: 'Darkling I listen'.

377 **aves:** 'Ave Marias' or 'Hail Marys', devotions to the Virgin Mary.

The Eve of St Mark (p. 201)
Written 13–17 Feb. 1819. K copied out a version of his poem on 20 Sept. in his journal letter to the George Keatses, 17–27 Sept. 1819 (*Letters*, 315–18), the basis of the text here. First published *L&L*, II. 279–83.

K began his poem shortly after returning from Chichester to Hampstead: see Gittings (1954), 86, who argues that Mrs Isabella Jones had provided K with the poem's subject. K's letter of 20 Sept. recalls: 'Some time since I began a Poem call'd "the Eve of St Mark" quite in the spirit of Town quietude. I think it will give you the sensation of walking about an old country Town in a coolish evening. I know not yet whether I shall ever finish it' (Letters, 315, see also 98 n. and 114 n. below). K probably intended the poem as a partner for The Eve of St Agnes; both recall sights and architecture at Chichester and at Stansted (see esp. 30–8 n. below). As with the superstition about St Agnes' Eve, K probably derived material about St Mark's Eve from John Brand's Popular Antiquities: 'It is customary in Yorkshire, for the common people to sit and watch in the church porch on St Mark's Eve, April 25th, from eleven o'clock at night till one in the morning. The third year (for this must be done thrice) they are supposed to see the ghosts of all those who are to die the next year, pass by into the church. . . . When any one sickens that is thought to have been seen in this manner, it is presently whispered about that he will not recover, for that such or such a one, who has watched St Mark's Eve, says so' (1849 edn, I. 192–3).

For further reading, see Gittings (1954), 83–92; Bate, 454–6; Sperry, 221–8.

5 Cf. the opening of the 'General Prologue' to The Canterbury Tales: 'Whan that Aprill with his shoures soote / The droghte of March hath perced to the roote'.

10 springtide sedge: cf. the 'withered' sedge in La belle dame sans merci, 3.

16 fireside oratries: K likens the large fireplaces in the citizens' houses to oratories – small rooms or chapels for private prayer.

24 Bertha: K may have taken this name from Chatterton's heroine Birtha in Ælla: A Tragycal Enterlude. See also 98–9 n. below.

30–8 Gittings (1954) shows that the decorations in Bertha's 'curious volume' were recalled from designs in the stained glass east windows at Stansted Chapel, near Bedhampton, visited by K in Jan. 1819. Cf. The Eve of St Agnes, 208–16 and n.

33 Aaron's breastplate: worn by the high priest of the Israelites; Aaron's consecration by Moses is described in Leviticus, 8. 1–13.

33–4 For St John's vision of the seven candlesticks, see Revelation, 1. 13–20.

35 St Mark's emblem, the winged lion, is derived from one of the four beasts of the apocalypse in Revelation, 4. 6–8.

36–8 For the ark of the covenant, and its 'cherubims of glory', see Hebrews, 9. 4–5.

38 golden mice: the Philistines captured the ark of the covenant after defeating the Israelites at Ebenezer; after various disasters, the Philistines returned the ark with a 'trespass offering', which included 'five golden mice'. See 1 Samuel, 4, 5, and 6. 1–4.

61–6 Recalling scenes at Chichester; see Gittings (1954), 90.

70 swart lamp: literally a 'dark lamp', but suggesting dim, dismal light.

76–82 It is possible that some details here, including the fire screen, are recalled from K's visit to Isabella Jones; in his letter of 14–31 Oct. 1818, K describes her sitting room ('a very tasty sort of place') with furniture which included 'Books, Pictures a bronze statue of Buonaparte, Music, aeolian Harp; a Parrot a Linnet' (*Letters*, 169, and Gittings (1954), 90–1). Besides the parrot, Mrs Jones's aeolian harp may have suggested – via Coleridge's *Eolian Harp*, 24–5, in *Sibylline Leaves* (1817) – K's 'legless birds of Paradise'.

79   **Lima Mice:** probably lemur mice.
80   See 76–82 n. above.
81   **Av'davat:** an Indian song-bird.
86   **Queen of Spades:** the card is associated with death.
93   **eremite:** see *The Eve of St Agnes*, 277 n.
94   **star . . . dagger:** denoting footnotes on the 'legend page'.
96   **crow quill:** for very fine writing.
98–9   Between these lines in K's letter of 20 Sept. is the comment: 'What follows is an imitation of the Authors in Chaucer's time – 'tis more ancient than Chaucer himself and perhaps between him and Gower' (*Letters*, 318). K's imitation is indebted to his reading of Chaucer and also to Chatterton's pseudo-mediaeval English; K discussed both in relation to Milton and the English language in his letter to Reynolds, 21 Sept. 1819 (*Letters*, 292). See also 24 n. above and 106 n. below.
99   **swevenis:** dreams.
102   **crimpide:** 'To crimp' is 'to compress or pinch into minute parallel plaits or folds' (*OED*).
105   **Gif:** if.
106   K quoted this line in his letter to Reynolds, 21 Sept. 1819. (*Letters*, 291); see also 98–9 n. above.
112   **Somedele:** something.
113   **auctoreth:** writes.
114   K's manuscript draft of the poem, now in the British Library, continues with the following lines before breaking off:

> At length her constant eyelids come
> Upon the fervent martyrdom;
> Then lastly to his holy shrine,
> Exalt amid the taper's shine
> At Venice

St Mark's shrine is at Venice.

Why did I laugh tonight (p. 204)
Written Mar. 1819, and copied into K's spring journal letter to the George Keatses, 19 Mar. 1819 (*Letters*, 231), the basis of the text here. First published *L&L*, II. 301.

K remarks on the sonnet in his letter: 'I am ever affraid that your anxiety for me will lead you to fear for the violence of my temperament continually smothered down: for that reason I did not intend to have sent you the following sonnet – but look over the two last pages and ask yourselves whether I have not that in me which will well bear the buffets of the world. It will be the best comment on my sonnet; it will show you that it was written with no Agony but that of ignorance; with no thirst of any thing but knowledge . . . the first steps to it were through my human passions – they went away, and I wrote with my Mind – and perhaps I must confess a little bit of my heart' (*Letters*, 230–31).

7   **O darkness! darkness!:** cf. K's letter to Haydon, 8 Mar. 1819: 'I will not spoil my love of gloom by writing an ode to darkness' (*Letters*, 201). K may have been thinking of Byron's *Darkness*, published in *The Prisoner of Chillon and Other Poems* (1816). Cf. also *Hyperion*, III. 86–7 n.

9–10   Cf. *Macbeth*, 4.1.98–9: 'Macbeth / Shall live the lease of Nature'.

11   Anticipating *Ode to a Nightingale*, 56: 'To cease upon the midnight with no pain'.

13–14   Cf. K's letter to his brothers, 21, 27 (?) Dec. 1817: 'the excellence of every Art is its intensity, capable of making all disagreeables evaporate, from their being in close relationship with Beauty & Truth' (*Letters*, 42).

La belle dame sans merci and *La Belle Dame sans Mercy* [*Indicator* version] (p. 206 and p. 207)
Written 21 or 28 Apr. 1819 (see *TKP*, 232), and drafted in K's spring journal letter to the George Keatses, 14 Feb.–3 May 1819 (*Letters*, 243–4). First published in Leigh Hunt's *Indicator* (10 May 1820), 248, signed 'Caviare'. Both texts are reproduced here.

The *Indicator* version of the poem has numerous variations from that in K's letter, which may be attributed to K's own revisions or to Leigh Hunt's influence as editor (Hunt introduced the poem with an account of Alain Chartier's fifteenth-century ballad 'La Belle Dame Sans Mercy'). There has been considerable controversy over which version of the poem is to be preferred. Sidney Colvin, *John Keats. His Life and Poetry* (1917), 469–70, condemned the *Indicator* revisions as 'Hunt's suggestion . . . slipshod and commonplace'. 'It is surely a perversion in textual criticism to perpetuate the worse version merely because it happens to be the one printed in Keats's lifetime' (cf. Bate, 479 and n.). Contrast McGann, *KHM*, 32–42, for whom K in the *Indicator* deliberately established an ironic, distanced attitude to the literary establishment of the day, which amounted to K's 'final, active intentions' for his poem. To facilitate a comparative reading, the texts from the letter and from the *Indicator* are presented in parallel here.

The poem owes much to K's feelings for Fanny Brawne. Literary influences include Alain Chartier's ballad cited above; the enchantresses of *The Faerie Queene*; Burton's *Anatomy of Melancholy*; Percy's *Reliques of Ancient English Poetry* (1765), and more recent ballads by Wordsworth and Coleridge.

For further reading see Robert Graves, *The White Goddess* (1948), 374–80; Gittings (1954), 113–23, and responses by F. W. Bateson and K. Muir in *Essays in Criticism*, 4 (1954), 432–40; Sperry, 231–41; Barnard, 91–4; Susan Wolfson, *The Questioning Presence* (1986), 296–300; Theresa Kelley, 'Poetics and the Politics of Reception: Keats's "La Belle Dame sans Merci"', *English Literary History* (1987), 333–62; K. Swann, 'Harassing the Muse' in *Romanticism and Feminism*, ed. A. K. Mellor (1988), 81–92; John Barnard, 'Keats's Belle Dame and the Sexual Politics of Leigh Hunt's *Indicator*', *Romanticism*, 1 (1994–5).

Title According to Hunt, *Indicator*, 10 May 1820, suggested by Chartier's poem (see headnote); cf. *The Eve of St Agnes*, 291–2.

1 *Indicator* text: **Ah, what can ail thee, wretched wight:** wight, archaic in K's time, means 'person'; according to *OED* 'often implying some contempt or commiseration'. See McGann, KHM, 34–5, for this revision as a calculated 'literary' effect by K.

3 Cf. *The Eve of St Mark*, 10: 'springtide sedge'.

5 See 1 n. above.

6 See the 'hapless pilgrim' in Chatterton's 'An Excelente Balade of Charitie', 23: 'Howe woe-be-gone, how withered, forwynd, deade'. Chatterton glosses 'forwynd' as dry, sapless.

14–16 K's lady resembles the fatal enchantresses in *The Faerie Queene*, as well as the 'Night-Mair LIFE-in-DEATH' in Coleridge's *Ancient Mariner* (1817 edn): 'Her lips were red, her looks were free, / Her locks were yellow as gold'.

17–24 Stanzas 5 and 6 in K's letter are transposed in the *Indicator* version. **fragrant zone:** a girdle of flowers.

26 **manna dew:** cf. *Endymion*, 1. 766 n., and Coleridge's *Kubla Khan* (1816), 53.

32 **kisses four:** see K's letter of 14 Feb.–3 May 1819: 'Why four kisses— you will say – why four because I wish to restrain the headlong impetuosity of my Muse – she would have fain said "score" without hurting the rhyme – but we must temper the Imagination as the Critics say with Judgment. I was obliged to choose an even number that both eyes might have fair play: and to speak truly I think two a piece quite sufficient – Suppose I had said seven; there would have been three and a half a piece – a very awkward affair – and well got out of on my side' (*Letters*, 244). Altered to 'So kiss'd to sleep' in the *Indicator* version; see McGann, KHM, 36, and Robert Graves, *English Poetry* (1922), 54 for comment.

41 **starv'd:** lean, emaciated. **gloam:** twilight, gloaming, first recorded usage in *OED*; altered to 'gloom' in the *Indicator* version.

CAVIARE: cf. *Hamlet*, 2.2.431–3: 'the play, I remember, pleased not the million, 'twas caviare to the general'. See Colvin, 468-9, and McGann, KHM, 35, for K's signature as part of a strategy to open 'a slightly critical distance from his subject'.

To Sleep (p. 210)
Written probably Apr. 1819; copied in K's spring journal letter to the George Keatses on 21 Apr., as one of 'two or three [poems] lately written' (*Letters*, 253), the basis of the text here. First published in *Plymouth and Devonport Weekly Journal*, 11 Oct. 1838.

This is the earliest of K's experimental sonnets written in spring 1819. It shows in particular K's developing independence from the Shakespearean sonnet form: note how the rhyme-scheme of the sestet is linked to that of the octet, and that K avoids the final couplet of the Shakespearean sonnet. For K's remarks on the sonnet, see headnote to 'If by dull rhymes'. For further reading, see H. W. Garrod, *Keats* (1926), 85-6; M. R. Ridley, *Keats's Craftsmanship* (1933), 196-210; Stuart Curran, *Poetic Form and British Romanticism* (1986), 52-4.

5 **soothest:** most soothing (K's own coinage).
13 **oiled wards:** the ridges of the mechanism inside a lock; sometimes, as here, used in reference to the cavity inside a lock.

Ode to Psyche (p. 210)
Written late Apr. 1819. First published *1820*, the text reproduced here. K copied out his poem in his spring journal letter to the George Keatses on or shortly after 30 Apr. with these comments: 'The following Poem – the last I have written is the first and the only one with which I have taken even moderate pains – I have for the most part dash'd off my lines in a hurry – This I have done leisurely – I think it reads the more richly for it and will I hope encourage me to write other things in even a more peaceable and healthy spirit. You must recollect that Psyche was not embodied as a goddess before the time of Apulieus [*sic*] the Platonist who lived after the Augustan age, and consequently the Goddess was never worshipped or sacrificed to with any of the ancient fervour – and perhaps never thought of in the old religion – I am more orthodox than to let a hethen Goddess be so neglected' (*Letters*, 253). K's letter recalls the account of Psyche in L:

a nymph whom Cupid married and carried into a place of bliss, where he long enjoyed her company. Venus put her to death because she had robbed the world of her son; but Jupiter, at the request of Cupid, granted immortality to Psyche. The word signifies *the soul*, and this personification of Psyche is posterior to the Augustan age, though still it is connected with ancient mythology. Psyche is generally represented with the wings of a butterfly, to intimate the lightness of the soul, of which the butterfly is the symbol.

Other sources include Apuleius's *Golden Ass*, tr. William Adlington (1566); the stanza concerning Psyche in the garden of Adonis in *The Faerie Queene*, 3.6.50; Mary Tighe's *Psyche, or, The Legend of Love* (1811). Other literary and pictorial sources are discussed in Jack, 201–13.

K had approached the myth of Cupid and Psyche in 'I stood tip-toe' 141–50. As an allegory of the suffering of the human soul, the myth has affinities with K's discussion of the world as a 'vale of Soul-making', shortly before he copies out the ode in his letter: 'Do you not see how necessary a World of Pains and troubles is to school an Intelligence and make it a soul?' (*Letters*, 249–50). The poem's extended, irregular stanza form grew out of K's recent experiments with the sonnet in *To Sleep* and 'If by dull rhymes', opening the way for the other odes of 1819.

For further reading, see H. W. Garrod, *Keats* (1926), 83–90; Gittings, (1954), 124–30; Bate, 487–98; Dickstein, 196–205; Sperry, 249–61; Vendler, 46–70; Stuart Curran, *Poetic Form and British Romanticism* (1986), 81–4; Barnard, 100–4; D. Watkins, 'History, Self, and Gender in *Ode to Psyche*', *K&H*, 88–106.

2 Cf. Milton's *Lycidas*, 4, 6: 'with forced fingers rude / . . . Bitter constraint, and sad occasion dear'.

4 **soft-conched**: like a seashell.

5–6 Suggesting the heightened consciousness associated with visionary power; cf. *Ode to a Nightingale*, 79: 'Was it a vision, or a waking dream?'

7 **thoughtlessly**: in an abstracted mood.

14 **Tyrian**: purple, after a dye made in the ancient Phoenician city of Tyre.

16 **pinions**: wings.

20 **eye-dawn . . . aurorean**: as the lovers tenderly awaken, their love is renewed with the brilliance of dawn.

21 **The winged boy**: Cupid.

22 **dove**: in Mary Tighe's *Psyche* (5 edn, 1816), II. 3: 'Oh, Psyche . . . / Pure spotless dove! seek thy safe nest again'.

24–5 As a latecomer, Psyche surpasses the Olympians in beauty; cf. 42 below, and *Hyperion*, II. 228–9: ''tis the eternal law / That first in beauty should be first in might'.

26 **Phœbe**: the moon; cf. *Endymion*, IV. 56 n. **sapphire-region'd star**: cf. *On Visiting the Tomb of Burns*, 7.

27 **Vesper**: the evening star, Venus.

28–35 Recalling Milton's account in *On the Morning of Christ's Nativity*, 173–80, of the demise of classical deities, oracles, and shrines.

30 **make delicious moan**: cf. 44 below, and *La belle dame sans merci*, 20: 'made sweet moan'.

41   lucent fans: shining wings.

50   fane: temple.

52–60 K's temple for Psyche created in the imagination; cf. the ceremony for Pan, *Endymion*, 1. 63–106.

61–3 Fancy as a gardener 'improving' nature was common in Renaissance accounts of the imagination.

62   feign: invent, but perhaps also with the sense of deception associated with fancy in *Ode to a Nightingale*, 73–4.

'If by dull rhymes our English must be chain'd' (p. 212)

Written late Apr. or early May 1819, and copied out on or before 3 May in K's spring journal letter to the George Keatses (*Letters*, 255–6), the basis of the text here.

In his letter K remarks: 'I have been endeavouring to discover a better sonnet stanza than we have. The legitimate [Petrarchan] does not suit the language over-well from the pouncing rhymes – the other kind [Shakespearean] appears too elegiac – and the couplet at the end of it has seldom a pleasing effect – I do not pretend to have succeeded – It will explain itself' (*Letters*, 255). K seeks to avoid the 'dull' regularity of rhymes in the Petrarchan and Shakespearean sonnets, seeking a form 'more interwoven and complete'. K's breaking the constraints of regular sonnet forms here and in *To Sleep* was directly related to his composition of the odes in spring 1819 (see headnotes to *To Sleep*, *Ode to Psyche*, *Ode to a Nightingale*).

2   Andromeda: chained to a rock to be devoured by a sea monster, to avenge Neptune's wrath at her mother's vanity.

11 Midas's avariciousness was proverbial.

Ode to a Nightingale (p. 212)

Written Hampstead, May 1819. First published in *Annals of the Fine Arts*, 4 (July 1819), and subsequently in *1820*. Text here based on *1820*.

Charles Brown recalled the occasion of the poem's composition: 'In the spring of 1819 a nightingale had built her nest near my house. Keats felt a tranquil and continual joy in her song; and one morning he took his chair from the breakfast-table to the grass-plot under a plum-tree, where he sat for two or three hours. When he came into the house, I perceived he had some scraps of paper in his hand, and these he was quietly thrusting behind the books. On inquiry, I found those scraps, four or five in number, contained his poetic feeling on the song of our nightingale' (*KC*, II. 65). The placing of the poem in relation to the other odes of spring 1819 is conjectured from formal evidence: the regular ten-line stanza form is retained in the other spring odes, but without the shortened line which *Ode to a Nightingale* shares with the irregular stanzas of *Psyche*. The nightingale was a popular subject with contemporary poets; among poems K would have known are Charlotte Smith's *To a Nightingale* and *On the Departure of the Nightingale*, from *Elegiac Sonnets* (1784), and Coleridge's *Effusion XXIII. To the Nightingale* (1796) and *The Nightingale; A Conversational Poem* (1798, rpt in *Sibylline Leaves*, 1817). Among the 'thousand things' broached by Coleridge when he met K on 11 Apr. 1819 were 'Nightingales, Poetry' (*Letters*, 237).

For further reading, see Gittings (1954), 131–41; Bate, 498–510; Jack, 46–57; H. Bloom, *The Visionary Company* (rev. edn, 1971), 407–13; Dickstein, 205–21; Jones, 214–30; Sperry, 262–7; Vendler, 77–109; Barnard, 108–11; Paul D. Sheats, 'Keats, the Greater Ode, and the Trial of Imagination', *Coleridge, Keats, and the Imagination*, ed. Barth and Mahoney (1990), 174–200.

2 **hemlock:** the plant hemlock can be used as a powerful sedative.

4 **Lethe-wards:** towards Lethe, or forgetfulness; from Lethe – 'one of the rivers of hell, whose waters . . . had the power of making [the dead] forget whatever they had done, seen, or heard before' (L).

11 **vintage:** wine.

14 Evoking the festival at the grape harvest. Cf. also *The Eve of St Agnes*, 291–2.

15 Wine from the Mediterranean.

16 **Hippocrene:** K associates wine with the poetic inspiration of Hippocrene, 'a fountain of Boeotia, near Mount Helicon, sacred to the Muses' (L).

17–18 Cf. *Endymion*, II. 441–4.

19 **leave the world unseen:** not seeing the world, and unseen by the world.

23–4 Cf. Wordsworth's *Tintern Abbey* (1798), 53–4: 'the fretful stir / Unprofitable, and the fever of the world'.

26 K's brother Tom had died of tuberculosis, 1 Dec. 1819. Cf. K's remark to Fanny Keats, 12 Apr. 1819: 'the City or any place very confined would soon turn me pale and thin' (*Letters*, 207).

29–30 Cf. *Ode on Melancholy*, 21–3.

32 'Pards' are leopards; see *Endymion* IV. 193–272, 241–2 and nn.

33 **viewless:** invisible; cf. Lamia's 'viewless servants', *Lamia*, II. 136.

36 **haply:** perhaps. **Queen-Moon:** cf. Coleridge's *To the Nightingale* (1796), 8: 'the full orb'd Queen, that shines above'.

37 **Fays:** fairies.

38–50 Cf. the 'balmy night' described in Coleridge's *The Nightingale; A Conversational Poem* (1798), 5–11:

> You see the glimmer of the stream beneath,
> But hear no murmuring: it flows silently
> O'er its soft bed of verdure. All is still,
> A balmy night! and tho' the stars be dim,
> Yet let us think upon the vernal showers

> That gladden the green earth, and we shall find
> A pleasure in the dimness of the stars.

42   Cf. Coleridge's *Kubla Khan* (1816), 9: 'Where blossom'd many an incense-bearing tree'.

44   **seasonable:** suitable to the time of year; the month was May. Cf. K's remark, 'this is the 3d of May & every thing is in delightful forwardness; the violets are not withered, before the peeping of the first rose' (*Letters*, 256).

51   **Darkling:** in the dark; cf. *Paradise Lost*, III. 38–40: 'the wakeful bird / Sings darkling, and in shadiest covert hid / Tunes her nocturnal note'.

55   **rich to die:** cf. 'rich anger', *Ode on Melancholy*, 18.

56   Cf. 'Why did I laugh tonight', 11: 'Yet could I on this very midnight cease'.

60   **requiem:** K imagines the nightingale singing a mass for the dead.

62   Cf. Wordsworth, *The Excursion* (1814), IV. 760–2: 'While man grows old, and dwindles, and decays; / And countless generations of Mankind / Depart; and leave no vestige where they trod'.

64   **clown:** peasant.

66–7   **Ruth:** 'Ruth the Moabitess' was driven from her native land by famine, to glean corn in the fields of her kinsman Boaz. See Ruth, 2. 3. Cf. also Wordsworth, *The Solitary Reaper* (1807), 9–12.

69–70   Cf. 'Dear Reynolds, as last night', 50: 'The windows as if latch'd by fays and elves'.

70–71   **forlorn . . . Forlorn:** for the shift in the sense of 'forlorn' from, in the first instance, 'utterly lost', to 'pitiable; left desolate' (as a description of the poet's own state), see Cleanth Brooks, *Modern Poetry and the Tradition* (1939), 31.

73–8   Cf. Charlotte Smith, *On the Departure of the Nightingale*, 1–2: 'Sweet poet of the woods – a long adieu! / Farewel, soft minstrel of the year'.

75   **plaintive anthem:** cf. *The Solitary Reaper*, 18: 'the plaintive numbers flow'.

76   **still stream:** cf. Coleridge, *The Nightingale; A Conversational Poem*, 5–6, in 38–50 n. above.

79   **waking dream:** cf. Wordsworth, *Yarrow Visited* (1815), 3: 'a waking dream', and *Ode* ('Intimations') (1807), 56–7: 'Whither is fled the visionary gleam? / Where is it now, the glory and the dream?'

Ode on a Grecian Urn (p. 215)

Written possibly May 1819; dating, and the position of the poem in the sequence of spring odes remains conjectural. It shares some thematic concerns with *Ode to a Nightingale*, but resembles the remaining spring odes in abandoning the short eighth line. First published in *Annals of the*

Fine Arts (Jan. 1820), and subsequently in *1820*. Text here based on *1820*.

The poem is eclectic in its range of possible sources, as Jack, 214–24, demonstrates. Certainly, K did not have any single Grecian urn or vase in mind. Reproductions of Greek vases were fashionable at this time, as were volumes of engravings containing images of classical urns. K is said to have made a drawing of the Sosibios Vase from an engraving in Henry Moses' *Collection of Antique Vases* (1814), see Jack, plate 30. Finally K's interest in Greek art was evident from his response to the Elgin Marbles, which contributed at least one image to the ode (see 33–4 and n.).

The ode has been the subject of wide critical and scholarly discussion. For further reading, see in particular Cleanth Brooks, 'Keats's Sylvan Historian; History Without Footnotes', in *The Well Wrought Urn* (UK edn, 1949), 139–52; Gittings (1954), 131–41; William Empson, *The Structure of Complex Words* (1957), 368–74; Bate, 510–20; Dickstein, 221–8; Jones, 214–30; Sperry, 267–78; Vendler, 116–52; Susan J. Wolfson, *The Questioning Presence* (1986), 317–32; Barnard, 104–8; Watkins, 104–20; Theresa M. Kelley, 'Keats, Ekphrasis, and History', *K&H*, 212–37.

3–4   The urn is a 'historian' in that its decorative surface expresses a pastoral, 'flowery tale' from the distant past. 'Sylvan' means 'of the woods' – cf. the 'leaf-fring'd' border in 5 below.

7   Tempe ... Arcady: Tempe, a fertile valley in Thessaly; 'poets have described it as the most delightful spot of the earth' (L). Arcadia, an idyllic pastoral 'inland country of Peloponnesus ... much celebrated by the poets, and ... famous for its mountains' (L).

10   timbrels: tambourines.

11–14   Cf. Wordsworth's *Excursion* (1814), II. 710–12: 'Music of finer frame; a harmony, / So do I call it, though it be the hand / Of silence, though there be no voice'.

28   The line focuses K's ambivalent feelings about the urn that had emerged at 15–20 above. K may have been recalling Hazlitt's comments on Greek statues in 'On Gusto', *The Round Table* (1817): 'By their beauty they are raised above the frailties of pain or passion; by their beauty they are deified' (Howe, IV. 79). See also Hazlitt's 1818 lecture 'On Poetry in General': 'Greek statues ... are marble to the touch and to the heart ... In their faultless excellence they appear sufficient to themselves. By their beauty they are raised above the frailties of passion or suffering. By their beauty they are deified' (Howe, V. 11). Cf. K's spring journal letter to the George Keatses, late Apr. 1819, where he affirms 'how necessary a World of Pains and troubles is to school an Intelligence and make it a soul' (*Letters*, 250).

31–4   Cf. the Greek sacrifice described in 'Dear Reynolds', 20–22 and n.

33–4   These lines probably recall the image in the Elgin Marbles of the

heifer led to sacrifice from the south frieze of the Parthenon, slab 40.
See Jack, plate 33.

41   **Attic:** Grecian. **brede:** anything plaited or interwoven.
44   **tease us out of thought:** cf. 'Dear Reynolds', 77.
45   **Cold Pastoral:** cf. *On Visiting the Tomb of Burns*, 8: 'All is cold beauty'.

Ode on Melancholy (p. 217)

Written probably May 1819. First published in *1820*, the text reproduced here.

The first stanza rejects the conventional trappings of a macabre, gothic imagination, in favour of a meditation on themes which had preoccupied K in *Ode to a Nightingale* and *Ode on a Grecian Urn*: beauty and its transience, and the interpenetration of melancholy and delight. The poem adopts the ten-line stanza of *Ode on a Grecian Urn*.

For further reading, see Gittings (1954), 142–4; Bate, 520–24; H. Bloom, *The Visionary Company*, (rev. edn, 1971), 413–6; Sperry, 278–86; Vendler, 157–90; Barnard, 112–16.

1   **Lethe:** L: 'one of the rivers of hell, whose waters . . . had the power of making [the dead] forget whatever they had done, seen, or heard before'. Cf. *Ode to a Nightingale*, 3.
2   **Wolf's-bane:** 'A plant of the genus *Aconitum*, . . . with dull yellow flowers, occurring in mountainous regions in Europe' (*OED*).
4   **nightshade:** deadly nightshade, or belladonna, has poisonous berries. For Proserpine, see *Endymion*, 1. 944 and n.
5   **yew-berries:** the berries of the yew are poisonous; the tree often grows in graveyards and is associated with death.
6   **beetle . . . death-moth:** the deathwatch beetle and death's-head moth. The moth has markings on its wings that resemble a human skull; Psyche, or the soul, was often represented as a butterfly.
11–20   Melancholy, so often associated with 'weeping' and the 'shroud' of death, is also creative; like rain it 'fosters' life.
15   **glut . . . on:** 'To take one's fill of thinking, gazing, etc. *on* something' (*OED*).
18   **rich anger:** cf. *Ode to a Nightingale*, 55: 'rich to die'.
30   Cf. Shakespeare, sonnet 31, 10: 'Hung with the trophies of my lovers gone'.

Ode on Indolence (p. 218)

Written spring 1819, probably in May. First published in *L&L*, II. 276–8, the basis of the text here.

K's poem has its origin in the mood K described to the George Keatses in his spring journal letter on 19 March: 'This morning I am in a sort of temper indolent and supremely careless . . . Neither Poetry, nor

Ambition, nor Love have any alertness of countenance as they pass by me: they seem rather like figures on a greek vase – a Man and two women – whom no one but myself could distinguish in their disguisement. This is the only happiness; and is a rare instance of advantage in the body overpowering the mind' (*Letters*, 228). Sometime between writing this and 9 June, K composed his poem, possibly after re-reading his journal letter; on 9 June he told Mary-Ann Jeffery, 'I have been very idle lately, very averse to writing; both from the overpowering idea of our dead poets and from abatement of my love of fame. I hope I am a little more of a Philosopher than I was, consequently a little less of a versifying Pet-lamb . . . You will judge of my 1819 temper when I tell you that the thing I have most enjoyed this year has been writing an ode to Indolence' (*Letters*, 259) The ode contains numerous echoes of the *Ode to Psyche*, *Ode to a Nightingale*, and *Ode on a Grecian Urn*; it uses the ten-line stanza of the latter poem, but is in many respects stylistically inferior.

For further reading, see Gittings (1954), 142–6; Bate, 527–30; Jack, 244–6; Sperry, 286–91; Vendler, 20–39; Barnard, 116–18.

Motto   Matthew, 6. 28: 'Consider the lilies of the field, how they grow; they toil not, neither do they spin'.

10   **Phidian lore**: Phidias was one of the most famous sculptors of ancient Greece; among his many works was the frieze around the Parthenon, subsequently known as the Elgin Marbles.

12   **mask**: disguise, but also masquerade.

18   Cf. K's spring journal letter, 19 Feb.: 'pleasure has no show of enticement and pain no unbearable frown' (*Letters*, 228).

33–4   **fever-fit**: probably recalling *Macbeth*, 3.2.22–3: 'Duncan is in his grave; / After life's fitful fever he sleeps well'.

54   Cf. K's letter to Mary-Ann Jeffery; see headnote.

Lamia (p. 220)
Written probably late June–5 Sept. 1819. K arrived at Shanklin, Isle of Wight, 28 June, and on 11 July told Reynolds he had 'proceeded pretty well with Lamia, finishing the 1st part which consists of about 400 lines' (*Letters*, 268). He began work again after arriving at Winchester on 12 Aug., and on 5 Sept. wrote to John Taylor 'I have finish'd Lamia' (*Letters*, 288). The poem was revised in Mar. 1820, and published in *1820* as the first poem in the volume, the text reproduced here.

K's principal source for his poem was the story in Burton's *Anatomy of Melancholy*, which was printed immediately following the poem in *1820*:

Philostratus, in his fourth book *de Vita Apollonii*, hath a memorable instance in this kind, which I may not omit, of one Menippus Lycius, a young man twenty-five years of age, that going betwixt Cenchreas and Corinth, met such a phantasm in the habit of a fair gentlewoman, which taking him by the hand,

carried him home to her house, in the suburbs of Corinth, and told him she was a
Phœnician by birth, and if he would tarry with her, he should hear her sing and
play, and drink such wine as never any drank, and no man should molest him;
but she, being fair and lovely, would live and die with him, that was fair and
lovely to behold. The young man, a philosopher, otherwise staid and discreet,
able to moderate his passions, though not this of love, tarried with her a while to
his great content, and at last married her, to whose wedding, amongst other
guests, came Apollonius; who, by some probable conjectures, found her out to
be a serpent, a lamia; and that all her furniture was, like Tantalus' gold,
described by Homer, no substance but mere illusions. When she saw herself
descried, she wept, and desired Apollonius to be silent, but he would not be
moved, and thereupon she, plate, house, and all that was in it, vanished in an
instant: many thousands took notice of this fact, for it was done in the midst of
Greece. Burton's 'Anatomy of Melancholy', *Part 3. Sect. 2. Memb. 1. Subs. 1.*

The episode of Hermes and the nymph (1. 1–145) may have been
influenced by the story of Mercury's courtship of Herse in Ovid's
Metamorphoses, 11, and Marlowe's *Hero and Leander* (1598), 1. 386–
464. The magical effects of the poem may be indebted to K's reading of
oriental tales such as the *Arabian Nights*, and the figure of Lamia
resembles Coleridge's Geraldine in *Christabel* (1816) and the enchantress
in Peacock's *Rhododaphne* (1818). The metre of the poem is based on
Dryden's heroic couplets.

K's placing *Lamia* first in *1820* reflects his feelings about the poem's
importance. He told Richard Woodhouse, 22 Sept. 1819, that in contrast
to the 'inexperience' and 'simplicity' of *Isabella*, there was 'no objection
of this kind to Lamia' (*Letters*, 298). For further reading, see Gittings
(1954), 151–8, 168–74; Bate, 543–61; Miriam Allott, '*Isabella, The Eve
of St Agnes*, and *Lamia*', *John Keats. A Reassessment*, ed. K. Muir
(1969), 40–63; Jones, 242–60; Dickstein, 233–42; Sperry, 292–309;
Barnard, 119–29; Marjorie Levinson, *Keats's Life of Allegory* (1988),
255–99; Watkins, 135–55; Lucy Newlyn, '*Paradise Lost' and the
Romantic Reader* (1993), 182–8; Nicola Trott, 'Keats and the Prison-
House of History', *K&H*, 262–79.

Part 1
1. 1–5   The poem opens by returning to the world of ancient Greece,
before the English 'faery broods' had displaced the classical nymphs,
satyrs, dryads and fauns.
1. 3   **King Oberon:** king of the fairies in *A Midsummer Night's
Dream*.
1. 7   **ever-smitten Hermes:** Hermes (Mercury) was famous for his love
affairs. L: 'His children were also numerous as well as his amours'. Cf.
1. 129–45 below.
1. 13   **sacred island:** Crete was sacred because Jupiter . . . was educated
in that island' (L).

l. 15–16 Tritons: L: 'Sea deities . . . half men and half fishes', who 'wither' out of water. For the powerful sea god Triton, see *Endymion*, I. 206.

l. 23 winged feet: Mercury had 'wings for his feet' (L); cf. 42 below.

l. 46 cirque-couchant: K's own coinage, meaning 'coiled in a circle'. brake: a thicket; cf. *Endymion*, I. 18.

l. 47 gordian: intricately entwined, like the 'gordian knot'; cf. *Endymion*, III. 494 and n.

l. 49 pard: leopard; cf. 'Bacchus and his pards', *Ode to a Nightingale*, 32 and n.

l. 50 Eyed: the brilliant patterns on a (male) peacock's tail are called 'eyes'.

l. 55 penanced . . . elf: a fairy transformed into an animal as a punishment; for 'elf', see *Endymion*, II. 277 and n.

l. 57–8 L: 'According to some writers, Bacchus loved [Ariadne] after Theseus had forsaken her, and he gave her a crown of seven stars, which, after her death, was made a constellation'.

l. 63 L: 'Proserpine made Sicily . . . her residence' before she was carried away to the underworld by Pluto; cf. *Endymion*, I. 944 and n.

l. 67 K describes Hermes hovering before descending, although 'stoop' actually describes a bird of prey diving for the kill.

l. 78 Phœbean dart: ray of sunlight.

l. 81 star of Lethe: Mercury conducted the souls of the dead to the underworld; for Lethe, see *Ode to a Nightingale*, 4 n.

l. 89 serpent rod: caduceus, a magic rod entwined at one end by two serpents; see *Endymion*, I. 563 n.

l. 103 For the lasciviousness of satyrs, see *Endymion*, IV. 228; for Silenus, see *Endymion*, IV. 215–17 n.

l. 107 weïrd: magic.

l. 114 psalterian: like the sound of a psaltery, an old stringed instrument.

l. 115 Circean: like the fatal enchantress Circe.

l. 130 Dash'd: confounded or abashed.

l. 143 to the lees: to the last drops.

l. 145 Cf. 'human passion' in *Ode on a Grecian Urn*, 28–30.

l. 146–64 As Sperry, 302, points out: 'The description [of the serpent's transformation] resembles nothing so much as the effects of a violent chemical reaction . . . the passage is marked by a brilliant, mocking irony . . . a sort of separation of elements takes place. Lamia's bright emblems and colors are overrun and dwindle to a little pile of charred remains'.

l. 158 brede: interwoven patterns. Cf. *Ode on a Grecian Urn*, 41 and n.

l. 163 rubious-argent: K's own coinage, meaning ruby-silver.

l. 174 Cenchreas: a harbour of Corinth.

l. 182 passioned: 'To show, express, or be affected by passion or deep feeling' (*OED*).

l. 191   **sciential:** wise.

l. 193   **pettish:** peevish, irksome.

l. 198   **unshent:** unspoiled.

l. 207–9   **Nereids ... Thetis ... Bacchus:** see *Endymion*, III. 888–9 n.; II. 611 n.; IV. 193–272 n. respectively.

l. 211–12   The gardens of Pluto's palace in the underworld where Mulciber (the infernal architect of Pandemonium in *Paradise Lost*, I. 710–40) has erected pillars in a colonnade. **piazzian:** comes from 'piazza', a square.

l. 238   **drear:** Lycius's 'indifference' is 'drear' to Lamia as she awaits him.

l. 248   Orpheus braved the underworld to rescue his beloved Eurydice; 'Pluto and Proserpine were moved with his sorrow, and consented to restore him Eurydice, provided he forbore looking behind till he had come to the extremest borders of hell' (L). Orpheus's glance back was fatal, as Lycius's will prove.

l. 265   **descended Pleiad:** Lycius imagines Lamia may be one of the 'seven sisters' of the Pleiades, come down to earth.

l. 274–5   Recalling Lear's rash challenge to Cordelia: 'what can you say to draw / A third more opulent than your sisters?' I.i.84–5.

l. 285   **sleights:** stratagems.

l. 293   **amenity:** pleasure.

l. 297–300   Cf. the enchanting 'faery's song' in *La belle dame sans merci*, 24.

l. 320   **Adonian feast:** the festival of Adonis, a fertility rite held in the temple of Venus, hence the 'amorous herbs and flowers' at l. 318 above. L adds the significant remark that the 'time of the celebration was supposed to be very unlucky'.

l. 329   **Peris:** 'In Persian Mythology, one of a race of superhuman beings, originally represented as of evil or malevolent character, but subsequently as good genii, fairies, or angels, endowed with grace and beauty' (*OED*).

l. 333   **Pyrrha's pebbles:** after Deucalion's flood (see *Endymion*, II. 197–8 n.), Deucalion and Pyrrha were directed by the oracle of Themis to 'repair the loss of mankind' by throwing stones behind their backs; 'the stones which Pyrrha threw were changed into women' (L).

l. 347   **comprized:** 'taken in', absorbed.

l. 352   **temples lewd:** see L on the festival of Adonis: 'Only women were admitted, and such as did not appear were compelled to prostitute themselves for one day'.

l. 375   **Apollonius:** Apollonius of Tyana, 'a Pythagorean philosopher, well skilled in the secret arts of magic' (L). He advocated moral and religious reform.

l. 386   **sounds Æolian:** like the sound of an aeolian harp.

Part II

II. 9   **clench'd it quite:** proved it conclusively.

II. 11–15   Cupid ('Love') hovers, jealously guarding their bed-chamber against intruders.

II. 24   **a tythe:** a small part.

II. 32   **bourn:** boundary.

II. 34   **penetrant:** acutely perceptive.

II. 36   **empery:** empire.

II. 52   **trammel:** enmesh. Cf. II. 210 below, and K's letter to Fanny Brawne, 1 July 1819: 'Ask yourself my love whether you are not very cruel to have so entrammelled me, so destroyed my freedom' (*Letters*, 263).

II. 73–4   Cf. *Ode on Melancholy*, 18–20: 'Or if thy mistress some rich anger shows, / Emprison her soft hand, and let her rave, / And feed deep, deep upon her peerless eyes'.

II. 76   **sanguineous:** 'bloody'; flushed with anger.

II. 78   **mitigated:** moderated.

II. 78–81   Alluding to the 'celebrated serpent' which 'sprung from the mud and stagnated waters . . . after the deluge of Deucalion. . . . Apollo, as soon as he was born, attacked the monster, and killed him with his arrows' (L).

II. 80   **certes:** certainly.

II. 102   **blind and blank:** obscure and empty (as a response to Lycius's questions).

II. 105   Lamia 'betrays' Lycius into a charmed sleep, by means of a magic spell.

II. 114   **pompousness:** love of show; cf. Lycius's wish to show off Lamia at II. 57–61.

II. 118   **subtle:** Lamia's servants are invisible spirits, like the 'viewless servants' at II. 136 below.

II. 122–62   K copied out a draft of this passage in his letter to John Taylor, 5 Sept. 1819 (*Letters*, 288–9).

II. 122–4   Cf. the 'moan' of the enchantress in *La belle dame sans merci*, 20.

II. 136   **viewless:** cf. 118 n. above, and *Ode to a Nightingale*, 33 and n.

II. 137   **fretted:** elaborately carved.

II. 151–5:   Cf. I. 388–93 above.

II. 155   **demesne:** territory, here referring to Lamia's magic palace.

II. 160   **daft:** played the fool with.

II. 164–9   Cf. the Ancient Mariner stopping the wedding-guest in Coleridge's ballad. See also II. 287 and n. below.

II. 175   **lucid:** shining.

II. 185   **libbard's:** leopard's.

II. 187   **Ceres' horn:** the horn of plenty.

II. 217   **osier'd**: plaited or woven like osiers (willow).

II. 224   **willow ... adder's tongue**: both emblems of grief. Adder's-tongue (a fern) also had medicinal properties, and was appropriate for the serpent Lamia.

II. 225–6   **thyrsus**: Lycius's wreath will be made from the ivy and vine leaves around Bacchus's staff (the thyrsus).

II. 229–37   Cf. William Hazlitt's remarks in his 1818 lecture 'On Poetry in General': 'It cannot be concealed ... that the progress of knowledge and refinement has a tendency to circumscribe the limits of the imagination, and to clip the wings of poetry' (Howe, v. 9). At Haydon's 'immortal dinner', 28 Dec. 1817, K and Lamb 'agreed [Newton] had destroyed all the Poetry of the rainbow, by reducing it to a prism', *The Diary of Benjamin Robert Haydon*, ed. W. B. Pope (5 vols, 1960–3), II. 173.

II. 268   The guests' hair bristled with fright (picking up the sense of 'horrid' in II. 267 above).

II. 275   **deep-recessed vision**: sunken eyes.

II. 277   **juggling**: conjuring.

II. 287   **gray-beard wretch**: cf. *The Ancient Mariner* (1798), 15: ' "Now get thee hence, thou grey-beard Loon!" '. Cf. II. 164–9 and n. above.

II. 291   **sophist**: a wise and learned man.

II. 301   **perceant**: piercing.

To Autumn (p. 238)
Written at Winchester, 19 Sept. 1819 (*Letters*, 291–2). First published *1820*, the text reproduced here.

K wrote to J. H. Reynolds, 21 Sept. 1819: 'How beautiful the season is now – How fine the air. A temperate sharpness about it. Really, without joking, chaste weather – Dian skies – I never lik'd stubble fields so much as now – Aye better than the chilly green of the spring. Somehow a stubble plain looks warm – in the same way that some pictures look warm – this struck me so much in my sunday's walk that I composed upon it' (*Letters*, 291–2). In his letter to Richard Woodhouse, 21–2 Sept., K copied out his poem (*Letters*, 294–5).

The form of the poem is related to the spring odes, but with the stanza extended from ten to eleven lines. The poem has often been cited as K's most 'perfect' lyric, expressing a 'true impersonality' (Geoffrey Hartman). Recently it has been the focus of critical debate about whether its idealised nature represents an 'escape' from the world, or a lyrical intervention at a time of acute political and social crisis following the Peterloo Massacre of Aug. 1819. For further reading, see Gittings (1954), 182–90; Bate, 580–85; Jack, 232–43; Geoffrey Hartman, 'Poem and Ideology: A Study of Keats's "To Autumn" ', *The Fate of Reading and Other Essays* (1975); Sperry, 336–42; Vendler, 233–88; Jerome

McGann, KHM (58–62); Barnard, 138–40; Paul Fry, 'History, Existence, and "To Autumn"', KP, 211–19; John Creaser, 'From "Autumn" to Autumn in Keats's Ode', *Essays in Criticism* (1988), 190–214; Nicholas Roe, 'Keats's Commonwealth', *K&H*, 194–211.

4   **thatch-eves:** cf. Coleridge's *Frost at Midnight* (1817 text), 68–9: 'the nigh thatch / Smokes in the sun-thaw . . . the eve-drops fall'.

5   Cf. Chatterton's *Ælla: A Tragycal Enterlude*, 184–5: 'Whann the fayre apple, rudde as even skie, / Do bende the tree unto the fructyle grounde'. See also K's letter to Reynolds, 21 Sept. 1819: 'I always somehow associate Chatterton with autumn' (*Letters*, 292).

12   **thee:** on personification in the ode, see Jack, Creaser and Roe, cited above.

18   **swath:** 'The space covered by a sweep of the mower's scythe; the width of grass or corn to cut' (*OED*).

25   **barred clouds:** cf. Coleridge's *Dejection: An Ode* (1817 text), 31: 'those thin clouds above, in flakes and bars'.

26   See K's letter to Reynolds, 21 Sept. 1819, quoted in headnote.

28   **sallows:** willows.

30   **hilly bourn:** hills forming the boundary of the horizon.

31–2   Cf. Coleridge's *Frost at Midnight* (1817 text), 67–9.

The Fall of Hyperion: A Dream (p. 239)
Begun late July 1819 at Shanklin, Isle of Wight. Abandoned by 21 Sept. 1819. First published by R. M. Milnes, 'Another Version of Keats's "Hyperion"', *Miscellanies of the Philobiblon Society* (1856–7), 3–24.

The poem is a reconstruction of *Hyperion* in the form of a dream-vision related by the priestess Moneta. The poem begins with an induction (1. 1–18); this is followed by an introductory passage (1. 19–294) in which K develops his concern with the relation of suffering to poetry, and the question of the poet's calling and function for human-kind. The original narrative of *Hyperion* reappears at 1. 294. Strong influences on the poem are Milton's *Paradise Lost* and Dante's *Divina Commedia*. One of K's reasons for abandoning the poem was his dissatisfaction at the Miltonic inflection of his blank verse; he told Reynolds, 21 Sept.: 'I have given up Hyperion – there were too many Miltonic inversions in it – Miltonic verse cannot be written but in an artful or rather artist's humour. I wish to give myself up to other sensations. It may be interesting to you to pick out some lines from Hyperion and put a mark X to the false beauty proceeding from art, and one || to the true voice of feeling. Upon my soul 'twas imagination I cannot make the distinction – Every now & then there is a Miltonic intonation – But I cannot make the division properly' (*Letters*, 292). For examples of Miltonic syntax, see 1. 140, 145–6, 184. Cf. also K's comment to the George Keatses: 'I have but lately stood on my guard against Milton. Life to him would be death to me' (*Letters*, 325). A further reason for abandoning the poem was K's deteriorating health; Bate, 614, suggests that by mid-Sept. tuberculosis had 'seriously begun . . . bringing with it periods of immense fatigue and some fever'.

For further reading, see M. R. Ridley, *Keats's Craftsmanship* (1933), 266–80; Gittings (1954), 176–85; K. Muir, 'The Meaning of *Hyperion*', *John Keats. A Reassessment*, ed. K. Muir (1969), 103–123; Bate, 585–605; Jack, 225–31; Dickstein, 242–62; Jones, 91–114, 159–64; Sperry, 310–35; K. K. Ruthven, 'Keats and *Dea Moneta*', *Studies in Romanticism* (Summer, 1975), 445–59; Vendler, 197–226; Barnard, 129–37; Watkins, 156–176; Terence Hoagwood, 'Keats, Fictionality, and Finance', *K&H*, 127–42; Michael O'Neill, ' "When this warm scribe my hand": Writing and History in *Hyperion* and *The Fall of Hyperion*', *K&H*, 143–164.

The text here is based on the transcript of the poem by Richard Woodhouse, (W₂) in Harvard Library, incorporating I. 1–11, 61–86; II. 1–4, 6, from passages K copied out in his letter to Woodhouse 21, 22 Sept. 1819 (*Letters*, 295–6).

Canto I

I. 24–6 Cf. *Ode to Psyche*, 59–61: 'A rosy sanctuary will I dress / With the wreath'd trellis of a working brain, / With buds, and bells, and stars without a name'.

I. 31 Cf. the meal prepared by Eve in *Paradise Lost*, v. 303–7.

I. 35 **fabled horn:** the horn of plenty or cornucopia, emblem of Ceres, goddess of corn and harvests, mother of Proserpine. Cf. *Lamia*, II. 187.

I. 37 For the legend of Proserpine, see *Endymion*, I. 944 n.

I. 47–51 K alludes to the jealous intrigues of ambitious religious men, for whom poisoning helped to remove competitors. A caliph is 'in Mohammedan countries . . . the chief civil and religious ruler, as successor to Mohammed' (*OED*). The 'scarlet conclave' refers to Cardinals of the Catholic church.

I. 56 **Silenus:** cf. *Endymion*, IV. 215–17 and n.

I. 74 **asbestus:** 'A mineral of fibrous texture capable of being woven into an incombustible fabric'; the finest is 'usually pearly white' (*OED*).

I. 75 **in that place:** heaven; cf. Matthew, 6: 20: 'lay up for yourselves treasures in heaven, where neither moth nor rust doth corrupt'.

I. 88 **image, huge:** a statue of Saturn; cf. I. 299–300 below.

I. 96 **one minist'ring:** Moneta, the priestess of the temple; see I. 226–7 below.

I. 103 **Maian incense:** scent as from May flowers. 'Maian' derives from Maia, the goddess of May celebrated by K in 'Mother of Hermes' – his fragment of an ode to May.

I. 116 **gummed leaves:** leaves with aromatic gum or sap.

l. 135–6   **fair angels . . . heaven:** alluding to Jacob's dream of a ladder that 'reached to heaven'; see Genesis, 28: 12.

l. 137   **horned shrine:** As in the ancient world, Moneta's altar was decorated with horns; cf. l. 237 below.

l. 141   **veiled shadow:** K's descriptions of Moneta as a shade or shadow may recall *ombra* from Dante's *Purgatorio*. See also L's description of the Egyptian goddess Isis: 'the inscriptions of the statues of that goddess were often in these words: *I am all that has been, that shall be, and none among mortals has hitherto taken off my veil*'.

l. 144   **dated on:** postponed.

l. 147–9   Cf. Apollo's deification in *Hyperion*, III. 113–20.

l. 155   **sooth:** smooth, and also true.

l. 157–9   Cf. *Sleep and Poetry*, 123–5.

l. 161–2   **vision'ries . . . dreamers:** here used synonymously.

l. 168–70   The dreamer 'fevers' himself with his awareness of suffering about which he does nothing; the true poet ministers to others, as Moneta points out at l. 201 below.

l. 189–90   On the poet's roles, see also *Sleep and Poetry*, 245–7.

l. 198–202   On the distinction between the dreamer and the poet, see also l. 168–70 n. above.

l. 203   **Pythia's spleen:** Pythia was 'the priestess of Apollo at Delphi. She delivered the answer of the god to such as came to consult the oracle . . . often with loud howlings and cries' (L).

l. 205   **misty pestilence:** Apollo 'was the deity who, according to the notions of the ancients, inflicted plagues, and in that moment he appeared surrounded with clouds' (L).

l. 226   **Moneta:** another name for Mnemosyne, mother of the Muses. See *Hyperion*, II. 29 n.

l. 245   **globed brain:** recalled from K's medical studies; cf. I. 276–9 below, and *Ode to Psyche*, 50–60.

l. 246   **electral:** electrical, as if charged with electricity.

l. 256–8   Cf. Coleridge's *Ancient Mariner* (1798): 'Her skin is white as leprosy, / And she is far liker death than he; / Her flesh makes the still air cold'.

l. 267   **visionless:** unseeing; Moneta's sight is turned inward upon her own visions.

l. 271–4   Possibly recalling the followers of Mammon in *Paradise Lost*, I. 684–8.

l. 282   **Shade of Memory:** Mnemosyne (Moneta) means 'memory'.

l. 294–6   Here K returns to *Hyperion*, I. 1–3.

l. 298–9   Cf. I. 88–9 above.

l. 302–4   Cf. *Hyperion*, III. 113: 'Knowledge enormous makes a God of me'.

l. 312   **zoning of a summer's day:** the extent of a summer's day.

l. 326   **antient mother:** Tellus; see *Hyperion*, I. 20–1 n.

I. 335   **Thea:** see *Hyperion*, I. 23 n. K has removed any reference to Thea's gigantic size and strength (see *Hyperion*, I. 27–33), since he now wishes to emphasise the kinship of her grief to 'human sorrows' (I. 257 above). Cf. I. 346 below.

I. 354   For Saturn and *King Lear*, see *Hyperion*, I. 98–103 n.

I. 362   **captious:** taking exception to.

I. 411   **solitary Pan:** suggesting the desolation of nature after the fall of Saturn and the Titans, the end of the Golden Age; cf. I. 285 above.

I. 425   **Cybele:** see *Hyperion*, II. 4 n.

I. 431   **those imps:** Saturn's rebellious children, the Olympians.

Canto II

II. 1–49   This passage reworks *Hyperion*, I. 158–204, with Moneta as narrator.

II. 50   **Mnemosyne:** Moneta; see I. 226 n. above.

II. 53–61   Reworking *Hyperion*, I. 213–20.

'Bright Star, would I were stedfast as thou art' (p. 253)

Written 1819; more precise dating has proved difficult. K copied the poem in Joseph Severn's copy of Shakespeare's *Poems* while on his way by sea to Italy, Sept.–Oct. 1820, and it was long thought to be his last composition. The discovery of a transcript by K's friend Charles Brown, dated 1819, complicated matters; see Sidney Colvin, *John Keats* (1917), 492–4. Scholars have offered various dates of composition from Oct. 1818–late 1819; see further reading and notes below. First published *Plymouth and Devonport Weekly Journal*, 27 Sept. 1838. Text here reproduced from K's fair copy of the poem in Severn's copy of Shakespeare, Keats House, Hampstead.

For further reading, see Gittings (1954), 25–36; Aileen Ward, 'The Date of Keats's "Bright Star" Sonnet', *Studies in Philology* (1955), 75–85; Bate, 618–20; Christopher Ricks, *Keats and Embarrassment* (1974), 111–14; Barnard, 127–9; Nicholas Roe ' "Bright Star, Sweet Unrest": Image and Consolation in Wordsworth, Shelley, and Keats', *History and Myth. Essays on English Romantic Literature*, ed. S. Behrendt (1990), 143–48.

1–4   Cf. K's letter to Tom Keats, 25–7 June 1818: 'There are many disfigurements to this Lake [Windermere] – not in the way of land or water. No; the two views we have had of it are of the most noble tenderness – they can never fade away – they make one forget the divisions of life; age, youth, poverty and riches; and refine one's vision into a sort of north star which can never cease to be open lidded and stedfast over the wonders of the great Power' (*Letters*, 101). Cf. also Wordsworth's 'Chaldean Shepherds' who in *The Excursion*, IV. 697–9: 'Looked on the Polar Star, as on a Guide / And Guardian of their course, that never closed / His steadfast eye'.

4 Eremite: see *The Eve of St Agnes*, 277 n.

6 pure ablution washing as part of a religious rite; cf. 'priestlike task' in 5 above. The tides of the sea mean that it 'washes' the shore twice a day.

14 Cf. K's letter to Fanny Brawne, 25 July 1819: 'I have two luxuries to brood over in my walks, your Loveliness and the hour of my death. O that I could have possession of them both in the same minute . . . I will imagine you Venus to night and pray, pray, pray to your star like a Hethen. Your's ever, fair Star, John Keats. My seal is mark'd like a family table cloth with my mother's initial F for Fanny: put between my Father's initials' (*Letters*, 271–2).

'In after-time a sage of mickle lore' (p. 253)

Written 1820, possibly in July when K was 'marking the most beautiful passages' in his copy of Spenser (now lost) for Fanny Brawne (*Letters*, 383). First published *Plymouth and Devonport Weekly Journal*, 4 July, 1839, from a transcript by Charles Brown, and subsequently in *L&L*, 1. 281. Text here based on *L&L*.

According to *L&L*, 1. 281, this stanza was written by K at the end of *Faerie Queene*, 5.2, as a response to Spenser's undemocratic views. In Spenser's poem, a 'mighty Gyant' proposes to 'equalize' the world: 'Tyrants that make men subject to their law, / I will suppresse, that they no more may raine; / And Lordings curbe, that commons over-aw; / And all the wealth of rich men to the poore will draw' (5.2.38). Sir Artegall (representing justice) and his squire Talus defeat the giant; in K's poem, the Giant, educated out of his 'brutishness' by 'Typographus' (the printed word), vanquishes Spenser's oppressive heroes. Milnes remarks in this poem '[K] expressed . . . his conviction of the ultimate triumph of freedom and equality by the power of transmitted knowledge' (*L&L*, 1. 281). When published by K's friend Charles Brown in 1839 (see above), the poem was described as 'the last stanza, of any kind, that [K] wrote before his lamented death'.

1 mickle lore: much learning.
2 Yclep'd: named (a Spenserian archaism). **Typographus:** the power of the printed word: see headnote.
8 Artegall and Talus: see headnote.

APPENDIX ONE

1 *The Preface to* Endymion *(1818)*

Keats had written a preface dated Teignmouth, 19 Mar. 1818, but
its apologetic and defensive manner brought objections from K's
friend J. H. Reynolds and from his publishers, Taylor and Hessey.
See K's letter to Reynolds, 9 Apr. 1818, for his response to their
criticism (*Letters*, 85). The preface published with *Endymion* was
dated Teignmouth, 10 Apr. 1818:

Knowing within myself the manner in which this Poem has been
produced, it is not without a feeling of regret that I make it public.

What manner I mean, will be quite clear to the reader, who must
soon perceive great inexperience, immaturity, and every error
denoting a feverish attempt, rather than a deed accomplished. The
two first books, and indeed the two last, I feel sensible are not of such
completion as to warrant their passing the press; nor should they if I
thought a year's castigation would do them any good; – it will not:
the foundations are too sandy. It is just that this youngster should die
away: a sad thought for me, if I had not some hope that while it is
dwindling I may be plotting, and fitting myself for verses fit to live.

This may be speaking too presumptuously, and may deserve a
punishment: but no feeling man will be forward to inflict it: he will
leave me alone, with the conviction that there is not a fiercer hell
than the failure in a great object. This is not written with the least
atom of purpose to forestall criticisms of course, but from the desire
I have to conciliate men who are competent to look, and who do
look with a zealous eye, to the honour of English literature.

The imagination of a boy is healthy, and the mature imagination
of a man is healthy; but there is a space of life between, in which the
soul is in a ferment, the character undecided, the way of life
uncertain, the ambition thick-sighted: thence proceeds mawkish-
ness, and all the thousand bitters which those men I speak of must
necessarily taste in going over the following pages.

I hope I have not in too late a day touched the beautiful mythology
of Greece, and dulled its brightness: for I wish to try once more,
before I bid it farewel.

2 The publishers' advertisement for 1820

This was probably written by John Taylor (*KC*. I. 115 n.). K remarked on it 'This is none of my doing – I was ill at the time'. He added with respect to the final sentence: 'This is a lie'. See Amy Lowell, *John Keats* (2 vols, 1925) II. 424–5.

ADVERTISEMENT

If any apology be thought necessary for the appearance of the unfinished poem of HYPERION, the publishers beg to state that they alone are responsible, as it was printed at their particular request, and contrary to the wish of the author. The poem was intended to have been of equal length with ENDYMION, but the reception given to that work discouraged the author from proceeding.

Fleet-Street, 26 June, 1820

KEATS AND HIS CRITICS

Leigh Hunt, 'Young Poets', from the *Examiner* (1 December 1816), rpt *KCH*, 42

Hunt's account of K in his liberal newspaper, the *Examiner*, brought K's poetry to wide public notice for the first time. K had first met Hunt in October 1816, although he had admired Hunt as politician and poet for many years, as his sonnet *Written on the day that Mr Leigh Hunt left Prison* shows. Hunt was well-intentioned, and he did much to encourage K's early poetic ambitions. In response K emulated some of the stylistic traits of Hunt's poetry, for example his fondness for decorative verbal texture and run-on couplets. K quickly recognised the weaknesses of Hunt's style and sought to banish them from his own poems. But his literary and political association with Hunt, announced in the 'Young Poets' essay, had a lasting effect on K's critical reception from this moment onwards.

> The last of these young aspirants whom we have met with, and who promise to help the new school to revive Nature and
>
> > To put a spirit of youth in every thing, –
>
> is, we believe, the youngest of them all, and just of age. His name is JOHN KEATS. He has not yet published any thing except in a newspaper; but a set of his manuscripts was handed us the other day, and fairly surprised us with the truth of their ambition, and ardent grappling with Nature. In the following Sonnet there is one incorrect rhyme, which might be easily altered, but which shall serve in the mean time as a peace-offering to the rhyming critics. The rest of the composition, with the exception of a little vagueness in calling the regions of poetry 'the realms of gold', we do not hesitate to pronounce excellent, especially the last six lines. The word *swims* is complete; and the whole conclusion is equally powerful and quiet:–
>
> [Quotes *On first looking into Chapman's Homer* in full.]
>
> We have spoken with the less scruple of these poetical promises, because we really are not in the habit of lavishing praises and

announcements, and because we have no fear of any pettier vanity on the part of young men, who promise to understand human nature so well.

John Gibson Lockhart, 'Cockney School of Poetry No. IV' *Blackwood's Edinburgh Magazine* (August 1818), rpt *KCH*, 103–4

Lockhart's series of 'Cockney School' essays began in October 1817, as an attack on Leigh Hunt and his associates – among whom K was numbered. Although Lockhart's motives were mainly political, the essays as a sequence form a brilliantly caustic commentary on a fundamental change in English cultural life. Hunt and William Hazlitt were the most prominent among a group of poets and journalists with strongly democratic, reformist sympathies, who had been educated outside the public schools and the universities at Oxford and Cambridge. Their writings, allied to their politics, represented an articulate challenge to the establishment of the day, such that their poetic style ('loose couplets') might be read as the signature of subversive ('liberal') politics and licentious morals. K's friend Benjamin Bailey had mentioned the poet's background and education in conversation with Lockhart, providing information used in this powerful, sarcastic reading of the 1817 collection and *Endymion*. Echoing Hunt's 'Young Poets' essay (see above), Lockhart caricatures K as a 'boy of pretty abilities', ridicules his classical education through translation, and damns *Endymion* as 'profane and vulgar'. Lockhart's brilliant, energetic disparagement of the 'young Cockney rhymester' actually betrays his recognition (and fear) that K's poetry is the music of the democratic world to come.

It is time to pass from the juvenile *Poems*, to the mature and elaborate *Endymion, a Poetic Romance*. The old story of the moon falling in love with a shepherd, so prettily told by a Roman Classic, and so exquisitely enlarged and adorned by one of the most elegant of German poets, has been seized upon by Mr John Keats, to be done with as might seem good unto the sickly fancy of one who never read a single line either of Ovid or of Wieland. If the quantity, not the quality, of the verses dedicated to the story is to be taken into account, there can be no doubt that Mr John Keats may now claim Endymion entirely to himself. To say the truth, we do not suppose either the Latin or the German poet would be very anxious to dispute about the property of the hero of the 'Poetic Romance.' Mr

Keats has thoroughly appropriated the character, if not the name.
His Endymion is not a Greek shepherd, loved by a Grecian goddess;
he is merely a young Cockney rhymester, dreaming a phantastic
dream at the full of the moon. Costume, were it worth while to
notice such a trifle, is violated in every page of this goodly octavo.
From his prototype Hunt, John Keats has acquired a sort of vague
idea, that the Greeks were a most tasteful people, and that no
mythology can be so finely adapted for the purposes of poetry as
theirs. It is amusing to see what a hand the two Cockneys make of
this mythology; the one confesses that he never read the Greek
Tragedians, and the other knows Homer only from Chapman, and
both of them write about Apollo, Pan, Nymphs, Muses, and
Mysteries, as might be expected from persons of their education. We
shall not, however, enlarge at present upon this subject, as we mean
to dedicate an entire paper to the classical attainments and attempts
of the Cockney poets. As for Mr Keats' *Endymion*, it has just as
much to do with Greece as it has with 'old Tartary the fierce;' no
man, whose mind has ever been imbued with the smallest knowledge
or feeling of classical poetry or classical history, could have stopped
to profane and vulgarise every association in the manner which has
been adopted by this 'son of promise.' Before giving any extracts, we
must inform our readers, that this romance is meant to be written in
English heroic rhyme. To those who have read any of Hunt's poems,
this hint might indeed be needless. Mr Keats has adopted the loose,
nerveless versification, and Cockney rhymes of the poet of *Rimini*;
but in fairness to that gentleman, we must add, that the defects of the
system are tenfold more conspicuous in his disciple's work than in
his own. Mr Hunt is a small poet, but he is a clever man. Mr Keats is
a still smaller poet, and he is only a boy of pretty abilities, which he
has done every thing in his power to spoil.

John Hamilton Reynolds, unsigned review from the *Alfred, West
of England Journal and General Advertiser* (October 1818),
reprinted in the *Examiner* (October 1818) and *KCH*, 120

In this review Reynolds defends his friend and fellow-poet against
the attack by John Wilson Croker in the *Quarterly Review*
(September 1818). The defence was intended to draw attention to
the unique qualities of K's poetry, and Hunt reprinted it in the
Examiner to ensure that it had a wide circulation. Reynolds also
reinforces the idea of K as a 'young' poet, and initiates the critical
tradition in which K's 'high mind' was held to be somehow isolated
from the contemporary world.

Mr Keats has certainly not perfected anything yet; but he has the power, we think, within him, and it is in consequence of such an opinion that we have written these few hasty observations. If he should ever see this, he will not regret to find that all the country is not made up of Quarterly Reviewers. All that we wish is, that our Readers could read the Poem, as we have done, before they assent to its condemnation – they will find passages of singular feeling, force, and pathos. We have the highest hopes of this young Poet. We are obscure men, it is true, and not gifted with that perilous power of mind, and truth of judgment which are possessed by Mr Croker, Mr Canning, Mr Barrow, or Mr Gifford, (all 'honourable men', and writers in the *Quarterly Review*). We live far from the world of letters, – out of the pale of fashionable criticism, – aloof from the atmosphere of a Court; but we are surrounded by a beautiful country, and love Poetry, which we read out of doors, as well as in. We think we see glimpses of a high mind in this young man, and surely the feeling is better that urges us to nourish its strength, than that which prompts the Quarterly Reviewer to crush it in its youth, and for ever. If however, the mind of Mr Keats be of the quality we think it to be of, it will not be cast down by this wanton and empty attack. Malice is a thing of the scorpion kind – It drives the sting into its own heart. The very passages which the *Quarterly Review* quotes as ridiculous, have in them the beauty that sent us to the Poem itself.

From an unsigned review of *Lamia, Isabella, The Eve of St Agnes, and other Poems*, published in Paris in *Galignani's Weekly Repository, or Literary Gazette* (3 and 10 September 1820), 22–3

This review was reprinted from the *Monthly Review* (July 1820), and it indicates one view of K circulated widely on the European continent. The reviewer takes K's poetry seriously, and is concerned that 'the poems should receive a 'fair trial' by the reading public. The passage below responds in particular to the unsettling qualities of K's poetry that had drawn Lockhart's abusive criticism in *Blackwood's* (see above) and which, much later, have received perceptive attention from John Bayley (see below). Like *Lyrical Ballads* in 1798, K's poems appear as a challenge to received ideas 'of the *manner* in which a poet ought to write'; throughout, remarks about the literary qualities of the poems carry an implicit political meaning.

This little volume must and ought to attract attention, for it displays the ore of true poetic genius, though mingled with a large portion of dross. Mr Keats is a very bold author, bold perhaps because (as we learn) he has yet but little more than touched the 'years of discretion'; and he has carried his peculiarities both of thought and manner to an extreme which, at the first view, will to many persons be very displeasing. [. . .]

Very few persons, probably, will admire Mr Keats on a short acquaintance; and the light and the frivolous never will. If we would enjoy his poetry, we must think it over; and on this very account, which is perhaps the surest proof of its merit, we are afraid that it will be slighted. Unfortunately, Mr Keats may blame himself for much of this neglect; since he might have conceded something to established taste, or (if he will) established prejudice, without derogating from his own originality of thought and spirit. On the contrary, he seems to have written directly in despite of our preconceived notions of the *manner* in which a poet ought to write; and he is continually shocking our ideas of poetical decorum, at the very time when we are acknowledging the hand of genius. In thus boldly running counter to old opinions, however, we cannot conceive that Mr Keats merits either contempt or ridicule; the weapons which are too frequently employed when liberal discussion and argument would be unsuccessful. At all events, let him not be pre-judged without a candid examination of his claims. A former work by this very young poet (*Endymion*) which escaped our notice, cannot certainly be said to have had a fair trial before the public; and now that an opportunity is afforded for correcting that injustice, we trust that the candour of all readers will take advantage of it.

William Hazlitt, 'On Effeminacy of Character' from *Table Talk* (1821–2), rpt Howe, VIII. 254–5

Hazlitt presents K as a representative example of 'effeminacy of style', offering a gendered response to the ambiguous qualities of K's poetic style, which had attracted hostile political comments elsewhere (see Lockhart above). Figuring K in the same gendered terms Burke had used to define 'beauty' (see the Introduction to this volume), Hazlitt anticipates nineteenth-century responses to K and his poetry which emphasise his 'exquisite fancy' as opposed to the 'action' and 'manhood of poetry' that might bear upon the actuality of the world. Hazlitt's comments should be compared with the extracts from Karen Swann and Anne Mellor below.

I cannot help thinking that the fault of Mr Keats's poems was a deficiency in masculine energy of style. He had beauty, tenderness, delicacy, in an uncommon degree, but there was a want of strength and substance. His Endymion is a very delightful description of the illusions of a youthful imagination, given up to airy dreams – we have flowers, clouds, rainbows, moonlight, all sweet sounds and smells, and Oreads and Dryads flitting by – but there is nothing tangible in it, nothing marked or palpable – we have none of the hardy spirit or rigid forms of antiquity. He painted his own thoughts and character; and did not transport himself into the fabulous and heroic ages. There is a want of action, of character, and so far, of imagination, but there is exquisite fancy. All is soft and fleshy, without bone or muscle. We see in him the youth, without the manhood of poetry. His genius breathed 'vernal delight and joy.' – 'Like Maia's son he stood and shook his plumes,' with fragrance filled. His mind was redolent of spring. He had not the fierceness of summer, nor the richness of autumn, and winter he seemed not to have known, till he felt the icy hand of death!

Elizabeth Barrett: three comments on Keats

Elizabeth Barrett's comments show how responses to K's poetry were prejudiced by the myth of the poet – 'Poor poor Keats' – which developed swiftly after his death. Her letter of 27 October 1841 repeats the story that K had been assassinated by reviewers, given currency twenty years earlier by Shelley's preface to *Adonais* (see Introduction to this volume).

Elizabeth Barrett, from her diary 18–19 August 1831, *The Barretts at Hope End. The Early Diary of Elizabeth Barrett Browning*, ed. Elizabeth Berridge (1974) 141–2

Thursday August 18
I finished Keats's Lamia, Isabella, Eve of St Agnes & Hyperion, before breakfast. The three first disappointed me. The extracts I had seen of them, were undeniably the finest things in them. But there is some surprising poetry – poetry of wonderful grandeur, in the Hyperion. The effect of the appearance of Hyperion, among the ruined Titans, is surpassingly fine. Poor poor Keats. His name shall be in my 'Poets Record.' Like his own Saturn, he was dethroned from the seat which his genius claimed: and in the radiance of his own Hyperion, will he appear to posterity – in

> 'splendour, like the morn,
> Pervading all the beetling gloomy steeps
> All the sad spaces of oblivion.'

Friday August 19
I finished the Endymion today. I do not admire it as a fine poem; but I do admire many passages of it, as being very fine poetry. As a whole, it is cumbrous & unwieldy. You dont know where to put it.

Your imagination is confused by it: & your feelings uninterested.
And yet a poet wrote it.

Elizabeth Barrett from letter of 27 October 1841, *Elizabeth
Barrett to Miss Mitford*, ed. Betty Miller (1954), 93

Keats — yes — Keats — *he was* a poet. That Jove is recognised by his
thunder. A true poet, from his first words to his last, when he said he
'felt the daisies growing over him'. Poor Keats! Do you know, did I
ever tell you, that Mr Horne was at school with him and that they
were intimate friends? 'The divine Keats' — he says of him — and will
not hear the common tale, which I for one thought deteriorative to
the dead poet's memory, that he suffered himself to be slain outright
and ingloriously by the Quarterly reviewer's tomahawk. No, said
Mr Horne to me once — 'He was already bending over his grave in
sweet and solemn contemplation, when the satyres *hoofed* him into
it'.

Leigh Hunt on *The Eve of St Agnes*, stanza 3, from *Imagination
and Fancy* (1844), rpt *KCH*, 276–7

Hunt had been influential by introducing K's poetry to the public
in his 'Young Poets' essay of 1816 (see the first extract above). In
this extract from his later essay on K, he offers a perceptive
psychological analysis of the phrase 'Flatter'd to tears' (21) in the
third stanza of *The Eve of St Agnes*. The passage is representative
of Hunt's literary criticism at its best.

A true poet is by nature a metaphysician; far greater in general than
metaphysicians professed. He feels instinctively what the others get
at by long searching. In this word 'flattered' is the whole theory of
the secret of tears; which are the tributes, more or less worthy, of
self-pity to self-love. Whenever we shed tears, we take pity on
ourselves; and we feel, if we do not consciously say so, that we
deserve to have the pity taken. In many cases, the pity is just, and the
self-love not to be construed unhandsomely. In many others, it is the
reverse; and this is the reason why selfish people are so often found
among the tear-shedders, and why they seem even to shed them for
others. They imagine themselves in the situation of the others, as
indeed the most generous must, before they can sympathize; but the
generous console as well as weep. Selfish tears are avaricious of
everything but themselves.

'Flatter'd to tears.' Yes, the poor old man was moved, by the sweet
music, to think that so sweet a thing was intended for his comfort as

well as for others. He felt that the mysterious kindness of heaven did not omit even his poor, old, sorry case, in its numerous workings and visitations; and, as he wished to live longer, he began to think that his wish was to be attended to. He began to consider how much he had suffered – how much he had suffered wrongly or mysteriously – and how much better a man he was, with all his sins, than fate seemed to have taken him for. Hence, he found himself deserving of tears and self-pity, and he shed them, and felt soothed by his poor, old, loving self. Not undeservedly either; for he was a pains-taking pilgrim, aged, patient, and humble, and willingly suffered cold and toil, for the sake of something better than he could otherwise deserve; and so the pity is not exclusively on his own side: we pity him too, and would fain see him well out of that cold chapel, gathered into a warmer place than a grave. But it was not to be. We must, therefore, console ourselves with knowing, that this icy endurance of his was the last, and that he soon found himself at the sunny gate of heaven.

Matthew Arnold, from a letter to Arthur Hugh Clough (after September 1848). *The Letters of Matthew Arnold to Arthur Hugh Clough*, ed. H. F. Lowry (1932), 97

Matthew Arnold's criticism sought to identify poetry of 'high seriousness', which might allow a society dominated by commercial imperatives to realise its moral and spiritual being. Arnold's conviction that poetry should have a moral purpose ('an Idea of the world') led him to recoil in horror from K's writing, with its attachment to sense, passion, and a relish for the 'multitudinousness' of the world.

What harm he has done in English Poetry. As Browning is a man with a moderate gift passionately desiring movement and fulness, and obtaining but a confused multitudinousness, so Keats with a very high gift, is yet also consumed by this desire: and cannot produce the truly living and moving, as his conscience keeps telling him. They will not be patient neither understand that they must begin with an Idea of the world in order not to be prevailed over by the world's multitudinousness: or if they cannot get that, at least with isolated ideas: and all other things shall (perhaps) be added unto them.

– I recommend you to follow up these letters with the Laocoön of Lessing: it is not quite satisfactory, and a little mare's nesty – but very searching.

– I have had that desire of fulness without respect of the means,

which may become almost maniacal: but nature had placed a bar
thereto not only in the conscience (as with all men) but in a great
numbness in that direction. But what perplexity Keats Tennyson et
id genus omne must occasion to young writers of the ὁπλίτης[1] sort:
yes and those d—d Elizabethan poets generally. Those who cannot
read G[ree]k sh[ou]ld read nothing but Milton and parts of
Wordsworth: the state should see to it: for the failures of the
σταθμοί[2] may leave them good citizens enough, as Trench: but the
others go to the dogs failing or succeeding.

1 'heavy-armed foot soldier'.
2 'march of the day'; in plural here it means 'stages along the royal road'.

Walter Bagehot on *Ode on a Grecian Urn* from 'Percy Bysshe
Shelley', *The National Review* (October 1856), rpt *Collected
Works of Walter Bagehot*, ed. Norman St John-Stevas (15 vols,
1965–86), I. 469–70

Bagehot's emphasis on 'chasteness' shows that he shared Arnold's
concern for the morality of poetry (see previous extract).
Although he recognised that K's poems infuse the 'cold' forms of
classical beauty with a 'shadowy warmth', a 'soft tint', he was
unwilling to grant those poems any higher purpose of 'abstract
labour . . . haunting speculations . . . attenuated thoughts'. Like
Shelley, he achieves a pure lyricism unmatched by Tennyson's
brooding, meditative verse. K's achievement was to write poems
of unreflective fancy; he celebrates the 'obvious beauty of the
world' in verse of 'simple rich melody'.

One of the most essentially modern of recent poets has an 'Ode on a
Grecian Urn': it begins —

> Thou still unravish'd bride of quietness,
>   Thou foster-child of silence and slow time,
> Silvan historian, who canst thus express
>   A flowery tale more sweetly than our rhyme:
> What leaf-fring'd legend haunts about thy shape
>   Of deities or mortals, or of both,
>   In Tempe or the dales of Arcady?
>   What men or gods are these? What maidens loth?
> What mad pursuit? What struggle to escape?
>   What pipes and timbrels? What wild ecstasy?

No ancient poet would have dreamed of writing thus. There would
have been no indistinct shadowy warmth, no breath of surrounding

beauty: his delineation would have been cold, distinct, chiselled like the urn itself. The use which such a poet as Keats makes of ancient mythology is exactly similar. He owes his fame to the inexplicable art with which he has breathed a soft tint over the marble forms of gods and goddesses, enhancing their beauty without impairing their chasteness.

Walter Bagehot, from 'Tennyson's Idylls', *The National Review* (October 1859), rpt *Collected Works*, II. 200–1

Mr Tennyson is deficient in the most marked peculiarity which Shelley and Keats have in common. Both of these poets are singularly gifted with a sustained faculty of lyrical expression. They seem hurried into song; and, what is more, kept there when they have been hurried there. Shelley's *Skylark* is the most familiar example of this. A rather young musician was once asked, what was Jenny Lind's charm in singing. 'Oh,' he replied, 'she went up so high, and staid up high so long.' There is something of this sustainment at a great height in all Shelley's lyrics. His strains are profuse. He is ever soaring; and whilst soaring, ever singing. Keats, it is true, did not ascend to so extreme an elevation. He did not belong to the upper air. He had no abstract labour, no haunting speculations, no attenuated thoughts. He was the poet of the obvious beauty of the world. His genius was of the earth – of the autumn earth – rich and mellow; and it was lavish. He did not carry his art high or deep; he neither enlightens our eyes much, nor expands our ears much; but pleases our fancies with a prolonged strain of simple rich melody. He does not pause, or stay, or hesitate. His genius is continuous; the flow of it is as obvious at the best moments as the excellence, and at inferior moments is more so. Mr Tennyson, on the other hand, has no tendencies of this kind. He broods, as we have said. There are undoubtedly several beautiful songs in his writings, – several in which the sentiment cleaves to the words, and cannot even in our memories be divorced from them. But their beauty is not continuous. A few lines fasten upon us with an imperious and evermastering charm; but the whole composition, as a whole, has not much value. The run of it, as far as it has a run, expresses nothing. The genius of Mr Tennyson is delineative; it muses and meditates; it describes moods, feelings, and objects of imagination; but it does not rush on to pour out passion, or express overwhelming emotion.

William Michael Rossetti, from his *Life of Keats* (1887), 207–9

This late Victorian estimate of K appears at the end of Rossetti's one-volume biography. It shows how the earlier accounts of K's 'youthfulness', 'effeminacy' and 'unworldliness' now defined a poetical character lacking in 'mental balance', 'substance' and 'control'. Hunt had introduced K as a 'young poet' (see first extract above); his premature death, and the critical consensus of the nineteenth century, had enforced the idea that K was 'doomed' to be the poet of youth, 'expectation', and 'delight'.

One of the most compendious and elegant phrases in which the genius of Keats has been defined is that of Leigh Hunt: 'He never beheld an oak tree without seeing the Dryad.' In immediate meaning Hunt glances here at the mythical sympathy or personifying imagination of the poet; but, if we accept the phrase as applying to the sensuous object-painting, along with its ideal aroma or sugges-tion in his finest work, we shall still find it full of right significance. [. . .] It seems to me true that not many of Keats's poems are highly admirable; that most of them, amid all their beauty, have an adolescent and frequently a morbid tone, marking want of manful thew and sinew and of mental balance; that he is not seldom obscure, chiefly through indifference to the thought itself and its necessary means of development; that he is emotional without substance, and beautiful without control; and that personalism of a wilful and fitful kind pervades the mass of his handiwork. We have already seen, however, that there is a certain not inconsiderable proportion of his poems to which these exceptions do not apply, or apply only with greatly diminished force; and, as a last expression of our large and abiding debt to him and to his well-loved memory, we recur to his own words, and say that he has given us many a 'thing of beauty,' which will remain 'a joy for ever.' By his early death he was doomed to be the poet of youthfulness; by being the poet of youthfulness he was privileged to become and to remain enduringly the poet of rapt expectation and passionate delight.

Algernon Charles Swinburne, 'John Keats', from *The Encyclo-paedia Britannica* (9th edn, 1875–89)

Swinburne did not admire K's earlier poetry or *Endymion*, but, in seeking to identify the 'credentials' of fame in K, he offers this rhapsody on his 'unequalled and unrivalled odes'. In this extract, Swinburne also affirms the poet's 'manhood' against those who perpetuated the 'degrading' myth that he had succumbed to hostile reviewers. Shelley's idea of his 'delicate and fragile genius' in the preface to *Adonais* is dismissed here by Swinburne as 'the false Keats'.

No little injustice has been done to Keats by such devotees as fix their mind's eye only on the more salient and distinctive notes of a genius which in fact was very much more various and tentative, less limited and peculiar, than would be inferred from an exclusive study of his more specially characteristic work. But within the limits of that work must we look of course for the genuine credentials of his fame; and highest among them we must rate his unequalled and unrivalled odes. Of these perhaps the two nearest to absolute perfection, to the triumphant achievement and accomplishment of the very utmost beauty possible to human words, may be that to Autumn and that on a Grecian Urn; the most radiant, fervent, and musical is that to a Nightingale; the most pictorial and perhaps the tenderest in its ardour of passionate fancy is that to Psyche; the subtlest in sweetness of thought and feeling is that on Melancholy. Greater lyrical poetry the world may have seen than any that is in these; lovelier it surely has never seen, nor ever can it possibly see. From the divine fragment of an unfinished ode to Maia we can but guess that if completed it would have been worthy of a place beside the highest. His remaining lyrics have many beauties about them, but none perhaps can be called thoroughly beautiful. He has certainly left us one perfect sonnet of the first rank; and as certainly he has left us but one.

Keats, on high and recent authority, has been promoted to a place beside Shakespeare; and it was long since remarked by some earlier critic of less note that as a painter of flowers his touch had almost a Shakespearean felicity, – recalling, a writer in our own day might have added, the hand of M. Fantin on canvass. The faultless force and the profound subtlety on this deep and cunning instinct for the absolute expression of absolute natural beauty can hardly be questioned or overlooked; and this is doubtless the one main distinctive gift or power which denotes him as a poet among all his equals, and gives him right to a rank for ever beside Coleridge and Shelley. As a man, the two admirers who have done best service to his memory are, first and far foremost, Lord Houghton, and secondly Mr Matthew Arnold. These alone, among all who have written of him without the disadvantage or advantage of a personal acquaintance, have clearly seen and shown us the manhood of the man. That ridiculous and degrading legend which imposed so strangely on the generous tenderness of Shelley, while evoking the very natural and allowable laughter of Byron, fell to dust at once for ever on the appearance of that admirable and unsurpassed biography which gave perfect proof to all time that 'men have died and worms have eaten them,' but not for fear of critics or through suffering inflicted by reviews. Somewhat too sensually sensitive he may have been in either capacity, but the nature of the man was as far as was the quality of the poet above the pitiful level of a creature whose soul could 'let itself be snuffed out by an article'; and in fact, owing doubtless to the accident of a death which followed so fast on his early appearance and his dubious reception as a poet, the insolence and injustice of his reviewers in general have been comparatively and even considerably exaggerated. Except from the chief fountainhead of professional ribaldry then open in the world of literary journalism, no reek of personal insult arose to offend his nostrils; and then as now the tactics of such unwashed malignants were inevitably suicidal; the references to his brief experiment of apprenticeship to a surgeon which are quoted from *Blackwood* in the shorter as well as in the longer memoir by Lord Houghton could leave no bad odour behind them save what might hang about men's yet briefer recollection of his assailant's unmemorable existence. The false Keats, therefore, whom Shelley pitied and Byron despised would have been, had he ever existed, a thing beneath compassion or contempt. That such a man could have had such a genius is almost evidently impossible; and yet more evident is the proof which remains on everlasting record that none was ever further from the chance of decline to such degradation than the real and actual man who made that name immortal.

H. W. Garrod, from *Keats* (1926), 68–73

This passage from Garrod's short monograph argues that K was a poet who had shared the 'revolutionary idea' of the age in which he lived. In *Hyperion* and *The Fall of Hyperion* (or *Hyperion: A Vision*) Garrod identifies the displacement of the Titans by the Olympians with revolutionary progress, but points out that the 'revolutionary idea' was not limited to politics. Hyperion lingers on as the poetic voice of a superseded culture; Apollo 'dies into life' as god of poetry, the sublime representative of '*the poet upon earth*' who articulates 'the beauty of the world through its sorrows'. Garrod finds a similar opposition between visionary and humanitarian poetry throughout K's work, and contends that the fragmentary status of the *Hyperion* poems shows that K was unable to resolve what 'order of life' a truly humane poetry might require.

I have spoken already of Keats' early revolutionary sympathies, of his Huntian or Wordsworthian politics. I said that these sympathies went deeper, and lasted longer, than is usually recognized. Keats, I said, is more the child of the Revolutionary Idea than we commonly suppose. That is true, even in politics. But the Revolutionary Idea is neither wholly, nor primarily, political. Of the multifarious manifestations of this idea Keats undertook to write, what no other of the romantics essayed, the epic. So at least I conceive *Hyperion* — as, under allegoric forms, the epic of the Revolutionary Idea. In history, as in mythology, the Revolutionary Idea begins when children refuse any longer to be eaten by their parents. There is that in nature which will not be eaten by custom; and there is that in poetry which will not be eaten by prose; and whether what happens be figured as Jove deposing Saturn, or the French Revolution dethroning the Ancien Regime, Apollo ousting Hyperion, or Wordsworth dispossessing Pope, or, again, beauty dispossessing order, imagination replacing reason, matters hardly at all; in each event the same causes operate. Somewhat thus, I take it, Keats conceived his epic of the Revolutionary Idea. Exactly how he had it in mind to distribute the emphasis, ingenuity may be harmlessly exercised in guessing; but if Keats himself stopped because he did not know how to go on, it would be nothing out of nature, and perhaps, indeed, out of nature if it were otherwise. It is notable that, in the story as he tells it, Apollo is the last of the gods to establish his power. The poem waits upon his advent; and upon his advent, and activity, depends, we feel, the unravelling of the dramatic complex. Neither can the New Order work without him, nor the reconciliation he brought about of new and old. Jove, we may suppose, figures the civil power, the institutions of political life. These are workable only so far as the context of them can be poetized; and so far as they are new, they require a new poetry. Hyperion is the last of the Titans to fall before the new order; of the old order, that is, there lives longest, and last leaves the heart, its poetry. It is in the nature of things that periodic storms of time should shatter material institutions, the laboriously built fabric of tradition and habit. But over the wreck there still lingers for awhile some ghost of beauty and poetry; the 'still undisgraced radiance' of Hyperion. But Hyperion cannot stay; or he stays only to view

> The misery his radiance has betrayed
> To the most hateful seeing of itself.

Saturn may boast that

> there shall be
> Beautiful things made new for the surprise
> Of the sky-children;

but he knows in his heart that this creation can be the work only of some new power of beauty, some new poetry, some Apollo. Hyperion has outlived his world. The hope which the elder gods repose in him is, say they what they may, half-hearted; and in fact the order which they represent has fallen from their want of faith in him, or from a mutual breach of sympathy.

Apollo, the usurping god of light, the new poetry, comes to deity in a fashion sufficiently significant. Keats carries the poem no farther than the beginnings of his god-head. But sufficiently far that we know that this godhead is not without its birth-pangs:

> Soon wild commotion shook him, and made flush
> All the immortal fairness of his limbs,
> Most like the struggle at the gates of death;

and he speaks of him plainly as 'dying into life'.

Of this birth-anguish of Apollo, with which *Hyperion* ends, we must fetch the interpretation, I should suppose, from *Hyperion: A Vision*. Alike of the god of poetry *and of the poet upon earth* this is true, that their living must be by dying. It is not by accident, I mean, that, on the one hand, *Hyperion* ends thus with the death-shriek of Apollo, with this anguish of the god dying into life, and that, on the other hand, all the emphasis of the later version is thrown on the necessity for the poet of seeing the beauty of the world through its sorrows, through human suffering:

> None can usurp this height, returned that Shade,
> But those to whom the miseries of the world
> Are misery, and will not let them rest.

In other words, I take the revolutionary Apollo to contrast, in Keats' imagination, with the god whom he dispossesses, as humanitarian with visionary. Again and again does Keats, as we have seen, carry us to this opposition of two kinds of poetry – and shrink back from his own conclusions. I will not say that *Hyperion* remains, and was bound to remain, the fragment that it is, merely because Keats cannot bring himself to point the moral which he has so far drawn. That fear of himself, that uneasiness, operates. But it is part of a wider perplexity. I should prefer to conceive that Keats, pursuing his epic of the Revolutionary Idea, trailing, as he went, clouds of indeterminate allegory, was held by that death-shriek, or birth-shriek, of his own Apollo; that he was startled into misgiving; that some disquiet of the creating imagination assailed him; that he felt himself brought up sharply against the need of defining, the need of clarifying his own conception. What truly was this god, who thus dies into life? and into what order of life does this dying in fact conduct him?

Hyperion, the *Hyperion* of the volume of 1820, leaves the question without answer; indeed, that it puts the question we should scarcely know except for *Hyperion: A Vision*. It is even possible that in the version printed in 1820 Keats was trying to save his work out of allegory. It could not be done, and he gave up, recurring in the last months of 1819 to allegory unshamed. The recoil of intention leaves the greater of the two poems a fragment of statuesque beauty. Some mist and soil allegory does throw about it. That this is not so much as to impair vitally its beauty of outline and largeness of conception – that is just God's mercy, never wanting to poets.

Cleanth Brooks, *The Well Wrought Urn* (UK edn, 1949), 31

This extract is drawn from one of the greatest volumes of American 'new criticism'. Brooks' close reading discovers in the repetition of 'forlorn' in the seventh and eighth stanzas of *Ode to a Nightingale* the new critical touchstones of value in poetry: irony and paradox. His account is valuable for the sense it gives of the poem in process, the psychic experience (for poet and for reader) of being 'wrenched out of reverie'.

Consider the transition from the seventh to the eighth stanzas of 'The Ode to a Nightingale':

> The same that oft-times hath
> Charmed magic casements, opening on the foam
> Of perilous seas, in faery lands forlorn.

> Forlorn! the very word is like a bell
> To toll me back from thee to my sole self –

In the first instance, 'forlorn' is being used primarily in its archaic sense of 'utterly lost.' The faery lands are those of a past which is remote and far away. But the meaning of 'forlorn' is definitely shifted as the poet repeats the word. In its meaning, 'pitiable; left desolate', 'forlorn' describes the poet's own state, and applies, as he suddenly realizes in the poem, to his own case. The very adjective which is used to describe the world of the imagination which the bird symbolizes, ironically enough can be used to describe his own situation. The psychological effect is that of a man in a reverie suddenly stumbling, and being wrenched out of the reverie. The real world makes its demands; no matter how beautiful the realm of the imagination, one cannot free himself from actuality and live in the imagination permanently. Indeed, the general theme of the poem may be described as that of the following paradox: the world of the imagination offers a release from the painful world of actuality, yet at the same time it renders the world of actuality more painful by contrast. Keats's repetition of 'forlorn' is thus a concentrated instance of the theme of the whole poem. Recognition of the irony makes the poem not less, but more, serious.

Christopher Ricks, *Keats and Embarrassment* (1974), 97–9

Ricks defends the 'erotic fervour' of *Isabella* by emphasising the physical integrity of the poem's language, finding K's imaginative richness allied with the potential for embarrassment. His close reading and attention to 'all the meaning' are acutely perceptive, celebrating an exultant 'nobleness of life' in poetry that earlier critics had found 'tasteless'.

It is therefore not an objection to Keats's erotic writing that it can cause a twinge of distaste, since the accommodation of distaste can be a humanly and artistically valuable thing, especially when it coexists with a frank delight. *The British Critic* deplored 'the following exquisite nonsense to describe a kiss' (the fifth and sixth lines of the stanza):

> 'Love! thou art leading me from wintry cold,
>   Lady! thou leadest me to summer clime,
> And I must taste the blossoms that unfold
>   In its ripe warmth this gracious morning time.'
> So said, his erewhile timid lips grew bold,
>   And poesied with hers in dewy rhyme:
> Great bliss was with them, and great happiness
> Grew, like a lusty flower in June's caress.
>
> ('Isabella', IX)

M. R. Ridley outdid *The British Critic*: ' "And poesied with hers in dewy rhyme", which, apart from conveying a sensation of somewhat tasteless lusciousness, seems to convey as little meaning as is possible for seven English words arranged in a grammatical clause.' But the line is tastelessly luscious only if one ignores all the meaning, and of course the meaning affects the sensation. The kiss is a rhyme because it rhymes (pairs) their lips ('And pair their rhymes as Venus yokes her doves', *Don Juan*, v. 1) and doubly so because the upper and lower lips already rhyme with each other. It is 'dewy' because the lips are wetted by saliva, a fact at once romantically expressed and attractive (as if the reader were either the kisser or the kissed), and also disconcerting (the reader is neither, and the saliva on lips is something which cannot but be faintly uneasy to contemplate unless one is not just contemplating it). The essential thing was for Keats to apply 'dewy' directly to 'lips', and not to allow any gap such as might allow the physical immediacy of the sense (saliva, after all) to slip away through a slackness; you can see the same complex of feelings, including the pair of lips and the song ('a glee'), coming to nothing elsewhere:

> a glee
> Circling from three sweet pair of Lips in Mirth;
> And haply you will say the dewy birth
> Of morning Roses—
>
> ('To the Ladies . . .', 3–6)

'Dewy', though at the opposite pole as a verbal device, works rather as the tautology does in Bob Dylan's exultant cry of memory, 'Her mouth was watery and wet'. And 'poesied'?: because a kiss is a creative act, like writing a poem; like a poem, it both recognizes what already exists and brings something new into existence; it both is bred from, and breeds love. ('Brown has been walking up and down the room a breeding – now at this moment he is being delivered of a couplet – and I dare say will be as well as can be expected – Gracious – he has twins!')

A kiss does not use words, but then 'poesied' and 'rhyme' are aware of that; it is a fine stroke of the poetical imagination which sees the simple creativity of a kiss as its honourable equal. The poet does not belittle his art, though he archaizes it with an effect of modesty ('to poesy' has a different effect from 'poesy' the noun). Poetry is a nobleness of life, and so is a kiss. The creativity fulfils itself in the last couplet:

> Great bliss was with them, and great happiness
> Grew, like a lusty flower in June's caress.

– where the tautology (like 'Her mouth was watery and wet') of bliss and happiness is an exultation, a cup running over, while at the same time indicating a difference of sense through the verbs. 'Great bliss was with them': bliss, an accompaniment, ecstatically out of the ordinary; 'and great happiness / Grew', as ordinary, continuing, and expansive. The erotic fervour is unmistakable and burgeoning, as in the choice of 'lusty', so sure to call up lust and so confident of holding it off.

John Bayley, 'The Vulgar and the Heroic in "Bad Poetry"', from The Uses of Division (1976), 120–22

Bayley admits that the opening passage of Endymion III is 'apparently terrible', and K's rhymes are 'deplorable'. Yet he argues that the unselfconsciousness of K's early poetry, and of Endymion in particular, creates a vitality and animation that has been lost in the more deliberately 'aesthetic' poetry of The Fall of Hyperion. K's development as a poet obscured his true poetic personality, which Bayley terms 'magnificently gemein', with the conscious artistry of the poet plotting 'a great line'.

Even at its most unpropitious, *Endymion* is packed with borrowed life which has become Keats.

> There are who lord it o'er their fellow-men
> With most prevailing tinsel; who unpen
> Their baaing vanities, to browse away
> The comfortable green and juicy hay
> From human pastures; or, O torturing fact!
> Who, through an idiot blink, will see unpack'd
> Fire-branded foxes to sear up and singe
> Our gold and ripe-ear'd hopes.

This is apparently terrible, but let us compare it with the opening of the second *Hyperion*.

> Fanatics have their dreams, wherewith they weave
> A paradise for a sect; the savage too
> From forth the loftiest fashion of his sleep
> Guesses at heaven: pity these have not
> Trac'd upon vellum or wild Indian leaf
> The shadow of melodious utterance.
> But bare of laurel they live, dream and die;
> For Poesy alone can tell her dreams,
> With the fine spell of words alone can save
> Imagination from the sable charm
> And dumb enchantment.

The passage seems to be treading gingerly, with a precarious confidence, secured by a careful abstention from anything that may jar. We miss the deplorable rhymes which wrench the sense so nakedly in their direction, and yet which – like Byron's – in fact give a greater vigour and forcefulness of meaning to the *Endymion* passage than the opening of *Hyperion* can show. In the latter, Keats's greater caution seems to blur and weaken sense; his voice survives only in the thoughtful, colloquial note of 'pity these have not . . .'; and the metaphors (*weave, spell, enchantment*) lie limply, and indeed decoratively, without pressing their conviction bois-terously in upon us. Without gathering itself consciously together, the animation of the *Endymion* style can leap into the discovery of

> Innumerable mountains rise, and rise,
> Ambitious for the hallowing of thine eyes.

('Rise, and rise' – the rhyme takes the mountain range in its stride; and *ambitious* is a perfect example of Keats's power to make use of a grand word without reflecting on it, as unself-consciously as he uses *baaing* or *comfortable*.) Or into a typically Keatsian argument:

> And, truly, I would rather be struck dumb
> Than speak against this ardent listlessness;
> For I have ever thought that it might bless
> The world with benefits unknowingly;
> As does the nightingale, upperched high,
> And cloistered among cool and bunched leaves –
> She sings but to her love, nor e'er conceives
> How tip-toe night holds back her dark-grey hood.
> Just so may love, although 'tis understood
> The mere commingling of passionate breath,
> Produce more than our searching witnesseth.

(The movement of that line – 'the mere commingling of passionate breath' is as subtle as anything in Pope or Tennyson, but is given without pretension or pause; and the nightingale, in its characteristically awkward setting, is far more real than Clare's more graceful bird, 'lost in a wilderness of listening leaves'.) Or it may be into a passage like this –

> Straying about, yet cooped up in the den
> Of helpless discontent, – hurling my lance
> From place to place, and following at chance,
> At last, by hap, through some young trees it struck,
> And, plashing among bedded pebbles, stuck
> In the middle of a brook.

– where being young has all the force that it might have in Byron, together with a most un-Byronic sense of the *feel* of an event, the moment in the wood when the spear clattered into the stream. (Contrast this, or 'the sodden turfed dell' of the murder in *Isabella*, with the Claude landscape of *Hyperion*.) Or Keats may launch a *sententia*:

> But this is human life? the war, the deeds,
> The disappointment, the anxiety,
> Imagination's struggles, far and nigh,
> All human, bearing in themselves this good,
> That they are still the air, the subtle food,
> To make us feel existence and to show
> How quiet death is.

The passage rises into a greatness of generality and at once presses onward; while the opening of the second *Hyperion* seems to be feeling its way, forward towards the plotted moment of a great line, followed by an appropriate rest for appreciation:

> When this warm scribe, my hand, is in the grave.

It is moving, and impressive, but it is also in a damaging sense aesthetic. We have seen it coming. Keats is no longer the Squire, writing with 'ful devout corage', but a nineteenth-century poet, nearly a Tennyson, feeling deeply and fashioning a line out of the feeling; the pause between feeling and making can be felt, and in the hush our sense of craftsmanship at work is embarrassingly strong.

Helen Vendler, *The Odes of John Keats* (1983), 291–2

Vendler argues that throughout the odes of 1819 K ponders complex questions – general and personal – which demonstrate his increasing power as a poet. In contrast to the 'structureless' *Endymion*, she finds K working much more 'consciously and sedulously' in the later poetry. Unlike Bayley, who argued in the previous extract that such a development weakened K's poetic vitality, Vendler finds in the sustained complexities of the odes evidence of K's growing ability to 'orchestrate' all aspects of his poetry ever more powerfully.

'A complex mind,' said Keats, 'is one that is imaginative and at the same time careful of its fruits'. Keats's complex mind, in the odes, is pondering complex questions. What, for the religious unbeliever, should be the 'system of salvation'? Are there objects or processes worthy of worship by the human mind? What is the modern poet's relation to classical myth and allegorical language? Is the dualistic description of man as composed of senses and spirit in conflict a true one? Does art originate in nature or is it opposed to nature? Can poetry be goaded by ambition or is it conceived in indolent reverie? Is art a process wholly conceptual or must it, to be called art, be embodied in a medium? Is abstract art to be preferred to representational art? Is there a hierarchy of arts, according to their medium, and if so, where does poetry rank in this hierarchy? Is the aesthetic act one in which we 'lose ourselves' in a better world, or one in which we actively work to represent and reproduce the entire world in which we live? Is it possible to attend to 'medium' and 'message' at one and the same time in confronting a work of art? Can aesthetic emotions be mixed as well as pure, and if so, which is the higher form? What is aesthetic temperance, and what is its relation to aesthetic and emotional intensity? Is the artist, or the artwork, a benefactor to man?

These and other general questions were preoccupying Keats as he composed the odes. At the same time he was working out in these great poems questions of a more private nature. These have to do with his feelings about women as brides, elusive objects of fancy, goddesses whose due was religious veneration, helpless beings needing rescue, patient mothers, and Muses. They also have to do with his feelings about sexuality – the irreconcilability of 'mad pursuit' and romantic love, the wish for an unravished bride, the paradoxical nature of human passion that left him both cloyed and parched, the tragic necessity that the grape of intensity be burst so that joy could be tasted, the presence of melancholy in the ultimate recesses of delight, the terror of a mistress's anger, the comparison of the mind to a womb, and the assertion of the possibility of a creative 'pregnancy' within the womb of the brain.

These religious, philosophical, aesthetic, and sexual problems were joined in Keats's mind, as he wrote the odes, by problems about expression in language. He is evidently engaged, throughout the odes, in experiments on his own linguistic and figurative resources, as he begins to work more consciously and sedulously the treasuries of language he had poured out in a fine profusion (and uneven coherence) in the relatively structureless *Endymion*. We see him in the odes pondering the relative value of various lyric structures, from the simplest to the most complex; we find him concentrating not only on one symbol at a time (a bird, an urn) but on one trope at a time, as a governing device for a poem. (He also chose a governing trope for the whole sequence, the trope of apostrophe, which is the figure for what is to be venerated.) We see him growing in power, until he learns to orchestrate the relations of theme, symbol, trope, syntax, and register of diction in ever more powerful ways.

Alan J. Bewell, 'The Political Implication of Keats's Classicist Aethetics', from KP, 227–9

Bewell finds the celebration of 'progress' in *Hyperion* complicated by K's use of Egyptian sculpture in the representation of Thea. K seems to empathise with the 'sorrow' of Egyptian sculpture, which carries within it the premonition of its own eclipse and loss of meaning as later cultures (such as classical Greece) gain ascendency. In this view history is not a progress towards increasing enlightenment, but a continuous displacement and supersession of one age by another. Bewell's essay makes very effective use of the materialist and political approaches associated with 'new historicism' in the 1980s.

If *Hyperion* is a poem that celebrates progress, the description of the face of Thea, like 'that of a Memphian sphinx, / Pedestal'd haply in a palace court, / When sages look'd to Egypt for their lore' (I. 31–3) is even more problematic. Rather than valorizing the beauty that succeeds sublimity, Keats values the 'sorrow' of Egyptian sculpture, a sorrow that derives from its ability to incorporate within itself a premonition of its eclipse and loss of meaning:

> How beautiful, if sorrow had not made
> Sorrow more beautiful than Beauty's self.
> There was a listening fear in her regard,
> As if calamity had but begun;
> As if the vanward clouds of evil days
> Had spent their malice, and the sullen rear
> Was with its stored thunder labouring up.
>
> (1. 35–41)

Thea's prophetic sorrow looks beyond 'the vanward clouds of evil days' to a time when Egypt will be invaded and destroyed by the artillery of advancing troops, 'a sullen rear ... with its stored thunder labouring up.'

Rather than depicting history as a progress towards increasing light and knowledge, a new sun rising in the west, Keats depicts it as a continuous process of displacement, of one sun supplanting and darkening another. Though a sign *as sign* can achieve a certain kind of permanence, its meaning is less resistant to change and loss. The Titans, as signs standing on the threshold of nonmeaning, are caught in a 'deathwards [progress] to no death.' This process, in which the gods of an earlier time progressively lose their meaning to become unspeaking signs, is epitomized by the fall of Hyperion, the sun-god of the Orient. Initially, Keats, aware that hieroglyphs were often carved onto the interior walls of Egyptian monuments, describes how Hyperion's 'winged minions,' that had stood 'within each aisle and deep recess' of his palace 'in close clusters' (1. 196–7) slowly pass from 'dreams,' 'monstrous forms,' 'effigies,' 'spectres,' and 'Phantoms' (1. 227–30), into hieroglyphs decorating the remnants of a palatial ruin:

> Hieroglyphics old
> Which sages and keen-eyed astrologers
> Then living on the earth, with labouring thought
> Won from the gaze of many centuries:
> Now lost, save what we find on remnants huge
> Of stone, or marble swart; their import gone,
> Their wisdom long since fled. –
>
> (1. 277–83)

Since the Rosetta Stone, though discovered by Napoleon's Expedition in 1799, was not deciphered until approximately two years after the composition of *Hyperion*, Keats's reference to hieroglyphs is to a dead language, whose meaning has been totally lost in time. Immediately thereafter, in a passage modelled upon Milton's description of Satan's incarnation in the serpent, Hyperion feels an agony gradually creep 'from the feet unto the crown / Like a lithe serpent vast and muscular / Making slow way' (1. 260–2) and, for the first time, we see him as statuary – as Laocoön. In our final view of him, he has become the Statue of Memnon, a sculpture that sings in the light of another sun:

> a vast shade,
> In midst of his own brightness, like the bulk
> Of Memnon's image at the set of sun
> To one who travels from the dusking East:
> Sighs, too, as mournful as that Memnon's harp
> He utter'd, while his hands contemplative
> He press'd together, and in silence stood.
>
> (II. 372–8)

Twilight and dawn converge upon Hyperion, stationed on a granite peak, ushering in the day of his supersession, singing in a voice that will be stifled or silenced by history.

Marjorie Levinson, *Keats's Life of Allegory. The Origins of a Style* (1988)

Levinson's criticism analyses K's poetry in terms of the social and sexual meanings of poetic style. She finds in K's 'blushing' poetry of 'adolescence and its special self-consciousness' the signature of the insecurities of 'the marginal, insecure, or immature bourgeoisie' of K's time. Levinson's K is a 'low' and unaccomplished bourgeois poet, whose 'awkward' poetry betrays an aspiration to the 'self-possession' of legitimate class-status.

Ricks's Keats is a poet who abolishes his own and his readers' self-consciousness by a poetics of conscious discomfiture. Through its aurally and visually embarrassing representations, Keats's poetry induces in its readers a painful, but, since this is art, a contained self-consciousness. By *entertaining* what is, in its natural form, a consuming state of mind, the reader learns to surpass rather than suppress his embarrassment. This is what Ricks means by his accolade, taken from Keats: 'unmisgiving'. Keats constructs a canon so psychically capacious that it accommodates even self-consciousness, which it thereby deconstructs. To use the idiom of the theory from which Ricks's argument implicitly derives, the acting-out is also a working-through for both the poet and his reader.

By setting Ricks's psychological construct in social space, we find within his own argument the shadow of an answer to the question we have raised. Why did Keats's early readers find the poetry so precisely *mis*giving: solipsistic, fraudulent, falsifying, and perverse?

Ricks studies Keats as a 'blushing' poet: a poet of adolescence and its special self-consciousness. We are reminded that blushing and genital engorgement, as by masturbation, are only nominally distinct processes. By reference to the social meanings we've teased from the early response to Keats's style, we associate one sort of self-consciousness (adolescent, sexual) with another: middle-class, social. Or, just as self-consciousness is the salient symptom of adolescence (signified by the blush and at once a cause and effect of masturbation), so does it signify the complex identity problems of a middle class in a middling stage, securing itself *and* its anxiety by its fetishistic possessive style. I'm suggesting that we draw an analogy between the marginal, insecure, or immature bourgeoisie of Keats's day and the modern state of adolescence. Both those middle classes are defined by memory (the longing for a childhood, working-class, 'gemein', or 'primitive' unself-consciousness: for example, Wordsworthian authenticity), and desire (a state beyond self-consciousness: Byron's adult, aristocratic coolness). Both, moreover, are *constituted* by that contradiction. In the accomplished bourgeois poet, this self-division translates into a 'high', philosophic self-consciousness, which is, we have seen, a good solution to two such identity problems (legitimacy / originality, pleasure / work). In Byron, the self-consciousness is also 'high', not in an intellectual sense but in a social register, where it signifies the political mastery that comes of self-possession. By the analogy, the 'low' self-consciousness of Keats's poetry – something like the awkwardness we feel in social situations – cannot be read as only the luckless effect of his ambitiousness, or as a reflection of ideal psychic processes. We must also construe this effect, the rhetorical form of a contradiction, as part of a project in its own right. Thus did Keats go about the business of making himself into that nonsense thing, the middle class.

Keats's poetry blushes more radically and purposively than Ricks suggests. It blushes at the level of style. This is a discourse which 'feeds upon' but does not assimilate its sources. It *engorges* – a transitive operation – in such a way as to make itself permanently, gesturally, *intransitively* engorged: 'stationed', in Keats's phrase. Keats's discursive procedures rehearse that protocol whereby the middle class of his day produced itself as a kind of collective, throbbing oxymoron: achieved by its ambitiousness, hardworking in its hedonism, a 'being' that defined itself strictly by its properties, or ways of having. In the style of Keats's poetry, we read the dream of masturbation: the fantasy of 'the perpetual cockstand', that solution to castration anxiety. In both the dream and the anxiety, we, like Byron, discern the genetic code of the middle class.

Karen Swann, 'Harassing the Muse', from *Romanticism and Feminism*, ed. Anne K. Mellor (1988), 88–9

In this extract Swann's feminist reading of *La belle dame sans merci* identifies a complicity between naive and knowing readers of romantic idealisation. Both attempt to contain and silence the feminine by disregarding the woman's perspective – a romantic scene that amounts to harassment. Here K's gender role as poet of romance is masculine, in contrast to his feminised presence in extracts by Hazlitt (above) and Mellor (below).

Like Robert Graves we know from books that it's a mistake for knights to allow themselves to be diverted from knightly tasks, particularly for the sake of ladies they find wandering in the woods –or, shifting to the terms of a popular romantic account of the poet's career, we know it's a mistake when aspirants to poetic fame dally too long with the poetry of wish-fulfilling fantasy and sensuous delight. The 'pale kings and princes' whose warning interrupts the knight's romantic interlude are figures of us. Crying 'La belle dame sans merci / Hath thee in thrall,' they simply declare what we already know to be true – that the knight has become caught up in a form whose pleasures, though great, are fatally circumscribed.

The naive reader of the lady, the knight, is caught up in idealizing fantasy; the knowing reader knows that such captivation is fatal – every ideal woman is also a deathly woman. Both of these readings attempt to contain the lady's significance with the assistance of a familiar romance plot; both limit certain ideal and/or fatal effects to the spliced term woman/poetry. Taken together, of course, these two readers present us with a woman we have already encountered, the woman of chivalry – both complement and absolute other, both she who delusively promises to overcome, and she who takes the blame for, the absence of relations. It remains for the feminist critic, less enchanted with romance, to defend the lady. One should try not to do this in a chivalrous fashion – it may not be in the lady's or the critic's best interests to assume she exists unproblematically, in a form one wants to champion. Yet a feminist critic listening to the knight's tale picks up threads of another story: the hint of physical compulsion ('I made a garland'), the suggestion of interpretive violence ('And sure in language strange she said – / I love thee true'); this critic might wonder if certain signs – moans, sighs, tears – don't indicate resistance more than love or duplicity. She might conclude that 'romance' is at least as fatal to the lady as the knight. Not only does its logic work toward her disappearance from the scene, romance blinds most readers to the woman's point of view – a point of view from which the exchange between lady and knight looks less like a domestic idyll or a fatal encounter and more like a scene of harassment.

Daniel P. Watkins, *Keats's Poetry and the Politics of the Imagination* (1989), 26–31

This account of political history in K's sonnet *On first looking into Chapman's Homer* is notable for the emphasis it places on the formative role of K's school reading in his imaginative life as a poet. Watkins associates K's poetic development with his serious wish 'to find a poetic voice to express his understanding of historical processes'. Like the extract from Bewell above, Watkins's criticism is a good example of the methods and concerns of current new historicist criticism of K.

In discussing *On first looking into Chapman's Homer*, critics often note that while Keats achieves an admirable consistency in tone and metaphor he gets his history wrong when he describes Cortez, rather than Balboa, staring 'at the Pacific . . . Silent, upon a peak in Darien' (12–14). This perhaps would be a minor matter, except that it contributes to the common misperception that Keats was not a serious student of history, encouraging us to disregard or to de-emphasize the way issues of historical importance shape and define his poetry, and thus eliding the historical anxiety permeating his work. The fact is, of course, that he was from his earliest school days an avid reader of history books, and the greater portion of his verse shows quite clearly the impact that these works had on his thinking and imagination. This is nowhere more evident than in his sonnet on Chapman's Homer, which is a concerted effort to bring poetry and history together into a single enterprise. [. . .]

One work that Keats read at the Clarke residence at the same time he was reading Chapman's Homer, and that probably is the most important historical source for the sonnet, is William D. Robertson's *History of America*, a highly readable, even exciting, three-volume account of adventures and discoveries in the New World. [. . .] If one reads the lengthy accounts in Robertson of Balboa and Cortez, however, the problem of historical reference becomes more complicated than it at first seems: the descriptions of the two explorers are virtually identical [. . .] Both men, for instance, recognized the importance of the Isthmus of Darien, looking to it as a field of potential discovery, although it was Balboa of course whose expedition proved more successful in this area. Both men struggled successfully against virtually insurmountable obstacles. Most importantly, both men, at the moment of discovery, are described as surveying a gulf that is part of the Pacific (Balboa surveyed the Gulf of St Michael; Cortez surveyed the Gulf of California). Given the closeness of these descriptions, it is easy to see that Keats, relying on memory, could have confused them, or that he may have combined them imaginatively, compressing them into a single, powerful image of one individual's awareness of a particular and tremendously significant moment in history, once again presenting his view of the primary importance of historical struggle and accomplishment.

When Keats sat down to write his sonnet after a night of reading Chapman's Homer, it is likely that his first aim was not simply to capture the excitement of discovery, but to suggest the excitement of historical inquiry and of the way imaginative literature can contribute to and participate in this inquiry. Taking this view, whether he meant actually to describe Balboa discovering the Pacific is less significant than his own discovery that the imagination and the intellect need not be entirely distinct faculties. As his subsequent poetry bears out – Isabella, Otho the Great, the Hyperion poems, even Lamia – this continued to be a primary concern as he worked with ever greater seriousness to find a poetic voice to express his understanding of historical processes.

At the same time, however, the Chapman sonnet is not entirely a moment of triumph for Keats the poet; in fact, the historical details in the poem reveal the extent to which Keats's thought is entrapped in what McGann has called the romantic ideology. The poetic mastery of a historical subject comes at the expense of history itself, creating a tension that Keats's poetry never entirely lays to rest. While the poem displays the poet's interest in historical texts and in the poetic handling of those texts, it establishes at the same time a rigid dichotomy between beauty and history. That is, the inspiration of the poem arises from Keats's sense of imaginative discovery; moreover, the beautifully expressed sense of wonder at this discovery actually elides much historical reality, and even much of what Robertson chronicles: the savage abuse by European explorers of native Americans; the violence and personal viciousness of Cortez; the imperialist drive for wealth and territory by the European invaders. These matters exist in the extreme margins of the poetic text, becoming visible through Keats's major historical source, and they reveal that the poetic triumph of the Chapman sonnet is in the celebration of the energy associated with discoveries of historical significance, rather than in the articulation or representation of history itself. While this fact in itself does not denigrate the young Keats's poem, it does suggest the kinds of vexing historical-poetic problems that will continue to surface in his poetry as he

confronts the facts of historical reality and attempts to find a way to
write poetically about them in a world where historical facts often
offered little cause for celebration.

Anne K. Mellor, 'Ideological Cross-Dressing', from *Romanticism
and Gender* (1993), 171–5

Mellor draws attention to K's capacity for 'reversing' gender
stereotypes in his poetry and in actual life. In an extract that
strikingly recalls Hazlitt's (negative) comments in 'On Effeminacy
of Character' (see above), Mellor celebrates the feminine aspects
of K's 'empathic', 'decentered' sensibility – qualities which K
himself had associated with Shakespeare and 'the true poet'.

Keats subtly complicates the issue of gender and ideology, as
others have remarked, either by occupying the position of the
woman in life or in discourse, or by blurring the distinction between
genders, between masculinity and femininity. Let us focus first on a
few aspects of Keats' life and death, which has been so fully
described by Walter Jackson Bate and others. Orphaned at the age of
fourteen, the second son in a family of four children, Keats
immediately took on the role of mother to his younger siblings. He
corresponded faithfully with his sister Fanny, comforting and
advising her. When his brother Tom fell sick of the family disease,
tuberculosis, he became Tom's nurse, tending Tom until his death.
Keats' first choice of a profession, that of apothecary or, in modern
terminology, a combination of pharmacist and lower-level general
practitioner, may also be significant. While the male medical
profession has long sought to cure disease, nursing the sick and the
dying has traditionally been an occupation associated with women,
and Keats' desire – to help others to bear their pain and suffering –
might be construed as feminine. [. . .]
    Keats' poetic theory is self-consciously positioned within the
realm of the feminine gender. Keats' famous definitions of the
'poetical character' and of 'negative capability,' as Barbara Gelpi
and Adrienne Rich recently reminded us, presuppose an anti-
masculine conception of identity. If we take the examples of William
and Dorothy Wordsworth as representative of a wider construction
of gendered subjectivity in the nineteenth century, the masculine self
was thought to have a strong sense of its own ego boundaries, the
feminine self was not. In his descriptions both of his own sense of
identity and of the appropriate consciousness of the true poet, Keats
reversed these gender stereotypes:

As to the poetical Character itself (I mean that sort of which, if I am any thing, I am a Member; that sort distinguished from the wordsworthian or egotistical sublime; which is a thing per se and stands alone) it is not itself – it has no self – it is every thing and nothing – It has no character – it enjoys light and shade; it lives in gusto, be it foul or fair, high or low, rich or poor, mean or elevated – It has as much delight in conceiving an Iago as an Imogen. What shocks the virtuous Philosopher delights the camelion Poet.

Keats here resists a masculinist construction of the self as bounded, unitary, complete, and instrumental – the consciousness of self-as-agent which he (perhaps unfairly) assigned to the William Wordsworth of *The Prelude*.

In its place Keats promotes a very different concept of self, one similar to Dorothy Wordsworth's floating island self. Like the contemporary Self-in-Relation school of psychology or the French psychoanalytic school inspired by Lacan and Kristeva, Keats images the self as unbounded, fluid, decentered, inconsistent – not 'a' self at all. Keats – like the Poet he describes – 'has no Identity – he is continually in for[ming] and filling some other Body.'

A self that continually overflows itself, that melts into the Other, that *becomes* the Other, is conventionally associated with the female, and especially with the pregnant woman who experiences herself and her child as one. Such a self erases the difference between one and two, and by denying the validity of logical, Aristotelian distinctions, has seemed to many rationalists to embrace irrationality and confusion. Keats advocates such 'confusion' (and appropriates such a self for the male sex) when he insists that the quality which forms 'a Man of achievement especially in literature and which Shakespeare possessed so enormously' is '*Negative Capability*, that is, when man is capable of being in uncertainties, Mysteries, doubts, without any irritable reaching after fact and reason.' Above all, Keats defines the true poet as empathic, a quality everywhere identified with femininity in the eighteenth century. The literature of sensibility, even as it developed the new image of 'the man of feeling,' appropriated to that man qualities traditionally defined as feminine: tears, heightened emotions, excessive passion or love, extreme irrationality, wasting diseases, suicidal impulses and madness.

SUGGESTIONS FOR FURTHER READING

Poetical Works

There are at present three editions of K's complete poetical works. *The Poems of John Keats*, ed. Miriam Allott (1970) has very full annotation for each poem, as does *John Keats: The Complete Poems*, ed. John Barnard (1973), which also contains a valuable glossary for K's classical references. The standard edition, with full textual apparatus detailing variations in manuscript and published sources for the poems, is *The Poems of John Keats*, ed. Jack Stillinger (1978). The scholarly groundwork for Stillinger's edition of the poems appeared in his study *The Texts of Keats's Poems* (1974).

Letters

Keats's letters have been well-served by editors in the latter half of this century. The fullest edition is *The Letters of John Keats 1814–1821*, ed. Hyder Edward Rollins (2 vols, 1958), although these volumes are no longer in print and difficult to obtain outside specialised libraries. More readily accessible is Robert Gittings's excellent *Letters of John Keats: A Selection* (1970), containing all of K's important letters; annotation in this Everyman selection has been keyed to Gittings's volume. In *The Keats Circle. Letters and Papers 1816–1878* (2 edn, 2 vols, 1965), Hyder Edward Rollins gathers a wealth of correspondence and other documentary evidence relating to K's life and times, forming an indispensable source of biographical and documentary information.

Biographies

Among modern biographies, Walter Jackson Bate's *John Keats* (1963) remains a massive and authoritative study, one of the best literary biographies ever published. Its only shortcoming, in scanting the social and political dimensions of the life, is redressed by Aileen Ward's *John Keats. The Making of a Poet* (1963). Robert Gittings's *John Keats. The Living Year* (1954) focuses (at times controversially) on the biographical contexts of K's intense creativity during 1819, complementing the same author's more extensive *John Keats* (1968). John Barnard's *John Keats*

(1987) is the best short introduction to the life and work.

Critical Studies

K has been the subject of numerous critical studies since the early reminiscences of K's contemporaries Charles Brown, CCC, Leigh Hunt, Richard Woodhouse and others (many of which are gathered in *The Keats Circle* cited above). The following is necessarily a very selective list, arranged chronologically, indicating some rewarding twentieth-century studies for additional reading.

H. W. Garrod, *Keats* (1926). A short study, with some particularly valuable comment on *Hyperion* and the development of the odes.

M. R. Ridley, *Keats's Craftsmanship: A Study in Poetic Development* (1933). The first extensive and detailed study of K's patterns of composition as revealed in the manuscripts.

Ian Jack, *Keats and the Mirror of Art* (1967). A marvellous study of the visual resources of K's imagination, this is also essential reading as a guide to literature and the visual arts in the first two decades of the nineteenth century.

John Keats. A Reassessment, ed. Kenneth Muir (1969). A valuable collection of essays, including Miriam Allott's '*Isabella*, *The Eve of St Agnes* and *Lamia*', and Kenneth Muir's 'The Meaning of *Hyperion*'.

John Jones, *John Keats's Dream of Truth* (1969). Complex, highly individual study of the evolution of K's poetry of 'feel'.

Harold Bloom, 'John Keats' in *The Visionary Company. A Reading of English Romantic Poetry* (rev. edn, 1971). Probably the best essay available as an introduction to the evolution of K's poetic career.

Jack Stillinger, *The Hoodwinking of Madeline and other Essays on Keats's Poetry* (1971). An influential and rewarding collection of essays, unified by the idea that K's poems treat the 'mutability inherent in nature and human life', turning from visionary transcendence to a 'naturalized imagination, embracing experience and process'.

Morris Dickstein, *Keats and His Poetry: A Study in Development* (1971). Traces 'the inner history of Keats's imagination', with particular attention to *Endymion*.

Keats. The Critical Heritage, ed. G. M. Matthews (1971). Gathers reviews from K's lifetime until the later nineteenth century. A valuable guide to the development of K's critical reception.

Stuart M. Sperry, *Keats the Poet* (1973). Ranging over the whole of K's poetry, this study is full of perceptive commentary. Highly recommended.

Christopher Ricks, *Keats and Embarrassment* (1974). Brilliant study exploring the ways in which K and his writings were 'especially sensitive to, and morally intelligent about, embarrassment'.

John Bayley, *The Uses of Division: Unity and Disharmony in Literature* (1976), 107–56. The chapter on K persuasively and wittily argues for the earlier poems, including *Endymion*, as the most articulate demonstration of K's 'magnificently *gemein*' poetic personality. This is an extended version of Bayley's Chatterton Lecture for the British Academy, 'Keats and Reality' (1962), and should be read alongside Ricks's study (see above).

Helen Vendler, *The Odes of John Keats* (1983). Argues for the linguistic, aesthetic and philosophical continuity of K's odes and *The Fall of Hyperion*. Humane and authoritative.

Jerome McGann, *The Beauty of Inflections. Literary Investigations in Historical Method and Theory* (1985), 17–65. McGann's essay 'Keats and the Historical Method in Literary Criticism' is important as a reminder about the uses of historical, contextual and bibliographic materials in the elucidation of Romantic poetry.

Susan J. Wolfson, *The Questioning Presence. Wordsworth, Keats, and the Interrogative Mode in Romantic Poetry* (1986). Studies the formal, rhetorical and stylistic possibilities of interrogative poetry in K, with particular concern for how Wordsworth's poetry affected and shaped K's work.

'Keats and Politics. A Forum', ed. Susan J. Wolfson, *Studies in Romanticism* (Summer 1986). Contains five essays which treat the political and historical aspects of K's writings. William Keach's 'Cockney Couplets: Keats and the Politics of Style' is particularly recommended.

John Barnard, *John Keats* (1987). The best short critical introduction available.

R. S. White, *Keats as a Reader of Shakespeare* (1987). A detailed account of what Shakespeare meant to K as 'a creative reader who happened also to be a great poet in his own right'.

Marjorie Levinson, *Keats's Life of Allegory. The Origins of A Style* (1988). Focusing on the 'uncanonical' poems, Levinson presents a social-stylistic analysis of K as a poet whose sense of disadvantage conditioned his literary ambitions.

Karen Swann, 'Harassing the Muse' in *Romanticism and Feminism*, ed. Anne K. Mellor (1988). A vigorous new look at K from a feminist perspective. Recommended.

Daniel P. Watkins, *Keats's Poetry and the Politics of the Imagination* (1989). A good example of materialist criticism of K associated with 'new historicism'.

Margaret Homans, 'Keats Reading Women, Women Reading Keats', *Studies in Romanticism* (Fall, 1990). Investigates 'some real, historical women readers of Keats, and his construction of women readers as it emerges in . . . his letters and poems'.

Susan J. Wolfson, 'Feminizing Keats' in *Critical Essays on John Keats*, ed.

H. de Almeida (1990). Explores the cultural processing of K during the nineteenth century, with particular concern for 'how the language of gender operates in the literary and social culture in which he wrote and was reviewed'.

Nicholas Roe, 'Keats's Lisping Sedition', *Essays in Criticism* (January 1992). Presents new material and commentary on the literary and political backgrounds to Lockhart's attack on K in the fourth 'Cockney School' essay in *Blackwood's Magazine*.

Carol Kyros Walker, *Walking North with Keats* (1992). A useful and well-illustrated study of K's 1818 walking tour in the English Lake District and Scottish Highlands.

Anne K. Mellor, 'Ideological Cross-Dressing: John Keats/Emily Brontë' in *Romanticism and Gender* (1993). Mellor shows how K 'complicates the issue of gender and ideology . . . by occupying the position of the woman in life or in discourse', before turning to the 'heroic, masculine' idiom of the Miltonic *Hyperion* poems. Does not oversimplify the fluidity of gender identities in Romantic writing.

David Pirie, 'Keats' in *The Penguin History of Literature. The Romantic Period*, ed. D. Pirie (1994). This is an up-to-date and perceptive essay on social-political dimensions of K's career and writings.

Keats and History, ed. Nicholas Roe (1995). This collection of thirteen essays gathers together the best of contemporary work on K, approaching his writings through politics, social history, feminism, economics, historiography, stylistics, aesthetics, and mathematical theory. Highly recommended.

ACKNOWLEDGEMENTS

The editor and publishers wish to thank the following for permission to use copyright material:

Associated University Presses for material from Daniel P. Watkins, *Keats's Poetry and the Politics of the Imagination*, 1989, pp. 26–31;

Blackwell publishers for material from Marjorie Levinson, *Keats's Life of Allegory: The Origins of a Style*, 1988, pp. 25–6;

Harvard University Press for material from Helen Vendler, *The Odes of John Keats*, 1983, pp. 291–2;

Oxford University Press for material from Christopher Ricks, *Keats and Embarrassment*, 1974, pp. 97–9; and H.W. Garrod, *Keats*, 1926, pp. 68–73;

Random Century Group for material from John Bayley, *The Uses of Division: Unity and Disharmony in Literature*, 1976, Chatto & Windus, pp. 120–22;

Routledge for material from Anne K. Mellor, *Romanticism and Gender*, 1993, pp. 171–5;

Studies in Romanticism for material from Alan J. Bewell, 'The Political Implication of Keats's Classicist Aesthetics', *Studies in Romanticism*, 25, 2, Summer 1986.

Every effort has been made to trace all the copyright holders but if any have been inadvertently overlooked the publishers will be pleased to make the necessary arrangement at the first opportunity.

INDEX OF TITLES

INDEX OF FIRST LINES